ICSA
STUDY TEXT

Foundation Paper 2

Quantitative Techniques

New in this September 2000 edition

- New user-friendly format

- Updated to reflect recent exam questions

FOR EXAMS IN DECEMBER 2000 AND JUNE 2001

BPP Publishing
September 2000

First edition 1993
Sixth edition September 2000

ISBN 0 7517 5126 X (Previous edition 0 7517 5022 0)

British Library Cataloguing-in-Publication Data
A catalogue record for this book
is available from the British Library

First published by

BPP Publishing Limited
Aldine House, Aldine Place
London W12 8AW

Reprinted in the UK under licence from BPP Publishing Limited by

ICSA Publishing Limited
16 Park Crescent
London W1B 1AH

Printed in Great Britain by The Basingstoke Press Limited

We are grateful to the Institute of Chartered Secretaries and Administrators for permission to reproduce in this text the syllabus of which the Institute holds the copyright.

We are grateful to the Institute of Chartered Secretaries and Administrators, the Association of Accounting Technicians, and the Chartered Institute of Management Accountants for permission to reproduce past examination questions. The suggested answers have been prepared by BPP Publishing Limited.

HOW TO USE THIS STUDY TEXT

Aims of this Study Text

To provide you with the knowledge and understanding, skills and application techniques that you need if you are to be successful in your exams

This Study Text has been carefully written around the official ICSA **Quantiative Techniques** syllabus.

- It is **comprehensive**. We do not omit sections of the syllabus: the examiner may examine any part of the syllabus from any angle- and you do not want to be left high and dry.

- It keeps you **up-to-date** with developments in the subject and the way in which the examiner is designing questions.

- It is **on-target**. We do not include any material which is not examinable. You can therefore rely on the BPP Study Text as the stand-alone source of all your information for the exam, without worrying that any of the material is irrelevant.

To allow you to study in the way that best suits your learning style and the time you have available, by following your personal Study Plan

You may be studying at home on your own until the date of the exam, or you may be attending a full-time course. You may like to read every word, or you may prefer to skim-read and devote the remainder of your time to question practice. Whatever your approach, you will find the BPP Study Text meets your needs in designing and following your personal Study Plan.

To tie in with the rest of the BPP Effective Study Package to ensure you have the best possible chance of passing the exam

The BPP Effective Study Package

Recommended period of use	Elements of the BPP Effective Study Package
3-12 months before exam	**Study Text** Use the Study Text to acquire knowledge, understanding, skills and the ability to use application techniques.

| 1-3 months before exam | **Practice & Revision Kit**
 Attempt the tutorial questions and read the helpful checklists which are provided for each topic area in the Kit. Then try the numerous examination questions, for which there are realistic suggested answers. |

Settling down to study

By this stage in your career you are probably very experienced at learning and taking exams. But have you ever thought about *how* you learn? Let's have a quick look at the key elements required for effective learning.

Key element of learning	Using the BPP Study Text
Motivation	You can rely on the comprehensiveness and technical quality of BPP material. You've chosen the right Study Text - so you're in pole position to pass your exam!
Clear objectives and standards	Do you want to be a prizewinner or simply achieve a pass? Only you can decide.
Feedback	Work through the examples in this text and do the Exercises and Test your knowledge quizzes. Evaluate your efforts critically - how are you doing?
Study Plan	You need to be honest with yourself about your progress - don't be over-confident, but don't be negative either. Make your Study Plan (see below) and try to stick to it. Focus on the short-term objectives - completing two chapters a week, say - but beware of losing sight of your study objectives.
Practice	Use the Test your knowledge quizzes and Chapter roundups to refresh your memory after you have completed your initial study of each chapter.

These introductory pages let you see exactly what you are up against. But however you study, there are two things you should do.

- **Read through the syllabus and syllabus commentary:** these will help you to identify areas you have already covered, perhaps at a lower level of detail, and areas that are totally new to you.
- **Study the examination paper section,** where we show you the format of the exam and analyse the recent papers **including the one set in June 2000.**

Developing your personal Study Plan

Preparing a Study Plan (and sticking closely to it) is one of the key elements in learning success. First you need to be aware of your style of learning. There are four typical learning styles. Consider yourself in the light of the following descriptions and work out which you fit most closely. You can then plan to follow the key study steps in the sequence suggested.

Learning styles	Characteristics
Theorist	Seeks to understand principles before applying them in practice
Reflector	Seeks to observe phenomena, thinks about them and then chooses to act
Activist	Prefers to deal with practical, active problems; does not have much patience with theory
Pragmatist	Prefers to study only if a direct link to practical problems can be seen; not interested in theory for its own sake

Key study steps

We have broken the learning process down into a series of key steps, which you can apply to each chapter in turn. We list them here in the order which seems to work best for **theorists** and **reflectors**. If you are an **activist** or a **pragmatist** you may prefer to use a different sequence. The various options are summarised after the table of steps. Tackle the chapters in the order you find them in the Study Text. Taking into account your individual learning style, follow these key study steps for each chapter.

Key study steps	Activity
Step 1 *Chapter topic list*	Study the list. Each numbered topic is a numbered section in the chapter.
Step 2 *Introduction*	Read through it. It is designed to show you *why* the topics in the chapter need to be studied - how they lead on from previous topics, and how they lead into subsequent ones.
Step 3 *Explanations*	Proceed methodically through the chapter, reading each section thoroughly and making sure you understand. Where a topic has been examined, we state the month and year of examination against the appropriate heading. You should pay particular attention to these topics.
Step 4 *Note taking*	Take brief notes if you wish, avoiding the temptation to copy out too much.
Step 5 *Examples*	Follow each through to its solution very carefully.
Step 6 *Case examples*	Study each one, and try to add flesh to them from your own experience - they are designed to show how the topics you are studying come alive (and often come unstuck) in the real world.
Step 7 *Exercises*	Make a very good attempt at each one in the chapter. These are designed to put your knowledge into practice.
Step 8 *Solutions*	Check yours against ours, and make sure you understand the reasons why they may differ.
Step 9 *Chapter roundup*	Work through it very carefully, to make sure you have grasped the major points it is highlighting.
Step 10 *Test your knowledge quiz*	When you are happy that you have covered the chapter, use the Test your knowledge quiz to check how much you have remembered of the topics covered. The answers are in the paragraphs in the chapter that we refer you to.
Step 11 *Illustrative questions*	Either at this point, or later when you are thinking about revising, make a full attempt at the question(s) suggested at the very end of the chapter. You can find these at the end of the Study Text, along with the answers so you can see how you did.

BPP
PUBLISHING

Learning style approaches

Learning style	Sequence of key study steps in the BPP Study Text
Theorist	1, 2, 3, 4, 6, 7, 8, 9, 10, 11, (4 continuous)
Reflector	
Activist	1, 2, 7/8 (read through), 5, 6, 9, 3, 7/8 (full attempt), 10, 11 (4 continuous)
Pragmatist	7/8 (read through), 2, 5, 6, 9, 1, 3, 7/8 (full attempt), 10, 11 (4 continuous)

Planning your studies

Next you should complete the following checklist.

Am I motivated? (a) ☐

Do I have an objective and a standard that I want to achieve? (b) ☐

Am I a theorist, a reflector, an activist or a pragmatist? (c) ☐

How much time do I have available per week, given: (d) ☐

- the standard I have set myself
- the time I need to set aside later for work on the Practice and Revision Kit
- the other exam(s) I am sitting, and (of course)
- practical matters such as work, travel, exercise, sleep and social life?

Now:

- take the time you have available per week for this Study Text (d), (e) ☐ and multiply it by the number of weeks available to give (e).
- divide (e) by the number of chapters to give (f) (f) ☐
- set about studying each chapter in the time represented by (f), following the key study steps in the order suggested by your particular learning style.

This is your personal Study Plan.

Moving on...

However you study, when you are ready to embark on the practice and revision phase of the BPP Effective Study Package, you should still refer back to this Study Text, both as a source of reference (you should find the index particularly helpful for this) and as a refresher (the Chapter roundups and Test your knowledge quizzes help you here).

And remember to keep careful hold of this Study Text - you will find it invaluable in your work.

SYLLABUS

Objective

To provide an introduction to quantitative techniques which are widely applicable in business administration with emphasis upon applications to business problems and interpretation.

	Covered in Chapter
Collection and Presentation of Numerical Data	
Official sources of economic and business data	1
Survey methods	1
Questionnaire design	1
Sampling methods	1
Interviews	1
Postal questionnaires	1
Tabulation	2
Graphs, charts and diagrams	2-3
Frequency Distribution	
Measures as they apply to different types of business and organisational type data	4
Measures of location: mean, median and mode	4
General awareness of other measures of location for specialist needs: geometric mean for averaging proportions, harmonic mean for averaging rates	4
Measures of dispersion: range, quartile deviation and standard deviation	5
Skewness: coefficient of variation	5
Relationships and Forecasting	
Changes in variables, including those of an economic or production nature	12
Correlation and regression	6
Product moment correlation coefficient	6
Rank correlation coefficient	6
Linear regression using the least squares method	6
Time series analysis: additive and multiplicative models	7
Components of a time series: trend, cyclical, seasonal and random	7
Moving averages	7
Simple methods of forecasting	7
Index Numbers	
The use of index numbers as a means of expressing average change in economic activity over a period of time	8
Price relative methods	8
Aggregate methods	8
Laspeyres, Paasche and Fishers index numbers	8
Problems involved in the use of index numbers	8

Syllabus

THE EXAMINATION PAPER

Paper requirements and format

The paper consists of eight questions. Four questions are to be attempted. All questions carry equal marks (25).

Analysis of past papers

The following topics have been examined in papers set under the syllabus for Paper 2 *Quantitative Techniques*.

June 2000

1 Averages
2 Data presentation, averages and dispersion
3 Time series analysis
4 Correlation and regression
5 Index numbers
6 Probability
7 Mathematical models and breakeven analysis
8 Linear programming

December 1999

1 Data presentation
2 Data presentation, averages and dispersion
3 Time series analysis
4 Correlation and regression
5 Index numbers
6 Probability
7 Mathematical models (including graphical representation of data)
8 Linear programming

June 1999

1 Sampling methods
2 Data presentation, averages and dispersion
3 Time series analysis
4 Correlation and regression
5 Index numbers
6 Probability
7 Discounting
8 Linear programming

December 1998

1 Questionnaires
2 Data presentation, averages and dispersion
3 Time series analysis
4 Correlation and regression
5 Index numbers
6 Probability
7 Investment appraisal
8 Linear programming

The examination paper

June 1998

1   Definition of terms
2   Data presentation, averages and dispersion
3   Time series analysis
4   Correlation and regression
5   Index numbers
6   Probability and probability distributions
7   Breakeven analysis
8   Linear programming

December 1997

1   Pictorial representation of data
2   Data presentation, averages and dispersion
3   Time series analysis
4   Correlation and regression
5   Index numbers
6   Probability
7   Interest and discounting
8   Linear programming

June 1997

1   Questionnaires and interviews
2   Data presentation and hypothesis testing
3   Time series analysis and forecasting
4   Correlation and regression
5   Index numbers
6   Probability and probability distributions
7   Mathematical models (including graphical representation)
8   Linear programming

December 1996

1   Sampling methods
2   Data presentation, averages and dispersion
3   Time series analysis
4   Correlation
5   Index numbers
6   Probability and statistical inference
7   Discounting
8   Linear programming

June 1996

1   Statistical terms
2   Data presentation, averages and dispersion
3   Time series analysis and index numbers
4   Correlation
5   Internal rate of return and sinking funds
6   Venn diagrams and probability distributions
7   Mathematical models and breakeven analysis
8   Linear programming

December 1995

1 Sampling methods
2 Data presentation, averages
3 Time series analysis and forecasting
4 Correlation and regression
5 Index numbers
6 Probability and statistical inference
7 Discounting and sinking funds
8 Linear programming

June 1995

1 Methods of data presentation
2 Data presentation, averages, dispersion, probability
3 Time series analysis
4 Correlation and regression
5 Index numbers
6 Probability
7 Mathematical models
8 Linear programming

December 1994

1 Averages and measures of dispersion
2 Data presentation, averages and measures of dispersion
3 Time series analysis
4 Correlation and regression
5 Index numbers
6 Probability and probability distributions
7 Interest
8 Linear programming

June 1994

1 Sampling methods
2 Histogram, averages and measures of dispersion
3 Time series analysis
4 Correlation and regression
5 Index numbers
6 Hypothesis testing, Venn diagrams and probability
7 Compound interest and discounting
8 Linear programming

Part A
The collection and presentation of numerical data

Chapter 1

THE COLLECTION OF NUMERICAL DATA

This chapter covers the following topics.

1   Data

2   Official sources of economic and business data

3   Survey methods of collecting data

4   Questionnaire design

5   Sampling

6   Random sampling

7   Quasi-random sampling

8   Non-random sampling

9   Interviews

10 Postal questionnaires

Introduction

The words 'quantitative techniques' often strike terror into the hearts of students. They conjure up images of complicated mathematical formulae, scientific analysis of reams of computer output and the drawing of strange graphs and diagrams. Such images are wrong. Quantitative techniques simply involve **collecting data**, their **presentation** in a useful form and their **interpretation**.

A study of the subject will demonstrate that quantitative techniques are nothing to be afraid of and that a knowledge of them are extremely advantageous in your working environment. The main advantage of quantitative techniques are that they offer methods which can be used to make sense of numbers. In a business environment, for example, a manager may collect all sort of data on production levels, costs or sales, but on their own the numbers are unlikely to mean very much. By using quantitative techniques, a manager can try to make sense out of the numbers which in turn should help in making sensible business decisions.

We will start our study of quantitative techniques by looking at data collection. In Chapters 2 and 3 we will consider how to present data once they have been collected.

1   DATA

6/98

What are data?

1.1   '**Data**' is a term that you will come across time and time again in your study of quantitative techniques but what does 'data' mean? 'Data' is simply a 'scientific' term for facts, figures, information and measurements. Data therefore include the number of people who pass their driving test each year with red hair, the number of goals scored by each football team in the second division in the current season to date, and the profit after tax for the past ten years of the four biggest supermarket chains.

Types of data

1.2   Data may be of several types, the first distinction being between **attributes** and **variables**.

Attributes and variables

1.3 **An attribute is something an object has either got or not got. It cannot be measured.** For example, an individual is either male or female. There is no measure of *how* male or *how* female somebody is: the sex of a person is an attribute.

1.4 **A variable is something which can be measured.** For example, the height of a person can be measured according to some scale (such as centimetres).

Discrete and continuous variables

1.5 Variables can be further classified as **discrete** or **continuous**.

(a) **Discrete variables** can only take a finite or countable number of values within a given range. Examples of such variables include ' goals scored by Chachont United against Willford City', 'shoe size' and 'number of people entering SupaSave SupaMarket in Rutminster between 9.05am and 9.10am on a particular day'. If we arbitrarily chose a range of 0 - 10, 2 goals could be scored but not $2\frac{1}{2}$, a (British) shoe size could be $5\frac{1}{2}$ but not 5.193 and 9 people could enter the supermarket but not 9.999.

(b) **Continuous variables** may take on any value. They are measured rather than counted. For example, it may be considered sufficient to measure the heights of a number of people to the nearest centimetre but there is no reason why the measurements should not be made to the nearest 1/100cm. Two people who are found to have the same height to the nearest cm could almost certainly be distinguished if more precise measurements were taken.

Exercise 1

Look through the following list of surveys and decide whether each is collecting data on attributes, discrete variables or continuous variables.

(a) A survey of statistics text books, to determine how many diagrams they contain
(b) A survey of cans in a shop, to determine whether or not each has a price sticker
(c) A survey of athletes to find out how long they take to run a mile
(d) A survey of the heights of telegraph poles in England

Solution

(a) The number of diagrams in a textbook is a discrete variable, because it can only be counted in whole number steps. You cannot, for example, have 26½ diagrams or 47.32 diagrams in a book.

(b) Whether or not a can possesses a sticker is an attribute. It is not something which can be measured. A can either possesses the attribute or it does not.

(c) How long an athlete takes to run a mile is a continuous variable, because the time recorded can, in theory, take any value, for example 4 minutes 2.0643 seconds.

(d) The height of a telegraph pole is a continuous variable.

Primary data and secondary data

1.6 The data used in a statistical survey, whether variables or attributes, can be either **primary data** or **secondary data**.

(a) **Primary data** are data collected especially for the purpose of whatever survey is being conducted. Raw data are primary data which have not been processed at all, but are still just (for example) a list of numbers.

(b) **Secondary data** are data which have already been collected elsewhere, for some other purpose, but which can be used or adapted for the survey being conducted.

1.7   An advantage of using primary data is that the investigator knows where the data came from, the circumstances under which they were collected, and any limitations or inadequacies in the data.

1.8   In contrast, note the following inadequacies of secondary data.

(a)   Any limitations in the data might not be known to the investigator, because he or she did not collect them.

(b)   The data might not be entirely suitable for the purpose they are being used for.

1.9   Secondary data are sometimes used despite their inadequacies, simply because they are available cheaply whereas the extra cost of collecting primary data would far outweigh their extra value.

Collecting the data

1.10   Now that we have some idea of the different types of data, we can address ourselves to the problem of getting hold of them.

1.11   Many textbooks defer their discussion of how data are obtained until after a consideration of the techniques available for analysing them. This approach is, however, like cooking a meal before buying the ingredients. We will therefore begin our study of collecting data with a look at the ways of obtaining data. We will then go on to consider the techniques available for analysing them.

2   OFFICIAL SOURCES OF ECONOMIC AND BUSINESS DATA

2.1   Secondary data are data that were originally collected as primary data for a particular purpose or for general use, but are now being used for another purpose. The Government, for example, collects data to help with making decisions about running the country, and makes these data available to the public.

2.2   Examples of secondary data include the following.

(a)   **Published statistics**. For example, the Government publishes statistics through the Central Statistical Office (CSO). The European Union and the United Nations also publish statistics. So do various newspapers and accountancy bodies.

(b)   **Historical records**. The type of historical record used for a survey obviously depends on what survey is being carried out. An accountant producing an estimate of future company sales might use historical records of past sales.

Sources of published statistics

2.3   You may be expected to identify the sources of certain published statistics. As you will probably be aware, the range of published economic, business and accounting data is very wide, and a comprehensive knowledge of sources is impracticable. In this chapter the better known sources will be described.

2.4   All published statistics are a source of secondary data. Great care must be taken in using them, since the data may not be obtained or classified in precisely the same way as primary data collected **specifically** for the purpose of the current statistical analysis would be.

2.5   Despite the general shortcomings of secondary data there are many circumstances in which published statistics can be of great value. Many Government statistics are compiled at least partly for the purpose of being used in further analysis and explanatory notes are given so that the user of the data knows to what extent they are relevant to his needs and what level of confidence he can have in the results of his analysis.

The Central Statistical Office and other bodies

2.6　The **Central Statistical Office (CSO)** publishes the following.

(a)　The *Monthly Digest of Statistics* (which gives data for the recent past)
(b)　The *Annual Abstract of Statistics* (which gives data over a much longer period)
(c)　*Economic Trends* (published monthly)
(d)　*Financial Statistics* (published monthly)

2.7　The **European Union** has a Statistical Office of the European Community (SOEC) which gathers statistics from each of the member countries. The SOEC has several statistical publications, including *Basic Statistics of the Community*.

2.8　The **United Nations** also publishes some statistics on the world economy (for example the Statistical yearbook), and a Yearbook of labour statistics is published by the International Labour Organisation.

2.9　In the remainder of this section, we shall concentrate on statistical publications in the UK.

The Department of Employment Gazette

2.10　The Department of Employment publishes statistics monthly about employment and unemployment, and about retail prices. The statistics which are published monthly in the *Department of Employment Gazette* include, for example, statistics on the following.

- Retail prices
- Employment
- Unemployment
- Unfilled job vacancies
- Wage rates
- Overtime
- Stoppages at work

2.11　Retail prices are very important to a wide variety of users.

(a)　For the **Government**, the Retail Prices Index (RPI) indicates the degree of success there has been in fighting inflation.

(b)　For **employees**, the RPI may give an indication of how much wages need to rise to keep pace with inflation.

(c)　For **consumers**, the RPI indicates the increases to be expected in the prices of goods in shops.

(d)　For **businesses**, the RPI may give a broad indication of how much costs should have been expected to rise over recent years and months.

(e)　For **pensioners** and **social security recipients**, the movement in the RPI is used to update benefit levels.

The Bank of England Quarterly Bulletin

2.12　The Bank of England issues a quarterly magazine which includes data on banks in the UK, the money supply and Government borrowing and financial transactions.

Population data

2.13　Data on the UK population, such as population numbers in total and by region, births, deaths and marriages, are produced monthly by the Office of Population Censuses and Surveys (OPCS) in a publication entitled *Population Trends*.

The OPCS also produces an **annual statistical review**.

Every ten years, there is a full **census** of the whole population, and results of the census are published. The last census was in April 1991.

The Blue Book and the Pink Book

2.14 *The Blue Book on National Income and Expenditure* is published annually by the CSO, giving details of the following.

(a) **Gross national product** (analysed into sections of the economy such as transport and communication, insurance, banking and finance, public administration and defence).

(b) **Gross national income** (analysed into income from self-employment, income from employment, profits of companies, income from abroad and so on).

(c) **Gross national expenditure** (analysed into expenditure on capital goods, expenditure by consumers and by public authorities, imports and so on).

2.15 This information is augmented by more detailed statistics, also provided in the Blue Book. There is also an annual *Pink Book, The UK Balance of Payments* which analyses the UK's external trade, external capital transactions (inflows and outflows of private capital) and official financing.

The Annual Abstract of Statistics

2.16 Most government statistics of economic and business data are brought together into a main reference book, the *Annual Abstract of Statistics*, which is published by the CSO. Notes about the data and definitions of the data provided are contained in the book.

The Monthly Digest of Statistics

2.17 The CSO's *Monthly Digest of Statistics* is an abbreviated version of the Annual Abstract, updated and published monthly. A January supplement provides definitions. The information included in the *Monthly Digest* covers a wide range of topics, such as industrial output, production costs, prices and wages, social services, law enforcement, national income, external trade, retailing, transport, construction, agriculture and food.

Financial Statistics

2.18 The CSO publishes a monthly compilation of financial data in *Financial Statistics*. This gives statistics on a variety of financial topics.

(a) Government income, expenditure and borrowing

(b) Assets and liabilities of banks and statistics on other financial institutions, such as building societies, unit trusts, investment trusts, insurance companies and pension funds

(c) Companies (profits, sources and uses of capital funds, acquisitions and mergers, share trading and so on)

(d) Personal sector finance (loans for home buying, consumer credit, personal income expenditure and saving and so on)

(e) The overseas sector

(f) The money supply

(g) Issues of capital and Stock Exchange transactions

(h) Exchange rates, interest rates and share prices

Economic Trends

2.19 Like the *Monthly Digest of Statistics* and *Financial Statistics*, *Economic Trends* is a monthly publication of the CSO. As its name implies, its main purpose is to indicate trends, and the publication includes graphs as well as numerical statistics.

The Financial Times

2.20 The *Financial Times* and other newspapers and investment journals provide statistics about the Stock Market. These include the following.

(a) The **FT-Actuaries All-Share Index** (compiled jointly by the *Financial Times*, the Institute of Actuaries in London and the Faculty of Actuaries in Edinburgh). This is an index of share prices quoted on the Stock Exchange.

(b) The **FTSE 100 index**. This is a stock market index of 100 leading shares, compiled by the *Financial Times* and the Stock Exchange.

The *Financial Times* also includes various other items of daily information on financial matters.

- Foreign exchange rates
- Interest rates
- Gilts and other stock prices

3 SURVEY METHODS OF COLLECTING DATA

3.1 There are two basic methods of collecting primary data from individuals: they can be asked questions or their behaviour can be observed. The latter method of collection is called observation and is outside the scope of this syllabus; the former involves the collection of data using surveys.

3.2 There are two main types of survey.

- **Interviews**
- **Postal questionnaires**

3.3 We will be looking at each type, and their respective advantages and disadvantages, in Sections 9 and 10.

3.4 Although surveys offer a quick, efficient and cost-effective way of obtaining the required data, they are not straightforward. Without skill, tact and expertise the results may easily become contaminated with bias and error and the conclusions subsequently drawn will be useless.

3.5 A famous example of this occurred years ago in the United States, when somebody was asked to conduct an **opinion poll** (which is a form of survey) on whether the next president was likely to be Democrat or Republican. The survey was carried out, but in a wrong way. The survey officer **telephoned** people, and far more Republicans than Democrats had telephones. The survey was useless, because it had not been planned properly.

3.6 The reason why the opinion poll turned out so badly was that the population for the survey had not been defined properly. In data collection, the word '**population**' refers to the **entire collection of items being considered**. The opinion poll should have used the population 'all Americans of voting age', whereas it actually used the population 'all Americans with a telephone'.

3.7 The following example will be used to illustrate the factors which need to be considered when planning a survey.

Example: planning a survey

3.8 You are asked to conduct a survey of the spending habits of the population of London. Before you speak to a single person, you need to think about all of the following.

(a) **The precise definition of the objectives of the survey.** This is essential in order to ensure that all necessary data are collected and time and expense are not wasted on superfluous material. For example, are mortgage repayments to be included in the survey? What about pension contributions?

(b) **The definition of units of measurement.** You could be collecting data about several variables. Data must be collected and measured in the same units. For our example this is easy: all figures will be in pounds sterling. But for a survey of, say, sales within a company, some figures could be in pounds sterling and others in quantities.

(c) **The accuracy of data required.** This will depend on the degree of accuracy required in the results and will affect the units of measurement and the size of sample (number of people to be investigated). For example, are items of spending to be listed to the nearest pound, to the nearest £10, or what? If the collected data are only correct to the nearest £10, then any conclusions eventually drawn from the data can only be accurate to the nearest £10. In fact, if you perform any calculations with the data, the final results may not even be accurate to the nearest £10.

(d) **The definition of the population.** The population is the field of all items under consideration. It will obviously depend on the objectives and must be carefully defined. For example, should it be the residents of all London boroughs, of the London postal districts, or just of the City of London?

(e) **The depth of enquiry.** Is a complete enquiry to be made of all the members of the population or will it be sufficient to take a sample?

(f) **Cost effectiveness.** The results must be worth the cost of collecting the data. Such considerations will affect the whole survey and in particular the accuracy and depth of enquiry. For example, we might estimate that the cost of our survey was £100,000, but that any information arising out of the survey is not worth £100,000 (because it could not be used in any way to gain that amount of money). If that were the case, the survey would not be cost-effective, and should be abandoned.

Errors in survey methods of collecting data

3.9 There are three main types of error that can appear in survey methods of collecting data.

- Sampling error
- Response error   **Non-sampling error**
- Non-response error

3.10 **Sampling error** arises when the sample of the population surveyed (if the entire population is not being investigated) is not representative of the population from which it is drawn. For example, if a sample of the population of a city was composed entirely of babies less than three months old, the sample would obviously not be representative of the population of the city.

3.11 **Response error** can occur even when all members of the population are surveyed and arises because respondents are either unable (through ignorance, forgetfulness or inarticulateness) or unwilling (due to time pressure, desire for privacy, guessing and so on) to respond.

3.12 **Non-response error** can occur either if respondents refuse to take part in the survey or are 'not at home'.

3.13 Non-response in survey methods of data collection is a particular problem if those who refuse to take part in the survey are likely to be different in some way to those who do take part. The easiest way to reduce the effect of this situation is to try and increase the percentage of those taking part (responding).

3.14 **Reducing non-response for interviews**

(a) The success of interviews relies on the quality of interaction between respondent and interviewer. Interviewers who appear/sound pleasant, interesting and interested in the respondent and who convincingly persuade the respondent that his/her views are important will produce lower rates of refusal.

(b) If someone is 'not at home' the interviewer should call back.

(c) Respondents can be promised gifts/monetary reward.

3.15 **Reducing non-response for postal questionnaires**

(a) Contact respondents prior to despatching the questionnaire to ask whether they would be prepared to aid the study by completing a questionnaire.

(b) Include a covering letter to explain why the data are being collected and to put the respondent in the appropriate frame of mind.

(c) Include a freepost/stamped addressed envelope for ease of reply.

(d) Provide a gift or monetary incentive upon questionnaire completion.

(e) Address the respondent by name. This not only increases the response rate but will encourage the named person to complete the questionnaire personally.

(f) Use postal or telephone follow up reminders.

(g) Carefully select a target audience who have particular interest in the topic.

4 QUESTIONNAIRE DESIGN
6/97, 12/98

4.1 The following factors should be considered when designing a questionnaire.

- Initial considerations
- Question content
- Question phrasing
- Types of response format
- Question sequence
- Questionnaire layout
- Pretest, revision and final version of questionnaire

Initial considerations

4.2 Three important considerations need to be borne in mind before starting to design a questionnaire.

- Type of information required
- Type/nature of respondents
- Type and method by which the survey is to be administered

Question content

4.3 When deciding on question content it is vital to think about the following.

(a) **Is the question necessary?**

(b) **Will the respondent understand the question?**

The language used should be that of the respondent group. Think about the different language used by managing directors and teenagers.

(c) **Will the question elicit the required data?**

A survey often fails to generate the required data because of badly-phrased questions or questions that are too ambiguous to elicit specific information. Double-barrelled questions ('Do you often go to pubs and restaurants?') should be split and words describing frequency ('often', 'slightly', 'somewhat') should be avoided as they have a wide range of interpretation.

Exercise 2

What might be a better way of asking 'Do you often go to the cinema?'

Solution

'Do you go to the cinema (a) once a week, (b) once a month, (c) twice a year?'

(d) **Does the respondent have the necessary data to be able to answer the question?**

The ability of the respondent to answer will depend on three factors.

(i) **Degree to which the respondent is informed.** If respondents do not know the answer to a question they may try to bluff their way out of, what is to them, an embarrassing situation by guessing. Such answers lead to errors in the conclusions drawn from the data collected. Questions should therefore be phrased so that is does *not* appear that the interviewer is suggesting that the respondent should know the answer.

(ii) **The state of the respondent's memory.** Questions relating to unimportant/ infrequent events or to events some time in the past, are likely to tempt respondents to guess. This may introduce error and so it is better to 'jog' respondents' memories in some way.

(iii) **The articulateness of the respondent.** Even the most articulate of respondents may find it difficult to be verbally adept about their feelings, beliefs, opinions and motivations. If such data are required other data collection methods better suited to uncovering such information (such as projective techniques) should be considered.

(e) **Is the respondent willing/able to answer the questions?**

A respondent may refuse to answer one or more questions on a questionnaire (non-response) or many 'refuse' by providing a wrong or distorted answer. Reasons for this unwillingness to provide accurate answers include the following.

- The situation is inappropriate for data disclosure.
- Data disclosure would prove embarrassing to the respondent.
- Data disclosure is a potential threat to the prestige of the respondent.

Certain techniques can be employed to eliminate distorted/wrong/inaccurate answers.

(i) Assess whether the question is really necessary (especially if it will cause embarrassment, a loss of prestige).

(ii) Reassure the respondent of the importance of the question and of the value of their response.

(iii) Begin a 'difficult' question with a statement which implies the topic of the question is common/quite usual.

(iv) Imply that the behaviour in which you are interested is an attribute of a third party.

(v) Provide respondents with a card on which are listed possible responses, identified by a letter or a number, to potentially embarrassing questions. Respondents need only provide a letter/number as their answer.

(vi) When analysing the data, replies to questions related to image/prestige should be upgraded or downgraded as necessary.

Question phrasing

4.4 Given below is a checklist of factors to consider when translating data requirements into words.

(a) **Use a style of language appropriate to the target population.**

(b) **Avoid long questions.**

Oppenheim (*Questionnaire Design and Attitude Measurement*) suggests that a question should be no more than 20 words in length.

(c) **Avoid vague and ambiguous words.** Payne (*The Art of Asking Questions*) suggests asking the following six questions about every word in a question.

   (i) Does it mean what is intended?
   (ii) Does it have any other meaning?
   (iii) If so, does the context make the meaning clear?
   (iv) Does it have more than one pronunciation?
   (v) Is there a word of similar pronunciation with which it might be confused?
   (vi) Is there a simpler word or phrase available?

(d) **Avoid biased words and leading questions.**

A pilot test of the questionnaire should identify any words which have emotional overtones for groups being questioned.

Leading questions are those that either suggest the way in which the respondent should answer, or strongly suggest what the position on the subject held by the person asking the question. Leading questions can be made less 'leading' by the inclusion of an appropriate number of alternative replies.

(e) **Do not use double-barrelled questions.**

(f) **Avoid negative questions.**

They can be confusing, make the respondent guess and hence introduce error. For example, if respondents are asked to agree or disagree with 'Naughty children are not the responsibility of parents', an answer of 'disagree' means that the respondent thinks that naughty children are the responsibility of parents. The mental gymnastics of sorting out such a question are best avoided.

(g) **Do not encourage respondents to guess.**

Questions which ask respondents to estimate or make generalisations are a potential source of error. For example, do not ask respondents how many glasses of wine they drink a *year*. Ask them how many they drink a month or week and do the mental arithmetic yourself.

(h) **Avoid questions which assume respondents have possession of all the relevant factors pertaining to the question.**

Types of response format

4.5 **Questions can be open or closed.** Open questions are difficult to analyse. An open question might be worded like this.

'How did you travel to work today?'

The responses may be so numerous that analysis becomes onerous and time consuming. The designer of the questionnaire should instead try to offer a full range of possible responses to the question, perhaps like this. 'Please indicate how you travelled to work today.

By bus	☐
By train	☐
By private car	☐
On foot	☐
By bicycle/motorcycle	☐
I did not go to work today (illness, holidays etc)	☐
I work at home	☐
I do not work	☐

Other (please give details)....................'

The responses from this closed question will be much easier to analyse. It is important, however, to avoid putting such lists of responses in order of supposed popularity.

4.6 The table on the next page gives examples of both types of question.

Exercise 3

What types of problem can you envisage arising from the use of multiple choice questions? How can such problems be overcome?

Solution

Here are some ideas. You may have thought of others.

(a) Capturing a full range of possible responses to a question such as 'In which store do you buy the majority of your clothes?' can be impractical.

This problem can be overcome by listing the most popular stores and using an 'other (please specify)' option

(b) The position of the alternative responses may introduce bias.

This problem can be overcome (but not entirely) by producing different versions of the questionnaire.

(c) An unbalanced set of alternative responses could be provided such as the following.

Q: What do you think of TV programme 'XXX'?

A:	1	2	3
	Too boring	Very dull	Indifferent

Obviously such response sets should not be used.

Question sequence

4.7 (a) Start with **quota control questions** so as to rapidly determine whether the interviewee is the right type of person. Quota control questions might identify whether the interviewee is employed or unemployed, under 40 or over 40 and so on. Such questions facilitate the termination of worthless interviews as early as possible.

(b) Move onto questions which will **engage interest, reassure and give a foretaste of what is to follow.**

Part A: The collection and presentation of numerical data

Name	Description	Example
	CLOSED-END QUESTIONS	

Dichotomous — A question with two possible answers.

'In arranging this trip, did you personally phone British Airways?'

Yes ☐   No ☐

Multiple choice — A question with three or more answers.

'With whom are you travelling on this flight?'

No one ☐   Children only ☐
Spouse ☐   Business associates/
Spouse and   friends/relatives ☐
children ☐   An organised tour
                group ☐

Likert scale — A statement with which the respondent shows the amount of agreement/

'Small airlines generally give better service

Strongly disagree 1	Disagree 2	Neither agree nor disagree 3	Agree 4	Strongly agree 5
☐	☐	☐	☐	☐

British Airways

Semantic differential — A scale connecting two bipolar words, where the respondent selects the point

Large _ _ _ _ _ _ _ _ _ _ _ _ _ _ _ Small
Experienced _ _ _ _ _ _ _ _ _ _ _ _ Inexperienced
_ _ _ _ _ _ _ _ _ _ _ _ _ _ _ _ _

Importance scale — A scale that rates the importance of some attribute.

Extremely important 1	Very important 2	Somewhat important 3	Not very important 4	Not at all important 5
☐	☐	☐	☐	☐

Rating scale — A scale that rates some attribute from 'poor' to 'excellent'.

Excellent   Very good   Good   Fair   Poor

Intention-to-buy scale — A scale that describes the respondent's intention to buy.

'If an inflight telephone was available on a long flight, I would'

Definitely buy 1	Probably buy 2	Not sure 3	Probably not buy 4	Definitely not buy 5
☐	☐	☐	☐	☐

| | **OPEN-END QUESTIONS** | |

Completely unstructured — A question that respondents can answer in an almost unlimited number of ways.

'What is your opinion of British Airways?'

Word association — Words are presented, one at a time, and respondents mention the first word that

'What is the first word that comes to mind when you hear the following'
Airline_____
British_____
Travel_____

Sentence completion — An incomplete sentence is presented and respondents complete the

'When I choose an airline, the most important consideration in my decision is _____ '

Story completion — An incomplete story is presented, and respondents are asked to complete it.

'I flew B.A. a few days ago. I noticed that the exterior and interior of the plane had bright colours. This aroused in me the following thoughts and feelings.' Now complete the story.

Picture completion — A picture of two characters is presented, with one making a statement. Respondents are asked to identify with the other and fill in the empty balloon.

Thematic Apperception Test (TAT) — A picture is presented and respondents are asked to make up a story about what they think is happening or may happen in the picture.

(c) Questions should be in **logical order** as far as possible, but if difficult questions are necessary it may be more appropriate to put them at the end.

(d) Avoid questions which suggest the answers to later questions. This will cause **bias**.

Questionnaire layout

4.8 (a) Use good quality paper.

(b) The questionnaire should be as short as possible. Questionnaires which are too long may discourage the respondent from even starting it.

(c) If respondents have to complete the questionnaire themselves, it must be as approachable as possible. Consider the use of lines, boxes, different type faces/print sizes and small pictures. Use plenty of space.

(d) Make sure that the instructions which guide the respondent through the questionnaire are as user friendly as possible and are kept to a minimum.

(e) Explain the purpose of the survey at the beginning of the questionnaire and where possible guarantee confidentiality. Emphasise the date by which it must be returned.

(f) At the end of the questionnaire, thank the respondent and make it clear what they should do with the completed questionnaire.

Pretest, revision and final version of the questionnaire

4.9 Pretesting the questionnaire will uncover faults in its design before it is too late and should therefore ensure that the final version of the questionnaire gathers the required data.

5 SAMPLING

6/94, 12/95, 12/96, 6/98

5.1 **Sampling** is one of the most important subjects in quantitative methods In most practical situations the population will be too large to carry out a complete survey and only a sample will be examined. A good example of this is a poll taken to try to predict the results of an election. It is not possible to ask everyone of voting age how they are going to vote: it would take too long and cost too much. So a sample of voters is taken, and the results from the sample are used to estimate the voting intentions of the whole population.

5.2 Occasionally a population is small enough that all of it can be examined: for example, the examination results of one class of students. When all of the population is examined, the survey is called a **census**. This type of survey is quite rare, however, and usually the investigator has to choose some sort of sample.

5.3 You may think that using a sample is very much a compromise, but you should consider the following points.

(a) In practice, a 100% survey (a census) never achieves the completeness required.

(b) A census may require the use of semi-skilled investigators, resulting in a loss of accuracy in the data collected.

(c) It can be shown mathematically that once a certain sample size has been reached, very little extra accuracy is gained by examining more items.

(d) It is possible to ask more questions with a sample.

(e) The higher cost of a census may exceed the value of results.

(f) Things are always changing. Even if you took a census it could well be out of date by the time you completed it.

BPP PUBLISHING

The choice of a sample

5.4 One of the most important requirements of sample data is that they should be **complete**. That is, the data should cover all areas of the population to be examined. If this requirement is not met, then the sample will be **biased**.

5.5 For example, suppose you wanted to survey the productivity of workers in a factory, and you went along every Monday and Tuesday for a few months to measure their output. Would these data be complete? The answer is no. You might have gathered very thorough data on what happens on Mondays and Tuesdays, but you would have missed out the rest of the week. It could be that the workers, keen and fresh after the weekend, work better at the start of the week than at the end. If this is the case, then your data will give you a misleadingly high productivity figure. Careful attention must therefore be given to the sampling method employed to produce a sample.

5.6 Sampling methods fall into three main groups.

- Random sampling
- Quasi-random sampling
- Non-random sampling

6 RANDOM SAMPLING
6/94, 12/95, 6/96, 6/99

6.1 To ensure that the sample selected is free from bias, **random sampling** must be used. Inferences about the population being sampled can then be made validly.

6.2 A **simple random sample** is a sample selected in such a way that every item in the population has an equal chance of being included.

6.3 For example, if you wanted to take a random sample of library books, it would not be good enough to pick them off the shelves, even if you picked them at random. This is because the books which were out on loan would stand no chance of being chosen. You would either have to make sure that all the books were on the shelves before taking your sample, or find some other way of sampling (for example, using the library index cards).

6.4 **A random sample is not necessarily a perfect sample.** For example, you might pick what you believe to be a completely random selection of library books, and find that every one of them is a detective thriller. It is a remote possibility, but it could happen. The only way to eliminate the possibility altogether is to take 100% survey (a census) of the books, which, unless it is a tiny library, is impractical.

Sampling frames

6.5 If random sampling is used then it is necessary to construct a **sampling frame. A sampling frame is simply a numbered list of all the items in the population.** Once such a list has been made, it is easy to select a random sample, simply by generating a list of random numbers.

6.6 For instance, if you wanted to select a random sample of children from a school, it would be useful to have a list of names:

```
0    J Absolam
1    R Brown
2    S Brown
...
```

Now the numbers 0, 1, 2 and so on can be used to select the random sample. It is normal to start the numbering at 0, so that when 0 appears in a list of random numbers it can be used.

6.7 Sometimes it is not possible to draw up a sampling frame. For example, if you wanted to take a random sample of Americans, it would take too long to list all Americans.

Exercise 4

You want to take a random sample of all people who live in a particular area. Why would the electoral register not be an adequate sampling frame?

Solution

Children and people who have recently moved into the area are omitted; people who have recently left the area are still included.

6.8 A sampling frame should have the following characteristics.

- **Completeness.** Are all members of the population included on the list?
- **Accuracy.** Is the information correct?
- **Adequacy.** Does it cover the entire population?
- **Up to dateness.** Is the list up to date?
- **Convenience.** Is the sampling frame readily accessible?
- **Non-duplication.** Does each member of the population appear on the list only once?

Exercise 5

Why is a telephone directory an unsuitable sampling frame of the human population?

Solution

Not everyone has a telephone and not all of those who do are listed.

Random number tables

6.9 Assuming that a sampling frame can be drawn up, then a random sample can be picked from it by one of the following methods.

(a) The **lottery method**, which amounts to picking numbered pieces of paper out of a box

(b) The use of **random number tables**

6.10 Set out below is part of a typical random number table.

93716	16894	98953	73231
32886	59780	09958	18065
92052	06831	19640	99413
39510	35905	85244	35159
27699	06494	03152	19121
92962	61773	22109	78508
10274	12202	94205	50380
75867	20717	82037	10268
85783	47619	87481	37220

You should note the following points.

(a) The sample is found by selecting groups of random numbers with the number of digits depending on the total population size, as follows.

Total population size	Number of random digits
1 - 10	1
1 - 100	2
1 - 1,000	3

The items selected for the sample are those corresponding to the random numbers selected.

(b) The starting point on the table should be selected at random. After that, however, numbers must be selected in a consistent manner. In other words, you should use the table row by row or column by column. By jumping around the table from place to place, personal bias may be introduced.

(c) In many practical situations it is more convenient to use a computer to generate a list of random numbers, especially when a large sample is required.

Example: random number tables

6.11 An investigator wishes to select a random sample from a population of 800 people, who have been numbered 000, 001, ...799. As there are three digits in 799 the random numbers will be selected in groups of three. Working along the first line of the table given earlier, the first few groups are as follows.

$$937 \quad 161 \quad 689 \quad 498 \quad 953 \quad 732$$

Numbers over 799 are discarded. The first four people in the sample will therefore be those numbered 161, 689, 498 and 732.

Drawbacks of random sampling

6.12 (a) The selected items are subject to the full range of variation inherent in the population.

(b) An unrepresentative sample may result.

(c) The members of the population selected may be scattered over a wide area, adding to the cost and difficulty of obtaining the data.

(d) An adequate sampling frame might not exist.

(e) The numbering of the population might be laborious.

Quasi- and non-random sampling

6.13 In many situations it might be too expensive to obtain a random sample, in which case quasi-random sampling is necessary, or else it may not be possible to draw up a sampling frame. In such cases, **non-random sampling** has to be used.

7 QUASI-RANDOM SAMPLING   *6/94, 12/95, 12/96, 6/98*

7.1 **Quasi-random sampling, which provides a good approximation to random sampling, necessitates the existence of a sampling frame.**

The main methods of quasi-random sampling are as follows.

- Systematic sampling
- Stratified sampling
- Multistage sampling

Systematic sampling

7.2 **Systematic sampling may provide a good approximation to random sampling. It works by selecting every nth item after a random start.** For example, if it was decided to select a sample of 20 from a population of 800, then every 40th (800 ÷ 20) item after a random start in the first 40 should be selected. The starting point could be found using the lottery method or random number tables. If (say) 23 was chosen, then the sample would include the 23rd, 63rd, 103rd, 143rd ... 783rd items.

The gap of 40 is known as the **sampling interval**.

The investigator must ensure that there is no regular pattern to the population which, if it coincided with the sampling interval, might lead to a **biased sample**. In practice, this problem is often overcome by choosing **multiple starting points** and using **varying sampling intervals** whose size is selected at random.

7.3　If the sampling frame is in **random order** (such as an alphabetical list of students) a **systematic sample** is essentially the same as a simple random sample.

A systematic sample does not, however, fully meet the criterion of **randomness** since some samples of the given size have zero probability of being chosen. The method is, however, easy and cheap and hence is widely used.

Stratified sampling

7.4　In many situations **stratified sampling** is the best method of choosing a sample. The population must be divided into strata or categories.

If we took a random sample of all chartered secretaries in the country, it is conceivable that the entire sample might consist of members of the ICSA working in local government. Stratified sampling removes this possibility as random samples could be taken from each type of employment, the number in each sample being proportional to the total number of chartered secretaries in each type (for example those in local government, those in public companies and those in private companies).

Example: stratified sampling

7.5　The number of chartered secretaries in each type of work in a particular country are as follows.

Local government	500
Public companies	500
Private companies	700
Public practice	800
	2,500

7.6　If a sample of 20 was required the sample would be made up as follows.

		Sample
Local government	$\dfrac{500}{2,500} \times 20$	4
Public companies	$\dfrac{500}{2,500} \times 20$	4
Private companies	$\dfrac{700}{2,500} \times 20$	6
Public practice	$\dfrac{800}{2,500} \times 20$	6
		20

7.7　**The strata frequently involve multiple classifications.** In social surveys, for example, there is usually stratification by age, sex and social class. This implies that the sampling frame must contain information on these three variables before the threefold stratification of the population can be made.

BPP PUBLISHING

7.8 **Advantages of stratification** are as follows.

(a) It ensures a representative sample since it guarantees that every important category will have elements in the final sample.

(b) The structure of the sample will reflect that of the population if the same proportion of individuals is chosen from each stratum.

(c) Each stratum is represented by a randomly chosen sample and therefore inferences can be made about each stratum.

(d) Precision is increased. Sampling takes place within strata and, because the range of variation is less in each stratum than in the population as a whole and variation between strata does not enter as a chance effect, higher precision is obtainable. (For this to occur, the items in each stratum must be as similar as possible and the difference between the individual strata must be as great as possible.)

7.9 Note, however, that **stratification requires prior knowledge of each item in the population**. Sampling frames do not always contain this information. Stratification from the electoral register as to age structure would not be possible because the electoral register does not contain information about age.

Exercise 6

A chartered secretary is selecting a sample of invoices for checking. The invoices are numbered sequentially. The first invoice is selected randomly and is invoice number 3. He then selects invoice numbers 7, 11, 15, 19 and 23 to complete the sample. Is this stratified sampling or systematic sampling? What would you have said if he had taken samples in the same way from invoices up to £500, invoices over £500 and up to £1,000 and invoices over £1,000?

Solution

Systematic sampling is being used. The alternative method proposed would be stratified sampling, with systematic sampling being used to select a sample from each stratum.

Multistage sampling

7.10 **Multistage sampling** is normally used to cut down the number of investigators and the costs of obtaining a sample. An example will show how the method works.

Example: multistage sampling

7.11 A survey of spending habits is being planned to cover the whole of Britain. It is obviously **impractical to draw up a sampling frame**, so random sampling is not possible. Multi-stage sampling is to be used instead.

7.12 The country is divided into a number of areas and a small sample of these is selected at random. Each of the areas selected is subdivided into smaller units and again, a smaller number of these is selected at random. This process is repeated as many times as necessary and finally, a random sample of the relevant people living in each of the smallest units is taken. A fair approximation to a random sample can be obtained.

7.13 Thus, we might choose a random sample of eight areas, and from each of these areas, select a random sample of five towns. From each town, a random sample of 200 people might be selected so that the total sample size is $8 \times 5 \times 200 = 8,000$ people.

7.14 The main advantage of this method is one of cost saving but there are a number of disadvantages.

(a) There is the possibility of bias if, for example, only a small number of regions are selected.

(b) The method is not truly random as once the final sampling areas have been selected the rest of the population cannot be in the sample.

(c) If the population is heterogeneous, the areas chosen should reflect the full range of the diversity. Otherwise, choosing some areas and excluding others (even if it is done randomly) will result in a biased sample.

7.15 The sampling methods looked at so far have necessitated the existence of a sampling frame (or in multistage sampling, sampling frames of areas, sub-areas and items within selected sub-areas). It is often impossible to identify a satisfactory sampling frame and, in such instances, other sampling methods have to be employed.

8 NON-RANDOM SAMPLING   *6/94, 12/95, 6/96, 12/96, 6/98, 6/99*

8.1 There are two main methods of **non-random sampling**, used when a sampling frame cannot be established.

- Quota sampling
- Cluster sampling

Quota sampling

8.2 In **quota sampling**, randomness is forfeited in the interests of cheapness and administrative simplicity. Investigators are told to interview all the people they meet up to a certain quota. A large degree of bias could be introduced accidentally. For example, an interviewer in a shopping centre may fill his quota by only meeting people who can go shopping during the week. In practice, this problem can be partly overcome by subdividing the quota into different types of people, for example on the basis of age, sex and income, to ensure that the sample mirrors the structure or stratification of the population. The interviewer is then told to interview, for example, 30 males between the ages of 30 and 40 from social class C 1. The actual choice of the individuals to be interviewed, within the limits of the **quota controls**, is left to the field worker.

8.3 **Advantages of quota sampling**

(a) It is cheap and administratively easy.

(b) A much larger sample can be studied, and hence more information can be gained at a faster speed for a given outlay than when compared with a fully randomised sampling method.

(c) Although a fairly detailed knowledge of the characteristics of a population is required, no sampling frame is necessary because the interviewer questions every person he meets up to the quota.

(d) Quota sampling may be the only possible approach in certain situations, such as television audience research.

(e) Given suitable, trained and properly briefed field workers, quota sampling yields enough accurate information for many forms of commercial market research.

8.4 **Disadvantages of quota sampling**

(a) The method can result in certain biases (although these can often be allowed for and/or may be unimportant for the purpose of the research).

(b) The non-random nature of the method rules out any valid estimate of the sampling error (a concept you will meet later in your studies) in estimates derived from the sample.

Conclusion

8.5 Quota sampling cannot be regarded as ultimately satisfactory in research where it is important that theoretically valid results should be obtained. It can be argued, however, that when other large sources of error, such as non response, exist, it is pointless to worry too much about sampling error.

Example: quota sampling

8.6 Consider the figures in Paragraph 7.5 above, but with the following additional information relating to the sex of the chartered secretaries.

	Male	*Female*
Local government	300	200
Public companies	400	100
Private companies	300	400
Public practice	300	500

8.7 An investigator's quotas might be as follows.

	Male	*Female*	*Total*
Local government	30	20	50
Public companies	40	10	50
Private companies	30	40	70
Public practice	30	50	80
			250

Using quota sampling, the investigator would interview the first 30 male chartered secretaries in local government that he met, the first 20 female chartered secretaries in local government that he met and so on.

Cluster sampling

8.8 **Cluster sampling involves selecting one definable subsection of the population as the sample, that subsection taken to be representative of the population in question.** The pupils of one school might be taken as a cluster sample of all children at school in one county.

Cluster sampling benefits from low costs in the same way as multistage sampling.

8.9 The advantages of cluster sampling are that it is a good alternative to multistage sampling if a satisfactory sampling frame does not exist and it is inexpensive to operate because little organisation or structure is involved. There is, however, the potential for considerable bias.

Exercise 7

A publishing company carries out a national survey of adults' reading habits. To reduce travelling costs, the country is first divided into constituencies. A sample of 50 constituencies is then selected at random. Within each of these constituencies, 5 polling districts are selected, again using random techniques. Interviewers will visit a random selection of 30 people on the electoral register in each of the districts selected. What sampling method is the company using?

Solution

Multistage sampling

---

9   INTERVIEWS   *12/98*

9.1   There are basically two types of interview that can be used to collect data, the **personal (face to face) interview** and the **telephone interview**.

Personal interviews

9.2   **Personal interviews can be classified according to their structure and directness.**

Structure

9.3   (a)   A **fully-structured interview** is controlled through the use of a structured questionnaire. The interviewer reads out the questions to the respondent in an unbiased manner and must note the responses exactly as they are given. The interviewer should not provide any additional inputs to the process, not even explanations of the questions. The responses to a fully-structured interview have been predetermined by the research design and may not be influenced by the interviewer or the respondent.

Fully-structured interviews are most useful in providing the data collector with quantitative data such as 'so many people said this, or think that or do this'. Fully-structured questions should be easy to ask and easy for respondents to answer. Proponents often argue that the use of such interviews removes bias, which is true in so far as during the interview neither the data collector nor the respondent should be able to influence the data. However, bias may have been in built to the process wittingly or otherwise by the survey designer. Responses can be pre-coded for ease of data analysis post-interview.

The major limitation of fully-structured questionnaires is in the structure. For example, if the data collector wanted to know which factors appeared to be most important in making choices about holiday destinations, a fully-structured questionnaire may provide the respondent with five choices which the data collector feels are important. The answers will make it possible to rank the five factors in order of importance. However, if the respondent identified other factors felt to be important, they would be overlooked since there is no opportunity to respond. Thus, the data collector may have missed an opportunity to discover factors which may be more important than those he/she had pre-determined. This particular problem may be overcome by adding a further category choice, but this too has its limitations. For example, how many of the previous respondents might have chosen the additional category listed by a respondent choosing this extra category? This may lead to errors in the data.

(b)   **Semi-structured interviews** consist of both closed questions offering pre-determined (pre-coded) choices such as those contained within the fully structured interviews, together with 'open ended' questions which offer respondents a free choice of responses. For example, 'Which factors do you consider most important when making a choice of holiday destination?' provides the respondent with an open question to which they may respond freely.

The interviewer may decide to use probing questions such as: 'What other factors are there?' This is useful after the respondent has listed a few factors but has partially dried up. Probing questions may trigger further responses and the interviewer may be more confident about the data provided. Semi-structured interviews allow for the collection of both qualitative and quantitative data in the same interview. The major difficulty is in analysing and interpreting responses to open-ended questions.

(c)   Neither interviewer or respondent is bound by the structure of a questionnaire in an **unstructured** interview. Interviewers may have a checklist of topics to cover in questioning, but they are free to word such questions as they wish. The order in which questions are covered may also be varied. This will allow the respondent to control the data flow and for the interviewer to explore more thoroughly particular views of the respondent and why they are held. Unstructured interviews are a very useful way of capturing data which is qualitative in nature.

Directness

9.4   Directness is the degree to which the respondent is aware of the purpose(s) of the survey.

9.5   **Advantages of personal interviews**

(a)   The interviewer is able to reduce respondent anxiety and allay potential embarrassment, thereby increasing the response rate and decreasing the potential for error.

(b)   The routing ('if yes go to question 7, if no go to question 10') of questions is made easier due to the experience of the interviewer.

(c)   Interviewers can ask, within narrow limits, for a respondent's answer to be clarified.

(d)   The questions can be given in a fixed order with a fixed wording and the answers can be recorded in a standard manner. If there is more than one interviewer involved in the survey this will reduce variability.

(e)   Standardised questions and ways of recording the responses mean that less skilled interviewers may be used, thereby reducing the cost of the survey.

(f)   Pictures, signs and objects can be used.

9.6   **Disadvantages of personal interviews**

- They can be time consuming.

- The cost per completed interview can be higher than with other survey methods.

- Questionnaires can be difficult to design.

- Fully-structured interviews have particular disadvantages.

    (a)   Questions must be kept relatively simple, thus restricting the depth of data collected.

    (b)   Questions must normally be closed because of the difficulties of recording answers to open questions.

    (c)   Interviewers cannot probe vague or ambiguous replies.

Telephone interviews

9.7   **Telephone interviews are a relatively fast and low-cost means of gathering data compared to personal interviews.** They are most useful when only a small amount of information is required. They also benefit the respondent in terms of the short amount of time taken up by the interview.

9.8   **CATI (computer-assisted telephone interviewing)** has been used successfully by insurance services and banks as well as consumer research organisations. The telephone interviewer calls up a questionnaire on screen and reads questions to the respondent. Answers are then recorded instantly on computer. Complex questions with questionnaire routing may be handled in this way.

9.9   **Advantages of telephone interviews**

(a)   The response is rapid.

(b)   A wide geographical area can be covered fairly cheaply from a central location. There is no need for the interviewer to travel between respondents.

(c)   It may be easier to ask sensitive or embarrassing questions.

9.10 **Disadvantages of telephone surveys**

(a) A biased sample may result from the fact that a proportion of people do not have telephones and many of those who do are ex-directory.

(b) It is not possible to use 'showcards' or pictures.

(c) The refusal rate is much higher than with face-to-face interviews.

(d) It is not possible to see the interviewee's expression or to develop the rapport that is possible with personal interviews.

(e) The interview must be short.

(f) Respondents may be unwilling to participate for fear of being sold something.

10 POSTAL QUESTIONNAIRES   *6/97, 12/98*

10.1 If the size of interviewer-induced error is likely to be large or its magnitude cannot be predicted with any degree of accuracy and if cost is an important factor when deciding on the data collection method, postal questionnaires should be given serious consideration.

10.2 As there is no one to clear up ambiguity in questions, their wording and sequence must be carefully thought out prior to use of the questionnaire.

10.3 **Advantages of postal questionnaires**

(a) The cost per person is likely to be less, so more people can be sampled.

(b) It is usually possible to ask more questions because the people completing the forms (the respondents) can do so in their own time.

(c) All respondents are presented with questions in the same way. There is no opportunity for an interviewer to influence responses (interviewer bias) or to misrecord them.

(d) It may be easier to ask personal or embarrassing questions in a postal questionnaire than in a personal interview.

(e) Respondents may need to look up information for the questionnaire. This will be easier if the questionnaire is sent to their home or place of work.

10.4 **Disadvantages of postal questionnaires**

(a) Large numbers of postal questionnaires may not be returned or may be returned only partly completed. This may lead to biased results if those replying are not representative of all people in the survey. Response rates are likely to be higher with personal interviews, and the interviewer can encourage people to answer all questions. Low response rates are a major problem with postal questionnaires.

(b) Misunderstanding is less likely with personal interviews because the interviewer can explain questions which the interviewee does not understand.

(c) Personal interviews are more suitable when deep or detailed questions are to be asked, since the interviewer can take the time required with each interviewee to explain the implications of the question. Also, the interviewer can probe for further information and encourage the respondent to think deeper.

Chapter roundup

- This chapter has concentrated on the practical problems of collecting data.

- An **attribute** is something an object has either got or not got. It cannot be measured. A **variable** is something which can be measured.

- **Variables** can be **discrete** (may take specific values) or **continuous** (may take any value).

- **Data** may be **primary** (collected specifically for the current purpose) or **secondary** (collected already).

- **Secondary data** can be collected from a number of official sources.

- One way of collecting primary data is the **survey method**. There are two main types of survey, **interviews** and **postal questionnaires**.

- Questionnaire design involves the following considerations.

  - Initial considerations
  - Question content
  - Question phrasing
  - Types of response format
  - Question sequence
  - Questionnaire layout
  - Pretest, revision and final version

- Data are often collected from a **sample** rather than from a **population**. A sample can be selected using **random sampling** (using random number tables or the lottery method), **quasi-random sampling** (systematic, stratified and multistage sampling) or **non-random sampling** (quota and cluster sampling). Ensure that you know the characteristics, advantages and disadvantages of each sampling method.

- Once data have been collected they need to be presented and analysed. It is important to remember that if the data have not been collected properly, no amount of careful presentation or interpretation can remedy the defect.

Test your knowledge

1   What is a discrete variable? (see para 1.5)

2   What are secondary data? (1.6)

3   List some of the UK official sources of economic and business data. (2.6-2.20)

4   How can the non-response rate for postal questionnaires be reduced? (3.15)

5   What factors should be considered when phrasing questions for questionnaires? (4.4)

6   List the arguments in favour of using a sample. (5.3)

7   What is a simple random sample? (6.2)

8   What is stratified sampling? (7.4)

9   What are the advantages of postal questionnaires over personal interviews? (10.3)

Now try illustrative questions 1 to 4 at the end of the Study Text

Chapter 2

THE PRESENTATION OF DATA: TABULATION AND CHARTS

This chapter covers the following topics

1   Tabulation

2   Frequency distributions

3   Charts

4   Histograms

Introduction

You now know how to collect data. So what do we do now? We have to **present** the data we have collected so that it can be of use. This chapter begins by looking at how data can be presented in **tables** and **charts**. Such methods are helpful in presenting key data in a concise and easy to understand way. They are, however, purely descriptive and offer little opportunity for further detailed numerical analysis of a situation. **Histograms**, on the other hand, provide the link between the purely diagrammatic approach to data analysis and the numerical approach covered in Chapters 4 and 5.

1   TABULATION

1.1   **Raw data** (the list of results from a survey) need to be summarised and analysed, to give them meaning. This chapter is concerned with several different ways of presenting data to convey their meaning. We will start with one of the most basic ways, the **preparation of a table.**

1.2   **Tabulation** means putting data into tables. A table is a matrix of data in rows and columns, with the rows and the columns having titles.

1.3   Since a table is **two-dimensional**, it can only show two variables. For example, the resources required to produce items in a factory could be tabulated, with one dimension (rows or columns) representing the items produced and the other dimension representing the resources.

Cost of resources required per unit of product

	Product items				
	A	*B*	*C*	*D*	*Total*
Resources					
Direct material A	X	X	X	X	X
Direct material B	X	X	X	X	X
Direct labour grade 1	X	X	X	X	X
Direct labour grade 2	X	X	X	X	X
Supervision	X	X	X	X	X
Machine time	X	X	X	X	X
Total	X	X	X	X	X

1.4 To tabulate data, you need to recognise what the two dimensions should represent, prepare rows and columns accordingly with suitable titles, and then insert the data into the appropriate places in the table.

Guidelines for tabulation

1.5 The table in Paragraph 1.3 illustrates certain guidelines which you should apply when presenting data in tabular form. These are as follows.

(a) The table should be given a clear title.

(b) All columns should be clearly labelled.

(c) Where appropriate, there should be clear sub-totals.

(d) A total column may be presented; this would usually be the right-hand column.

(e) A total figure is often advisable at the bottom of each column of figures.

(f) Tables should not be packed with too much data so that reading the information is difficult.

(g) Eliminate non-essential information, rounding large numbers to two or three significant figures.

(h) Do not hide important figures in the middle of the table. Consider ordering columns/rows by order of importance/magnitude.

Example: tables

1.6 The total number of employees in a certain trading company is 1,000. They are employed in three departments: production, administration and sales. 600 people are employed in the production department and 300 in administration. There are 110 male juveniles in employment, 110 female juveniles, and 290 adult females. The remaining employees are adult males.

In the production department there are 350 adult males, 150 adult females and 50 male juveniles, whilst in the administration department there are 100 adult males, 110 adult females and 50 juvenile males.

Required

Draw up a table to show all the details of employment in the company and its departments and provide suitable secondary statistics to describe the distribution of people in departments.

Solution

1.7 The basic table required has the following two dimensions.

- Departments
- Age/sex analysis

1.8 **Secondary statistics** (not the same thing as secondary data) are supporting figures that are supplementary to the main items of data, and which clarify or amplify the main data. A major example of secondary statistics is **percentages**. In this example, we could show one of the following.

(a) The percentage of the total work force in each department belonging to each age/sex group

(b) The percentage of the total of each age/sex group employed in each department

In this example, (a) has been selected but you might consider that (b) would be more suitable. Either could be suitable, depending of course on what purposes the data are being collected and presented for.

1.9

Analysis of employees

	Production		Administration		Sales		Total	
	No	%	No	%	No	%	No	%
Adult males	350	58.4	100	33.3	**40	40	*490	49
Adult females	150	25.0	110	36.7	**30	30	290	29
Male juveniles	50	8.3	50	16.7	**10	10	110	11
Female juveniles	* 50	8.3	* 40	13.3	**20	20	110	11
Total	600	100.0	300	100.0	100	100	1,000	100

*   Balancing figure to make up the column total

**   Balancing figure then needed to make up the row total

Rounding errors

1.10   **Rounding errors** may become apparent when, for example, a percentages column does not add up to 100%. To avoid bias, any rounding should be to the nearest unit and the potential size of errors should be kept to a tolerable level by rounding to a small enough unit (for example to the nearest £10, rather than to the nearest £1,000).

Tally marks

1.11   **Tally marks** are another simple way of presenting data. If we measured the number of jobs completed by each employee in a department during one week, the data could be collected and presented as follows.

Employee	Jobs completed	
A	₦₦ ////	= 9
B	₦₦ ₦₦ ////	= 14
C	₦₦ //	= 7
D	///	= 3

Exercise 1

The expenditure of the Borough Council of Numac on school dinners for the year 20X0/X1 was £2,496,000 made up as follows.

Personnel:	administration £108,800; meals supervision £195,200; kitchen staff £944,000.
Operating expenses:	provisions £812,800; crockery and utensils £73,600; protective clothing £3,200; laundering £6,400.
Buildings:	maintenance £32,000; fuel £83,200; cleaning £19,200; equipment and furniture £9,600; rent £48,000.

Central establishment charges £160,000.

During the year 3,200,000 school dinners were served.

Required

Present the foregoing information in the form of a table showing the following.

(a)   The expenditure, item by item, with subtotals for the separate categories of expenditure

(b)   The information specified in (a) expressed as costs per school dinner

Solution

The two dimensions (the rows and columns) to be represented in the table are expenditure items and the amount of expenditure per item in total and as a cost per school dinner. Expenditure items must be sub-analysed, but this forms part of the 'expenditure items' dimension. Sub-totals are easily included, but it might make the table clearer if sub-totals are presented in a separate column. When one dimension includes a larger number of items, it is better to present these items as the rows of the table, to make better use of the space on the page. The number of school dinners served is an important figure, but one which does not fit into the rows or columns of the table. We should show it as a separate item, either just below the table heading or at the foot of the table.

BOROUGH COUNCIL OF NUMAC
SCHOOL DINNER EXPENSES 20X0/X1

Number of school dinners served in the year: 3,200,000

	(a) Expenditure		(b) Cost/school dinner	
	£	£	pence	pence
Personnel				
Administration	108,800		3.4	
Meals supervision	195,200		6.1	
Kitchen	944,000		29.5	
Total		1,248,000		39.0
Operating expenses				
Provisions	812,800		25.4	
Crockery and utensils	73,600		2.3	
Protective clothing	3,200		0.1	
Laundering	6,400		0.2	
Total		896,000		28.0
Buildings				
Maintenance	32,000		1.0	
Fuel	83,200		2.6	
Cleaning	19,200		0.6	
Equipment and furniture	9,600		0.3	
Rent, rates and so on	48,000		1.5	
Total		192,000		6.0
Central establishment charges		160,000		5.0
Grand total		2,496,000		78.0

2 FREQUENCY DISTRIBUTIONS

12/97

2.1 If a large number of measurements of a particular variable are taken (for example the number of units produced per employee per week) some values may occur more than once. A **frequency distribution** (or **frequency table**) is obtained by recording the number of times each value occurs.

Example: a frequency distribution

2.2 The output in units of 20 employees during one week was as follows.

65	69	70	71	70	68	69	67	70	68
72	71	69	74	70	73	71	67	69	70

2.3 If the number of occurrences is placed against each output quantity, a frequency distribution is produced.

Output of employees in one week in units

Output Units	Number of employees (frequency)
65	1
66	0
67	2
68	2
69	4
70	5
71	3
72	1
73	1
74	1
	20

2.4 The number of employees corresponding to a particular volume of output is called a **frequency**. When the data are arranged in this way it is immediately obvious that 69 and 70 units are the most common volumes of output per employee per week.

Grouped frequency distributions

2.5 It is often convenient to group frequencies together into bands or classes. For example, suppose that the output produced by each of 20 employees during one week was as follows, in units.

1,087	850	1,084	792
924	1,226	1,012	1,205
1,265	1,028	1,230	1,182
1,086	1,130	989	1,155
1,134	1,166	1,129	1,160

2.6 An **ungrouped frequency distribution** would not be a helpful way of presenting the data, because each employee has produced a different number of units in the week.

2.7 The range of output from the lowest to the highest producer is 792 to 1,265, a range of 473 units. This range could be divided into classes of say, 100 units (the class width or class interval), and the number of employees producing output within each class could then be grouped into a single frequency, as follows.

Output Units	Number of employees (frequency)
700 - 799	1
800 - 899	1
900 - 999	2
1,000 - 1,099	5
1,100 - 1,199	7
1,200 - 1,299	4
	20

Grouped frequency distributions of continuous variables

2.8 **Grouped frequency distributions** (or grouped frequency tables) **can be used to present data for continuous variables**.

Example: a grouped frequency distribution for a continuous variable

2.9   Suppose we wish to record the heights of 50 different individuals. The information might be presented as a grouped frequency distribution, as follows.

Height	Number of individuals (frequency)
cm	
Up to and including 154	1
Over 154, up to and including 163	3
Over 163, up to and including 172	8
Over 172, up to and including 181	16
Over 181, up to and including 190	18
Over 190	4
	50

2.10   Note the following points.

   (a)   It would be wrong to show the ranges as 0 - 154, 154 - 163, 163 - 172 and so on, because 154 cm and 163 cm would then be values in two classes, which is not permissible.

   (b)   There is an *open ended* class at each end of the range. This is because heights up to 154 cm and over 190 cm are thought to be uncommon, so that a single 'open ended' class is used to group all the frequencies together.

Preparing grouped frequency distributions

2.11   To prepare a grouped frequency distribution, a decision must be made about **how wide each class should be**. In an examination, you might be told how many classes to use, or what the class interval should be. You should, however, generally observe the following guidelines.

   (a)   The size of each class should be appropriate to the nature of the data being recorded, and the most appropriate class interval varies according to circumstances.

   (b)   The upper and lower limits of each class interval should be suitable 'round' numbers for class intervals which are in multiples of 5, 10, 100, 1,000 and so on. For example, if the class interval is 10, and data items range in value from 23 to 62 (discrete values), the class intervals should be 20-29, 30-39, 40-49, 50-59 and 60-69, rather than 23-32, 33-42, 43-52 and 53-62.

   (c)   With continuous variables, either:

      (i)   the upper limit of a class should be 'up to and including ...' and the lower limit of the next class should be 'over ...'; or

      (ii)   the upper limit of a class should be 'less than...', and the lower limit of the next class should be 'at least ...'.

Exercise 2

The commission earnings for May 20X3 of the assistants in a department store were as follows (in pounds).

60	35	53	47	25	44	55	58	47	71
63	67	57	44	61	48	50	56	61	42
43	38	41	39	61	51	27	56	57	50
55	68	55	50	25	48	44	43	49	73
53	35	36	41	45	71	56	40	69	52
36	47	66	52	32	46	44	32	52	58
49	41	45	45	48	36	46	42	52	33
31	36	40	66	53	58	60	52	66	51
51	44	59	53	51	57	35	45	46	54
46	54	51	39	64	43	54	47	60	45

Required

Prepare a grouped frequency distribution classifying the commission earnings into categories of £5 commencing with '£25 and under £30'.

Solution

We are told what classes to use, so the first step is to identify the lowest and highest values in the data. The lowest value is £25 (in the first row) and the highest value is £73 (in the fourth row). This means that the class intervals must go up to '£70 and under £75'.

We can now set out the classes in a column, and then count the number of items in each class using tally marks.

Class interval	Tally marks	Total
£25 and less than £30	///	3
£30 and less than £35	////	4
£35 and less than £40	//// ////	10
£40 and less than £45	//// //// ////	15
£45 and less than £50	//// //// //// ///	18
£50 and less than £55	//// //// //// ////	20
£55 and less than £60	//// //// ///	13
£60 and less than £65	//// ///	8
£65 and less than £70	//// /	6
£70 and less than £75	///	3
	Total	100

2.12 You should be able to interpret a grouped frequency distribution and express an interpretation in writing. In the example in Paragraph 2.9, an interpretation of the data is fairly straightforward.

(a) Most heights fell between 154 cm and 190 cm.

(b) Most heights were in the middle of this range, with few people having heights in the lower and upper ends of the range.

Cumulative frequency distributions

2.13 A **cumulative frequency distribution** (or **cumulative frequency table**) **can be used to show the total number of times that a value above or below a certain amount occurs.**

Example: cumulative frequency distributions

2.14 The volume of output produced in one day by each of 20 employees is as follows, in units.

18	29	22	17
30	12	27	24
26	32	24	29
28	46	31	27
19	18	32	25

2.15 We could present a grouped frequency distribution as follows.

Output Units	Number of employees (frequency)
Under 15	1
15 or more, under 20	4
20 or more, under 25	3
25 or more, under 30	7
30 or more, under 35	4
35 or more	1
	20

BPP PUBLISHING

2.16 The two possible cumulative frequency distributions for the same data are as follows.

	Cumulative frequency		Cumulative frequency
≥ 0	20	<15	1
≥ 15	19	<20	5
≥ 20	15	<25	8
≥ 25	12	<30	15
≥ 30	5	<35	19
≥ 35	1	<47	20

Notes

(a) The symbol > means 'greater than' and ≥ means 'greater than or equal to'. The symbol < means 'less than' and ≤ means 'less than or equal to'. These symbols provide a convenient method of stating classes.

(b) The first cumulative frequency distribution shows that of the total of 20 employees:

 • 19 produced 15 units or more
 • 15 produced 20 units or more
 • 12 produced 25 units or more and so on

(c) The second cumulative frequency distribution shows that of the total of 20 employees:

 • One produced under 15 units
 • Five produced under 20 units
 • Eight produced under 25 units and so on

3 CHARTS
6/95, 12/97, 6/98, 12/99

3.1 Instead of presenting data in a table, it might be preferable to give a visual display in the form of a **chart**.

3.2 The purpose of a chart is to convey the data in a way that will demonstrate its meaning or significance more clearly than a table of data would. Charts are not always more appropriate than tables, and the most suitable way of presenting data will depend on the following.

 (a) **What the data are intended to show**. Visual displays usually make one or two points quite forcefully, whereas tables usually give more detailed information.

 (b) **Who is going to use the data**. Some individuals might understand visual displays more readily than tabulated data.

3.3 There are three types of chart that might be used to present data.
 • Pictograms
 • Pie charts
 • Bar charts
We shall look at each of these in turn.

Pictograms

3.4 **A pictogram is a statistical diagram in which quantities are represented by pictures or symbols.**

Example: pictograms

3.5 A pictogram showing the number of employees at a factory would represent the quantities of employees using pictures of people.

Number of employees

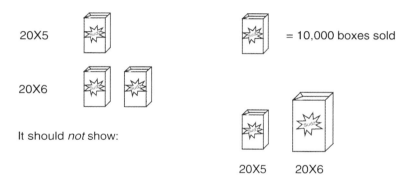

In this example, each picture represents ten employees, and to represent a smaller quantity, a part-picture can be drawn. Here, there were 45 men employed in 20X6.

3.6 The **guidelines for drawing a pictogram** are as follows.

(a) The symbols should be clear and simple.

(b) The quantity that each symbol represents should be clearly shown in a key to the pictogram.

(c) Bigger quantities ought to be shown by more symbols, not by bigger symbols. For example, if sales of boxes of dishwasher powder double between 20X5 and 20X6, a pictogram should show:

In this pictogram, the bigger symbol does not give a true impression of sales growth.

3.7 **The advantage of pictograms is that they present data in a simple, readily understood way.** Pictograms convey their message to the reader at a glance, and are consequently often used on television and in advertisements.

3.8 **The disadvantages of pictograms are that they can only convey a limited amount of information, and that they lack precision.** Each symbol must represent quite a large number of items, otherwise a pictogram would contain too many symbols. Using portions of a symbol to represent smaller quantities gives some extra precision, but not much.

represents 1,000 men then

represents less than 1,000 men, but how many exactly? 400? 500? 600?

Pie charts

3.9 **A pie chart is used to show pictorially the relative sizes of component elements of a total.** It is called a pie chart because it is circular, and so has the shape of a pie in a round pie dish and because the 'pie' is then cut into slices. Each slice represents a part of the total.

3.10 Pie charts have sectors of varying sizes, and you need to be able to draw sectors fairly accurately. To do this, you need a protractor. Working out sector sizes involves converting parts of the total into equivalent degrees of a circle.

Example: pie charts

3.11 The costs of production at Factory A and Factory B during March 20X2 were as follows.

	Factory A		Factory B	
	£'000	%	£'000	%
Direct materials	70	35	50	20
Direct labour	30	15	125	50
Production overhead	90	45	50	20
Office costs	10	5	25	10
	200	100	250	100

Required

Show the costs for the factories in pie charts.

Solution

3.12 To convert the components into degrees of a circle, we can use either the percentage figures or the actual cost figures.

(a) Using the percentage figures, the total percentage is 100%, and the total number of degrees in a circle is 360°. To convert from one to the other, we multiply each percentage value by 360/100 = 3.6.

	Factory A		Factory B	
	%	Degrees	%	Degrees
Direct materials	35	126	20	72
Direct labour	15	54	50	180
Production overhead	45	162	20	72
Office costs	5	18	10	36
	100	360	100	360

(b) Using the actual cost figures, we would multiply each cost by

	Factory A	Factory B
$\dfrac{\text{Number of degrees}}{\text{Total cost}}$	$\dfrac{360}{200} = 1.8$	$\dfrac{360}{250} = 1.44$

	Factory A		Factory B	
	£'000	Degrees	£'000	Degrees
Direct materials	70	126	50	72
Direct labour	30	54	125	180
Production overhead	90	162	50	72
Office costs	10	18	25	36
	200	360	250	360

3.13 A pie chart could be drawn for each factory, as follows. A protractor is used to measure the degrees accurately to obtain the correct sector sizes.

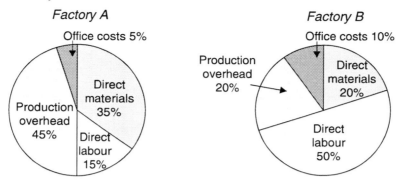

3.14 The **advantages of pie charts** are as follows.

(a) They give a simple pictorial display of the relative sizes of elements of a total.

(b) They show clearly when one element is much bigger than others.

(c) They can sometimes clearly show differences in the elements of two different totals. In the example above, the pie charts for factories A and B show how factory A's costs mostly consist of production overhead and direct materials, whereas at factory B, direct labour is the largest cost element.

3.15 The **disadvantages of pie charts** are as follows.

(a) They show only the relative sizes of elements. In the example of the two factories, for instance, the pie charts do not show that costs at Factory B were £50,000 higher in total than at Factory A.

(b) They involve calculating degrees of a circle and drawing sectors accurately, and this can be time consuming.

(c) It is sometimes difficult to compare sector sizes accurately by eye.

Bar charts

3.16 **The bar chart is one of the most common methods of presenting data in a visual form. It is a chart in which quantities are shown in the form of bars.**

3.17 There are three main types of bar chart.

• Simple bar charts
• Component bar charts, including percentage component bar charts
• Multiple (or compound) bar charts

Simple bar charts

3.18 **A simple bar chart is a chart consisting of one or more bars, in which the length of each bar indicates the magnitude of the corresponding data item.**

Example: a simple bar chart

3.19 A company's total sales for the years from 20X1 to 20X6 are as follows.

Year	Sales
	£'000
20X1	800
20X2	1,200
20X3	1,100
20X4	1,400
20X5	1,600
20X6	1,700

The data could be shown on a simple bar chart as follows

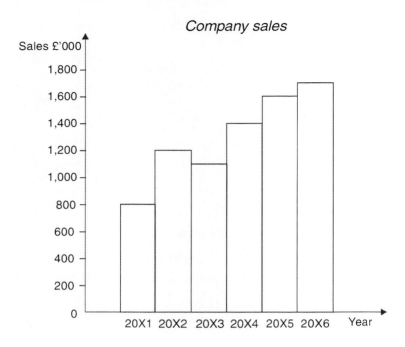

3.20 Each axis of the chart must be clearly labelled, and there must be a scale to indicate the magnitude of the data. Here, the y axis includes a scale for the amount of sales, and so readers of the bar chart can see not only that sales have been rising year by year (with 20X3 being an exception) but also what the actual sales have been each year.

3.21 Simple bar charts serve two purposes.

(a) They show the **actual magnitude** of each item.

(b) They enable one to **compare magnitudes**, by comparing the lengths of bars on the chart.

Component bar charts

3.22 **A component bar chart is a bar chart that gives a breakdown of each total into its components.**

Example: a component bar chart

3.23 Charbart plc's sales for the years from 20X7 to 20X9 are as follows.

	20X7	20X8	20X9
	£'000	£'000	£'000
Product A	1,000	1,200	1,700
Product B	900	1,000	1,000
Product C	500	600	700
Total	2,400	2,800	3,400

3.24 A component bar chart would show the following.

- How total sales have changed from year to year
- The components of each year's total

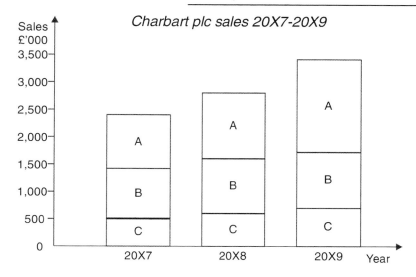

3.25 The bars in a bar chart can either be drawn side by side, with no gap between them, or with gaps between them, as in the diagram here. It does not matter which method is used.

3.26 In this diagram the growth in sales is illustrated and the significance of growth in product A sales as the reason for the total sales growth is also fairly clear. The growth in product A sales would have been even clearer if product A had been drawn as the bottom element in each bar instead of the top one.

Percentage component bar charts

3.27 The difference between a component bar chart and a percentage component bar chart is that with a **component bar chart**, the **total length of each bar** (and the length of each component in it) **indicates magnitude**. A bigger amount is shown by a longer bar. With a **percentage component bar chart, total magnitudes are not shown**. If two or more bars are drawn on the chart, the total length of each bar is the same. The only varying lengths in a percentage component bar chart are the lengths of the sections of a bar, which vary according to the relative sizes of the components.

Example: a percentage component bar chart

3.28 The information in the previous example of sales of Charbart plc could have been shown in a percentage component bar chart as follows.

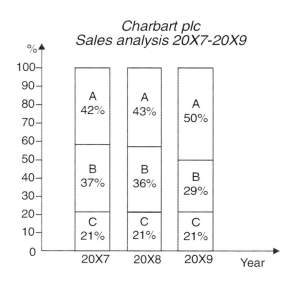

Working

	20X7		20X8		20X9	
	£'000	%	£'000	%	£'000	%
Product A	1,000	42	1,200	43	1,700	50
Product B	900	37	1,000	36	1,000	29
Product C	500	21	600	21	700	21
Total	2,400	100	2,800	100	3,400	100

3.29 This chart shows that sales of C have remained a steady proportion of total sales, but the proportion of A in total sales has gone up quite considerably, while the proportion of B has fallen correspondingly.

Multiple bar charts (compound bar charts)

3.30 **A multiple bar chart (or compound bar chart) is a bar chart in which two or more separate bars are used to present sub-divisions of data.**

Example: a multiple bar chart

3.31 The output of Rodd Ltd in the years from 20X6 to 20X8 is as follows.

	20X6	20X7	20X8
	'000 units	'000 units	'000 units
Product X	180	130	50
Product Y	90	110	170
Product Z	180	180	125
Total	450	420	345

The data could be shown in a multiple bar chart as follows.

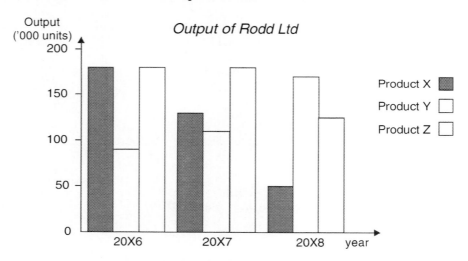

3.32 A multiple bar chart uses several bars for each total. In the above example, the sales in each year are shown as three separate bars, one for each product, X, Y and Z.

Multiple bar charts are sometimes drawn with the bars horizontal instead of vertical.

3.33 Multiple bar charts present similar information to component bar charts, except for the following.

(a) **Multiple bar charts do not show the grand total** (in the above example, the total output each year) **whereas component bar charts do.**

(b) **Multiple bar charts illustrate the comparative magnitudes of the components more clearly than component bar charts.**

Exercise 3

Income for Lemmi Bank in 20X0, 20X1 and 20X2 is made up as follows.

	20X0	*20X1*	*20X2*
	£'000	*£'000*	*£'000*
Interest income	3,579	2,961	2,192
Commission income	857	893	917
Other income	62	59	70

Required

Using the above data, draw the following.

(a)   A simple bar chart
(b)   A component bar chart
(c)   A percentage component bar chart
(d)   A compound bar chart

Solution

(a)

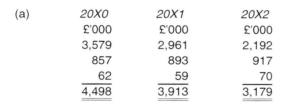

20X0	*20X1*	*20X2*
£'000	*£'000*	*£'000*
3,579	2,961	2,192
857	893	917
62	59	70
4,498	3,913	3,179

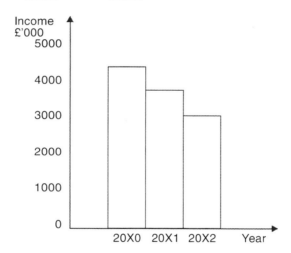

(b)   Income

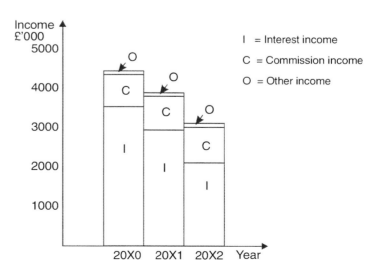

I = Interest income

C = Commission income

O = Other income

BPP
PUBLISHING

(c)

	20X0		20X1		20X2	
	£'000	%	£'000	%	£'000	%
	3,579	80	2,961	76	2,192	69
	857	19	893	23	917	29
	62	1	59	1	70	2
	4,498	100	3,913	100	3,179	100

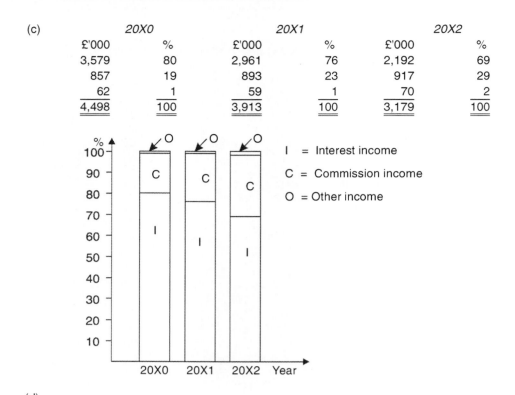

I = Interest income

C = Commission income

O = Other income

(d)

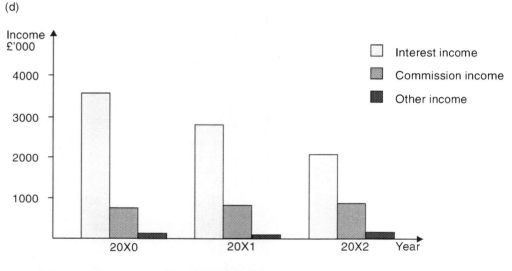

Interest income

Commission income

Other income

Line charts

3.34 **A line chart is similar to a bar chart but with lines instead of bars. The length of the line is proportional to the value represented. It is often used for discrete variables.**

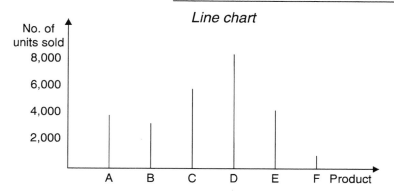

Line chart

Gantt charts

3.35 **Gantt charts** are named after their creator, Henry Gantt, a management scientist working in the early years of this century. They are a **form of bar chart or line chart**.

3.36 **The purpose of a Gantt chart is to record progress over time**. A chart can show the following.

- Progress in a given period, for example each month
- Cumulative progress to date, for example in the year to date

3.37 Actual progress can be compared with planned progress, and so a Gantt chart gives a quick visual indication as to whether actual progress is ahead of or behind schedule.

Constructing a Gantt chart

3.38 The lines or bars are usually drawn horizontally, and vertical lines divide them, separating them into time periods. Each time period of equal length is shown by an equal length of line or bar.

Example: Gantt charts

3.39 Suppose that budgeted sales of Fred Ltd are as follows.

Month	Sales	Cumulative sales for the year to date
	Units	Units
January	1,000	1,000
February	1,500	2,500
March	2,000	4,500
April	2,500	7,000
May	1,500	8,500
June	500	9,000

3.40 A Gantt chart would be constructed as follows.

Gantt chart of
sales, half year January - June

Month	Jan	Feb	March	April	May	June
Budgeted sales in month	1,000	1,500	2,000	2,500	1,500	500
Budgeted cumulative sales for year to date	1,000	2,500	4,500	7,000	8,500	9,000
Budget						

The Gantt chart can show a budget line, with the line representing both sales in the month and cumulative sales for the year to date: that is, target figures for the individual time periods and also cumulative target figures.

The budget line represents time, but also these budgeted quantities. Since the sales budget varies from month to month, the length of the line does not relate to quantities of sales. (The length of the line relates to time.)

3.41 We can construct a Gantt chart as at the end of January, February and March, as follows, supposing that actual sales were 600, 1,800 and 1,600 in those months. Monthly sales are shown by a line and cumulative sales by a bar.

(a)

Gantt chart at end of January

	Jan	Feb	Mar	Apr	May	Jun
Budget						
Actual sales in month	● 600					
Cumulative actual sales	▭ 600					

The length of each 'actual' line is $\dfrac{600}{1,000}$ or 60% of budget.

(b)

Gantt chart at end of February

	Jan	Feb	Mar	Apr	May	Jun
Budget						
Actual sales in month	● 600	● 1,800				
Cumulative actual sales		2,400				

The length of the 'actual sales in February' line is 1,600/1,500 = 120% of the budget, which means drawing a second line which is 20% of the length of the February section of the budget line.

Cumulative sales are 2,400/2,500 = 96% of budget and so the bar is 96% of the length of the January plus February budget line.

(c)

Gantt chart at end of March

	Jan	Feb	Mar	Apr	May	Jun
Budgeted sales in month	1,000	1,500	2,000	2,500	1,500	500
Budgeted cumulative sales for year to date	1,000	2,500	4,500	7,000	8,500	9,000
Budget						
Actual sales in month	● 600	● 1,800	1,600 ●			
Cumulative actual sales			4,000			

The length of the 'actual sales in March' line is 1,600/2,000 = 80% of the budget line.

Cumulative sales are 4,000/4,500 = 8/9 of the length of the January to March budget line.

Venn diagrams

3.42   **A Venn diagram may be used to show divisions and sub-divisions of a category.** Here is an example.

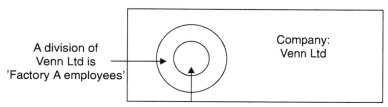

Venn diagram showing divisions and sub-divisions of a category

3.43   If we use the following symbols:

U   (Universal) = the set of all the company's employees;
A   = the set of Factory A employees;
B   = the set of direct production workers in Factory A;

the Venn diagram can be shown as follows.

Venn diagram using symbols

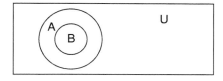

3.44   If we used B to represent the set of all direct production workers, whether inside Factory A or in other factories of Venn Ltd, we could draw Venn diagrams as follows.

Venn diagrams of sets of Factory A employees and direct production workers

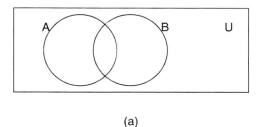

(a)

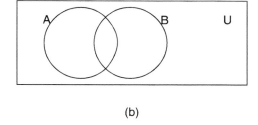

(b)

(a)   The shading on this diagram picks out the company's production workers within Factory A, that is those who are both employed in Factory A and employed as production workers. This area is called the intersection of A and B and is written A ∩ B.

(b)   The shading on this diagram picks out those employees who are either direct production workers or who work in Factory A (or who come into both categories). This area is called the union of A and B and is written A ∪ B.

Statistical maps or cartograms

3.45   **Statistical maps, or cartograms, may be used to display geographical data.** Here is an example.

Unemployment in England and Wales, 20X3

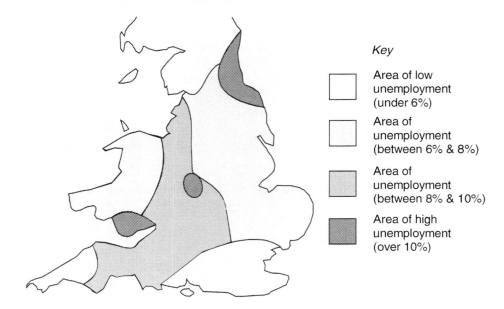

Key

☐ Area of low unemployment (under 6%)

☐ Area of unemployment (between 6% & 8%)

▨ Area of unemployment (between 8% & 10%)

▉ Area of high unemployment (over 10%)

A key is needed to explain the meaning of different shadings on the map.

4 HISTOGRAMS

6/94, 6/95, 12/95, 6/96, 12/96, 6/97, 12/97, 6/98, 12/98, 6/99, 12/99, 6/00

4.1 **Histograms** look rather like bar charts, but there are important differences. They are used when **grouped data of a continuous variable** are presented. They can also be used for **discrete data,** by **treating the data as continuous** so there are no gaps between class intervals: for example with a cricketer's scores in various games, using $\geq 0 < 10, \geq 10 < 20$ and so on, instead of 0-9, 10-19 and so on.

4.2 The number of observations in a class is represented by the **area** covered by the bar, rather than by its height.

Example: a histogram

4.3 The weekly wages of employees of Salt Lake Ltd are as follows.

Wages per employee	Number of employees
> £40 ≤ £60	4
> £60 ≤ £80	6
> £80 ≤ £90	6
> £90 ≤ £120	6
> £120 ≤ £150	3

The class intervals for wages per employee are not all the same, and range from £10 to £30.

4.4 **A histogram is drawn as follows.**

(a) The width of each bar on the chart must be proportionate to the corresponding class interval. In other words, the bar representing wages of > £40 ≤ £60, a range of £20, will be twice as wide as the bar representing wages of > £80 ≤ £90, a range of only £10.

(b) A standard width of bar must be selected. This should be the size of class interval which occurs most frequently. In our example, class intervals of £20 and £30 each occur twice. An interval of £20 will be selected as the standard width.

(c) Each frequency is then divided by the actual class interval and multiplied by the standard class interval to obtain the *height* of the bar in the histogram.

4.5

Class interval	Size of interval	Frequency	Adjustment	Height of bar
> £40 ≤ £60	20	4	× 20/20	4
> £60 ≤ £80	20	6	× 20/20	6
> £80 ≤ £90	10	6	× 20/10	12
> £90 ≤ £120	30	6	× 20/30	4
> £120 ≤ £150	30	3	× 20/30	2

(a) The first two bars will be of normal height.

(b) The third bar will be twice as high as the class frequency (6) would suggest, to compensate for the fact that the class interval, £10, is only half the standard size.

(c) The fourth and fifth bars will be two thirds as high as the class frequencies (6 and 3) would suggest, to compensate for the fact that the class interval, £30, is 150% of the standard size.

4.6

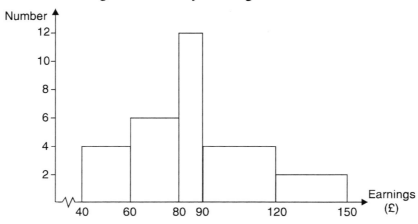

Histogram of weekly earnings: Salt Lake Ltd

Exercise 4

The sales force of a company have just completed a successful sales campaign. The performances of individual sales staff have been analysed as follows, into a grouped frequency distribution.

Sales	Number of sales staff
Up to £10,000	1
> £10,000 ≤ £12,000	10
> £12,000 ≤ £14,000	12
> £14,000 ≤ £18,000	8
> £18,000 ≤ £22,000	4
> £22,000	1

Required

Draw a histogram from this information.

Solution

Before drawing the histogram, we must decide on the following.

(a) A standard class width: £2,000 will be chosen.

(b) An open-ended class width. It is usual for the width to be the same as that of the adjoining class. In this example, the open-ended class width will therefore be £2,000 for class 'up to £10,000' and £4,000 for the class '> £22,000'.

BPP PUBLISHING

Class interval	Size of width £	Frequency	Adjustment	Height of block
Up to £10,000	2,000	1	× 2/2	1
> £10,000 ≤ £12,000	2,000	10	× 2/2	10
> £12,000 ≤ £14,000	2,000	12	× 2/2	12
> £14,000 ≤ £18,000	4,000	8	× 2/4	4
> £18,000 ≤ £22,000	4,000	4	× 2/4	2
> £22,000	4,000	1	× 2/4	¹/₂

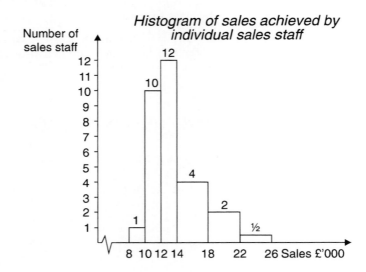

Histogram of sales achieved by individual sales staff

The advantages and disadvantages of histograms

4.7 **Histograms are frequently used to display grouped frequency distributions graphically**.

(a) They display clearly the comparative frequency of occurrence of data items within classes.

(b) They indicate whether the range of values is wide or narrow, and whether most values occur in the middle of the range or whether the frequencies are more evenly spread.

Consider these two histograms.

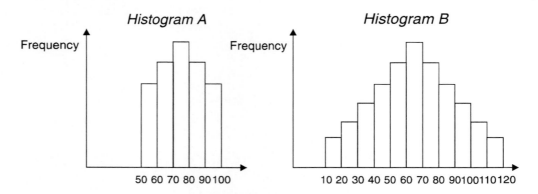

In (A) there is a narrower range of values than in (B). Both have the most frequently occurring value somewhere in the middle of the range (70-80 with A and 60-70 with B).

Now compare these two histograms.

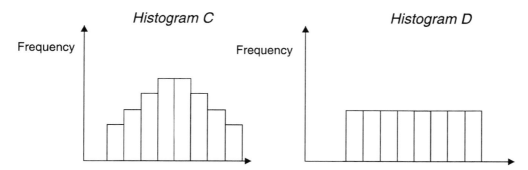

The most frequently occurring values in histogram C are towards the middle of the range, whereas in histogram D, values occur with equal frequency across the entire range.

4.8 The **main disadvantages of histograms** are as follows.

(a) If a histogram represents sample data, the measurements in the histogram might give a false sense of accuracy. The sample data will not be an exact representation of the population as a whole.

(b) If the histogram is showing data about a **continuous** variable, the sharp steps of the histogram blocks would be a little misleading.

(c) Histograms in which the class widths vary may not be readily understood by the lay person.

Frequency polygons

4.9 **A histogram can be converted into a frequency polygon**, which is drawn on the assumption that within each class interval, the frequency of occurrence of data items is not evenly spread. There will be more values at the end of each class interval nearer the histogram's peak (if any), and so the flat top on a histogram bar should be converted into a rising or falling line.

4.10 A frequency polygon is drawn from a histogram, in the following way.

Step 1. Mark the mid-point of the top of each bar in the histogram.
Step 2. Join up all these points with straight lines.

4.11 The ends of the diagram (the mid-points of the two end bars) should be joined to the base line at the mid-points of the next class intervals outside the range of observed data. These intervals should be taken to be of the same size as the last class intervals for observed data.

Example: a frequency polygon

4.12 The following grouped frequency distribution relates to the number of occasions during the past 40 weeks that a particular cost has been a given amount.

Cost £	*Number of occasions*
> 800 ≤ 1,000	4
> 1,000 ≤ 1,200	10
> 1,200 ≤ 1,400	12
> 1,400 ≤ 1,600	10
> 1,600 ≤ 1,800	4
	40

Required

Prepare a frequency polygon.

Solution

4.13 A histogram is first drawn, in the way described earlier. All classes are of the same width.

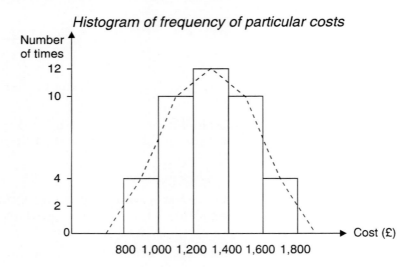

Histogram of frequency of particular costs

The mid-points of the class intervals outside the range of observed data are 700 and 1,900.

4.14 If a histogram is drawn with many narrow classes, the frequency polygon may become virtually a smooth curve, a **frequency curve**.

Chapter roundup

- This chapter has considered a number of ways of presenting data.

- **Tables** are a simple way of presenting information about two variables.

- **Frequency distributions** are used if values of particular variables occur more than once. Make sure that you know the difference between **grouped frequency** and **cumulative frequency** distributions.

- **Charts** often convey the meaning or significance of data more clearly than would a table. Make sure that you are able to construct the following

Pictograms	Line charts
Pie charts	Venn diagrams
Bar charts	Statistical maps
Gantt charts	

- There are three main types of bar chart: **simple**, **component** (including percentage component) and **multiple** (or compound).

- **Histograms** are used to present grouped data of a **continuous** variable. They can also be used for **discrete variables** by **treating the variables as continuous** so there are no gaps between class intervals. The number of observations in a class is represented by the area covered by the block, rather than by its height.

- Make sure that you are able to present data in all of the formats covered in this chapter and that you are aware of the information available from each method of presentation. When selecting a method of data presentation remember to consider the type of information which must be shown and the presentation which the ultimate user of the information will find most helpful.

Test your knowledge

1   What are the main guidelines for tabulation? (see para 1.5)

2   How would you prepare a grouped frequency distribution? (2.11)

3   What is a cumulative frequency distribution? (2.13)

4   What is the advantage of pictograms? (3.7)

5   What are the disadvantages of pie charts? (3.15)

6   Name the three main types of bar chart. (3.17)

7   What is the purpose of a Gantt chart? (3.36)

8   Describe a Venn diagram. (3.42 - 3.44)

9   What are the computations needed to draw a histogram? (4.4)

10   How would you draw a frequency polygon from a histogram? (4.10)

Now try illustrative questions 5 and 6 at the end of the Study Text

BPP PUBLISHING

Chapter 3

THE PRESENTATION OF DATA: GRAPHS

This chapter covers the following topics.

1   Ogives

2   Lorenz curves

3   Z charts

4   Band curves

5   Frequency distribution curves

6   Scattergraphs

Introduction

Tabulation and charts, including the statistically useful histogram, were covered in Chapter 2. In this chapter we will look at **graphical data presentation methods**. Just as there are statistically useful charts, there are statistically useful graphs. **Ogives**, **Lorenz curves** and **Z charts use cumulative frequencies** and provide additional statistical information.

This chapter also considers **band curves**, **frequency distribution curves**, **semi-logarithmic graphs** and **scattergraphs**.

---

1   OGIVES   *12/94, 12/95, 6/98*

1.1   **An ogive shows the cumulative number of items with a value less than or equal to, or alternatively greater than or equal to, a certain amount.**

Example: ogives

1.2   Consider the following frequency distribution.

Number of faulty units rejected on inspection	Frequency	Cumulative frequency
1	5	5
2	5	10
3	3	13
4	$\underline{1}$	14
	$\underline{\underline{14}}$	

An ogive would be drawn as follows.

Ogive of rejected items

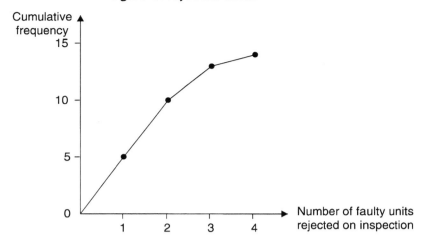

1.3 The ogive is drawn by plotting the cumulative frequencies on the graph, and joining them with straight lines. Although many ogives are more accurately curved lines, you can use straight lines in drawing an ogive in an examination. An ogive drawn with straight lines may be referred to as a **cumulative frequency polygon**, whereas one drawn as a curve may be referred to as a **cumulative frequency curve**.

1.4 For grouped frequency distributions, where we work up through values of the variable, the cumulative frequencies are plotted against the **upper limits** of the classes. For example, for the class 'over 200, up to and including 250', the cumulative frequency should be plotted against 250.

Exercise 1

A grouped frequency distribution for the volume of output produced at a factory over a period of 40 weeks is as follows.

Output (units)	Number of times output achieved
> 0 ≤ 200	4
>200 ≤ 400	8
>400 ≤ 600	12
>600 ≤ 800	10
>800 ≤1,000	6
	40

Required

Draw an appropriate ogive, and estimate the number of weeks in which output was 550 units or less.

Solution

Upper limit of interval	Frequency	Cumulative frequency
200	4	4
400	8	12
600	12	24
800	10	34
1,000	6	40

BPP PUBLISHING

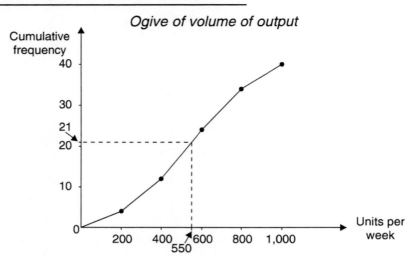

Ogive of volume of output

The dotted lines indicate that output of up to 550 units was achieved in 21 out of the 40 weeks.

1.5 **We can also draw ogives to show the cumulative number of items with values greater than or equal to some given value.**

Example: downward-sloping ogives

1.6 Output at a factory over a period of 80 weeks is shown by the following frequency distribution.

Output per week Units	*Number of times output achieved*
> 0 ≤100	10
> 100 ≤200	20
> 200 ≤300	25
> 300 ≤400	15
> 400 ≤500	10
	80

1.7 If we wished to draw an ogive to show the number of weeks in which output exceeded a certain value, the cumulative total would begin at 80 and drop to 0.

In drawing an ogive when we work down through values of the variable, the descending cumulative frequency should be plotted against the lower limit of each class interval.

Lower limit of interval	*Frequency*	*Cumulative ('more than') frequency*
0	10	80
100	20	70
200	25	50
300	15	25
400	10	10
500	0	0

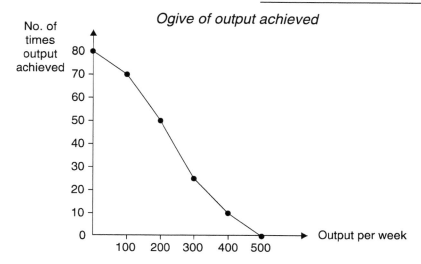

Ogive of output achieved

Make sure that you understand what this curve shows.

For example, 350 on the x axis corresponds with about 18 on the y axis. This means that output of 350 units or more was achieved 18 times out of the 80 weeks.

Exercise 2

If you wanted to produce an ogive showing the cumulative number of students in a class with an exam mark of 55% or more, would you need an upward-sloping or a downward-sloping ogive?

Solution

A downward-sloping ogive

What information does an ogive provide?

1.8 **An ogive represents a cumulative frequency distribution** and it can be used to show what range of values contain given proportions of the total population. For example, it can be used to find the following.

- The range of values of the first 50% of the population
- Within what range of values the middle 50% of the population falls

1.9 These particular pieces of information can be obtained by finding the following from the ogive.

(a) The value of the middle item in the range, corresponding to a cumulative frequency of 50% of the *total*. For example, if there are 11 data items, the middle item would be the sixth. If there are ten data items, we would take the fifth item.

The middle item of n data items is the $[(n + 1)/2]$th where n is an odd number and the $(n/2)$th where n is an even number (it is not usually worth worrying about the fact that when n is even, there are two items which are equally 'in the middle').

The value of the middle item is called the median value.

(b) The value of the item which is a quarter (25%) of the way through the cumulative frequencies (running from low values up to high values). For example, if there are 11 data items, this would be the third item. If there are ten data items, it would be taken as the mid-way point between the second and third items: the '$2\frac{1}{2}$ th' item. However, one might decide to approximate and take the third item.

This quarter-way-through item is called the lower quartile or the first quartile.

(c) The value of the item which is three quarters (75%) of the way through the cumulative frequencies. For example, if there are 11 data items, this would be the value of the ninth item.

This **three-quarters-way-through** value is called the **upper quartile** or the **third quartile**. (The second quartile is the median.)

Example: the median and quartiles

1.10 The production of each manufacturing department of your company is monitored weekly to establish productivity bonuses to be paid to the members of that department.

250 items have to be produced each week before a bonus will be paid. The production in one department over a 40 week period is shown below.

382	367	364	365	371	370	372	364	355	347
354	359	359	360	357	362	364	365	371	365
361	380	382	394	396	398	402	406	437	456
469	466	459	454	460	457	452	451	445	446

Required

(a) Form a frequency distribution of five groups for the number of items produced each week.

(b) Construct the ogive for the frequency distribution established in (a).

(c) Establish the value of the median from the ogive.

(d) Establish the values of the upper and lower quartiles.

(e) Interpret the results that you obtain in (c) and (d).

Solution

1.11 The first step is to decide on the size of class intervals for a grouped frequency distribution, given that the requirement here is for five classes.

Highest value amongst the data	469
Less lowest value amongst the data	347
Range of values	122

This gives a minimum average class interval of $\dfrac{122}{5}$ = 24.4, say 25.

However, it is not obvious what the lowest and highest values of each class would be, and it might be easier to take class intervals of 30. This would give a range of values of $30 \times 5 = 150$, which is 28 more than the range of 122 that we need. By sharing the 'excess' between the low and high ends of the range and also looking for suitable lower and upper limits to each class, we arrive at classes from 341 – 370 to 461 – 490.

Class	Frequency	Cumulative frequency
341 - 370	17	17
371 - 400	9	26
401 - 430	2	28
431 - 460	10	38
461 - 490	2	40
	40	

1.12 The ogive is now constructed by marking units along the x axis and cumulative frequency along the y axis. The first class interval is 341 – 370, and so the x axis starts at 340.

Ogive of weekly production

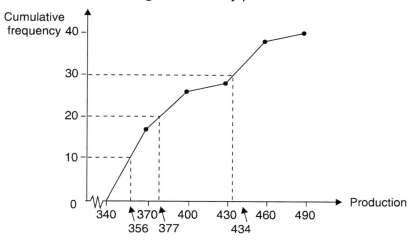

1.13 The **median** is the $\frac{1}{2} \times 40 = $ 20th value. Reading off from the ogive, this value is 377 units per week.

The **upper quartile** is the $\frac{3}{4} \times 40 = $ 30th value. The lower quartile is the $\frac{1}{4} \times 40 = $ 10th value. Reading off from the ogive, these values are 434 units and 356 units respectively.

1.14 These values show that in half of the weeks production was in the range 356 to 434 units, with the **middle-of-the-range value** (the **median**) being 377, which is closer to the lower quartile than to the upper quartile.

2 LORENZ CURVES

2.1 **A Lorenz curve also makes use of cumulative frequencies; it measures one cumulative amount against another.** It is normal, though not essential, for both the x axis and the y axis to be shown in terms of percentages (each up to 100%).

2.2 **A Lorenz curve shows degree of concentration.** A common application of the Lorenz curve is to show the distribution of wealth. If the distribution is completely even, then there is no concentration of wealth in the population, and everyone has the same wealth.

Example: Lorenz curves

2.3 The national wealth of Ruritania is spread as follows.

Wealth in roubles per person	No of people	Wealth '000 roubles
< 500	13,000	5,200
≥ 500 < 1,000	16,000	12,800
≥ 1,000 < 5,000	16,000	48,000
≥ 5,000 < 40,000	2,000	50,000
≥ 40,000	500	25,000
	47,500	141,000

2.4 From these figures the cumulative number of people and the cumulative wealth can be calculated.

No of people	Cumulative no of people	%	Wealth '000 roubles	Cumulative wealth '000 roubles	%
13,000	13,000	27	5,200	5,200	4
16,000	29,000	61	12,800	18,000	13
16,000	45,000	95	48,000	66,000	47
2,000	47,000	99	50,000	116,000	82
500	47,500	100	25,000	141,000	100

2.5   The graph is plotted from the percentage columns.

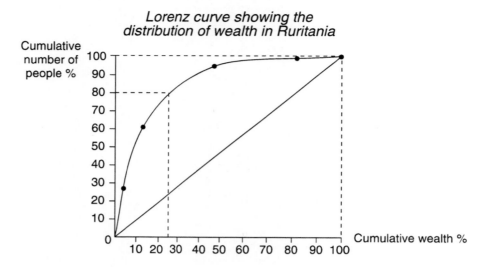

2.6   A straight line is also drawn, joining the origin of the graph with the point (100%, 100%). This is the line we would expect if there were no concentration of wealth in the population, that is, if everyone had the same wealth. It is drawn to show how much concentration there actually is. The more the curve deviates from this diagonal line (called the **line of uniform distribution**), the greater the concentration.

2.7   In this case it appears that a large proportion of the wealth of Ruritania belongs to a fairly small section of the population. The dotted lines on the graph show that 80% of the population own only 25% of the wealth, so the richest 20% of the population own 75% of the wealth.

2.8   **The main application of Lorenz curves is in making comparisons.** For instance, researchers may wish to see whether in subsequent years the concentration of wealth in Ruritania changes. If Lorenz curves for subsequent years are plotted on the same graph it can be seen whether the degree of concentration has increased (in which case the curve will be further from the diagonal) or decreased (in which case the curve will be nearer the diagonal).

Exercise 3

The following table shows the distribution of the levels of turnover of the companies in a certain industry.

Turnover £'000	Number of companies
over 500 - 1,000	32
over 1,000 - 1,500	58
over 1,500 - 2,000	41
over 2,000 - 2,500	33
over 2,500 - 3,000	28
over 3,000 - 3,500	16

Required

(a)   Construct a Lorenz curve from these data. Use the mid-point of each class as the turnover of each company in the class.

(b)   State what this chart shows.

Solution

(a)   *Calculation of figures for Lorenz curve*

Turnover £'000	Class midpoint,x £'000	No of cos,f	Total turnover,fx	Cumulative turnover	%	Cumulative companies	%
over 500 - 1,000	750	32	24,000	24,000	6.46	32	15.38
over 1,000 - 1,500	1,250	58	72,500	96,500	25.98	90	43.27
over 1,500 - 2,000	1,750	41	71,750	168,250	45.29	131	62.98
over 2,000 - 2,500	2,250	33	74,250	242,500	65.28	164	78.85
over 2,500 - 3,000	2,750	28	77,000	319,500	86.00	192	92.30
over 3,000 - 3,500	3,250	16	52,000	371,500	100.00	208	100.00

The Lorenz curve is now drawn. The number of companies has been recorded on the y axis and turnover on the x axis, but it would be equally suitable to have turnover on the y axis and the number of companies on the x axis.

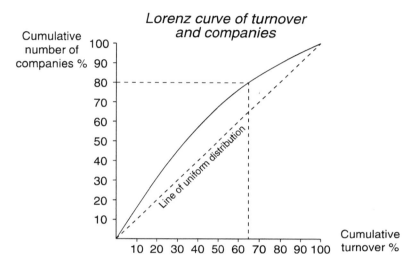

(b) The Lorenz curve in this example shows the degree of concentration of total revenue within the population of companies. The further the curve is away from the diagonal the greater is the degree of concentration of revenue.

In this case it appears that there is a moderate degree of concentration of turnover. Approximately 80% of companies share only about 65% of the total turnover, so the top 20% of companies have 35% of total turnover.

3   Z CHARTS

3.1 **A Z chart is a time series graph which can be very useful for presenting business data.** It shows the following.

- The value of a variable plotted against time over the year
- The cumulative sum of values for that variable over the year to date
- The annual moving total for that variable

3.2 The **annual moving total** is the sum of values of the variable for the 12 month period up to the end of the month under consideration.

A line for the budget for the year to date may be added to a Z chart, for comparison with the cumulative sum of actual values.

Example: Z charts

3.3   The sales figures for a company for 20X2 and 20X3 are as follows.

	20X2 sales £m	20X3 sales £m
January	7	8
February	7	8
March	8	8
April	7	9
May	9	8
June	8	8
July	8	7
August	7	8
September	6	9
October	7	6
November	8	9
December	8	9
	90	97

Required

Draw a Z chart to represent these data.

Solution

3.4   The first thing to do is to calculate the cumulative sales for 20X3 and the annual moving total for the year.

	Sales 20X2 £m	Sales 20X3 £m	Cumulative sales 20X3 £m	Annual moving total £m
January	7	8	8	91
February	7	8	16	92
March	8	8	24	92
April	7	9	33	94
May	9	8	41	93
June	8	8	49	93
July	8	7	56	92
August	7	8	64	93
September	6	9	73	96
October	7	6	79	95
November	8	9	88	96
December	8	9	97	97

The first figure in the annual moving total is arrived at by taking the sales for the year ended December 20X2, adding those for January 20X3 and subtracting those for January 20X2. This gives the sales for a 12 month period to the end of January 20X3 as 90 + 8 – 7 = 91.

A similar approach is used for the rest of the year, by adding on the new 20X3 month and deducting the corresponding 20X2 month.

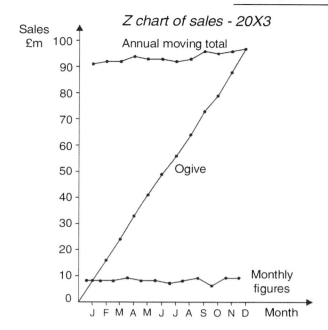

Z chart of sales - 20X3

3.5 You will notice that while the values of the annual moving total and the cumulative values are plotted on month-end positions, the values for the current monthly figures are plotted on mid-month positions. This is because the monthly figures represent achievement over a particular month whereas the annual moving totals and the cumulative values represent achievement up to a particular month end.

The interpretation of Z charts

3.6 The popularity of Z charts in practical applications derives from the wealth of information which they can contain.

(a) **Monthly totals** show the monthly results at a glance together with any seasonal variations.

(b) **Cumulative totals** show the performance to date, and can be easily compared with planned or budgeted performance by superimposing a budget line.

(c) **Annual moving totals** compare the current levels of performance with those of the previous year. If the line is rising then this year's monthly results are better than the results of the corresponding month last year. The opposite applies if the line is falling. The annual moving total line indicates the long-term trend in values of the variable, whether rising, falling or steady.

3.7 **You should note that Z charts do not have to cover 12 months of a year.** They could also be drawn for (for example) four quarters of a year, or seven days of a week. The method would be exactly the same.

Exercise 4

Why does the annual moving total line on a Z chart show the long-term trend, unaffected by seasonal effects such as sales being higher in summer than winter?

Solution

One example of each month is included in the annual moving total. Thus although July might be a very good month, but January a very bad month, there will be one July and one January in the total, balancing each other.

---

4 BAND CURVES

4.1 **A band curve, also known as a layer graph, is a form of time series graph in which the total figure is broken down into its components.**

Example: band curves

4.2 The costs of administration at the head office of STU Ltd might be shown as follows.

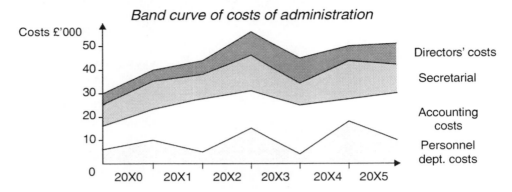

5 FREQUENCY DISTRIBUTION CURVES   12/97, 12/99, 6/00

5.1 A histogram is not a particularly accurate method of presenting a frequency distribution, because in grouping frequencies together in a class interval, it is assumed that these frequencies occur evenly throughout the class interval, which is unlikely. A frequency polygon is also somewhat unrepresentative, because it has straight lines between points.

5.2 One method of obtaining greater accuracy would be to make the class intervals smaller, and to draw a **histogram** or a **frequency polygon of the grouped frequency distribution** with these small intervals, as follows.

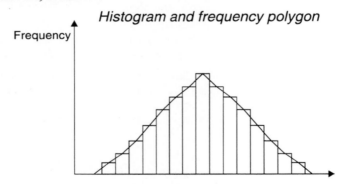

5.3 If the class intervals were made small enough, the frequency polygon would become very smooth. It would become a curve. A **frequency distribution curve** from the histogram and polygon in Paragraph 5.2 might be as follows.

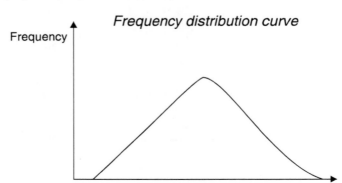

6   SCATTERGRAPHS

6.1   **Scattergraphs are graphs which are used to exhibit data, rather than equations which produce simple lines or curves, in order to compare the way in which two variables vary with each other. The x axis of the graph is used to represent the independent variable** (its value affects the value of the dependent variable) **and the y axis represents the dependent variable.**

6.2   To construct a scattergraph or scatter diagram, we must have several pairs of data, with each pair showing the value of one variable and the corresponding value of the other variable. Each pair is plotted on a graph. The resulting graph will show a number of points, scattered over the graph. The scattered points might or might not appear to follow a trend.

Example: scattergraphs

6.3   The output at a factory each week for the last ten weeks, and the cost of that output, were as follows.

Output (units)	10	12	10	8	9	11	7	12	9	14
Cost (£)	42	44	38	34	38	43	30	47	37	50

The data could be shown on a scattergraph.

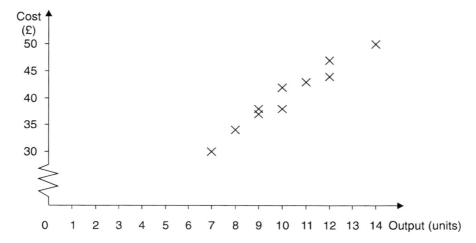

The cost depends on the volume of output: volume is the independent variable and is shown on the x axis.

6.4   You will notice from the graph that the plotted data, although scattered, lie approximately on a rising trend line, with higher total costs at higher output volumes. (The lower part of the y axis has been omitted, so as not to waste space. The break in the y axis is indicated by the jagged line.)

BPP
PUBLISHING

Chapter roundup

- This chapter has considered the ways of **presenting** and **summarising** data using graphs.

- An **ogive** shows the cumulative number of items with a value less than or equal to, or alternatively greater than or equal to, a certain amount. An ogive provides information on the **median** and **quartiles** of a population.

- A **Lorenz curve** is a form of cumulative frequency curve which measures one cumulative amount against another. Both the x and y axes are often shown in terms of percentages. This type of graph is used to show **degrees of concentration**.

- A **Z chart** shows the value of a variable plotted against time over the period, the cumulative sum of values for that variable over the period to date and the period moving total for that variable.

- Other types of graph include **band curves, frequency distribution curves, semi-logarithmic graphs** and **scattergraphs**.

- You should not only ensure that you can draw and interpret each type of graph looked at in this chapter, but you should also think carefully about the different situations in which the various types of graph would be appropriate.

Test your knowledge

1   How would you draw an ogive? (1.2 - 1.4)

2   Explain the meaning of the lower quartile and the upper quartile of a frequency distribution. (1.9)

3   What is the purpose of a Lorenz curve? (2.2)

4   What three lines are drawn on a Z chart? (3.1)

5   How is a scattergraph constructed? (6.2)

Now try illustrative questions 7 to 9 at the end of the Study Text

Part B
Measures of location and dispersion

Chapter 4

MEASURES OF LOCATION

This chapter covers the following topics.

1 The arithmetic mean

2 The mode

3 The median

4 The geometric mean and the harmonic mean

5 Weighted averages

Introduction

In Chapters 2 and 3 we saw how data can be summarised as, for example, a frequency distribution, or presented in some diagrammatical form such as histogram. While these are useful, it is sometimes desirable to summarise data in the form of a numerical value.

There are two initial numerical measures that we might require from a set of data: a measure of **location** and a **measure of dispersion**. In Chapter 5 we will study measures of dispersion, in this chapter measures of location, or averages.

An **average** is a **representative figure** that is used to give some impression of the size of all the items in a population. There are three main types of average.

- Mean
- Mode
- Median

An average, whether it is a mean, a mode or a median, is a **measure of central tendency**. By this we mean that while a population may cover a range of values, these values will be distributed around a central point. This central point, or average, is therefore in some way representative of the population as a whole.

As well as looking at the most commonly used averages, we will consider the **geometric** and **harmonic** means, which are specialised measures of location.

---

1   THE ARITHMETIC MEAN   6/94,12/94,6/95,12/95,6/96,12/96,6/98, 12/98, 6/99, 12,99, 6/00

1.1   This is the best known type of average. For ungrouped data, it is calculated by the formula

$$\textbf{Arithmetic mean} = \frac{\text{Sum of values of items}}{\text{Number of items}}$$

For example, the mean wage of a work force of ten men is the amount each worker would receive if all their earnings were pooled and then shared out equally among them.

Example: the arithmetic mean

1.2   The demand for a product on each of 20 days was as follows (in units).

3   12   7   17   3   14   9   6   11   10   1   4   19   7   15   6   9   12   12   8

BPP PUBLISHING

The arithmetic mean of daily demand is

$$\frac{\text{Sum of demand}}{\text{Number of days}} = \frac{185}{20} = 9.25 \text{ units}$$

1.3 **The arithmetic mean of a variable x is shown as $\overline{x}$ ('x bar').**

Thus in the above example $\overline{x}$ = 9.25 units.

1.4 In the above example, demand on any one day is never actually 9.25 units. The arithmetic mean is merely an average representation of demand on each of the 20 days.

The arithmetic mean of data in a frequency distribution

1.5 It is more likely that an arithmetic mean of a frequency distribution will be required. In our previous example, the frequency distribution would be shown as follows.

Daily demand *x*	*Frequency* *f*	*Demand × frequency* *fx*
1	1	1
3	2	6
4	1	4
6	2	12
7	2	14
8	1	8
9	2	18
10	1	10
11	1	11
12	3	36
14	1	14
15	1	15
17	1	17
19	1	19
	20	185

$$\overline{x} = \frac{185}{20} = 9.25$$

Sigma, Σ

1.6 The statistical notation for the arithmetic mean of a set of data uses the symbol Σ (sigma). Σ **means 'the sum of'** and is used as shorthand to mean the sum of a set of values.

Thus, in the previous example:

(a) Σ **f** would mean the sum of all the frequencies, which is 20;

(b) Σ **fx** would mean the sum of all the values of 'frequency multiplied by daily demand', that is, all 14 values of fx, so Σ fx = 185.

The symbolic formula for the arithmetic mean

1.7 Using the Σ sign, the formula for the arithmetic mean of a frequency distribution is

$$\overline{x} = \frac{\Sigma fx}{n} \text{ or } \frac{\Sigma fx}{\Sigma f}$$

where n is the number of values recorded, or the number of items measured.

The arithmetic mean of grouped data in class intervals

1.8   Another common problem is to calculate (or at least approximate) the arithmetic mean of a frequency distribution, where the frequencies are shown in class intervals.

Example: grouped data

1.9   Using the example in Paragraph 1.5, the frequency distribution might have been shown as follows.

Daily demand	Frequency
> 0 ≤ 5	4
> 5 ≤ 10	8
>10 ≤ 15	6
>15 ≤ 20	2
	20

1.10   **An arithmetic mean is calculated by taking the mid-point of each class interval, on the assumption that the frequencies occur evenly over the class interval range.** Note that the variable is discrete, so the first class includes 1, 2, 3, 4 and 5, giving a mid-point of 3. With a continuous variable (such as quantities of fuel consumed in litres), the mid-points would have been 2.5, 7.5 and so on.

Daily demand	Mid point x	Frequency f	fx
> 0 ≤ 5	3	4	12
> 5 ≤ 10	8	8	64
>10 ≤ 15	13	6	78
>15 ≤ 20	18	2	36
		$\Sigma f = 20$	$\Sigma fx = 190$

Arithmetic mean $\overline{x} = \dfrac{\Sigma fx}{\Sigma f} = \dfrac{190}{20} = 9.5$ units

1.11   Because the assumption that frequencies occurred evenly within each class interval is not quite correct in this example, our approximate mean of 9.5 is not exactly correct, and is in error by 0.25.

As the frequencies become larger, the size of this approximating error should become smaller.

The advantages and disadvantages of the arithmetic mean

1.12   The **advantages of the arithmetic mean** are as follows.

- It is widely understood.
- The value of every item is included in the computation of the mean.
- It is supported by mathematical theory and is suited to further statistical analysis.

1.13   The **disadvantages of the arithmetic mean** are as follows.

(a)   Its value may not correspond to any actual value. For example, the 'average' family might have 2.3 children, but no family has exactly 2.3 children.

(b)   An arithmetic mean might be distorted by extremely high or low values. For example, the mean of 3, 4, 4 and 6 is 4.25, but the mean of 3, 4, 4, 6 and 15 is 6.4. The high value, 15, distorts the average and in some circumstances the mean would be a misleading and inappropriate figure. (Note that extreme values are not uncommon in economic data.)

Exercise 1

For the week ended 15 November, the wages earned by the 69 operators employed in the machine shop of Mermaid Ltd were as follows.

Wages	Number of Operatives
under £ 60	3
£60 and under £70	11
£70 and under £80	16
£80 and under £90	15
£90 and under £100	10
£100 and under £110	8
£110 and under £120	6
	69

Required

Calculate the arithmetic mean wage of the machine operators of Mermaid Ltd for the week ended 15 November.

Solution

The mid point of the range 'under £60' is assumed to be £55, since all other class intervals are £10. This is obviously an approximation which might result in a loss of accuracy; nevertheless, there is no better alternative assumption to use. Note that the mid-points of the classes are half way between their end points, because wages can vary in steps of only 1p so are virtually a continuous variable.

Mid point of class x £	Frequency f	fx
55	3	165
65	11	715
75	16	1,200
85	15	1,275
95	10	950
105	8	840
115	6	690
	69	5,835

$$\text{Arithmetic mean} = \frac{£5,835}{69} = £84.57$$

2 THE MODE

12/94, 12/98, 12/99, 6/00

2.1 **The mode is an average which means 'the most frequently occurring value'.**

Example: the mode

2.2 The daily demand for stock in a ten day period is as follows.

Demand Units	Number of days
6	3
7	6
8	1
	10

The mode is 7 units, because it is the value which occurs most frequently.

The mode in grouped frequency distributions

2.3 **In a grouped frequency distribution, the mode can only be estimated approximately.**

2.4   The method of making this estimate is as follows.

(a)   Establish which is the class with the highest value of frequency ÷ class width (the modal class).

(b)   The mode is taken as

$$L + \frac{(F_1 - F_0) \times c}{2F_1 - F_0 - F_2}$$

where   L   =   the lower limit of the modal class
         F_0 =   the frequency of the next class below the modal class
         F_1 =   the frequency of the modal class
         F_2 =   the frequency of the next class above the modal class
         c   =   the width of the modal class

This formula only works if the modal class, the next class below it and the next class above it all have the same width (class interval).

Example: the formula for the mode

2.5   Calculate the mode of the following frequency distribution.

Value		Frequency
At least	Less than	
10	25	6
25	40	19
40	55	12
55	70	7
70	85	3

Solution

2.6   All classes have the same width, so the modal class is the class interval with the highest frequency, that is, the class ≥ 25 and < 40. The class interval is 15. F_1 is 19, the frequency of the modal class. F_0 is the frequency of the class below 25-40, the class 10-25, which is 6. F_2 is the frequency of the class 40-55, which is 12.

The estimated mode is

$$25 + \frac{(19-6) \times 15}{(2 \times 19) - 6 - 12}$$

$$= \quad 25 + \frac{(13 \times 15)}{(38-18)}$$

$$= \quad 25 + 9.75$$

$$= \quad 34.75$$

Exercise 2

An analysis of sales invoices outstanding at the end of February is as follows.

Invoice value		Number of invoices
at least	less than	
£	£	
10	25	4
25	40	8
40	55	18
55	70	9
70	85	3

What is the approximate modal value of invoices outstanding at the end of February?

Solution

The modal class is $\geq 40 < 55$.

An estimate of the mode is: $40 + \dfrac{(18-8) \times 15}{(2 \times 18) - 8 - 9} = 40 + \dfrac{150}{19} = £47.89$

Finding the mode from a histogram

2.7 **The mode of a grouped frequency distribution can also be calculated from a histogram.** Using this method, it does not matter if the class intervals vary.

Example: finding the mode from a histogram

2.8 Consider the following histogram.

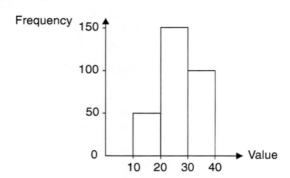

The mode is in the range 20-30. The modal class is the class with the tallest bar (which may not be the class with the highest frequency if the classes do not all have the same width).

2.9 We can **estimate the mode graphically** as follows.

(a) Join with a straight line the top left hand corner of the bar for the modal class and the top left hand corner of the next bar to the right.

(b) Join with a straight line the top right hand corner of the bar for the modal class and the top right hand corner of the next bar to the left.

2.10 Where these two lines intersect, we find the **estimated modal value**. In this example it is 26.7.

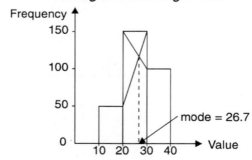

Histogram showing mode

Using the formula for the mode, we would arrive at the same answer.

$$\textbf{Mode} = 20 + \frac{(150-50) \times 10}{(2 \times 150) - 50 - 100}$$

$$= 20 + \frac{1,000}{150}$$

$$= 26.7$$

2.11 Again, using both the formula and the graphical approach, we are assuming that the frequencies occur evenly within each class interval but this may not always be correct. It is unlikely that the 150 values in the modal class occur evenly. Hence the mode in a grouped frequency distribution is only an estimate.

The advantages and disadvantages of the mode

2.12 The **mode** will be a more appropriate average to use than the mean in situations where it is useful to know the most **common value**. For example, if a manufacturer wishes to start production in a new industry, it might be helpful to know what sort of product made by the industry is most in demand with customers. The mode is **easy to find**, it is **uninfluenced by a few extreme values** and it can be used for data which are **not even numerical** (unlike the mean and median). The main disadvantage of the mode is that it **ignores dispersion around the modal value**, and unlike the mean, **does not take every value into account**. There can also be **two or more modes** within a set of data and, if the modal class is only very slightly bigger than another class, just a few more items in this other class could mean a substantially different result, suggesting some instability in this measure. It is also **unsuitable for further statistical analysis**.

3 THE MEDIAN   *12/95, 12/97, 12/98, 12/99, 6/00*

3.1 The third type of average is the median **The median is the value of the middle member of a distribution or array.**

3.2 The median of a set of ungrouped data is found by **arranging the items in ascending or descending order** of value, and selecting the item in the **middle of the range**. A list of items in order of value is called an **array**.

Example : the median

3.3 The median of the following nine values:

| 8 | 6 | 9 | 12 | 15 | 6 | 3 | 20 | 11 |

is found by taking the middle item (the fifth one) in the array:

| 3 | 6 | 6 | 8 | 9 | 11 | 12 | 15 | 20 |

The median is 9.

The median of the following ten values would be the fifth item in the array.

| 1 | 2 | 2 | 2 | 3 | 5 | 6 | 7 | 8 | 11 |

The median is 3.

With an even number of items, we could take the arithmetic mean of the two middle ones (in this example, $(3 + 5)/2 = 4$), but when there are many items it is not worth doing this.

The median of an ungrouped frequency distribution

3.4 The median of an ungrouped frequency distribution is found in a similar way. Consider the following distribution.

BPP PUBLISHING

Value	Frequency	Cumulative frequency
x	*f*	
8	3	3
12	7	10
16	12	22
17	8	30
19	5	35
	35	

(a) We came across the median in Chapter 3 when we were considering the information which may be obtained from an ogive. We can therefore use the formula given on page 55 for finding the middle item, or median of n data items of an ungrouped frequency distribution.

(b) In our example, there are 35 data items. Since this is an odd number, the median would be the (35 + 1)/2 = 18th item. The 18th item has a value of 16, as we can see from the cumulative frequencies in the right hand column of the above table.

The median of a grouped frequency distribution

3.5 **The median of a grouped frequency distribution**, like the arithmetic mean and the mode, **can only be estimated approximately.**

3.6 First, we must find the class interval to which the middle item belongs.

3.7 We then use the following formula.

Median = value of lower limit to the class + $\left(\dfrac{R}{f} \times c\right)$

where   c   is the size of the class interval

           f   is the frequency of the class

           R   is the difference between the middle member (n/2 (see below)) and the cumulative total of frequencies up to the end of the preceding class.

Note. For odd n, the middle member is taken to be n/2 and not (n + 1)/2 because, in assuming that the items are evenly spread throughout the distribution, we imagine a number of subdivisions, each with 1 in it. The formula (n+1)/2 finds the upper end of a subdivision not the end of it, and we must drop back half a division to n/2.

3.8 It is worth noting here that the formula used above to calculate the median of a grouped frequency distribution can also be used to find the value of an item at any position in a grouped frequency distribution.

3.9 **A grouped frequency distribution may be divided into percentiles.** There are 99 percentiles which divide data into 100 equal parts. If we wish to find the value of the nth percentile, we must first identify the class interval to which the nth percentile belongs. Once we have done this, we can use the following generalised formula.

nth percentile =   Value of lower limit to the class in which the nth percentile belongs.   + $\left(\dfrac{R}{f} \times c\right)$

See paragraph 3.7 for the meanings of the symbols used.

Example: the median of a grouped frequency distribution

3.10 The average monthly earnings of 135 employees of CD Ltd have been analysed as a grouped frequency distribution as follows.

Average monthly earnings		No of employees	Cumulative frequency
More than	Not more than		
£	£		
120	140	12	12
140	160	49	61
160	180	25	86
180	200	18	104
200	220	17	121
220	240	14	135

Required

Calculate the median monthly earnings of employees of CD Ltd.

Solution

3.11 The middle member is the 135/2 = 67.5th item. This occurs in the class £160 – £180.

$$\textbf{Median} = £160 + \left(\frac{67.5 - 61}{25} \times £20 \right)$$

$$= £165.20$$

Note that, because we are assuming that the values are spread out evenly within each class, the median calculated is only approximate.

Finding the median from an ogive

3.12 Instead of using the formula to estimate the median of a grouped frequency distribution, we could **establish the median from an ogive**. We saw how to do this in Chapter 3.

Exercise 3

The following grouped frequency distribution gives the annual wages of 200 employees in an engineering firm.

Wages	Number of employees
£	
5,000 and less than 5,500	4
5,500 and less than 6,000	26
6,000 and less than 6,500	133
6,500 and less than 7,000	35
7,000 and less than 7,500	2

Required

Calculate the mean, the median and the mode of annual wages.

Solution

(a) The mean

Mid point	Frequency		Cumulative frequency
x	f	fx	
£			
5,250	4	21,000	4
5,750	26	149,500	30
6,250	133	831,250	163
6,750	35	236,250	198
7,250	2	14,500	200
	200	1,252,500	

$$\textbf{Mean} = \frac{1,252,500}{200} = £6,262.50$$

(b) **The median value** is the value of the 100th item. This is estimated as

$$£6,000 + \frac{100 - 30}{133} \times £500$$

= £6,000 + £263.16

= £6,263.16

(c) The **modal value** is in the range £6,000 and less than £6,500. It is estimated as

$$£6,000 + \frac{(133 - 26) \times £500}{(2 \times 133) - 26 - 35}$$

= $£6,000 + \dfrac{£53,500}{205}$

= £6,260.98

The advantages and disadvantages of the median

3.13 The median is only of interest where there is a range of values and the middle item is of some significance. Perhaps the most suitable application of the median is in comparing changes in a 'middle of the road' value over time.

The **median** (like the mode) is **unaffected by extremely high or low values**. On the other hand, it **fails to reflect the full range of values**, and is **unsuitable for further statistical analysis**.

Exercise 4

Give a specific business, commercial or industrial example of when:

(a) the median would be used in preference to the arithmetic mean;
(b) the mode would be used in preference to the median;
(c) the arithmetic mean would be used in preference to any other average.

Solution

(a) Whenever a distribution is significantly skewed or expensive to measure, the median will be the most appropriate measure: salaries of employees, turnover of a large set of companies, time to destruction in tests of components.

(b) The mode is the most useful measure of location when the most common/popular item is required: number of customers in a queue, number of defects in a sample, sales of shirts by neck sizes.

(c) The mean should always be chosen in symmetric distributions or where further statistical calculations or analysis might be required: number of items produced per day on a large assembly line, number of orders received per month by a firm.

4 THE GEOMETRIC MEAN AND THE HARMONIC MEAN   *12/94, 6/00*

Geometric mean

4.1 **The geometric mean is a specialised measure of location. It is used to measure proportional changes** in, for example, wages or prices of goods.

4.2 **The geometric mean of n items is the nth root of their combined product.** The general formula which is used to calculate the geometric mean is as follows.

Geometric mean $= \sqrt[n]{x_1 \times x_2 \times x_3 \ldots x_n}$

where n   = the number of items to be averaged
$x_1, x_2, x_3 \ldots$ = the individual values of the items to be averaged

The best way to demonstrate the geometric mean when it is used to calculate proportional increases is by means of an example.

Example: geometric mean

4.3 The price of a particular commodity has been increasing over a four-year period as follows.

£84   £97   £116   £129

The proportional increases from each year to the next are

$$\frac{97-84}{84} = 0.155 = p_1$$

$$\frac{116-97}{97} = 0.196 = p_2$$

$$\frac{129-116}{116} = 0.112 = p_3$$

$$\textbf{Geometric mean} = \sqrt[n]{(1+p_1)(1+p_2)(1+p_3)...(1+p_n)}$$

$$= \sqrt[3]{1.155 \times 1.196 \times 1.112}$$

$$= 1.154$$

Average proportional increase = $1 - 1.154 = 0.154 = 15.4\%$

Note that £84 $\times 1.154^3$ = £129

Exercise 5

The population of a country has risen by 0.6%, 0.13%, 0.11% and 0.15% in each of four successive years. Calculate the (geometric) average rise.

Solution

Geometric mean = $\sqrt[4]{1.006 \times 1.0013 \times 1.0011 \times 1.0015}$ = 1.0025

(Geometric) average rise = 0.0025 = 0.25%

4.4 **Note that the geometric mean cannot be applied if the data contains zero values.**

Harmonic mean

4.5 The **harmonic mean** is another specialised measure of location. It **is used when the data consists of a set of rates such as prices** (£/kg), **speeds** (km/hr) or **production** (output/manhour).

4.6 **The harmonic mean of n items is the number of items (n) divided by the sum of the reciprocal of each individual item.**

The general formula for calculating the harmonic mean may be given as follows.

$$\textbf{Harmonic mean} = \frac{n}{\dfrac{1}{x_1} + \dfrac{1}{x_2} + \dfrac{1}{x_3} + ... \dfrac{1}{x_n}}$$

Where n = the number of items to be averaged

$x_1, x_2, ..., x_n$ = the individual values of the items to be averaged.

An example is the best way of demonstrating the harmonic mean.

Example: harmonic mean

4.7 An organisation owns three lorries. Over a distance of 100 miles, one does 14 miles per gallon, one 18 miles per gallon and one 20 miles per gallon.

$$\text{Harmonic mean} = \frac{3}{(\frac{1}{14} + \frac{1}{18} + \frac{1}{20})} = 16.95$$

Average consumption = 16.95 miles per gallon.

When to use the harmonic mean

4.8 When averaging rates (such as miles/gallon), the **harmonic mean** should be used if the rates are being averaged over **constant numerator units** (such as over a number of miles) whereas the **arithmetic mean** should be used if the rates are being averaged over **constant denominator units** (such as over a number of gallons).

Advantages of harmonic and geometric means

4.9 **Both means have the advantage of taking little account of extreme values** (whereas the arithmetic mean is often severely affected by extremes).

5 WEIGHTED AVERAGES

6/00

What is a weighted average?

5.1 Suppose you went shopping and spent £16.70 as follows.

Item	Cost £
Record	6.00
Tape	2.00
Book	2.50
Battery	1.20
Lunch	5.00
	16.70

On average, what was the cost of an item you bought?

5.2 The total cost was £16.70, and five items were purchased, so the average unit cost was £16.70/5 = £3.34.

5.3 But now suppose that instead of £16.70, you spent a total of £50 as follows.

Item	Number purchased	Cost per item £	Total cost £
Record	3	6.00	18
Tape	5	2.00	10
Book	2	2.50	5
Batteries	10	1.20	12
Lunch	1	5.00	5
	21		50

Now what is the average cost of one of your purchases?

5.4 The total cost was £50, and 21 items were purchased, so the average unit cost was £50/21 = £2.38.

5.5 In the first example, the average cost was £3.34 but in the second example the average cost dropped to £2.38. This is because in the first example, only one of each item was purchased. So the record, the tape, the book, the battery and the lunch were all given equal **weight** when it came to working out the average cost. In the second example, different numbers of each item were purchased, so they were given different weights when the average cost was calculated. For instance, twice as many batteries were bought as tapes, so the 'weight' for batteries was twice that for tapes. The average cost came down in the second example, because more weight was given to the items which cost less per unit.

5.6 If somebody had asked us to work out the simple average cost of a book, a record, a tape, a battery and a lunch, we would have calculated £3.34 as in Paragraph 5.2. This would be a **simple average**.

5.7 If somebody had asked us to work out the average cost per item of two books, three records, five tapes, ten batteries and a lunch, we would first have to multiply the cost of each item by a weight. In this example, the appropriate weights are just the numbers of items bought (two, three, five, ten and one). The result of our calculation is called a **weighted average.**

5.8 **A weighted average should be used whenever a simple average fails to give an accurate reflection of the relative importance of the items being averaged.** If, for example, a manufacturer buys various components, in working out the average cost of a component he should attach greatest weight to the types of component he buys most of.

Exercise 6

What type of average would be used in each of the following circumstances?

(a) Average output per hour of a machine over five hours.

(b) Average output per hour of a machine over 5,000 units of output.

(c) The most popular holiday destination of the residents of a country in a twelve-month period.

(d) The average life of 100 light bulbs.

(e) The average weekly wages of supermarket checkout assistants in three different stores.

(f) Average number of employees of an expanding firm over a five-year period.

Solution

(a) Arithmetic mean (constant denominator)

(b) Harmonic mean (constant numerator)

(c) Mode

(d) Median (by using the life of the 50th light bulb to go out as the average there is no necessity to wait until the 100th bulb goes out)

(e) Arithmetic mean (all values should be similar)

(f) Geometric mean

Exercise 7

Look out for mentions in the press, TV and radio of the word 'average' and try to work out which particular form of average or typical value is actually being used in each case.

Chapter roundup

- This chapter has looked at the main types of average.

- The **arithmetic mean** is the best known type of average and hence is widely understood. The mean is used for further statistical analysis and hence it is vital that you understand how it is calculated, its advantages and disadvantages and its significance.

- The **mode** is the most frequently occurring value.

- The **median** is the value of the middle member of an array.

- The **arithmetic mean**, **mode and median** of a grouped frequency distribution can only be estimated approximately.

- You should now be able to calculate any of the three commonly-used averages for a basic set of values, an ungrouped frequency distribution and a grouped frequency distribution.

- The **geometric mean** measures proportional changes. The **harmonic mean** is an average of rates which are being averaged over constant numerator units.

- A **weighted average** should be used if a simple average fails to give an accurate reflection of the relative importance of the items being averaged.

Test your knowledge

1   State a formula for the arithmetic mean of a frequency distribution. (see para 1.7)

2   Define the mode. (2.1)

3   Explain how to estimate the mode from a histogram of a distribution. (2.7- 2.10)

4   Define the median. (3.1)

5   State the formula for estimating the median of a grouped frequency distribution. (3.7)

6   How is a harmonic mean calculated? (4.6)

7   Explain the difference between a simple average and a weighted average. (5.6, 5.7)

Now try illustrative questions 10 and 11 at the end of the Study Text

Chapter 5

MEASURES OF DISPERSION

This chapter covers the following topics.

1   The range, quartiles and other quantiles

2   The mean deviation

3   The variance and the standard deviation

4   Relative measures of dispersion

5   Skewness

Introduction

In Chapter 4 we introduced the first type of statistic that can be used to describe certain aspects of a set of data - measures of location. **Averages** are a method of determining the '**location**' or **central point of a distribution**, but they give no information about the dispersion of values in the distribution. For example, consider the following frequency distributions.

Value	Distribution X Frequency	Distribution Y Frequency
x	f	f
1	3	0
2	6	0
3	10	10
4	12	30
5	10	10
6	6	0
7	3	0
	50	50

Both distributions have the same mean, median and mode (4) but, although distributions X and Y have the same averages, they are noticeably different. Distribution X is more spread out, and values range from 1 to 7; in distribution Y, the range of values is restricted to 3, 4 and 5. The differences between the distributions are caused by their **spread** or **dispersion**.

Measures of dispersion give some idea of the spread of a variable about its average. The main measures are discussed below.

1   THE RANGE, QUARTILES AND OTHER QUANTILES

6/94,12/94,6/96,12/97,6/98, 12/98, 6/00

The range

1.1   **The range is the difference between the highest observation and the lowest observation.**

The main properties of the range as a measure of spread are as follows.

- It is easy to find and to understand.
- It is easily affected by one or two extreme values.
- It gives no indication of spread between the extremes.
- It is not suitable for further statistical analysis.
- One of its common practical uses is for quality control purposes.

BPP PUBLISHING

Like its companion measure the mode, the range is really only useful when we want a quick idea of the variability in a set of data without having to go to the trouble of doing any calculations.

Exercise 1

Calculate the mean and the range of each of the following sets of data.

(a) x_1 =   4   8   7   3   5   16   24   5

(b) x_2 =   10   7   9   11   11   8   9   7

Solution

(a) $\bar{x}_1$ $= \dfrac{72}{8} = 9$

The figures have a mean of 9 and a range of 24 -3 = 21.

(b) $\bar{x}_2$ $= \dfrac{72}{8} = 9$

The figures have a mean of 9 and a range of 11 - 7 = 4.

The set of data x_1 is more widely dispersed than the set of data x_2.

Quartiles and other quantiles

1.2 **Quartiles are one means of identifying the range within which most of the values in the population occur.** The **lower quartile (Q_1)** is the value **below** which 25% of the population fall and the **upper quartile (Q_3)** is the value **above** which 25% of the population fall. It follows that 50% of the total population fall between the lower and the upper quartiles. The **quartiles** and the **median** divide the population into four groups of equal size.

1.3 In a similar way, a population could be divided into **ten equal groups,** and the value of each dividing point is referred to, not as a quartile, but as a **decile**. When a population is divided into 100 parts, the value of each dividing point is referred to as a **percentile**. For example, in a population of 200 values, the percentiles would be the second, fourth, sixth, eighth and so on, up to the 198th item, in rising order of values.

Quartiles, deciles and **percentiles**, and any other similar dividing points for analysing a frequency distribution, are referred to collectively as **quantiles**. The purpose of quantiles is to **analyse the dispersion of data values**. All quantiles can be found easily from an ogive. Quantiles are best suited to types of business data that are particularly susceptible to extremes (wages, turnover), have distributions that have open-ended classes or are difficult, expensive or impossible to obtain at extremes. These are just the type of data that are best suited for analysis using the median.

The quartile deviation and the inter-quartile range

1.4 **A measure of spread in a frequency distribution is the quartile deviation.** The quartile deviation is half the difference between the lower and upper quartiles and is sometimes called the **semi inter-quartile range**. The formula provided in your exam is $(Q_3 - Q_1)/2$.

1.5 For example, if the lower and upper quartiles of a frequency distribution were 6 and 11, the quartile deviation of the distribution would be $(11 - 6)/2 = 2.5$ units.

This shows that the average distance of a quartile from the median is 2.5. The smaller the quartile deviation, the less dispersed is the distribution.

1.6 As with the range, the quartile deviation may be misleading. If the majority of the data are towards the lower end of the range then the third quartile will be considerably further above the median than the first quartile is below it, and when the two distances from the median are averaged the difference is disguised. This is likely to be the case with a country's personal income distribution. In such circumstances, it is better to quote the actual values of the two quartiles, rather than the quartile deviation.

1.7   We could also have used the **inter-quartile range**, which in the above example would be 11 – 6 = 5. This would show that the range of values of the middle half of the population is 5 units. (The semi-interquartile range is half of the inter-quartile range).

Example: quartiles

1.8   Calculate the following of the grouped frequency distribution below.

(a)   The lower and upper quartiles and the median
(b)   The quartile deviation

Value x		Frequency f	Cumulative frequency
more than £	*not more than* £		
0	10	3	3
10	20	6	9
20	30	11	20
30	40	15	35
40	50	12	47
50	60	7	54
60	70	6	60
		$\overline{60}$	

Solution

1.9   (a)   The **lower quartile (Q_1)** is the ¼ × 60th = 15th item, which is in the class £20 – £30.

It is calculated in the same way as the median of a grouped frequency distribution (which we studied in Chapter 4) using the formula

$$Q_1 = \text{value of lower limit of class} + \left(\frac{R}{f} \times c \right)$$

where Q_1 is the lower quartile

f is the frequency of occurrences in the quartile class

R is the quartile member minus the cumulative frequency up to the end of the preceding class

c is the width of the quartile class.

Lower quartile Q_1 $= 20 + \left(\frac{15-9}{11} \times 10 \right)$

$= 25.45$, say 25

The **median (Q_2)** is the 30th item, which is in the class £30 – £40.

It is $30 + \left(\frac{30-20}{15} \times 10 \right) = 36.67$, say 37.

The **upper quartile (Q_3)** is the 45th item, which is in the class interval £40 – £50.

$Q_3 = 40 + \left(\frac{45-35}{12} \times 10 \right) = 48.33$, say 48.

(b)   The **quartile deviation** is $\dfrac{Q_3 - Q_1}{2} = \dfrac{48-25}{2} = 11.5$ units

2 THE MEAN DEVIATION

2.1 Another measure of dispersion is the **mean deviation**. This is a **measure of the average amount by which the values in a distribution differ from the arithmetic mean.**

$$\textbf{Mean deviation} = \frac{\Sigma f|x - \overline{x}|}{n}$$

2.2 (a) $|x - \overline{x}|$ is the difference between each value (x) in the distribution and the arithmetic mean $\overline{x}$ of the distribution. When calculating the mean deviation for grouped data the deviations should be measured to the midpoint of each class: that is, x is the midpoint of the class interval. The vertical bars mean that all differences are taken as positive. Thus if x = 3 and $\overline{x}$ = 5, then $x - \overline{x}$ = −2 but $|x - \overline{x}|$ = 2.

(b) $f|x - \overline{x}|$ is the value in (a) above, multiplied by the frequency for the class.

(c) $\Sigma f|x - \overline{x}|$ is the sum of the results of all the calculations in (b) above.

(d) n (which equals Σf) is the number of items in the distribution.

Example: the mean deviation

2.3 Calculate the mean deviation of the following frequency distribution.

Value x Units	Frequency of occurrence f	fx
6	4	24
7	6	42
8	10	80
9	11	99
10	8	80
11	1	11
	40	Σfx = 336

Solution

2.4 First we must calculate the arithmetic mean.

$$\overline{x} = \frac{\Sigma fx}{\Sigma f} = \frac{336}{40} = 8.4$$

Value x	$|x - \overline{x}|$	Frequency f	$f|x - \overline{x}|$
6	2.4	4	9.6
7	1.4	6	8.4
8	0.4	10	4.0
9	0.6	11	6.6
10	1.6	8	12.8
11	2.6	1	2.6
			44.0

$$\textbf{Mean deviation} = \frac{44.0}{40} = 1.1 \text{ units}$$

Thus the mean is 8.4 units, and the mean deviation is 1.1 units.

Exercise 2

Calculate the mean deviation of the following grouped frequency distribution.

Value		Frequency of
More than	Not more than	occurrence
0	10	4
10	20	6
20	30	8
30	40	20
40	50	6
50	60	6
		50

Solution

Mid point

x	f	fx	$|x - \bar{x}|$	$f|x - \bar{x}|$
5	4	20	27.2	108.8
15	6	90	17.2	103.2
25	8	200	7.2	57.6
35	20	700	2.8	56.0
45	6	270	12.8	76.8
55	6	330	22.8	136.8
	50	1,610		539.2

Arithmetic mean $\bar{x} = \dfrac{1,610}{50} = 32.2$

Mean deviation $= \dfrac{539.2}{50} = 10.784$ units, say 10.8 units.

The usefulness of the mean deviation

2.5 **The mean deviation is a measure of dispersion which shows by how much, on average, each item in the distribution differs in value from the arithmetic mean of the distribution.**

Unlike quartiles, it uses all values in the distribution to measure the dispersion, but it is not greatly affected by a few extreme values because an average is taken.

The mean deviation is not, however, suitable for further statistical analysis.

3 THE VARIANCE AND THE STANDARD DEVIATION

6/94, 12/94, 6/95, 12/95, 12/96, 12/98, 6/99, 12/99, 6/00

3.1 The most important measure of dispersion in statistics is the **standard deviation**. It is denoted by s or σ. σ is the lower case Greek letter sigma. The symbol s is used for the standard deviation of a sample, and σ is used for the standard deviation of a population.

3.2 **The standard deviation is the square root of the variance**.

The variance is the average of the squared deviation $(x - \bar{x})^2$ for each value in the distribution. It is denoted by s^2 or σ^2.

3.3 Thus the **variance** $= \dfrac{\Sigma f(x - \bar{x})^2}{n} = \dfrac{\Sigma f(x - \bar{x})^2}{\Sigma f}$

$$= \dfrac{\Sigma fx^2}{n} - \left(\dfrac{\Sigma fx}{n}\right)^2 = \dfrac{\Sigma fx^2}{\Sigma f} - \left(\dfrac{\Sigma fx}{\Sigma f}\right)^2 = \dfrac{\Sigma fx^2}{n} - (\bar{x})^2$$

The last of these formulae can be easily remembered as 'mean of squares minus square of mean'. All the formulae will always give the same value for the variance.

3.4 The **standard deviation (s)** $= \sqrt{\dfrac{\Sigma f(x-\overline{x})^2}{n}} = \sqrt{\dfrac{\Sigma f(x-\overline{x})^2}{\Sigma f}}$

$$= \sqrt{\dfrac{\Sigma fx^2}{n} - \left(\dfrac{\Sigma fx}{n}\right)^2} = \sqrt{\dfrac{\Sigma fx^2}{\Sigma f} - \left(\dfrac{\Sigma fx}{\Sigma f}\right)^2} \; \star$$

$$= \sqrt{\dfrac{\Sigma fx^2}{\Sigma f} - \overline{x}^2}$$

★ Formula provided in the examination

Example: the variance and the standard deviation

3.5 Calculate the variance and the standard deviation of the frequency distribution below.

Value x	Frequency f
6	4
7	6
8	10
9	11
10	8
11	1
	40

It has a mean, $\overline{x}$, of 8.4 units.

Solution

3.6 Using the formula provided in the examination, the calculation is as follows.

Value x	f	fx	x^2	fx^2
6	4	24	36	144
7	6	42	49	294
8	10	80	64	640
9	11	99	81	891
10	8	80	100	800
11	1	11	121	121
	40	336		2,890

Variance $= \dfrac{\Sigma fx^2}{\Sigma f} - \left(\dfrac{\Sigma fx}{\Sigma f}\right)^2 = \dfrac{2,890}{40} - \left(\dfrac{336}{40}\right)^2 = 72.25 - 70.56 = 1.69$

Standard deviation $= \sqrt{1.69} = 1.3$ units

Exercise 3

The durations of the telephone calls made by an employee were recorded for a month. The results are shown in the following table.

Duration	Number of calls
Minutes	
Under 3	45
3 and under 6	59
6 and under 9	38
9 and under 12	31
12 and under 15	19
15 and under 18	8
18 and over	0

Required

Calculate the arithmetic mean, the variance and the standard deviation of the durations of these calls.

Solution

Mid point				
x	f	fx	x^2	fx^2
Minutes				
1.5	45	67.5	2.25	101.25
4.5	59	265.5	20.25	1,194.75
7.5	38	285.0	56.25	2,137.50
10.5	31	325.5	110.25	3,417.75
13.5	19	256.5	182.25	3,462.75
16.5	8	132.0	272.25	2,178.00
	200	1,332.0	643.50	12,492.00

$$\bar{x} = \frac{\Sigma fx}{\Sigma f} = \frac{1,332}{200} = 6.66$$

$$\textbf{Variance} = \frac{12,492}{200} - \left(\frac{1,332}{200}\right)^2 = 18.1044$$

Standard deviation $= \sqrt{18.1044} = 4.255$ minutes

The main properties of the standard deviation

3.7 The **standard deviation's main properties** are as follows.

(a) It is based on all the values in the distribution and so is more comprehensive than dispersion measures based on quantiles, such as the quartile deviation.

(b) It is suitable for further statistical analysis.

(c) It is more difficult to understand than some other measures of dispersion.

(d) It emphasises the effect of larger deviations rather more than the mean deviation because it squares all the deviations: $x - \bar{x}$

The importance of the standard deviation lies in its suitability for further statistical analysis.

The variance and the standard deviation of several items together

3.8 You may need to calculate the variance and standard deviation for n items together, given the variance and standard deviation for one item alone.

Example: several items together

3.9 The daily demand for an item of stock has a mean of 6 units, with a variance of 4 and a standard deviation of 2 units. Demand on any one day is unaffected by demand on previous days or subsequent days.

Required

Calculate the arithmetic mean, the variance and the standard deviation of demand for a five-day week.

Solution

3.10 The **mean** is simply 6 units a day × 5 days = 30 units.

The **variance** is also calculated as the sum of the variances for each day of the week: 4 a day × 5 days = 20.

The **standard deviation** is $\sqrt{20}$ = 4.47 units. (It is *not* 2 units a day × 5 days = 10 units.)

3.11 The rules demonstrated in this example apply whenever we have values of variables which are independent of each other: **add means, add variances** and **take the square root of the total variance to get the total standard deviation.**

Exercise 4

The weights of three items X, Y and Z vary independently and have the following means and standard deviations.

	Mean weight	Standard deviation
	kg	kg
X	10	2
Y	14	2
Z	6	1

The three items are sold together in a single packet.

Required

Calculate the mean weight of a packet of one unit each of X, Y and Z, and the standard deviation of the weights of packets.

Solution

Mean of X + Y + Z	= (10 + 14 + 6) kg = 30 kg
Variance of X + Y + Z	= $(2^2 + 2^2 + 1^2)$ = 9kg
Standard deviation of X + Y + Z =	$\sqrt{9}$ = 3 kg.

Packets of one of each of X, Y and Z have a mean weight of 30 kg and a standard deviation of weights of 3 kg.

---

4 RELATIVE MEASURES OF DISPERSION

The coefficient of variation

4.1 It is sometimes useful to be able to **compare the spreads of two distributions.**

This comparison can be done using the **coefficient of variation.**

$$\text{Coefficient of variation} = 100 \times \frac{\text{standard deviation}}{\text{mean}} = \frac{100s}{\bar{x}}$$

The coefficient of variation is sometimes known as the **coefficient of relative dispersion.** The formula is provided in the examination.

4.2 **The bigger the coefficient of variation, the wider the dispersion.** For example, suppose that two sets of data, A and B, have the following means and standard deviations.

	A	*B*
Mean	120	125
Standard deviation	50	51
Coefficient of variation	41.7	40.8

Although B has a higher standard deviation in absolute terms (51 compared to 50) its relative dispersion is a bit less than A's since the coefficient of variation is a bit smaller.

Exercise 5

A maintenance manager has recorded the time taken by maintenance staff to repair a particular type of equipment fault. The following table shows the time taken in minutes to repair 250 recent faults.

Time taken Minutes	Frequency
Under 10	28
10 and under 20	54
20 and under 30	81
30 and under 40	57
40 and under 50	23
50 and under 60	7
60 and over	0

Required

(a) Calculate the mean and the standard deviation of the time taken.

(b) Calculate the coefficient of variation.

Solution

Mid point x	f	fx	x^2	fx^2
5	28	140	25	700
15	54	810	225	12,150
25	81	2,025	625	50,625
35	57	1,995	1,225	69,825
45	23	1,035	2,025	46,575
55	7	385	3,025	21,175
*65	0	0	4,225	0
	250	6,390	11,375	201,050

* assumed, but irrelevant, since f = 0

(a) **Mean** $= \dfrac{6,390}{250} = 25.56$ minutes

Standard deviation $= \sqrt{\dfrac{201,050}{250} - \left(\dfrac{6,390}{250}\right)^2} = 12.28$ minutes

(b) **Coefficient of variation** $= \dfrac{12.28 \times 100}{25.56} = 48$

The quartile coefficient of dispersion

4.3 **The quartile coefficient of dispersion is another measure of dispersion using quartiles.** It differs from the quartile deviation because it is expressed as a **proportion** and not in units of the value of the variable. The lower the proportion, the less dispersed the distribution.

BPP PUBLISHING

4.4 **Quartile coefficient of dispersion** $= \dfrac{Q_3 - Q_1}{Q_3 + Q_1}$

where Q_1 is the lower quartile
Q_3 is the upper quartile

The coefficient of mean deviation

4.5 **The coefficient of mean deviation is simply the mean deviation expressed as a proportion of the arithmetic mean.**

For Exercise 2, for example, this would be $10.784/32.2 = 0.335$

This may be a useful measure because it shows the **relative size** of the mean deviation. In this case, the mean deviation of the value of items in the frequency distribution is about one third of the mean of the distribution.

5 SKEWNESS

5.1 As well as being able to calculate the average and spread of a frequency distribution, you should be aware of the skewness of a distribution. A frequency distribution must be either **symmetrical** or **asymmetrical**, that is, **skewed**.

Positive and negative skewness

5.2 A **symmetrical frequency distribution** is one which can be divided into two halves which are mirror images of each other. The arithmetic mean, the median and the mode will all have the same value.

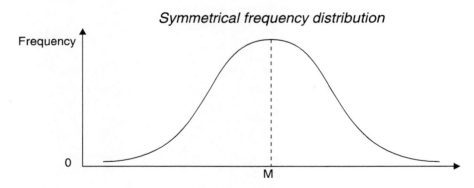

Symmetrical frequency distribution

The mean, the mode and the median will all have the same value, M.

5.3 A **positively skewed distribution's graph** will lean towards the left hand side, with a tail stretching out to the right.

The mean, the median and the mode will have different values.

Positively skewed distribution graph

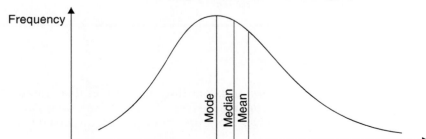

5.4 In **a positively skewed distribution,** the mode will be a lower value than the median and the mean will be a higher value than the median. The value of the mean is, in fact, higher than a great deal of the distribution.

5.5 A **negatively skewed distribution's graph** will lean towards the right hand side, with a tail stretching out to the left.

Once again, the mean, median and mode will have different values.

Negatively skewed distribution graph

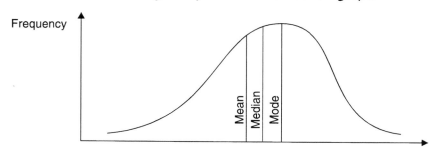

5.6 In a negatively skewed distribution, the mode will have a higher value than the median and the mean will have a lower value than the median. The value of the mean is lower than a great deal of the distribution.

5.7 It is a criticism of the mean as an average that for very skewed distributions its value **may not be representative** of the majority of the items in the distribution since it is affected by extreme values.

5.8 When a distribution is skewed, either positively or negatively, the mean and the median are always on the side of the long tail, the mean being further from the mode than the median. The more the distribution is skewed, the more spread out will be the three averages.

It can be shown that (approximately) **mean – mode = 3(mean – median)**

Pearson's coefficient of skewness

5.9 This coefficient (a relative measure) measures the amount of skewness.

$$\text{Pearson's coefficient of skewness} = \frac{3(\text{mean - mode})}{\text{standard deviation}} = \frac{\text{absolute measure of skewness}}{\text{absolute measure of dispersion}}$$

The formula will automatically give the right sign: a negative value means negative skewness and a positive value means positive skewness.

The version of the formula provided in the exam is: **Pearson measure** $= \dfrac{3(\overline{x} - \text{median})}{s}$

Example: Pearson's coefficient of skewness

5.10 The mean and the median of a frequency distribution are 4 and 7 respectively. The standard deviation is 8. Calculate Pearson's coefficient of skewness.

Solution

5.11 **Pearson's coefficient of skewness** $= \dfrac{3(4 - 7)}{8} = -1.125$

The frequency distribution is negatively skewed with a coefficient of skewness of –1.125

The quartile measure of skewness

5.12 The quartile measure of skewness is an alternative relative measure of skewness.

$$\textbf{Quartile measure of skewness} = \frac{Q_1 + Q_3 - 2(Q_2)}{Q_3 - Q_1} = \frac{\text{absolute measure of skewness}}{\text{absolute measure of dispersion}}$$

where Q_1 = the lower quartile
$\quad\quad\quad\ Q_2$ = the median
$\quad\quad\quad\ Q_3$ = the upper quartile

This formula is provided in the examination.

Example: the quartile measure of skewness

5.13 A frequency distribution is as follows.

Value	Frequency
At least 0, under 5	2
At least 5, under 8	30
At least 8, under 11	10
At least 11, under 14	4
At least 14, under 17	2
	48

The **lower quartile** (item 12) is $5 + \left(\dfrac{10}{30} \times 3\right) = 6$

The **median** (item 24) is $5 + \left(\dfrac{22}{30} \times 3\right) = 7.2$

The **upper quartile** (item 36) is $8 + \left(\dfrac{4}{10} \times 3\right) = 9.2$

The **quartile measure of skewness** is $\dfrac{6 + 9.2 - 2 \times 7.2}{9.2 - 6} = \dfrac{0.8}{3.2} = 0.25$

The distribution is positively skewed.

The J curve

5.14 One extreme form of a skewed distribution is a **J curve**, which may be **positive** or **negative**.

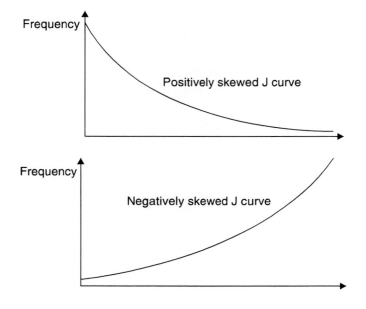

5.15 Positively skewed distributions with a J shape might include the number of firms of different sizes or the number of people earning a given wage.

Negatively skewed distributions with a J shape are less common, but include supply curves in economics.

Chapter roundup

- **Measures of dispersion** give some idea of the spread of variables about the average.

- The **range** is the difference between the highest and lowest observations.

- The **quartiles** and the **median** divide the population into four groups of equal size.

- The **quartile deviation** is half the difference between the two quartiles.

- The **mean deviation** is a measure of the average amount by which the values in a distribution differ from the **arithmetic mean**.

- The **standard deviation**, which is the square root of the variance, is the most important measure of dispersion used in statistics. Make sure you understand how to calculate the standard deviation of a set of data.

- The spreads of two distributions can be compared using the **coefficient of variation**. Other relative measures of dispersion include the **quartile coefficient of dispersion** and the **coefficient of mean deviation**.

- **Skewness** is the asymmetry of a frequency distribution curve. It affects the worth of averages. If a distribution is very skewed, so that the mean and mode are far apart, both the mean and mode could be misleading on their own. The median and quartiles should be used as measures of location and dispersion if you have a noticeably skewed distribution.

Test your knowledge

1 What are quantiles? (see para 1.3)

2 When calculating the mean deviation for grouped data, to where should the deviations be measured? (2.2)

3 What is the most important measure of spread used in statistics? (3.1)

4 Give a formula for the variance. (3.3)

5 Define the coefficient of variation of a distribution. (4.1)

6 Distinguish between positive skewness and negative skewness. (5.3 - 5.6)

Now try illustrative questions 12 and 13 at the end of the Study Text

Part C
Relationships and forecasting

Chapter 6

CORRELATION AND REGRESSION

This chapter covers the following topics.

1   Correlation

2   The product moment correlation coefficient and the coefficient of determination

3   Spearman's rank correlation coefficient

4   Lines of best fit

5   The scattergraph method

6   Linear regression using the least squares method

7   Interpretation of the regression coefficients

8   Reliability of estimates

9   The advantages and disadvantages of regression analysis

Introduction

In Chapters 4 and 5 we looked at the statistical analysis of one-variable data (age, turnover, salary, production levels and so on). We are now going to turn our attention to the **statistical analysis of two-variable data** (sales over time, advertising expenditure and sales revenue, output and costs and so on). Measures of **correlation** and **regression** can be thought of as the two-variable equivalents of the one-variable measures of location and dispersion: **regression** locates two-variable data in terms of a **mathematical relationship** which can be graphed as a **curve** or a **line** and **correlation** describes the **nature of the spread** of the items about the curve or line. The overall basic aim of correlation and regression is to **ascertain the extent to which one variable is related to another**.

---

1   CORRELATION   *6/94,12/94,6/95,12/95,12/96,6/97, 12/97, 6/98*

1.1   **When the value of one variable is related to the value of another, they are said to be correlated. Correlation therefore means an inter-relationship or correspondence.**

1.2   Examples of variables which might be correlated are as follows.

- A person's height and weight
- The distance of a journey and the time it takes to make it

1.3   One way of showing the correlation between two related variables is on a **scattergraph** or **scatter diagram**, plotting a number of pairs of data on the graph.

1.4   For example, a scattergraph showing monthly selling costs against the volume of sales for a 12-month period might be as follows.

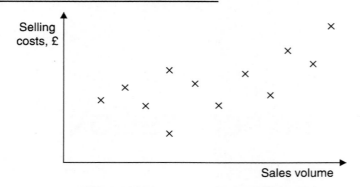

This scattergraph suggests that there is some **correlation** between selling costs and sales volume, so that as sales volume rises, selling costs tend to rise as well.

Degrees of correlation

1.5   Two variables can be one of the following.

- Perfectly correlated
- Partly correlated
- Uncorrelated

These differing degrees of correlation can be illustrated by scatter diagrams.

1.6   **Perfect correlation**

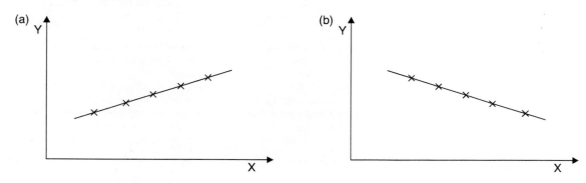

All the pairs of values lie on a straight line. An **exact linear relationship** exists between the two variables.

1.7   **Partial correlation**

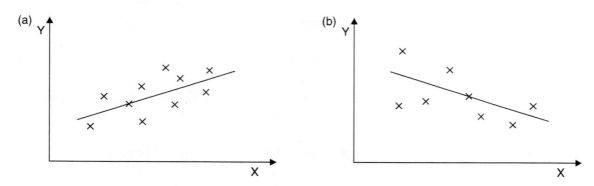

In (a), although there is **no exact relationship**, low values of X tend to be **associated** with low values of Y, and high values of X with high values of Y.

In (b) again, there is **no exact relationship**, but low values of X tend to be **associated** with high values of Y and vice versa.

1.8 No correlation

The values of these two variables are **not correlated** with each other.

Positive and negative correlation

1.9 **Correlation, whether perfect or partial, can be positive or negative.**

1.10 **Positive correlation** means that low values of one variable are associated with low values of the other, and high values of one variable are associated with high values of the other.

Negative correlation means that low values of one variable are associated with high values of the other, and high values of one variable with low values of the other.

Exercise 1

Which of the diagrams in Paragraphs 1.6 and 1.7 demonstrate negative correlation?

Solution

Diagrams in Paragraphs 1.6 (b) and 1.7 (b)

---

2 THE PRODUCT MOMENT CORRELATION COEFFICIENT AND THE COEFFICIENT OF DETERMINATION *6/94 - 6/99, 6/00*

The correlation coefficient

2.1 The degree of correlation between two variables can be measured, and we can decide, using actual results in the form of pairs of data, whether two variables are perfectly or partially correlated, and if they are partially correlated, whether there is a high or low degree of partial correlation.

2.2 **This degree of correlation is measured by the product moment correlation coefficient (the coefficient of correlation), r (also called the 'Pearsonian correlation coefficient').**

There are several formulae for the correlation coefficient, although each formula will give the same value. These include the following.

2.3 **Correlation coefficient, r** $= \dfrac{n\Sigma xy - \Sigma x \Sigma y}{\sqrt{[n\Sigma x^2 - (\Sigma x)^2]\,[n\Sigma y^2 - (\Sigma y)^2]}}$

where x and y represent pairs of data for two variables x and y, and n is the number of pairs of data used in the analysis.

This is the formula which will be used in subsequent examples and is provided in the examination.

2.4 **r must always fall between –1 and +1**. If you get a value outside this range you have made a mistake.

$r = +1$ means that the variables are **perfectly positively correlated**
$r = -1$ means that the variables are **perfectly negatively correlated**
$r = \ 0$ means that the variables are **uncorrelated**

Example: the correlation coefficient

2.5 The cost of output at a factory is thought to depend on the number of units produced. Data have been collected for the number of units produced each month in the last six months, and the associated costs, as follows.

Month	Output '000s of units x	Cost £'000 y
1	2	9
2	3	11
3	1	7
4	4	13
5	3	11
6	5	15

Required

Assess whether there is there any correlation between output and cost.

Solution

2.6 $$r = \frac{n\Sigma xy - \Sigma x\Sigma y}{\sqrt{[n\Sigma x^2 - (\Sigma x)^2][n\Sigma y^2 - (\Sigma y)^2]}}$$

We need to find the values for the following.

(a) Σxy Multiply each value of x by its corresponding y value, so that there are six values for xy. Add up the six values to get the total.

(b) Σx Add up the six values of x to get a total. $(\Sigma x)^2$ will be the square of this total.

(c) Σy Add up the six values of y to get a total. $(\Sigma y)^2$ will be the square of this total.

(d) Σx^2 Find the square of each value of x, so that there are six values for x^2. Add up these values to get a total.

(e) Σy^2 Find the square of each value of y, so that there are six values for y^2. Add up these values to get a total.

Workings

x	y	xy	x^2	y^2
2	9	18	4	81
3	11	33	9	121
1	7	7	1	49
4	13	52	16	169
3	11	33	9	121
5	15	75	25	225
$\Sigma x = 18$	$\Sigma y = 66$	$\Sigma xy = 218$	$\Sigma x^2 = 64$	$\Sigma y^2 = 766$

$$(\Sigma x)^2 = 18^2 = 324 \qquad (\Sigma y)^2 = 66^2 = 4{,}356$$

$$n = 6$$

$$r = \frac{(6 \times 218) - (18 \times 66)}{\sqrt{((6 \times 64) - 324) \times ((6 \times 766) - 4{,}356)}}$$

$$= \frac{1{,}308 - 1{,}188}{\sqrt{(384 - 324) \times (4{,}596 - 4{,}356)}}$$

$$= \frac{120}{\sqrt{60 \times 240}} = \frac{120}{\sqrt{14{,}400}} = \frac{120}{120} = 1$$

2.7   There is **perfect positive correlation** between the volume of output at the factory and costs.

Correlation in a time series

2.8   **Correlation exists in a time series if there is a relationship between the period of time and the recorded value for that period of time.** The correlation coefficient is calculated with time as the x variable although it is convenient to use simplified values for x instead of year numbers.

For example, instead of having a series of years 1987 to 1991, we could have values for x from 0 (1987) to 4 (1991).

Note that whatever starting value you use for x (be it 0, 1, 2 ... 721, ... 953), the value of r will always be the same.

Exercise 2

Sales of product A between 20X7 and 20Y1 were as follows.

Year	Units sold ('000s)
20X7	20
20X8	18
20X9	15
20Y0	14
20Y1	11

Required

Determine whether there is a trend in sales. In other words, decide whether there is any correlation between the year and the number of units sold.

Solution

Workings

Let 20X7 to 20Y1 be years 0 to 4.

	x		y		xy		x^2		y^2
	0		20		0		0		400
	1		18		18		1		324
	2		15		30		4		225
	3		14		42		9		196
	4		11		44		16		121
$\Sigma x =$	10	$\Sigma y =$	78	$\Sigma xy =$	134	$\Sigma x^2 =$	30	$\Sigma y^2 =$	1,266

BPP PUBLISHING

$(\Sigma x)^2 = 100$ $(\Sigma y)^2 = 6,084$

$n = 5$

$$r = \frac{(5 \times 134) - (10 \times 78)}{\sqrt{((5 \times 30) - 100) \times ((5 \times 1,266) - 6,084)}}$$

$$= \frac{670 - 780}{\sqrt{(150 - 100) \times (6,330 - 6,084)}} = \frac{-110}{\sqrt{50 \times 246}}$$

$$= \frac{-110}{\sqrt{12,300}} = \frac{-110}{110.90537} = -0.992$$

There is **partial negative correlation** between the year of sale and units sold. The value of r is close to −1, therefore a **high degree of correlation** exists, although it is not quite perfect correlation. This means that there is a clear **downward trend** in sales.

The coefficient of determination, r^2

2.9 Unless the correlation coefficient r is exactly or very nearly +1, −1 or 0, its meaning or significance is a little unclear. For example, if the correlation coefficient for two variables is +0.8, this would tell us that the variables are **positively correlated**, but the correlation is not perfect. It would not really tell us much else. A more meaningful analysis is available from the square of the **correlation coefficient, r^2,** which is called the **coefficient of determination.**

2.10 r^2 (alternatively R^2) **measures the proportion of the total variation in the value of one variable that can be explained by variations in the value of the other variable.** In the exercise above, r = −0.992, therefore r^2 = 0.984. This means that over 98% of variations in sales can be explained by the passage of time, leaving 0.016 (less than 2%) of variations to be explained by other factors.

2.11 Similarly, if the correlation coefficient between a company's output volume and maintenance costs was 0.9, r^2 would be 0.81, meaning that 81% of variations in maintenance costs could be **explained by** variations in output volume, leaving only 19% of variations to be explained by other factors (such as the age of the equipment).

2.12 Note, however, that if r^2 = 0.81, we would say that 81% of the variations in y can be explained by variations in x. We do not necessarily conclude that 81% of variations in y are caused by the variations in x. We must beware of reading too much significance into our statistical analysis.

Non-linear relationships

2.13 The formulae used above for r and r^2 only work for **linear** or **near linear relationships**. All the points on a scatter diagram might lie on a smooth curve as follows.

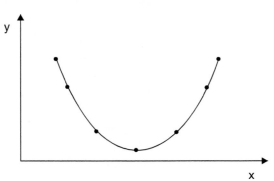

If the formula for r were used in a situation such as this, a low value of r would be obtained, suggesting that very little correlation exists, whereas in fact the two sets of variables are **perfectly correlated** by a **non-linear relationship**. There are methods of testing correlations of this type, but they are outside the scope of the syllabus.

Correlation and causation

2.14 If two variables are well correlated, either positively or negatively, this may be due to pure chance or there may be a reason for it. The larger the number of pairs of data collected, the less likely it is that the correlation is due to chance, though that possibility should never be ignored entirely.

2.15 If there is a reason, it may not be causal. For example, monthly net income is well correlated with monthly credit to a person's bank account, for the logical (rather than causal) reason that for most people the one equals the other.

2.16 Even if there is a causal explanation for a correlation, it does not follow that variations in the value of one variable cause variations in the value of the other. For example, sales of ice cream and of sunglasses are well correlated, not because of a direct causal link but because the weather influences both variables.

2.17 Having said this, it is of course possible that where two variables are correlated, there is a direct causal link to be found.

3   SPEARMAN'S RANK CORRELATION COEFFICIENT   *6/96, 12/96, 6/98, 6/99, 12/99*

3.1 In the examples considered above, the data were given in terms of the values of the relevant variables, such as the number of hours. Sometimes however, they are given in terms of **order** or **rank** rather than actual values. When this occurs, a correlation coefficient known as **Spearman's rank correlation coefficient, R**, should be calculated using the following formula.

Coefficient of rank correlation $r_s = 1 - \left[\dfrac{6\Sigma d^2}{n(n^2 - 1)} \right]$

where   n = number of pairs of data
d = the difference between the rankings in each set of data.

The coefficient of rank correlation can be interpreted in exactly the same way as the ordinary correlation coefficient. Its value can range from **–1 to +1**.

The formula is provided in the examination.

Example: the rank correlation coefficient

3.2 The examination placings of seven students were as follows.

Student	Statistics placing	Economics Placing
A	2	1
B	1	3
C	4	7
D	6	5
E	5	6
F	3	2
G	7	4

Required

Judge whether the placings of the students in statistics correlate with their placings in economics.

Solution

3.3 Correlation must be measured by Spearman's coefficient because we are given the placings of students, and not their actual marks.

$$R = 1 - \frac{6\Sigma d^2}{n(n^2 - 1)}$$

where d is the difference between the rank in statistics and the rank in economics for each student.

Student	Rank Statistics	Rank Economics	d	d^2
A	2	1	1	1
B	1	3	2	4
C	4	7	3	9
D	6	5	1	1
E	5	6	1	1
F	3	2	1	1
G	7	4	3	9
			$\Sigma d^2 =$	26

$$R = 1 - \frac{6 \times 26}{7 \times (49 - 1)} = 1 - \frac{156}{336} = 0.536$$

The correlation is positive, 0.536, but the correlation is not strong.

Tied ranks

3.4 If in a problem some of the items **tie for a particular ranking**, these must be given an **average place** before the coefficient of rank correlation is calculated. Here is an example.

Position of students in examination			Express as
A	1 =	average of 1 and 2	1.5
B	1 =		1.5
C	3		3
D	4		4
E	5 =		6
F	5 =	average of 5, 6 and 7	6
G	5 =		6
H	8		8

Exercise 3

Five artists were placed in order of merit by two different judges as follows.

Artist	Judge P Rank	Judge Q Rank
A	1	4 =
B	2 =	1
C	4	3
D	5	2
E	2 =	4 =

Required

Assess how the two sets of rankings are correlated.

Solution

	Judge P Rank	Judge Q Rank	d	d^2
A	1.0	4.5	3.5	12.25
B	2.5	1.0	1.5	2.25
C	4.0	3.0	1.0	1.00
D	5.0	2.0	3.0	9.00
E	2.5	4.5	2.0	4.00
				28.50

$$R = 1 - \frac{6 \times 28.5}{5 \times (25 - 1)} = -0.425$$

There is a slight negative correlation between the rankings.

4 LINES OF BEST FIT

4.1 **The correlation coefficient measures the degree of correlation between two variables, but it does not tell us how to predict values for one variable (y) given values for the other variable (x).** To do that, we need to find a line which is a good fit for the points on a scattergraph, and then use that line to find the value of y corresponding to each given value of x.

4.2 We will be looking at two ways of doing this, the **scattergraph method** and **linear regression using the least squares method.**

5 THE SCATTERGRAPH METHOD   *6/00*

5.1 **The scattergraph method is to plot pairs of data for two related variables on a graph, to produce a scattergraph, and then to *use judgement* to draw what seems to be a line of best fit through the data.**

5.2 For example suppose we have the following pairs of data about sales revenue and advertising expenditure.

Period	Advertising expenditure £	Sales revenue £
1	17,000	180,000
2	33,000	270,000
3	34,000	320,000
4	42,000	350,000
5	19,000	240,000
6	41,000	300,000
7	26,000	320,000
8	27,000	230,000

These pairs of data would be plotted on a **scattergraph** (the horizontal axis representing the independent variable and the vertical axis the dependent) and a **line of best fit** might be judged as the one shown below. It was drawn to pass through the middle of the data points, thereby having as many data points below the line as above it.

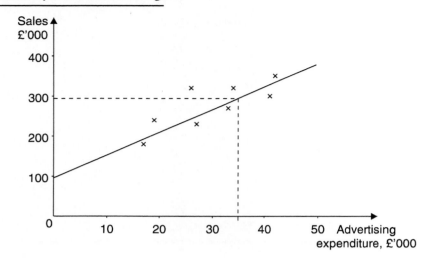

5.3 Suppose the company to which this data relates wants a forecast sales figure given a marketing decision to spend £35,000 on advertising. An estimate of sales can be read directly from the scattergraph as shown (£290,000).

6 LINEAR REGRESSION USING THE LEAST SQUARES METHOD

6/94 – 12/95, 6/97 – 6/00

6.1 **The least squares method of linear regression analysis provides a technique for estimating the equation of a line of best fit.**

6.2 The equation of a straight line has the form **y = a + bx**

where x and y are related variables
       x is the independent variable
       y is the dependent variable
       a is the intercept of the line on the vertical axis
and   b is the gradient of the line.

6.3 The least squares method provides estimates for the values of a and b using the following formulae (which are provided in the examination).

$$b = \frac{n\Sigma xy - \Sigma x \Sigma y}{n\Sigma x^2 - (\Sigma x)^2}$$

$$a = \frac{\Sigma y}{n} - \frac{b\Sigma x}{n}$$

where n is the number of pairs of data.

6.4 There are some points to note about these formulae.

(a) The line of best fit that is derived represents the **regression of y upon x.**

A different line of best fit could be obtained by interchanging x and y in the formulae. This would then represent the **regression of x upon y** (x = a + by) and it would have a slightly different slope. For examination purposes, always use the regression of y upon x, where x is the independent variable, and y is the dependent variable whose value we wish to forecast for given values of x. In a time series, x will represent time.

(b) Since $a = \frac{\Sigma y}{n} - \frac{b\Sigma x}{n}$, it follows that the line of best fit must **always** pass through the point $\left(\frac{\Sigma y}{n}, \frac{\Sigma x}{n}\right)$.

(c) If you look at the formula for b and compare it with the formula we gave for the correlation coefficient (Paragraph 2.3) you should see some similarities between the two formulae.

The formulae are provided in the examination.

Example: the least squares method

6.5 You are given the following data for output at a factory and costs of production over the past five months.

Month	Output x '000 units	Costs y £'000
1	20	82
2	16	70
3	24	90
4	22	85
5	18	73

There is a high degree of correlation between output and costs, and so it is decided to calculate fixed costs and the variable cost per unit of output using the least squares method.

Required

(a) Calculate an equation to determine the expected level of costs, for any given volume of output.

(b) Prepare a budget for total costs if output is 22,000 units.

(c) Confirm that the degree of correlation between output and costs is high by calculating the correlation coefficient.

Solution

6.6 (a) *Workings*

x	y	xy	x^2	y^2
20	82	1,640	400	6,724
16	70	1,120	256	4,900
24	90	2,160	576	8,100
22	85	1,870	484	7,225
18	73	1,314	324	5,329
$\Sigma x = 100$	$\Sigma y = 400$	$\Sigma xy = 8,104$	$\Sigma x^2 = 2,040$	$\Sigma y^2 = 32,278$

n = 5 (There are five pairs of data for x and y values)

$$b = \frac{n\Sigma xy - \Sigma x \Sigma y}{n\Sigma x^2 - (\Sigma x)^2}$$

$$= \frac{(5 \times 8,104) - (100 \times 400)}{(5 \times 2,040) - 100^2}$$

$$= \frac{40,520 - 40,000}{10,200 - 10,000} = \frac{520}{200}$$

$$= 2.6$$

$$a = \frac{\Sigma y}{n} - \frac{b\Sigma x}{n}$$

$$= \frac{400}{5} - 2.6 \times \left(\frac{100}{5}\right)$$

$$= 28$$

y = 28 + 2.6x

BPP
PUBLISHING

where y = total cost, in thousands of pounds
x = output, in thousands of units.

(b) If the output is 22,000 units, we would expect costs to be

28 + 2.6 × 22 = 85.2 = £85,200.

(c) $r = \dfrac{520}{\sqrt{200 \times (5 \times 32{,}278 - 400^2)}}$

$= \dfrac{520}{\sqrt{200 \times 1{,}390}} = \dfrac{520}{527.3} = +0.99$

Exercise 4

The expense claims and recorded car mileages on company business, relating to a particular day, of a sample of salesmen of a company are as follows.

Salesman	Mileage	Expenses £
A	100	60
B	80	48
C	20	20
D	120	55
E	70	38
F	50	38
G	80	44
H	40	30
I	50	40
J	60	50

Required

(a) Plot the data on a scatter diagram.

(b) Determine, by the method of least squares, a linear model to predict expenses, mileage having been given.

(c) Plot the model on your scatter diagram.

(d) Three further salesmen submit expense claims with mileages as follows.

Salesman	Mileage	Expenses £
K	110	64
L	30	48
M	160	80

Discuss in each case whether or not the claim is reasonable.

Solution

(a)

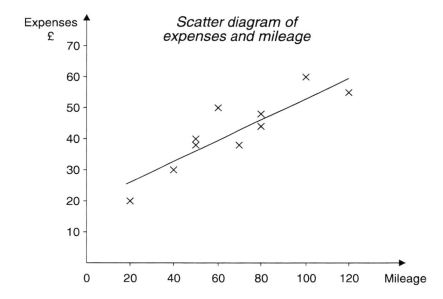

(b) The independent variable, x, is the mileage. The dependent variable, y, is the expenses in pounds.

x	y	x^2	xy
100	60	10,000	6,000
80	48	6,400	3,840
20	20	400	400
120	55	14,400	6,600
70	38	4,900	2,660
50	38	2,500	1,900
80	44	6,400	3,520
40	30	1,600	1,200
50	40	2,500	2,000
60	50	3,600	3,000
670	423	52,700	31,120

$$b = \frac{(10 \times 31,120) - (670 \times 423)}{10 \times 52,700 - 670^2}$$

$$= \frac{311,200 - 283,410}{527,000 - 448,900}$$

$$= \frac{27,790}{78,100}$$

$$= 0.36$$

$$a = \frac{423}{10} - 0.36 \times \frac{670}{10} = 18.18$$

The linear model is y = 18.18 + 0.36x.

(c) The line may be plotted using two points as follows.

x = 20, y = 25.38
x = 120, y = 61.38

The line is plotted on the graph above.

(d) For mileage of 110 miles, the model would predict expenses of 18.18 + (0.36 × 110) = £57.78, so K's claim of £64 is not unreasonably high.

For mileage of 30 miles, the model would predict expenses of 18.18 + (0.36 × 30) = £28.78, so L's claim of £48 is very high and should be investigated.

The model is based on data for mileages from 20 to 120 miles. It should not be used to extrapolate to 160 miles, but if it were to be so used it would predict expenses of 18.18 + (0.36 × 160) = £75.78. On this basis, M's claim for £80 is not unreasonable.

Regression lines and time series

6.7 The same technique can be applied to calculate a **regression line** (**a trend line**) for a time series. This is particularly useful for purposes of **forecasting**. As with correlation, years can be numbered from 0 upwards.

Exercise 5

Sales of product B over the seven year period from 20X1 to 20X7 were as follows.

Year	Sales of B
	'000 units
20X1	22
20X2	25
20X3	24
20X4	26
20X5	29
20X6	28
20X7	30

There is high correlation between time and the volume of sales.

Required

Calculate the trend line of sales, and forecast sales in 20X8 and 20X9.

Solution

Workings

Year		x		y		xy		x^2
20X1		0		22		0		0
20X2		1		25		25		1
20X3		2		24		48		4
20X4		3		26		78		9
20X5		4		29		116		16
20X6		5		28		140		25
20X7		6		30		180		36
	$\Sigma x =$	21	$\Sigma y =$	184	$\Sigma xy =$	587	$\Sigma x^2 =$	91

$n = 7$

Where $y = a + bx$

$$b = \frac{(7 \times 587) - (21 \times 184)}{(7 \times 91) - (21 \times 21)}$$

$$= \frac{245}{196}$$

$$= 1.25$$

$$a = \frac{184}{7} - \frac{1.25 \times 21}{7}$$

$$= 22.5357, \text{ say } 22.5$$

$y = 22.5 + 1.25x$ where $x = 0$ in 20X1, $x = 1$ in 20X2 and so on.

Using this trend line, predicted sales in 20X8 (year 7) would be

$22.5 + 1.25 \times 7 = 31.25 = 31,250$ units.

Similarly, for 20X9 (year 8) predicted sales would be

$22.5 + 1.25 \times 8 = 32.50 = 32,500$ units.

The meaning of 'least squares'

6.8 The term 'squares' in 'least squares regression analysis' refers to the squares of the differences between actual values of the dependent variable (y) and predicted values given by the regression line of best fit. These differences are referred to as **residuals** or **residual errors**. 'Least squares' means that the line of best fit that is calculated is the one that minimises the sum of the squares of all the residuals. The differences are measured vertically on a graph, not at an angle to take the shortest route to the regression line.

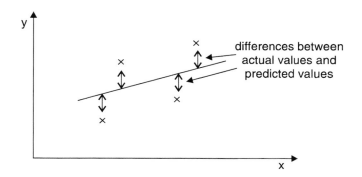

7 INTERPRETATION OF THE REGRESSION COEFFICIENTS   *6/94 – 12/95*

7.1 We said at the beginning of Chapter 6 that the least squares method of linear regression analysis provides estimates for a and b and, given values for x and y, you should now be able to determine a and b yourself.

7.2 a and b are known as the coefficients of the regression line **y = a + bx** but what do they actually mean?

7.3 We explained in Paragraph 6.2 that **a is the intercept of the line of best fit on the vertical axis**. The scatter diagram from Exercise 4 has been reproduced after Paragraph 7.6 but the regression line has been extended so that it meets the y axis. The intercept of this line on the y axis would appear to be approximately 18 or 19; the value of a was calculated as 18.18 using linear regression analysis. This means that when mileage is zero, expenses are £18.00. In other words, there are other costs, unrelated to the distance travelled, of £18 per day. These might include subsistence costs.

7.4 **b is the gradient or slope of the line of best fit.** The slope of a line is dependent upon the change in y for an increase in x. In diagram (a) below, an increase in the value of x from 5 to 6 produces an increase in y of 10 from 10 to 20. In diagram b, a similar increase in x produces an increase of 5 in y.

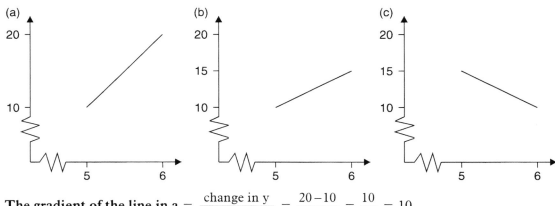

$$\text{The gradient of the line in a} = \frac{\text{change in y}}{\text{increase in x}} = \frac{20-10}{6-5} = \frac{10}{1} = 10$$

$$\text{The gradient of the line in b} = \frac{\text{change in y}}{\text{increase in x}} = \frac{15-10}{6-5} = 5$$

$$\text{The gradient of the line in c} = \frac{\text{change in y}}{\text{increase in x}} = \frac{10-15}{6-5} = -5$$

In (a) and (b), **y increases as x** increases and the gradient is **positive.** In (c), however, **y decreases as x increases** and hence the gradient is **negative.**

7.5   In numerical terms the gradient gives the rate of change in y for an increase in x.

7.6   In the scatter diagram below the gradient $= \dfrac{\text{change in y}}{\text{increase in x}} = \dfrac{61-18}{120} = 0.36$

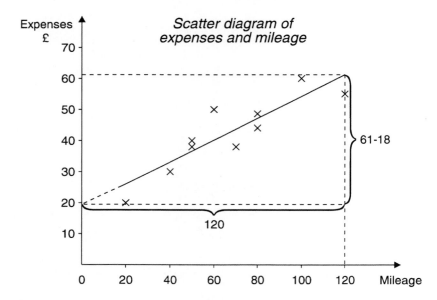

This mean that an increase of one mile travelled produces an increase in costs of £0.36. The coefficient 0.36 therefore indicates that there is a variable motoring cost of 36p per mile on average.

Exercise 6

Interpret the coefficients of the regression line determined in Paragraph 6.6.

Solution

The coefficient a = 28 indicates that when there is no output costs of £28,000 will still be incurred. In other words, fixed costs are £28,000.

The coefficient b = 2.6 indicates as output levels increase by one unit, costs increase by £2.60. The variable cost per unit is therefore £2.60.

8   RELIABILITY OF ESTIMATES   *6/94 – 12/95, 12/97, 6/00*

8.1   A check on the reliability of the estimates given by linear regression analysis is to calculate the **product moment correlation coefficient.** For Exercise 5, we have the following. ($\Sigma y^2 = 4,886$ for the data given.)

$$r = \frac{(7 \times 587)-(21 \times 184)}{\sqrt{[(7 \times 91)-(21 \times 21)] \times [(7 \times 4,886)-(184 \times 184)]}}$$

$$= \frac{4,109-3,864}{\sqrt{(637-441) \times (34,202-33,856)}}$$

$$= \frac{245}{\sqrt{196 \times 346}} = \frac{245}{260.4}$$

$$= 0.94$$

This is a **high positive correlation**, and $r^2 = 0.884$, indicating that 88.4% of the variation in sales can be explained by the variation in time. This would suggest that a fairly large degree of reliance can probably be placed on the estimates for 20X8 and 20X9.

8.2 If there is a **perfect linear relationship** between x and y (r = ±1) then we can predict y from any given value of x with great confidence.

8.3 If **correlation is high** (for example r = 0.9) the actual values will all lie quite close to the regression line and so predictions should not be far out. If correlation is below about 0.7, predictions will only give a very rough guide as to the likely value of y.

8.4 As with any analytical process, the amount of data available is very important. Even if correlation is high, if we have fewer than about ten pairs of values, we must regard any estimate as being somewhat unreliable.

8.5 When calculating a line of best fit, there will be a range of values for x. In the example in Paragraphs 6.5 and 6.6, the line y = 28 + 2.6x was predicted from data with output values ranging from x = 16 to x = 24. Depending on the degree of correlation between x and y, we might safely use the estimated line of best fit to predict values for y, provided that the value of x remains within the range 16 to 24. We would be on less safe ground if we used the formula to predict a value for y when x = 10, or 30, or any other value outside the range 16 to 24, because we would have to assume that the trend line applies outside the range of x values used to establish the line in the first place.

(a) **Interpolation** means using a line of best fit to predict a value within the two extreme points of the observed range.

(b) **Extrapolation** means using a line of best fit to predict a value outside the two extreme points.

9 THE ADVANTAGES AND DISADVANTAGES OF REGRESSION ANALYSIS
6/94 – 12/95

9.1 The **advantages of the least squares method of regression analysis** are as follows.

(a) It can be used to estimate a line of best fit using all the data available. It is likely to provide a more reliable estimate than any other technique of producing a straight line of best fit (for example, estimating by eye).

(b) The reliability of the estimated line can be evaluated by calculating the correlation coefficient r.

9.2 The **disadvantages of the least squares method of regression analysis** are as follows.

(a) It assumes a linear relationship between the two variables, whereas a non-linear relationship may exist.

(b) It assumes that what has happened in the past will provide a reliable guide to the future. For example, if a line is calculated for total costs of production, based on historical data, the estimate could be used to budget for future costs. However, if there has been cost inflation, a productivity agreement with the workforce, a move to new premises, the dismissal of large numbers of office staff and the introduction of new equipment, future costs of production might bear no relation to costs in the past.

(c) The technique assumes that the value of one variable, y, can be predicted or estimated from the value of one other variable, x. In reality, the value of y might depend on several other variables, not just on x.

Chapter roundup

- When the value of one variable is related to the value of another, they are said to be **correlated**.

- Two variables might be **perfectly correlated**, **partly correlated** or **uncorrelated**. Correlation can be **positive** or **negative**.

- The **degree of correlation** between two variables is measured by the **product moment correlation coefficient, r**. The nearer r is to +1 or -1, the stronger the relationship.

- The **coefficient of determination, r^2**, measures the proportion of the total variation in the value of one variable that can be explained by the variation in the value of the other variable.

- **Spearman's rank correlation coefficient** is used when data is given in terms of order or rank rather than actual values.

- The **scattergraph method** involves the use of judgement to draw what seems to be a **line of best fit** through plotted data.

- **Linear regression analysis** (the least squares method) is one technique for estimating a line of best fit. Ensure that you know how to use the formulae to calculate a and b in **y = a + bx**.

- Correlation and regression analysis do not indicate **cause** and **effect**. Even if r = 1, the correlation could still be spurious, both variables being influenced by a third.

Test your knowledge

1   Give some examples of variables which might be correlated. (see para 1.2)

2   Distinguish between positive and negative correlation. (1.10)

3   What range of values can the product moment correlation coefficient take? (2.4)

4   How should the coefficient of determination be interpreted? (2.10 - 2.12)

5   When should Spearman's rank correlation coefficient be used? (3.1)

6   What is the scattergraph method for finding a line of best fit? (5.1)

7   When using the least squares method of linear regression, does it matter which variable is chosen as x? (6.2)

8   What is a residual? (6.8)

9   What are the advantages and disadvantages of the least squares method of linear regression? (9.1, 9.2)

Now try illustrative questions 14 to 16 at the end of the Study Text

Chapter 7

TIME SERIES ANALYSIS

This chapter covers the following topics.

1   The components of time series

2   Finding the trend

3   Moving averages

4   Finding the seasonal variations

5   Forecasting

6   Deseasonalisation

Introduction

In Chapter 6 we looked at how the relationship between two variables, and the strength of that relationship, can be assessed. This chapter looks at how the relationship between a variable (such as turnover, customer levels, output) and time can be **analysed** so as to **forecast future values** for the variable.

---

1   THE COMPONENTS OF TIME SERIES

6/94 - 6/00

1.1   **A time series is a series of figures or values recorded over time.** The following are examples of time series.

- Output at a factory each day for the last month
- Monthly sales over the last two years
- Total annual costs for the last ten years
- The Retail Prices Index each month for the last ten years
- The number of people employed by a company each year for the last 20 years

1.2   **A graph of a time series is called a historigram.** (Note the 'ri'; this is not the same as a histogram.) For example, consider the following time series.

Year	Sales £'000
20X0	20
20X1	21
20X2	24
20X3	23
20X4	27
20X5	30
20X6	28

BPP PUBLISHING

The historigram is as follows.

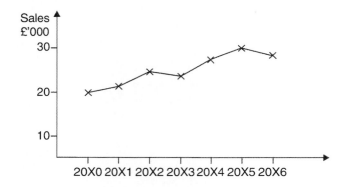

The horizontal axis is always chosen to represent time, and the vertical axis represents the values of the data recorded.

1.3 There are several features of a time series which it may be necessary to identify.

(a) A **trend**

(b) **Seasonal variations** or **fluctuations**

(c) **Cycles, or cyclical variations**

(d) **Non-recurring, random variations**. These may be caused by unforeseen circumstances, such as a change in the government of the country, a war, the collapse of a company, technological change or a fire.

The trend

1.4 **The trend is the underlying long-term movement over time in the values of the data recorded**. In the following examples of time series, there are three types of trend.

	Output per labour hour Units	Cost per unit £	Number of employees
20X4	30	1.00	100
20X5	24	1.08	103
20X6	26	1.20	96
20X7	22	1.15	102
20X8	21	1.18	103
20X9	17	1.25	98
	(A)	(B)	(C)

(a) In time series (A) there is a downward trend in the output per labour hour. Output per labour hour did not fall every year, because it went up between 20X5 and 20X6, but the long-term movement is clearly a downward one.

(b) In time series (B) there is an upward trend in the cost per unit. Although unit costs went down in 20X7 from a higher level in 20X6, the basic movement over time is one of rising costs.

(c) In time series (C) there is no clear movement up or down, and the number of employees remained fairly constant around 100. The trend is therefore a static, or level one.

Seasonal variations

1.5 **Seasonal variations are short-term fluctuations in recorded values, due to different circumstances which affect results at different times of the year, on different days of the week, at different times of day, or whatever**. Here are some examples.

(a) Sales of ice cream will be higher in summer than in winter, and sales of overcoats will be higher in autumn than in spring.

(b) Shops might expect higher sales shortly before Christmas, or in their winter and summer sales.

(c) Sales might be higher on Friday and Saturday than on Monday.

(d) The telephone network may be heavily used at certain times of the day (such as mid-morning and mid-afternoon) and much less used at other times (such as in the middle of the night).

1.6 '**Seasonal**' is a term which may appear to refer to the seasons of the year, but its meaning in time series analysis is somewhat broader, as the examples given above show.

Example: a trend and seasonal variations

1.7 The number of customers served by a company of travel agents over the past four years is shown in the following historigram.

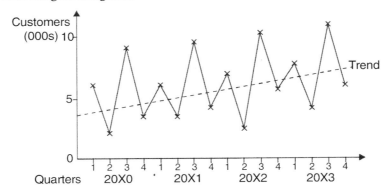

In this example, there would appear to be large seasonal fluctuations in demand, but there is also a **basic upward trend**.

Exercise 1

What seasonal variations would you expect to see in sales of video recorders?

Solution

Sales of video recorders might peak at Christmas and also before major sporting events such as Wimbledon.

Cyclical variations

1.8 **Cyclical variations are medium-term changes in results caused by circumstances which repeat in cycles.** In business, cyclical variations are commonly associated with **economic cycles**, successive **booms** and **slumps** in the economy. Economic cycles may last a few years. Cyclical variations are longer term than seasonal variations.

1.9 '**Periodicity**' is a term which is used to indicate **the length of a cycle in a time series**. For example, the graph in paragraph 1.7 has a one-year cycle or a periodicity of one year.

Summarising the components

1.10 In practice a time series could incorporate all four features and, to make reasonably accurate forecasts, the four features often have to be **isolated**. We can begin the process of isolating each feature by summarising the components of a time series by the following equation

$$Y = T + S + C + R$$

where Y = the actual time series
        T = the trend series
        S = the seasonal component
        C = the cyclical component
        R = the residual component

1.11 Though you should be aware of the cyclical component, it is unlikely that you will be expected to carry out any calculation connected with isolating it. The mathematical model which we will use, the **additive model**, therefore excludes any reference to C and is

$$Y = T + S + R$$

We will begin by isolating the trend.

2 FINDING THE TREND

6/94 - 6/00

2.1 **There are three principal methods of finding a trend.**

(a) **Inspection**. As we saw in Chapter 6, the trend line can be drawn by eye on a graph in such a way that it appears to lie evenly between the recorded points, that is, a line of best fit is drawn by eye. It should be drawn to pass through the middle of the recorded points, thereby having as many data points below it as above it. The line on the historigram in Paragraph 1.7 is an example.

(b) **Regression analysis by the least squares method**. This method, which we looked at in Chapter 6, makes the assumption that the trend line, whether up or down, is a straight line. Periods of time (such as quarters for which sales figures are given) are numbered, commonly from 0, and the regression line of the data on those period numbers is found. That line is then taken to be the trend.

(c) **Moving averages**. This method attempts to remove seasonal (or cyclical) variations by a process of averaging and is looked at in detail in the next section.

3 MOVING AVERAGES

6/94 - 6/00

Finding the trend by moving averages

3.1 **A moving average is an average of the results of a fixed number of periods**. Since it is an average of several time periods, it is related to the mid-point of the overall period.

3.2 Moving averages could cover the sales of a shop over periods of seven days (Monday to the next Sunday for example) or a business's costs over periods of four quarters, or whatever else was appropriate to the circumstances.

Example: moving averages

3.3

Year	Sales
	Units
20X0	390
20X1	380
20X2	460
20X3	450
20X4	470
20X5	440
20X6	500

Required

Take a moving average of the annual sales over a period of three years.

Solution

3.4 (a) Average sales in the three year period 20X0 – 20X2 were

$$\left(\frac{390 + 380 + 460}{3} \right) = \frac{1,230}{3} = 410$$

This average relates to the middle year of the period, 20X1.

(b) Similarly, average sales in the three year period 20X1 – 20X3 were

$$\left(\frac{380 + 460 + 450}{3} \right) = \frac{1,290}{3} = 430$$

This average relates to the middle year of the period, 20X2.

(c) The average sales can also be found for the periods 20X2 - 20X4, 20X3 - 20X5 and 20X4 - 20X6, to give the following.

Year	Sales	Moving total of 3 years' sales	Moving average of 3 years' sales (÷ 3)
20X0	390		
20X1	380	1,230	410
20X2	460	1,290	430
20X3	450	1,380	460
20X4	470	1,360	453
20X5	440	1,410	470
20X6	500		

Note the following points.

(i) The moving average series has five figures relating to the years from 20X1 to 20X5. The original series had seven figures for the years from 20X0 to 20X6.

(ii) There is an **upward trend** in sales, which is more noticeable from the series of moving averages than from the original series of actual sales each year.

3.5 The above example averaged over a three-year period. Over what period should a moving average be taken? The answer to this question is that the moving average which is most appropriate will depend on the circumstances and the nature of the time series. Note the following points.

(a) A moving average which takes an average of the results in many time periods will represent results over a longer term than a moving average of two or three periods.

(b) On the other hand, with a moving average of results in many time periods, the last figure in the series will be out of date by several periods. In our example, the most recent average related to 20X5. With a moving average of five years' results, the final figure in the series would relate to 20X4.

(c) When there is a known cycle over which seasonal variations occur, such as all the days in the week or all the seasons in the year, the most suitable moving average would be one which covers one full cycle.

Exercise 2

Using the following data, what is the three-month moving average for April?

Month	No of new houses finished
January	500
February	450
March	700
April	900
May	1,250
June	1,000

Solution

$$\frac{700 + 900 + 1,250}{3} = 950$$

Moving averages of an even number of results

3.6 In the previous example, moving averages were taken of the results in an **odd number of time periods**, and the average then related to the mid-point of the overall period.

3.7 If a moving average were taken of results in an even number of time periods, the basic technique would be the same, but the mid-point of the overall period would not relate to a single period. For example, suppose an average were taken of the following four results.

Spring	120	
Summer	90	average 115
Autumn	180	
Winter	70	

The **average** would relate to the **mid-point** of the period, between summer and autumn.

3.8 The trend line average figures need to relate to a particular time period; otherwise, seasonal variations cannot be calculated. To overcome this difficulty, we take a **moving average of the moving average**. An example will illustrate this technique.

Example: moving averages over an even number of periods

3.9 Calculate a moving average trend line of the following results.

Year	Quarter	Volume of sales '000 units
20X5	1	600
	2	840
	3	420
	4	720
20X6	1	640
	2	860
	3	420
	4	740
20X7	1	670
	2	900
	3	430
	4	760

Solution

3.10 A moving average of four will be used, since the volume of sales would appear to depend on the season of the year, and each year has four quarterly results.

The moving average of four does not relate to any specific period of time; therefore we will take a moving total of pairs of four-quarter totals and divide that moving total by 8 (ie the number of data items which contributed to the total).

Year	Quarter	Actual volume of sales '000 units	Moving total of 4 quarters' sales '000 units	Moving total of 8 quarters' sales '000 units	Mid-point of 2 moving averages Trend line '000 units
20X5	1	600			
	2	840			
	3	420	2,580	5,200	650.00
	4	720	2,620	5,260	657.50
20X6	1	640	2,640	5,280	660.00
	2	860	2,640	5,300	662.50
	3	420	2,660	5,350	668.75
	4	740	2,690	5,420	677.50
20X7	1	670	2,730	5,470	683.75
	2	900	2,740	5,500	687.50
	3	430	2,760		
	4	760			

3.11 The final moving averages are related to specific quarters (from the third quarter of 20X5 to the second quarter of 20X7).

4 FINDING THE SEASONAL VARIATIONS

6/94 - 6/00

4.1 Once a trend has been established, by whatever method, we can find the **seasonal variations**.

4.2 **The additive model for time series analysis is Y = T + S + R.** We can therefore write Y − T = S + R. In other words, if we deduct the trend series from the actual series, we will be left with the seasonal and residual components of the time series. If we assume that the residual component is relatively small, and hence negligible, the seasonal component can be found as **S = Y − T**, the **de-trended series.**

4.3 We will use two examples to illustrate the process.

Example: the trend and seasonal variations

4.4 Output at a factory appears to vary with the day of the week. Output over the last three weeks has been as follows.

	Week 1 '000 units	Week 2 '000 units	Week 3 '000 units
Monday	80	82	84
Tuesday	104	110	116
Wednesday	94	97	100
Thursday	120	125	130
Friday	62	64	66

Required

Find the seasonal variation for each of the 15 days, and the average seasonal variation for each day of the week using the moving averages method.

Solution

4.5 Actual results fluctuate up and down according to the day of the week and so a moving average of five will be used. The difference between the actual result on any one day (Y) and the trend figure for that day (T) will be the seasonal variation (S) for the day.

4.6 The seasonal variations for the 15 days are as follows.

121

		Actual (Y)	Moving total of five days' output	Trend (T)	Seasonal variation (Y–T)
Week 1	Monday	80			
	Tuesday	104			
	Wednesday	94	460	92.0	+2.0
	Thursday	120	462	92.4	+27.6
	Friday	62	468	93.6	–31.6
Week 2	Monday	82	471	94.2	–12.2
	Tuesday	110	476	95.2	+14.8
	Wednesday	97	478	95.6	+1.4
	Thursday	125	480	96.0	+29.0
	Friday	64	486	97.2	–33.2
Week 3	Monday	84	489	97.8	–13.8
	Tuesday	116	494	98.8	+17.2
	Wednesday	100	496	99.2	+0.8
	Thursday	130			
	Friday	66			

4.7

	Monday	Tuesday	Wednesday	Thursday	Friday
Week 1			+2.0	+27.6	–31.6
Week 2	–12.2	+14.8	+1.4	+29.0	–33.2
Week 3	–13.8	+17.2	+0.8		
Average	–13.0	+16.0	+1.4	+28.3	–32.4

You will notice that the variation between the actual results on any one particular day and the trend line average is not the same from week to week. This is because Y – T contains not only seasonal variations but **random variations** (**residuals**). In calculating the averages of the deviations, Y – T, for each day of the week, the residual components are expected to cancel out, or at least to be reduced to a negligible level.

4.8 Our estimate of the 'seasonal' or daily variation is almost complete, but there is one more important step to take. Variations around the basic trend line should cancel each other out, and add up to 0. In practice this is rarely the case because of random variation. The average seasonal estimates must therefore be corrected so that they add up to zero.

	Monday	Tuesday	Wednesday	Thursday	Friday	Total
Estimated average daily variation	–13.00	+16.00	+1.40	+28.30	–32.40	0.30
Adjustment to reduce total variation to 0	–0.06	–0.06	–0.06	–0.06	–0.06	–0.30
Final estimate of average daily variation	–13.06	+15.94	+1.34	+28.24	–32.46	0.00

These might be rounded up or down as follows.

Monday –13; Tuesday +16; Wednesday +1; Thursday +28; Friday –32; Total 0.

Exercise 3

Calculate a four-quarter moving average trend centred on actual quarters and then find seasonal variations from the following.

	Spring	Summer	Autumn	Winter
		Sales in £000		
20X7	200	120	160	280
20X8	220	140	140	300
20X9	200	120	180	320

Solution

		Sales (Y)	4-quarter total	8-quarter total	Moving average (T)	Seasonal variation (Y-T)
20X7	Spring	200				
	Summer	120				
			760			
	Autumn	160		1,540	192.5	−32.5
			780			
	Winter	280		1,580	197.5	+82.5
			800			
20X8	Spring	220		1,580	197.5	+22.5
			780			
	Summer	140		1,580	197.5	−57.5
			800			
	Autumn	140		1,580	197.5	−57.5
			780			
	Winter	300		1,540	192.5	+107.5
			760			
20X9	Spring	200		1,560	195.0	+5.0
			800			
	Summer	120		1,620	202.5	−82.5
			820			
	Autumn	180				
	Winter	320				

We can now average the seasonal variations.

	Spring	Summer	Autumn	Winter	Total
20X7			−32.5	+82.5	
20X8	+22.5	−57.5	−57.5	+107.5	
20X9	+5.0	−82.5			
	+27.5	−140.0	−90.0	+190.0	
Average variation (in £'000)	+13.75	−70.00	−45.00	+95.00	−6.25
Adjustment so sum is zero	+1.5625	+1.5625	+1.5625	+1.5625	+6.25
Adjusted average variations	+15.3125	−68.4375	−43.4375	+96.5625	0

These might be rounded up or down to:

Spring £15,000, Summer −£68,000, Autumn −£43,000, Winter £96,000

Seasonal variations using the multiplicative model

4.9 The method of estimating the seasonal variations in the above example was to use the differences between the trend and actual data. This is called the **additive mode**. This model assumes that the components of the series are **independent** of each other, an increasing trend not affecting the seasonal variations for example.

The alternative is to use the **multiplicative model**. whereby each actual figure is expressed as a **proportion** of the trend. Sometimes this method is called the **proportional model** The model summarises a time series as $Y = T \times S \times R$. Note that the trend component will be the same whichever model is used but the values of the seasonal and residual components will vary according to the model being applied.

4.10 The example in Paragraph 4.4 can be reworked on this alternative basis. The trend is calculated in exactly the same way as before but we need a different approach for the seasonal variations.

The multiplicative model is $Y = T \times S \times R$ and, just as we calculated $S = Y - T$ for the additive model (Paragraph 4.2) we can calculate $Y/T = S$ for the multiplicative model.

		Actual (Y)	Trend (T)	Seasonal percentage (Y/T)
Week 1	Monday	80		
	Tuesday	104		
	Wednesday	94	92.0	1.022
	Thursday	120	92.4	1.299
	Friday	62	93.6	0.662
Week 2	Monday	82	94.2	0.870
	Tuesday	110	95.2	1.155
	Wednesday	97	95.6	1.015
	Thursday	125	96.0	1.302
	Friday	64	97.2	0.658
Week 3	Monday	84	97.8	0.859
	Tuesday	116	98.8	1.174
	Wednesday	100	99.2	1.008
	Thursday	130		
	Friday	66		

4.11 The summary of the seasonal variations expressed in proportional terms is as follows.

	Monday %	Tuesday %	Wednesday %	Thursday %	Friday %
Week 1			1.022	1.299	0.662
Week 2	0.870	1.155	1.015	1.302	0.658
Week 3	0.859	1.174	1.008		
Total	1.729	2.329	3.045	2.601	1.320
Average	0.8645	1.1645	1.0150	1.3005	0.6600

Instead of summing to zero, as with the absolute approach, these should sum (in this case) to 5 (an average of 1).

They actually sum to 5.0045 so 0.0009 has to be deducted from each one. This is too small to make a difference to the figures above, so we should deduct 0.002 and 0.0025 to each of two seasonal variations. We could arbitrarily decrease Monday's variation to 0.8625 and Tuesday's to 1.162.

4.12 The averages in paragraph 4.11 have been calculated using the **arithmetic mean**. The examiner has stated that the **geometric mean** should be used for calculating the adjustment in **multiplicative models**. In an examination therefore, you should use the **geometric mean** for determining the average.

4.13 **Note that the multiplicative model is better than the additive model for forecasting when the trend is increasing or decreasing over time.** In such circumstances, seasonal variations are likely to be increasing or decreasing too. The additive model simply adds absolute and unchanging seasonal variations to the trend figures whereas the multiplicative model, by multiplying increasing or decreasing trend values by a constant seasonal variation factor, takes account of changing seasonal variations.

4.14 The following graphs demonstrate how the additive model is most appropriate where variations about the trend are within a constant band width ie of a similar magnitude, and how the multiplicative model is most appropriate where variations about the trend are not of within a constant band width, but instead increase as the trend increases.

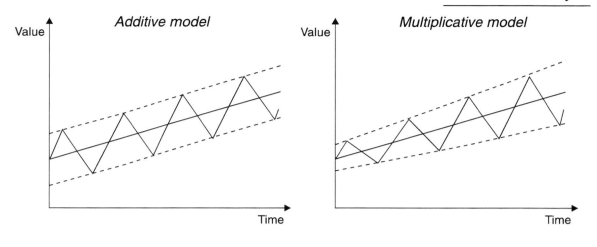

Additive model / Multiplicative model

Exercise 4

A company's quarterly sales figures have been analysed into a trend and seasonal variations using moving averages. Here is an extract from the analysis.

Year	Quarter	Actual £'000	Trend £'000
20X1	1	350	366
	2	380	370
	3	400	380
	4	360	394
20X2	1	410	406
	2	430	414
	3	450	418
	4	370	423

Required

Find the average seasonal variation for each quarter, using the multiplicative model.

Solution

Quarter	1 %	2 %	3 %	4 %
Variation, 20X1	0.956	1.027	1.053	0.914
Variation, 20X2	1.010	1.039	1.077	0.875
Average variation	0.983	1.033	1.065	0.895
Adjustment	0.006	0.006	0.006	0.006
Adjusted average variation	0.989	1.039	1.071	0.901

5 FORECASTING

6/94 - 6/00

5.1 Forecasting is an essential, but difficult task of management. Many forecasts are made by guessing, but they are unlikely to be reliable.

5.2 There are several mathematical techniques of forecasting which could be used. These techniques will not necessarily provide accurate forecasts but, on the whole, they are likely to provide more reliable estimates than guesswork. Techniques cannot eliminate uncertainty about the future, but they can help to ensure that managers take account of all currently-known facts in the preparation of their forecasts.

5.3 The technique which will be discussed here is that of **extrapolating a trend** and then **adjusting for seasonal variations**.

5.4 Forecasts of future values should be made as follows.

(a) **Calculate a trend line**. (In an examination you may be asked to plot the trend line on a scatter diagram. It should be drawn as a straight line using the first and last available trend line figures.)

(b) **Use the trend line to forecast future trend line values.**

(c) **Adjust these values by the average seasonal variation applicable to the future period, to determine the forecast for that period**. With the additive model, add (or subtract for negative variations) the variation. With the multiplicative model, multiply the trend value by the variation proportion.

5.5 Extending a trend line outside the range of known data, in this case forecasting the future from a trend line based on historical data, is known as **extrapolation**.

Example: forecasting

5.6 Sales of product X each quarter for the last three years have been as follows (in thousands of units). Trend values, found by a moving averages method, are shown in brackets.

Year	1st quarter	2nd quarter	3rd quarter	4th quarter
1	18	30	20 (18.75)	6 (19.375)
2	20 (20)	33 (20.5)	22 (21)	8 (21.5)
3	22 (22.125)	35 (22.75)	25	10

Average seasonal variations for quarters 1 to 4 are –0.1, +12.4, +1.1 and –13.4 respectively.

Required

Use the trend line and estimates of seasonal variations to forecast sales in each quarter of year 4.

Solution

5.7 The trend line indicates an increase of about 0.6 per quarter. This can be confirmed by calculating the average quarterly increase in trend line values between the third quarter of year 1 (18.75) and the second quarter of year 2 (22.75). The average rise is

$$\frac{22.75 - 18.75}{7} = \frac{4}{7} = 0.57, \text{ say } 0.6$$

5.8 Taking 0.6 as the quarterly increase in the trend, the forecast of sales for year 4, before seasonal adjustments (the trend line forecast) would be as follows.

Year	Quarter			Trend line
3	*2nd	(actual trend)	22.75, say	22.8
	3rd			23.4
	4th			24.0
4	1st			24.6
	2nd			25.2
	3rd			25.8
	4th			26.4

* last known trend line value.

5.9 Seasonal variations should now be incorporated to obtain the final forecast.

	Quarter	Trend line forecast '000 units	Average seasonal variation '000 units	Forecast of actual sales '000 units
Year 4	1st	24.6	−0.1	24.5
	2nd	25.2	+12.4	37.6
	3rd	25.8	+ 1.1	26.9
	4th	26.4	−13.4	13.0

5.10 If we had been using the **multiplicative model**, with an average variation for (for example) quarter 3 of 1.057, our prediction for the third quarter of year 4 would have been 25.8 × 1.057 = 27.3.

5.11 **All forecasts are, however, subject to error**, but the likely errors vary from case to case.

(a) The further into the future the forecast is for, the more unreliable it is likely to be.

(b) The less data available on which to base the forecast, the less reliable the forecast.

(c) The pattern of trend and seasonal variations cannot be guaranteed to continue in the future.

(d) There is always the danger of random variations upsetting the pattern of trend and seasonal variation.

Exercise 5

The percentage of employees absent from work was recorded over a four-week period as follows.

Week	Mon	Tues	Weds	Thurs	Fri
1	8.4	5.1	5.7	4.8	6.3
2	8.1	5.5	6.0	4.6	6.5
3	8.4	5.6	6.2	5.0	6.8
4	8.6	5.6	6.3	4.9	6.9

Required

(a) Draw a graph of the time series of absenteeism.

(b) By means of a moving average and the additive model, find the trend and the seasonal adjustments.

(c) Plot the trend line by eye and use it as a basis to forecast daily absenteeism for week 5.

(d) Personnel have suggested that the absenteeism figure for Friday of week 8 could be as high as 8%. Discuss whether or not you would support this.

Solution

(a)

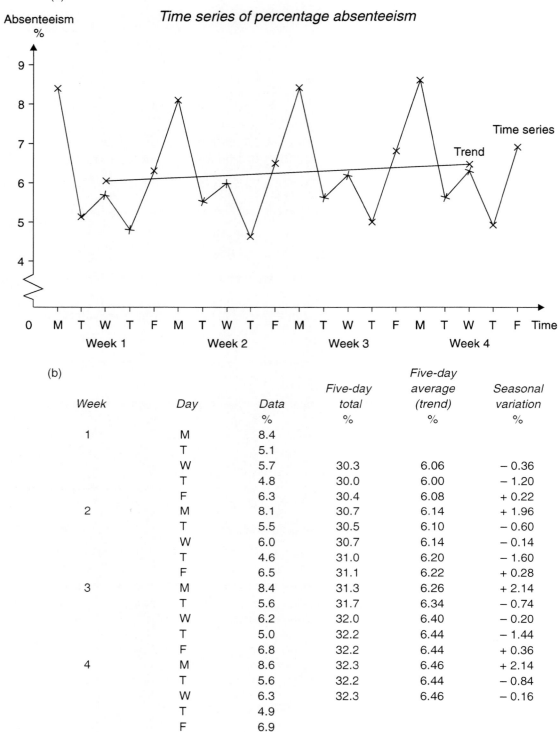

Time series of percentage absenteeism

(b)

Week	Day	Data %	Five-day total %	Five-day average (trend) %	Seasonal variation %
1	M	8.4			
	T	5.1			
	W	5.7	30.3	6.06	− 0.36
	T	4.8	30.0	6.00	− 1.20
	F	6.3	30.4	6.08	+ 0.22
2	M	8.1	30.7	6.14	+ 1.96
	T	5.5	30.5	6.10	− 0.60
	W	6.0	30.7	6.14	− 0.14
	T	4.6	31.0	6.20	− 1.60
	F	6.5	31.1	6.22	+ 0.28
3	M	8.4	31.3	6.26	+ 2.14
	T	5.6	31.7	6.34	− 0.74
	W	6.2	32.0	6.40	− 0.20
	T	5.0	32.2	6.44	− 1.44
	F	6.8	32.2	6.44	+ 0.36
4	M	8.6	32.3	6.46	+ 2.14
	T	5.6	32.2	6.44	− 0.84
	W	6.3	32.3	6.46	− 0.16
	T	4.9			
	F	6.9			

Week	M	T	W	T	F	Total
	%	%	%	%	%	
1			− 0.36	− 1.20	+ 0.22	
2	+ 1.96	− 0.60	− 0.14	− 1.60	+ 0.28	
3	+ 2.14	− 0.74	− 0.20	− 1.44	+ 0.36	
4	+ 2.14	− 0.84	− 0.16			
	6.24	−2.18	−0.86	−4.24	0.86	
Average	+ 2.08	− 0.73	− 0.22	− 1.41	+ 0.29	+ 0.01
Adjustment					− 0.01	− 0.01
Adjusted average						
	+ 2.08	− 0.73	− 0.22	− 1.41	+ 0.28	0

The seasonal adjustments are as shown in the last line of the above table.

(c) The trend line has been plotted on the graph above, using the figures for Wednesday of week 1 (6.06%) and Wednesday of week 4 (6.46%).

The trend rose by 0.4% over this period, an average daily rise of 0.4/15 = 0.027%. This average will be used to derive the trend for week 5.

Week 5 predictions

Day	Trend	Seasonal variation	Prediction	Rounded prediction
	%	%	%	%
Monday	6.541*	+ 2.08	8.621	8.6
Tuesday	6.568	− 0.73	5.838	5.8
Wednesday	6.595	− 0.22	6.375	6.4
Thursday	6.622	− 1.41	5.212	5.2
Friday	6.649	+ 0.28	6.929	6.9

* 6.46 + (3 × 0.027)

(d) A forecast for Friday of week 8, based on the above computations, would be 6.46 + (22 × 0.027) + 0.28 = 7.334%, which is significantly below the personnel department's forecast. It is probable that the personnel department have estimated a more steeply rising trend. However, no forecast so far into the future and based on only four weeks data is likely to be reliable. The estimate of 8% cannot be supported.

Residuals

5.12 **A residual is the difference between the results which would have been predicted** (for a past period for which we already have data) **by the trend line adjusted for the average seasonal variation and the actual results**.

5.13 **The residual is therefore the difference which is not explained by the trend line and the average seasonal variation.** The residual gives some indication of how much actual results were affected by other factors. Large residuals suggest that any forecast is likely to be unreliable. It is a good idea to calculate the residual series $(Y − T − S)$ in order to assess the adequacy of predictions. This will also test whether the assumption (made in Paragraph 4.2) is reasonable.

5.14 In the example in Paragraph 5.6, the 'prediction' for the third quarter of year 1 would have been 18.75 + 1.1 = 19.85. As the actual value was 20, the residual was only 20 − 19.85 = 0.15. The residual for the fourth quarter of year 2 was 8 − (21.5 − 13.4) = 8 − 8.1 = −0.1. An analysis of all the residuals associated with a particular time series will indicate whether the predictions based on the time series are reliable.

6 DESEASONALISATION

6.1 Economic statistics, such as unemployment figures, are often in 'seasonally adjusted' or 'deseasonalised' so as to ensure that the overall trend (rising, falling or stationary) is clear.

All this means is that **seasonal variations** (S) (derived from previous data) have **been taken out**, to leave a figure (Y – S) which might be taken as indicating the trend.

Example: deseasonalisation

6.2 Actual sales figures for four quarters, together with appropriate seasonal adjustment factors derived from previous data, are as follows.

		Seasonal adjustments	
	Actual	*Additive*	*Multiplicative*
Quarter	*sales*	*model*	*model*
	£'000	£'000	
1	150	+3	1.02
2	160	+4	1.05
3	164	–2	0.98
4	170	–5	0.95

Required

Deseasonalise these data.

Solution

6.3 We are reversing the normal process of applying seasonal variations to trend figures, so with the **additive model** we **subtract positive seasonal variations** (and add negative ones), and with the **multiplicative model** we **divide by the seasonal variation** factors (expressed as proportions).

			Deseasonalised sales
	Actual	*Additive*	*Multiplicative*
Quarter	*sales*	*model*	*model*
	£'000	£'000	£'000
1	150	147	147
2	160	156	152
3	164	166	167
4	170	175	179

Chapter roundup

- A **time series** is a series of figures or values recorded over time.

- A time series has four features: a **trend**, **seasonal variations**, **cyclical variations** and **random variations** (residuals).

- A time series can be summarised by the **additive model (Y = T + S + R)** or the **multiplicative (or proportion) model (Y = T × S × R)**.

- The most commonly used method in practice for finding the trend is the moving averages method. Once the trend has been established, the **seasonal component** can be calculated as **Y − T** (if the **additive model** is being used) or **Y/T** (if the **multiplicative model** is being used).

- A process of averaging and adjusting the individual seasonal components is necessary to remove the effect of any residuals and to arrive at seasonal components for each season of the year, day of the week as necessary.

- By **extrapolating** the trend line and adjusting the resulting figures for the seasonal component of the time series, **forecasts** can be obtained

- Calculating the **residuals** of the time series assesses the adequacy and reliability of the predictions made using the trend and seasonal components.

- **Deseasonalised data (Y − S)** are often used by economic commentators.

Test your knowledge

1   What is the definition of a time series? (see para 1.1)

2   What are the four components that combine to form a time series? (1.3)

3   How can trend lines be found? (2.1)

4   How are trend values calculated when moving averages of an even number of results are taken? (3.10)

5   Why are average seasonal variations adjusted to sum to zero? (4.8)

6   Distinguish between the additive model and the multiplicative model of time series. (4.9).

7   In what circumstances should the proportional model rather than the additive model be used? (4.13)

8   Describe how the additive model may be used in forecasting. (5.4 - 5.9)

9   What is extrapolation? (5.5)

10 What is the term for the difference which is not explained by the trend line and the average seasonal variation? (5.13)

Now try illustrative questions 17 and 18 at the end of the Study Text

Part D
Index numbers

Chapter 8

INDEX NUMBERS

This chapter covers the following topics.

1 Basic terminology

2 Simple indices

3 Index relatives

4 Composite index numbers

5 Laspeyre, Paasche and Fisher indices

6 Practical issues

7 Special published indices

Introduction

Index numbers provide a standardised way of comparing the values, over time, of prices, wages, volume of output and so on. They are used extensively in business, government and commerce.

No doubt you will be aware of some index numbers - for example, the RPI and the Financial Times All Share Index. This chapter will explain how to construct indices and will look at associated issues such as their limitations.

---

1 BASIC TERMINOLOGY
6/97

1.1 **An index is a measure, over time, of the average changes in the values** (prices or quantities) **of a group of items. An index comprises a series of index numbers**. Although it is possible to prepare an index for a single item, for example the price of an ounce of gold, such an index would probably be unnecessary. It is only when there is a group of items that a simple list of changes in their values over time becomes rather hard to interpret, and an index provides a useful single measure of comparison.

Price indices and quantity indices

1.2 **An index may be a price index or a quantity index.**

(a) **A price index measures the change in the money value of a group of items over time.** Perhaps the best known price index in the UK is the Retail Prices Index (RPI) which measures changes in the costs of items of expenditure of the average household.

(b) **A quantity index** (also called a volume index) **measures the change in the non-monetary values of a group of items over time.** An example is a productivity index, which measures changes in the productivity of various departments or groups of workers.

BPP PUBLISHING

Index points

1.3 The term 'points' refers to the difference between the index values in two years.

For example, suppose that the index of food prices in 20X1 – 20X6 was as follows.

20X1	180
20X2	200
20X3	230
20X4	250
20X5	300
20X6	336

The index has risen 156 points between 20X1 and 20X6. This is an increase of $(156/180) \times 100 = 86.7\%$.

Similarly, the index rose 36 points between 20X5 and 20X6, a rise of 12%.

The base period, or base year

1.4 Index numbers normally take the value for a **base date**, usually the starting point of the series though it could be part way through the series, as 100.

2 SIMPLE INDICES

2.1 When one commodity only is under consideration, we have the following formulae.

(a) **Price index** $= \dfrac{P_n}{P_o} \times 100$

where P_n is the price for the period under consideration and P_0 is the price for the base period.

(b) **Quantity index** $= \dfrac{Q_n}{Q_o} \times 100$

where Q_n is the quantity for the period under consideration and Q_0 is the quantity for the base period.

Example: single-item indices

2.2 If the price of a cup of coffee was 40p in 20X0, 50p in 20X1 and 76p in 20X2, then using 20X0 as a base year the price index numbers for 20X1 and 20X2 would be as follows.

20X1 price index $= \dfrac{50}{40} \times 100 = 125$

20X2 price index $= \dfrac{76}{40} \times 100 = 190$

2.3 If the number of cups of coffee sold in 20X0 was 500,000, in 20X1 700,000 and in 20X2 600,000, then using 20X0 as a base year, the quantity index numbers for 20X1 and 20X2 would be as follows.

20X1 quantity index $= \dfrac{700,000}{500,000} \times 100 = 140$

20X2 quantity index $= \dfrac{600,000}{500,000} \times 100 = 120$

3 INDEX RELATIVES

6/94, 12/94, 12/95, 6/96, 12/96, 12/97, 6/98, 6/99, 12/99, 6/00

3.1 An **index relative** (sometimes just called a relative) **is the name given to an index number which measures the change in a single distinct commodity**.

3.2 A **price relative** is calculated as $P_n/P_o \times 100$. We calculated price relatives for a cup of coffee in Paragraph 2.2.

3.3 A **quantity relative** is calculated as $Q_n/Q_o \times 100$. We calculated quantity relatives for cups of coffee in Paragraph 2.3.

Time series of relatives

3.4 Given the values of some commodity over time (a time series), there are two ways in which index relatives can be calculated.

3.5 In the **fixed base method**, a base year is selected (index 100), and all subsequent changes are measured against this base. Such an approach should only be used if the basic nature of the commodity is unchanged over time.

3.6 In the **chain base method**, changes are calculated with respect to the value of the commodity in the period immediately before. This approach can be used for any set of commodity values but must be used if the basic nature of the commodity is changing over time.

Example: fixed base and chain base methods

3.7 The price of commodity was £2.70 in 20X0, £3.11 in 20X1, £3.42 in 20X2 and £3.83 in 20X3. Construct both a chain base index and a fixed base index for the years 20X0 to 20X3 using 20X0 as the base year.

Solution

3.8

Chain base index	20X0	100	
	20X1	115	$(3.11/2.70 \times 100)$
	20X2	110	$(3.42/3.11 \times 100)$
	20X3	112	$(3.83/3.42 \times 100)$
Fixed base index	20X0	100	
	20X1	115	
	20X2	127	$(3.42/2.70 \times 100)$
	20X3	142	$(3.83/2.70 \times 100)$

The chain base relatives show the rate of change in prices from year to year, whereas the fixed base relatives show changes relative to prices in the base year.

Changing the base of fixed base relatives

3.9 It is sometimes necessary to change the base of a time series of fixed base relatives, perhaps because the base time point is too far in the past. The following time series has a base date of 1970 which would probably be considered too out of date.

	1990	1991	1992	1993	1994	1995
Index (1970 = 100)	451	463	472	490	499	505

To change the base date (to **rebase**), divide each relative by the relative corresponding to the new base time point and multiply the result by 100.

Exercise 1

Rebase the index in Paragraph 3.9 to 1993.

	1990	*1991*	*1992*	*1993*	*1994*	*1995*
Index (1993 = 100)	92*	94	96	100**	102***	103

* 451/490 × 100
** 490/490 × 100
*** 499/490 × 100

Comparing sets of fixed base relatives

3.10 You may be required to compare two sets of time series relatives. For example, an index of the annual number of advertisements placed by an organisation in the press and the index of the number of the organisation's product sold per annum might be compared. If the base years of the two indices differ, however, comparison is extremely difficult (as the illustration below shows).

	20W8	*20W9*	*20X0*	*20X1*	*20X2*	*20X3*	*20X4*
Number of advertisements placed (20X0 = 100)	90	96	100	115	128	140	160
Volumes of sales (20W0 = 100)	340	347	355	420	472	515	572

3.11 From the figures above it is impossible to determine whether sales are increasing at a greater rate than the number of advertisements placed, or vice versa. This difficulty can be overcome by rebasing one set of relatives so that the base dates are the same. For example, we could rebase the index of volume of sales to 20X0.

	20W8	*20W9*	*20X0*	*20X1*	*20X2*	*20X3*	*20X4*
Number of advertisements placed (20X0 = 100)	90	96	100	115	128	140	160
Volumes of sales (20X0 = 100)	96	98★	100	118	133★★	145	161

★ 347/355 × 100
★★ 472/355 × 100

3.12 The two sets of relatives are now much easier to compare. They show that volume of sales is increasing at a slightly faster rate, in general, than the number of advertisements placed.

Splicing

3.13 Consider the following selection of values from the Wholesale Price Index for Ruritania.

1 September 20X3	115.2	(1 March 20X0 = 100)
1 March 20X4	133.7	(1 March 20X0 = 100)
1 September 20X4	102.1	(1 March 20X4 = 100)
1 March 20X5	141.1	(1 March 20X4 = 100)

3.14 Suppose that we wished to make a comparison between the value of the index at 1 September 20X3 and the value of the index at 1 September 20X4. It is impossible to make a direct comparison because the index numbers at the two dates have different base dates. We therefore need to **convert**, or **splice**, the 1 September 20X3 figure to an index number with 1 March 20X4 as the base date by dividing by the figure for March 20X4 using March 20X0 as a base date.

New figure for September 20X3 = (115.2/133.7) × 100 = 86.2

This can now be compared with the figure of 102.1 for September 20X4, showing an increase of 15.9 points.

Time series deflation

3.15 The **real value** of a commodity can only be measured in terms of some 'indicator' such as the **rate of inflation** (normally represented by the Retail Prices Index) or the Index of Output of Production Industries. For example the cost of a commodity may have been £10 in 20X0 and £11 in 20X1, representing an increase of 10%. However, if we are told the prices in general (as measured by the RPI) increased by 12% between 20X0 and 20X1, we can argue that the **real cost** of the commodity has decreased.

Example: deflation

3.16 Mack Johnson works for Pound of Flesh Ltd. Over the last five years he has received an annual salary increase of £500. Despite his employer assuring him that £500 is a reasonable annual salary increase, Mack is unhappy because, although he agrees £500 is a lot of money, he finds it difficult to maintain the standard of living he had when he first joined the company.

Consider the figures below.

Year	(a) Wages £	(b) RPI	(c) Real wages £	(d) Real wages index
1	12,000	250	12,000	100.0
2	12,500	260	12,019	100.2
3	13,000	275	11,818	98.5
4	13,500	295	11,441	95.3
5	14,000	315	11,111	92.6

(a) This column shows Mack's wages over the five-year period.

(b) This column shows the current RPI.

(c) This column shows what Mack's wages are worth taking prices, as represented by the RPI, into account. The wages have been deflated relative to the new base period (year 1). Economists call these deflated wage figures **real wages**. The real wages for years 2 and 4, for example, are calculated as follows.

Year 2: £12,500 × 250/260 = £12,019
Year 4: £13,500 × 250/295 = £11,441

(d) This column is calculated by dividing the entries in column (c) by £12,000:

$$\textbf{Real index} = \frac{\text{current value}}{\text{base value}} \times \frac{\text{base indicator}}{\text{current indicator}}$$

So, for example, the **real wage index** in year 4 $= \frac{13,500}{12,000} \times \frac{250}{295} = 95.3$

3.17 The real wages index shows that the real value of Mack's wages has fallen by 7.4% over the five-year period. In real terms he is now earning £11,111 compared to £12,000 in year 1. He is probably justified, therefore, in being unhappy.

Exercise 2

The mean weekly take-home pay of the employees of Staples Ltd and a price index for the 11 years from 20X0 to 20Y0 are as follows.

Year	Weekly wage £	Price index (20X0 = 100)
20X0	150	100
20X1	161	103
20X2	168	106
20X3	179	108
20X4	185	109
20X5	191	112
20X6	197	114
20X7	203	116
20X8	207	118
20X9	213	121
20Y0	231	123

Required

Construct a time series of real wages for 20X0 to 20Y0 using a price index with 20X6 as the base year.

Solution

The index number for each year with 20X6 as the base year will be the original index number divided by 1.14, and the real wages for each year will be (money wages × 100)/index number for the year.

Year	Index	Real wage £
20X0	88	170
20X1	90	179
20X2	93	181
20X3	95	188
20X4	96	193
20X5	98	195
20X6	100	197
20X7	102	199
20X8	104	199
20X9	106	201
20Y0	108	214

4   COMPOSITE INDEX NUMBERS   *12/94, 6/97, 12/99*

4.1   Most practical indices cover more than one item and are hence termed **composite index numbers**. The RPI, for example, considers components such as food, alcoholic drink, tobacco and housing. An index of motor car costs might consider components such as finance payments, service costs, repairs, insurance and so on.

4.2   Suppose that the cost of living index is calculated from only three commodities: bread, tea and caviar, and that the prices for 20X1 and 20X2 were as follows.

	20X1	*20X2*
Bread	20p a loaf	40p a loaf
Tea	25p a packet	30p a packet
Caviar	450p a jar	405p a jar

4.3   A simple index could be calculated by adding the prices for single items in 20X2 and dividing by the corresponding sum relating to 20X1 (if 20X1 is the base year). In general, if the sum of the prices in the base year is ΣP_0 and the sum of the prices in the new year is ΣP_n, the index is $\dfrac{\Sigma P_n}{\Sigma P_0} \times 100$. The index, known as a **simple aggregate price index**, would therefore be calculated as follows.

	P_0	P_n
	20X1	*20X2*
	£	£
Bread	0.20	0.40
Tea	0.25	0.30
Caviar	4.50	4.05
	$\Sigma P_0 = 4.95$	$\Sigma P_n = 4.75$

Year	$\Sigma P_n / \Sigma P_0$	Simple aggregate price index
20X1	4.95/4.95 = 1.00	100
20X2	4.75/4.95 = 0.96	96

4.4 This type of index has a number of disadvantages. It ignores the amounts of bread, tea and caviar consumed (and hence the **importance** of each item), and the units to which the prices refer. If, for example, we had been given the price of a cup of tea rather than a packet of tea, the index would have been different.

4.5 To overcome these problems we can use **weighting**. A weighting factor can be thought of as an **indicator of the importance of the component** (such as alcohol in the RPI) with respect to the type of index being calculated.

4.6 There are two types of index which give different weights to different components, **weighted aggregate indices** and **weighted means of relatives indices**.

Weighted means of relatives indices

4.7 This method of weighting involves calculating index relatives for each of the components and using the weights given to obtain a weighted average of the relatives.

4.8 The general form of a **weighted means of relatives index** number is

$$\frac{\Sigma wI}{\Sigma w}$$

where w is the weighting factor
and I is the index relative

This is provided in the examination.

4.9 Values (price × quantity) relating to some point in time are usually used as weights.

4.10 Note that the weights may be from a year other than the base year. This is the method used for the index of wholesale prices. We could, for example, produce a weighted means of relatives index using 20X4 as base year, 20X6 as the given year and 20X5 values as weights.

4.11 Weighted means of relatives are very important in practice, the great majority of indices published in the UK being of this type.

Example: weighted means of relatives indices

4.12 Use both the information in Paragraph 4.2 and the following details about quantities purchased by each household in a week in 20X1 to determine a weighted means of price relatives index number for 20X2 using 20X1 as the base year.

	Quantity
Bread	6
Tea	2
Caviar	0.067

Solution

4.13	*Price relatives* (I)	Bread	$40/20 =$	2.00
		Tea	$30/25 =$	1.20
		Caviar	$405/450 =$	0.90
	Weightings (w)	Bread	$6 \times 0.20 =$	1.20
		Tea	$2 \times 0.25 =$	0.50
		Caviar	$0.067 \times 4.50 =$	0.30
		$\Sigma w =$		$\overline{2.00}$
	Index	Bread	$2 \times 1.2 =$	2.40
		Tea	$1.2 \times 0.5 =$	0.60
		Caviar	$0.9 \times 0.3 =$	0.27
		$\Sigma wI =$		$\overline{3.27}$

$$\text{Index number} = \frac{3.27}{2} \times 100 = 163.5$$

Weighted aggregate indices

4.14 This method of weighting involves multiplying each component value by its corresponding weight and adding these products to form an aggregate. This is done for both the base period and the period in question. The aggregate for the period under consideration is then divided by the base period aggregate.

4.15 The general form of a **weighted aggregate index** is

$$\frac{\Sigma wv_n}{\Sigma wv_o}$$

where w is the weighting factor

v_o is the value of the commodity in the base period

v_n is the value of the commodity in the period in question

4.16 **Price indices are usually weighted by quantities and quantity indices are usually weighted by prices.**

Exercise 3

What are the formulae for calculating price and quantity weighted aggregate indices if base year weights are used?

Solution

Price index: $\dfrac{\Sigma Q_o P_n}{\Sigma Q_o P_o} \times 100$

where P_0 represents the prices of items in the base year

P_n represents the prices of items in the new year

Q_0 represents the quantities of the items consumed in the base year

Quantity index: $\dfrac{\Sigma P_0 Q_n}{\Sigma P_0 Q_0} \times 100$

where Q_0 represents the quantities consumed in the base year
Q_n represents the quantities consumed in the new year
P_0 represents the prices in the base year

Example: a price index

4.17 In the previous example of the cost of living index (Paragraph 4.12), the 20X5 index value could have been calculated as follows.

Item	Quantity	Price in 20X1		Price in 20X5	
	Q_0	P_0	P_0Q_0	P_n	P_nQ_0
Bread	6	20	120	40	240
Tea	2	25	50	30	60
Caviar	0.067	450	30	405	27
			200		327

Index in 20X5 $= \dfrac{327}{200} \times 100 = 163.5$

4.18 Note that we get the same result as in Paragraph 4.13. This is because in the weights we used there were **percentages of total expenditure in the base year**, so the index number we computed was

$$\Sigma\left(\frac{P_n}{P_0} \times \frac{P_0Q_0}{\Sigma P_0Q_0}\right) = \Sigma\left(\frac{P_nQ_0}{\Sigma P_0Q_0}\right) = \frac{\Sigma P_nQ_0}{\Sigma P_0Q_0}$$

If we had weighted our price relatives in Paragraph 4.13 on a different basis, we would have got a different result.

4.19 We will now look at an example of a **quantity index**, which measures **changes in quantities** and uses **prices as weights**.

Example: a quantity index

4.20 The Falldown Construction Company uses four items of materials and components in a standard production job.

In 20X0 the quantities of each material or component used per job and their cost were as follows.

	Quantity	Price per unit
	Units	£
Material A	20	2
Material B	5	10
Component C	40	3
Component D	15	6

In 20X2 the quantities of materials and components used per job were as follows.

	Quantity
	Units
Material A	15
Material B	6
Component C	36
Component D	25

Using 20X0 as a base year, calculate the quantity index value in 20X2 for the amount of materials used in a standard job.

Solution

4.21

	Price	Quantity used in 20X0			Quantity used in 20X2	
	P_o £2	Q_o	P_oQ_o		Q_n	P_oQ_n
Material A	£2	20	40		15	30
Material B	£10	5	50		6	60
Component C	£3	40	120		36	108
Component D	£6	15	90		25	150
			300			348

$$\text{Quantity index} = \frac{348}{300} \times 100 = 116$$

This would suggest that the company is using 16% more materials in 20X2 than in 20X0 on a standard job.

5   LASPEYRE, PAASCHE AND FISHER INDICES

5.1   **Laspeyre and Paasche indices are special cases of weighed aggregate indices.**

Laspeyre indices

5.2   **Laspeyre indices use weights from the base period and are therefore sometimes called base weighted indices.**

Laspeyre price index

5.3   A **Laspeyre price index** uses **quantities** consumed in the base period as weights. In the notation already used it can be expressed as follows.

$$\text{Laspeyre price index} = \frac{\Sigma P_n Q_o}{\Sigma P_o Q_o} \times 100$$

Laspeyre quantity index

5.4   A **Laspeyre quantity index** uses **prices** from the base period as weights and can be expressed as follows.

$$\text{Laspeyre quantity index} = \frac{\Sigma P_o Q_n}{\Sigma P_o Q_o} \times 100$$

Paasche indices

5.5   **Paasche indices** use **current time period weights**. In other words the weights are changed every time period.

Paasche price index

5.6   A **Paasche price index** uses **quantities** consumed in the current period as weights and can be expressed as follows.

$$\text{Paasche price index} = \frac{\Sigma P_n Q_n}{\Sigma P_o Q_n} \times 100$$

Paasche quantity index

5.7 A **Paasche quantity index** uses **prices** from the current period as weights and can be expressed as follows.

Paasche quantity index $= \dfrac{\Sigma P_n Q_n}{\Sigma P_n Q_o} \times 100$

5.8 You are provided with the formulae for Paasche and Laspeyre indices in your examination.

Example: Laspeyre and Paasche price indices

5.9 The wholesale price index in Ruritania is made up from the prices of five items. The price of each item, and the average quantities purchased by manufacturing and other companies each week were as follows, in 20X0 and 20X2.

Item	Quantity 20X0 '000 units	Price per unit 20X0 Roubles	Quantity 20X2 '000 units	Price per unit 20X2 Roubles
P	60	3	80	4
Q	30	6	40	5
R	40	5	20	8
S	100	2	150	2
T	20	7	10	10

Required

Calculate the price index in 20X2, if 20X0 is taken as the base year, using the following.

(a) A Laspeyre index
(b) A Paasche index

Solution

5.10 *Workings*

Item	Q_o	P_o	Q_n	P_n	Laspeyre $P_o Q_o$	Laspeyre $P_n Q_o$	Paasche $P_n Q_n$	Paasche $P_n Q_o$
P	60	3	80	4	180	240	320	240
Q	30	6	40	5	180	150	200	240
R	40	5	20	8	200	320	160	100
S	100	2	150	2	200	200	300	300
T	20	7	10	10	140	200	100	70
					900	1,110	1,080	950

20X2 index numbers are as follows.

(a) Laspeyre index $= 100 \times \dfrac{1{,}110}{900} = 123.3$

(b) Paasche index $= 100 \times \dfrac{1{,}080}{950} = 113.7$

The Paasche index for 20X2 reflects the decline in consumption of the relatively expensive items R and T since 20X0. The Laspeyre index for 20X2 fails to reflect this change.

Exercise 4

A baker has listed the ingredients he used and their prices, in 20X3 and 20X4, as follows.

	Kgs used 20X3 '000s	Price per kg 20X3 £	Kgs used 20X4 '000s	Price per kg 20X4 £
Milk	3	1.20	4	1.50
Eggs	6	0.95	5	0.98
Flour	1	1.40	2	1.30
Sugar	4	1.10	3	1.14

Required

Calculate the following quantity indices for 20X4 (with 20X3 as the base year).

(a) A Laspeyre index
(b) A Paasche index

Solution

Workings

					Laspeyre		Paasche	
	Q_o	P_o	Q_n	P_n	P_oQ_o	P_oQ_n	P_nQ_n	P_nQ_o
Milk	3	1.20	4	1.50	3.60	4.80	6.00	4.50
Eggs	6	0.95	5	0.98	5.70	4.75	4.90	5.88
Flour	1	1.40	2	1.30	1.40	2.80	2.60	1.30
Sugar	4	1.10	3	1.14	4.40	3.30	3.42	4.56
					15.10	15.65	16.92	16.24

Quantity index numbers for 20X4 are as follows.

(a) **Laspeyre method** $= 100 \times \dfrac{15.65}{15.10} = 103.64$

(b) **Paasche method** $= 100 \times \dfrac{16.92}{16.24} = 104.19$

Which to use - Paasche or Laspeyre ?

5.11 Both patterns of consumption and prices change and a decision therefore has to be made as to whether a Paasche or a Laspeyre index should be used.

5.12 The following points should be considered when deciding which type of index to use.

(a) A **Paasche index requires quantities to be ascertained each year**. A Laspeyre index only requires them for the base year. Constructing a Paasche index may therefore be costly.

(b) For the **Paasche index the denominator has to be recalculated each year** because the quantities/prices must be changed to current year consumption/price levels.

For the **Laspeyre index, the denominator is fixed**. The Laspeyre index can therefore be calculated as soon as current prices/quantities are known. The Paasche index, on the other hand, cannot be calculated until the end of a period, when information about current quantities/prices becomes available.

(c) The denominator of a Laspeyre index is fixed and therefore the Laspeyre index numbers for several different years can be **directly compared**. With the Paasche index, on the other hand, comparisons can only be drawn directly between the current year and the base year (although indirect comparisons can be made).

(d) The weights for a Laspeyre index become **out of date**, whereas those for the Paasche index are updated each year.

(e) A **Laspeyre price index** implicitly assumes that, whatever the price changes, the quantities purchased will remain the same. In terms of economic theory, no substitution of cheaper alternative goods and services is allowed to take place. Even if goods become relatively more expensive, it assumes that the same quantities are bought. As a result, the **index tends to overstate inflation**.

(f) The effect of current year weighting when using the Paasche price index means that greater importance is placed on goods that are relatively cheaper now than they were in the base year. As a consequence, the **Paasche price index** tends to **understate inflation**.

In practice, it is common to use a Laspeyre index and revise the weights every few years. (Where appropriate, a new base year may be created when the weights are changed.)

Fisher's ideal index

5.13 Because Laspeyre's index uses base period weights it tends to overstate any change in prices or quantities. When prices increase there is usually a reduction in the quantities consumed. The index numerator is therefore likely to be too large. Likewise, when prices decrease, quantities consumed increase, resulting in an under-weighting of those prices which have decreased and hence an overstatement of change. The Paasche index, on the other hand, tends to understate change.

To overcome these difficulties some statisticians prefer to use **Fisher's ideal index**. This index is found by taking the **geometric mean of the Laspeyre index and the Paasche index**.

Fisher's ideal index $= \sqrt{\text{Laspeyre} \times \text{Paasche}}$

Exercise 5

The Laspeyre index of retail prices for 20X7 (with a base year of 20X1) is 137.2. The corresponding Paasche index is 134.9.

Required

Calculate Fisher's ideal index.

Solution

$\sqrt{(137.2 \times 134.9)} = 136.0$

---

6 PRACTICAL ISSUES

6/95

What items to include

6.1 The purpose to which the index is to be put must be carefully considered. Once this has been done, the items selected must be as **representative** as possible, taking into account this purpose. Care must be taken to ensure that the items are **unambiguously defined** and that their values are **readily ascertainable**.

6.2 For some indices, the choice of items might be relatively straightforward. For example, the **FT Actuaries All-Share Index**, compiled jointly by the Financial Times, the Institute of Actuaries and the Faculty of Actuaries, is made up of the share prices of approximately 800 companies quoted on The Stock Exchange. The weights are based on the market capitalisations of the companies (the number of shares in issue multiplied by their market value).

6.3 For other indices, the choice of items will be more difficult. The Retail Prices Index is an excellent example of the problem. It would be impossible to include all items of domestic spending and a selective, **representative basket of goods** and services must be found, ranging from spending on mortgages and rents, to cars, public transport, food and drink, electricity, gas, telephone, clothing, leisure activities and so on.

Collecting the data

6.4 Data are required to determine the following.

- The values for each item
- The weight that will be attached to each item

Consider as an example a **cost of living index**. The prices of a particular commodity will vary from place to place, from shop to shop and from type to type. Also the price will vary during the period under consideration. The actual prices used must obviously be some sort of **average**. The way in which the average is to be obtained should be clearly defined at the outset.

6.5 When constructing a price index, it is common practice to use the **quantities consumed** as **weights**; similarly, when constructing a quantity index, the **prices** may be used as **weights**. Care must be taken in selecting the basis for the weighting. For example, in a cost of living index, it may be decided to use the consumption of a typical family as the weights, but some difficulty may be encountered in defining a typical family.

The choice of a base year

6.6 The **choice of a base date**, or base year is not significant, except that it should be **representative**. In the construction of a price index, the base year must not be one in which there were abnormally high or low prices for any items in the basket of goods making up the index. For example, a year in which there is a potato famine would be unsuitable as a base period for the Retail Prices Index.

The limitations and misinterpretation of index numbers

Limitations

6.7 Index numbers are usually only **approximations** of changes in price or quantity over time, and must be interpreted with care.

(a) As we have seen, weightings become **out of date over time**. Unless a Paasche index is used, the weightings will gradually cease to reflect current reality.

(b) **New products or items may appear, and old ones may cease to be significant.** For example, spending has changed in recent years, to include new items such as personal computers and video recorders, whereas the demand for twin tub washing machines has declined. These changes would make the weightings of a price index for such goods out of date.

(c) **The data used to calculate index numbers might be incomplete, out of date, or inaccurate.** For example, the quantity indices of imports and exports are based on records supplied by traders which may be prone to error or even deliberate falsification.

(d) **The base year of an index should be a normal year**, but there is probably no such thing as a perfectly normal year. Some error in the index will be caused by atypical values in the base period.

(e) The '**basket of items**' in an index is often **selective**. For example, the Retail Prices Index (RPI) is constructed from a sample of households and from a basket of less than 400 items.

(f) A **national index** may not be very relevant to an individual town or region. For example, if the national index of wages and salaries rises from 100 to 115, we cannot conclude that the wages and salaries of people in, say, Glasgow, have gone up by 15%.

(g) An index may **exclude important items**: for example, the RPI excludes payments of income tax out of gross wages.

Misinterpretation

6.8 You must be careful not to misinterpret index numbers. Several possible mistakes will be explained using the following example of a retail prices index.

20X0		*20X1*		*20X2*	
January	340.0	January	360.6	January	436.3
		February	362.5	February	437.1
		March	366.2	March	439.5
		April	370.0	April	442.1

(a) It would be wrong to say that prices rose by 2.6% between March and April 20X2. It is correct to say that prices rose 2.6 points, or

$$\frac{2.6}{439.5} = 0.6\%$$

(b) It would be correct to say that the annual rate of price increases (the rate of inflation) fell between March and April 20X2. It would be a mistake, however, to suppose that a fall in the rate of inflation means that prices are falling, therefore the price index is falling.

The rate of price increases has **slowed down**, but the trend of prices is still **upwards**.

(i) The annual rate of inflation from March 20X1 to March 20X2 is

$$\left(\frac{439.5 - 366.2}{366.2} \right) = 20\%$$

(ii) The annual rate of inflation from April 20X1 to April 20X2 is

$$\left(\frac{442.1 - 370.0}{370.0} \right) = 19.5\%$$

Thus the annual rate of inflation has dropped from 20% to 19.5% between March and April 20X2, even though prices went up in the month between March and April 20X2 by 0.6%. (The price increase between March and April 20X1 was over 1%. This is included in the calculation of the rate of inflation between March 20X1 and March 20X2, but is excluded in the comparison between April 20X1 and April 20X2 where it has been replaced by the lower price increase, 0.6%, between March and April 20X2.)

7 SPECIAL PUBLISHED INDICES

6/94, 6/95, 12/96, 6/98

The Retail Prices Index (RPI)

7.1 **The Retail Prices Index measures the change in the cost of living**. It is published monthly (on a Tuesday) near the middle of the month by the Department of Employment and is displayed (to different levels of complexity) in the *Monthly Digest of Statistics*, the *Annual Abstract of Statistics*, the *Department of Employment Gazette* and *Economic Trends*. Since it measures the monthly change in the cost of living its principle use is as a **measure of inflation**.

7.2 The index measures the percentage changes, month by month, in the **average level of prices of 'a representative basket of goods'** purchased by the great majority of households in the United Kingdom. It takes account of practically all wage earners and most small and medium salary earners.

7.3 Each month the 350 items in the basket and the quantities bought of those items are listed in the **Family Expenditure Survey**. The Family Expenditure Survey is a continuing enquiry conducted by the Department of Employment into the general characteristics of households, their income and their expenditures. From this information the representative basket of goods is **divided into main groups**. Each group is divided into sections and these sections may be further split into separate items. Each group, section and specific item is weighted according to information from the Family Expenditure Survey to account for its relative importance in the basket.

7.4 Prices are collected from all over the United Kingdom by **Department of Employment** staff from different types of retail outlet each month. To ensure uniformity, the same ones are used each month. Price relatives are calculated for each item covered by the RPI for each retail outlet and averaged for a local area. The averages of local areas are averaged to obtain a national average (for each of the 350 items covered by the RPI).

7.5 The weights are then used to calculate **composite indices** using the **average of relatives method** for items in the sections, sections within groups and finally groups. The RPI is therefore a weighted average of relatives of each group with base date January 1987.

7.6 Each month, an **overall index** is published, as well as indices for each group, section and specific item.

7.7 The representative basket of goods is divided into the following main groups, which in 1993 had the weights as shown.

• Food and catering	189
• Alcohol and tobacco	113
• Housing and household expenditure	336
• Personal expenditure	97
• Travel and leisure	265
	1,000

The weights are always calculated to add to 1000.

7.8 **Certain items of expenditure are not included in the RPI.** These include the following.

(a) Income tax and National Insurance payments

(b) Insurance and pension payments

(c) Mortgage payments for house purchase (except for interest payments which are included)

(d) Gambling, gifts, charity

The items and their weights in the basket of goods are **continually revised** to ensure that they remain as **representative** as possible.

The Purchasing Power of the Pound Index (PPP)

7.9 This index is based solely on the annual average of the RPI. The basic idea behind the index is that when prices go up, the amount which can be purchased with a given sum of money goes down. The index is described in terms of two particular years. If the purchasing power of the pound is taken to be 100p in the first year (20X0) and the comparable purchasing power in the second year is calculated as, for example, 90p (20X5), this can be interpreted as the pound in 20X5 is worth only 90% of its 20X0 value or 100p in 20X5 buys what would have cost only 90p in 20X0.

The Tax and Price Index (TPI)

7.10 The TPI is published monthly and is another index which is linked to the RPI. It measures the **increase in gross taxable income** needed to compensate taxpayers for any increase in retail prices as measured by the RPI.

7.11 The TPI is considered to be a more comprehensive index than the RPI because the RPI simply measures changes in retail prices but the TPI also takes account of the changes in liability to direct taxes (including employees' national insurance contributions) facing a representative cross-section of taxpayers. Whether it is a better measure of the cost of living than the RPI because it takes direct taxes into account depends on the meaning of the phrase 'cost of living', which means different things to different people.

Index numbers of producer prices (PPI)

7.12 The PPI measure **manufacturers' prices**, the data for them being collected by the Business Statistics Office.

7.13 Indices are produced for a wide range of prices including output (home sales), materials and fuel purchased, commodities produced and imported. They are quoted for main industrial groupings, such as motor vehicles and parts, food manufacturing industries, the textile industry and so on. The various index numbers produced are calculated from the price movements of about 10,000 closely defined materials and products representative of goods purchased and manufactured by United Kingdom industry. All the indices express the current prices as a percentage of their annual average price in 1980, the base year.

Indices of Average Earnings

7.14 The **Indices of Average Earnings** are supplied on a monthly basis by the Department of Employment and measure the changes in average gross income.

Index of Output of Production Industries

7.15 **This index provides a general measure of monthly changes in the volume of output of the production industries in the United Kingdom**. Energy, water supply and manufacturing are included in the index but agriculture, transport, finance, construction, communications, distribution and all other public and private services are excluded.

7.16 The index is calculated as a weighted average of 328 separate relatives, each of which describes the change in the volume of output of a small sector of industry.

7.17 Many of the indices are **seasonally adjusted**, excluding any changes in production due to public and other holidays and other seasonal factors. The adjustments are designed to eliminate normal month to month fluctuations and thus show the trend more clearly.

Index of Retail Sales

7.18 Published monthly by the **Business Statistics Office**, this index covers the **retail trades** (excluding the motor trades) in Great Britain. Indices are given for both volume and value of sales as a result of major enquires into retailing. A voluntary panel of about 3,200 small retailers and about 350 large retailers (who account for about 80% of sales of this sector) fill out statistical returns covering volume and value of sales. Mail order firms are included in the panel.

Other index numbers

7.19 The following index numbers are given in publications such as the *Monthly Digest of Statistics* and the *Annual Abstract of Statistics*.

- Index Numbers of Output
- Index Numbers of Expenditure
- Volume Index of Sales of Manufactured Goods
- Indices of Labour Costs

There is also a very important **non-official index**, the **Financial Times Ordinary Share Index**.

Chapter roundup

- An **index** is a measure, over time, of the average changes in the value (price or quantity) of a group of items relative to the situation at some period in the past.

- An **index relative** is an index number which measures the change in a single distinct commodity.

- Index relatives can be calculated using the **fixed base method** or the **chain base method**.

- In order to compare two time series of relatives, each series should have the same base period and hence one (or both) may need **rebasing**.

- The **real value** of a commodity can only be measured in terms of some 'indicator' (such as the RPI).

- **Time series deflation** is a technique used to obtain a set of index relatives that measure the changes in the real value of some commodity with respect to some given indicator.

- **Composite indices** cover more than one item.

- **Weighting** is used to reflect the importance of each item in the index.

- There are two types of composite index number.
  - Weighted means of relatives indices
  - Weighted aggregate indices

- **Weighted means of relatives indices** are found by calculating indices and then applying weights.

- **Weighted aggregate indices** are found by applying weights and then calculating the index.

- There are two types of weighted aggregate index, the **Laspeyre** (which uses quantities/prices from the base period as the weights) and the **Paasche** (which uses quantities/prices from the current period as weights).

- **Fisher's ideal index** is the geometric mean of the Laspeyre and Paasche indices.

- Index number are a very useful way of summarising a large amount of data in a single series of numbers. You should remember, however, that any summary hides some detail and that index numbers should therefore be interpreted with caution.

Test your knowledge

1   How are index relatives calculated using the chain base method? (see para 3.8)

2   How is a time series of relatives rebased? (3.9)

3   What is splicing? (3.14)

4   Why must the real value of a commodity be measured in terms of some indicator? (3.15)

5   What is the general form of

   (a)   a weighted means of relatives index (4.8)
   (b)   a weighted aggregate index? (4.15)

6   What do Laspeyre indices use as weights? (5.2)

7   Why might Fisher's ideal index be used? (5.13)

8   What is excluded from the RPI? (7.8)

Now try illustrative questions 19 and 20 at the end of the Study Text

Part E
Probability and statistical inference

Chapter 9

PROBABILITY

> **This chapter covers the following topics.**
>
> 1 Uncertainty
>
> 2 The concept of probability
>
> 3 Permutations and combinations
>
> 4 The laws of probability
>
> 5 Venn diagrams
>
> 6 Expected values
>
> 7 Prior and posterior probabilities
>
> 8 Decision trees
>
> ## Introduction
>
> We are now going to move away from the collection, presentation and analysis of data and look at a new topic area, **probability**. This chapter will demonstrate how vital the role of probability is in business operations and planning and will explain the various techniques for assessing probability. In Chapter 10 we will build upon the basics learnt in this chapter and look at **probability distributions**. Chapter 11 will expand on one of the probability distributions introduced in Chapter 10, the **normal distribution**.

1 UNCERTAINTY

1.1 Mrs Cracked is responsible for product development at Lovely Lips Ltd, a cosmetics company. She has recently been working hard to perfect 'Perky Pink', a copy of the lipstick that Luscious, the number one popstar of the moment, is rumoured to be going to wear on her forthcoming world tour. She is naturally very upset to read in the music press that Luscious may be cancelling her world tour.

1.2 Although she reckons that this rumour may only have a 40% chance of being true, it presents her with a difficult choice. Sales of Perky Pink are estimated to be 10,000 units, each earning a profit of £1. This projection was, however, based on the assumption of Luscious going on her world tour. If this is not the case, Mrs Cracked reckons sales might be as low as 1,000 units. She is therefore forced to consider abandoning the project now, although £3,000 has already been invested in it.

1.3 To make matters worse, the marketing director then rings to let her know that Lovely Lips Ltd's arch competitor, Kissable and Co, may be planning to launch a similar colour lipstick which would sell for less and would cut Lovely Lips Ltd's sales to 6,000 units. Admittedly the marketing director estimates that the chance of Kissable and Co launching their product is only 50-50 but the possibility must still be taken into account.

1.4 Mrs Cracked and Lovely Lips Ltd therefore have two alternatives: to abandon Perky Pink altogether or to go ahead and market the lipstick regardless of whether the tour goes ahead or not and take the risk that Kissable and Co will bring out its own product.

1.5 Such a scenario is typical of situations facing countless organisations everyday. Ideally the business community would know with certainty what was going to happen. The real world is, however, not normally helpful! The future is uncertain. Those running organisations must therefore be able to tackle and take account of this uncertainty. They must understand what '50-50' means, what 'a 40% chance means'. They must be able to evaluate choices by quantifying the 'expected' or 'most likely' future results and, in addition, be able to make some attempt to quantify the possible variations.

1.6 There are a number of ways of analysing **uncertainty** (which as specific methods are outside the scope of this syllabus). Underlying all of these methods is, however, one concept: **probability**. An understanding of the concept of probability is vital if you are to take account of **uncertainty**.

2 THE CONCEPT OF PROBABILITY

6/95

2.1 'The **likelihood** of rain this afternoon is fifty percent' warns the weather report from your radio alarm clock. 'There's **no chance** of you catching that bus' grunts the helpful soul as you puff up the hill. The headline on your newspaper screams '**Odds** of Rainbow Party winning the election rise to one in four'.

2.2 '**Likelihood**' and '**chance**' are expressions used in our everyday lives to denote a level of uncertainty. **Probability**, a word which often strikes fear into the hearts of students, is simply the mathematical term used when we need to imply a **degree of uncertainty**.

2.3 **Probability is a measure of likelihood and can be stated as a percentage, a ratio, or more usually as a number from 0 to 1**. Zero probability corresponds to impossibility, whereas a probability of one corresponds to certainty. A 50% chance of something happening is a probability of ½. A chance of 1 in 4 is equivalent to a probability of ¼ and we express 'there's no chance of catching the bus' as P(catching the bus) = 0.

2.4 In statistics, probabilities are more commonly expressed as **proportions** than as percentages: for example, if there are six possible different outcomes in a certain situation, the probabilities might be expressed as follows.

Possible outcome	Probability as a percentage	Probability as a proportion
A	15.0%	0.150
B	20.0%	0.200
C	32.5%	0.325
D	7.5%	0.075
E	12.5%	0.125
F	12.5%	0.125
	100.0%	1.000

2.5 It is useful to consider how probability can be quantified. A businessman might estimate that if the selling price of a product is raised by 20p, there would be a 90% probability that demand would fall by 30%, but how would he have reached his estimate of 90% probability?

2.6 **There are several ways of assessing probabilities.**

(a) **They may be measurable with mathematical certainty**.

  (i) If a coin is tossed, there is a 0.5 probability that it will come down heads, and a 0.5 probability that it will come down tails.

  (ii) If a die is thrown, there is a one-sixth probability that a 6 will turn up.

(b) **They may be measurable from an analysis of past experience**. For example, suppose that an analysis of the last 300 working days shows that on 180 days there were no machine breakdowns. Given no change in the average reliability of machinery, we would therefore be able to estimate that the probability of no machine breakdowns during a day is 180/300 = 0.6 (so the probability of at least one breakdown during the day must be 0.4).

(c) **Probabilities can be estimated from research or surveys.** For example, a new product might be test-marketed in selected trial areas, and from the results of the test it might be estimated that there is a 70% chance that demand would be sufficient to earn a satisfactory profit for the company if the product were sold nationally.

2.7 A final introductory point about probability is that it is **a measure of the likelihood of an event happening in the long run, or over a large number of times.** If we toss a coin eight times, we cannot predict that it will necessarily come down heads four times and tails four times. The coin may come down heads eight times, or not once in the eight throws; heads may occur any number of times between zero and eight. We can say, however, that in the long run heads will occur about 50% of the time if a coin is tossed a sufficiently large number of times.

3 PERMUTATIONS AND COMBINATIONS

Permutations

3.1 **A permutation is an ordered arrangement of items**, and is best explained by means of an example.

Example: simple permutations

3.2 If you have three pieces of fruit, an apple, a banana and a pear, you can eat them in a number of different orders, or **permutations**. The permutations for eating these fruit are as follows.

Order in which fruit is eaten

Permutation	*1st*	*2nd*	*3rd*
1	apple	pear	banana
2	apple	banana	pear
3	pear	apple	banana
4	pear	banana	apple
5	banana	apple	pear
6	banana	pear	apple

Permutation 1 shows that the apple is eaten first, followed by the pear and then the banana. Permutation 5 shows that the banana is eaten first, followed by the apple and then the pear. For three pieces of fruit there are therefore six different permutations or orders in which they may be eaten. Note how each different permutation (1 - 6) has the fruits in a unique arrangement.

3.3 Statisticians will often need to work out the **number of ways that an event can occur** in order to calculate probabilities. Listing each permutation or order can be very time consuming and possibly inaccurate. Formulae may be used in order to calculate the number of permutations or orders.

3.4 In general, the number of permutations of n objects is written as n! (n factorial).

$$n! = n(n-1)(n-2)(n-3)\ldots\ldots$$

3.5 In our fruit example, 3 pieces of fruit may be arranged in 3! ways.

$$3! = 3 \times 2 \times 1 = 6 \text{ arrangements}$$

Note that this is the same answer as the one which was obtained by writing out all of the different arrangements or permutations in paragraph 3.2.

Permutations of groups

3.6 It is possible that we may wish to calculate the number of permutations of eating only two of the fruits from the apple, banana and pear. The ways in which these fruits may be arranged are as follows.

Permutation	1st	2nd
1	apple	pear
2	pear	apple
3	apple	banana
4	banana	apple
5	pear	banana
6	banana	pear

There are therefore six permutations of eating two pieces of fruit from a possible three pieces of fruit, where **order matters**.

3.7 (a) It probably won't surprise you to learn that there is also a formula which may be used to calculate the number of **permutations of n items, selecting x at a time**. The number is denoted by the term $_nP_x$ and the formula is as follows.

$$_nP_x = \frac{n!}{(n-x)!}$$

(b) In the fruit example above, there are three pieces of fruit (n = 3) and we wish to select two pieces of fruit, therefore x = 2

$$_3P_2 = \frac{3!}{(3-2)!} = \frac{3!}{1!} = \frac{3 \times 2 \times 1}{1} = 6 \text{ permutations}$$

3.8 **A permutation is therefore an arrangement of items in which the order matters. An arrangement of items where the order does not matter is known as a combination.**

Combinations

3.9 It is important to understand the difference between combinations and permutations. The main distinction is that order matters for permutations, but does not matter for combinations.

Example: simple combinations

3.10 (a) Let us consider the apple, banana and pear example in paragraph 3.2. Where we have three pieces of fruit, how many ways can we select the fruit where order does not matter?

(b) The answer is only 1, since the arrangement apple, pear, banana is the same as apple, banana, pear which is the same as banana, apple, pear and so on. In fact the different permutations listed (1-6) are all the same combination of fruit.

(c) The following formula can be used for calculating the number of combinations of n items, x at a time.

$$^nC_x = \frac{n!}{x!(n-x)!}$$

where n = total number of items

x = the number of items per arrangement

(d) If we use the formula to calculate the number of ways of combining three fruit out of three fruit, we get the following answer.

Let n = 3 and let x = 3

$$^3C_3 = \frac{3!}{3!(3-3)!} = \frac{3!}{3!0!} = \frac{3 \times 2 \times 1}{3 \times 2 \times 1 \times 1} = 1$$

Note that $0! = 1$ (always).

3.11   In paragraph 3.6 we considered the permutations of eating two pieces of fruit. The combinations of eating two pieces of fruit out of three pieces of fruit may be calculated by using the formula in the above example. We wish to calculated $^3C_2$.

$$^3C_2 = \frac{3!}{(3-2)!2!} = \frac{3!}{1!2!} = \frac{3 \times 2 \times 1}{1 \times 2 \times 1} = 3$$

3.12   We can list the three combinations of selecting the pieces of fruit out of a possible three pieces. Remember that **order does not matter**, so the permutations 1 and 2 in paragraph 3.6 are the same combination of fruit. **Combinations do not worry about the order of things** and therefore apple 1st, pear 2nd is the same combination as pear 1st, apple 2nd.

Combination of fruit eaten

apple	pear
apple	banana
pear	banana

The number of combinations is three which is the same as the answer which was calculated by using the formula in paragraph 3.11.

Example: combinations of one or two items

3.13   A hardware storekeeper sells paint which he mixes himself in pairs to get the right colours. If we assume that by mixing two of the basic paints he always gets a colour different to any of the other mixtures and different to any of the basic colours, how many different shades can he obtain by stocking n basic paints? (*Note.* Any one basic paint itself counts as one shade.)

Solution

3.14   The total number of mixtures (combinations) of two paints will be:

$$^nC_2 = \frac{n!}{(n-2)!2!} = \frac{n \times (n-1)}{2 \times 1} = \frac{n^2 - n}{2}$$

If we add to this the number of paints stocked, n, (which are themselves different shades) we get a total of

$$\frac{n^2 - n}{2} + n$$

Exercise 1

A class of 15 students is about to sit a statistics examination. They will subsequently be listed in descending order by reference to the marks scored. Assume that there are no tied positions with two or more students having the same mark.

Required

Calculate the following.

(a)   The number of different possible orderings for the whole class

BPP PUBLISHING

(b)   The number of different possible results for the top three places

(c)   The number of different possible ways of having three people taking the top three places (irrespective of order)

Solution

(a)   The number of different possible orderings of the whole class is

$$_{15}P_{15} = \frac{15!}{(15-15)!} = \frac{15!}{0!} = 15! = 1,307,674,368,000$$

(b)   The number of different possible results for the top three places is given by the number of permutations of three out of 15.

$$_{15}P_3 = \frac{15!}{(15-3)!} = \frac{15!}{12!} = 15 \times 14 \times 13 = 2,730$$

(c)   The number of ways of having three people taking the top three places is given by the number of combinations of three out of 15.

$$^{15}C_3 = \frac{15!}{(15-3)!3!} = \frac{15 \times 14 \times 13}{3 \times 2 \times 1} = 455$$

---

4   THE LAWS OF PROBABILITY   *12/96, 6/97, 12/97, 12/98, 6/99, 12/99, 6/00*

4.1   It is the year 2020 and examiners are extinct. A mighty but completely fair computer churns out examinations that are equally likely to be easy or difficult. There is no link between the number of questions on each paper, which is arrived at on a fair basis by the computer, and the standard of the paper. You are about to take five examinations.

Simple probability

4.2   It is vital that the first examination is easy as it covers a subject which you have tried, but unfortunately failed, to understand. What is the probability that it will be an easy examination?

4.3   Obviously (let us hope), the probability of an easy paper is ½ (or 50% or 0.5). This reveals a very important principle (which holds if each result is equally likely).

Probability of achieving the desired result

=   Number of ways of achieving desired result
      ―――――――――――――――――――――――――――
         Total number of possible outcomes

Let us apply the principle to our example.

Total number of possible outcomes = 'easy' or 'difficult'   = 2
Total number of ways of achieving the desired result (which is 'easy')   = 1

The probability of an easy examination, or P(easy examination)   = ½

Example: simple probability

4.4   Suppose that a coin is tossed in the air. What is the probability that it will come down heads?

Solution

4.5   P(heads)   =   Number of ways of achieving desired result (heads)
                              ―――――――――――――――――――――――――――――――――――
                              Total number of possible outcomes (heads or tails)

                      =   ½ or 50% or 0.5.

Complementary outcomes

4.6 **Complementary outcomes may be thought of as being opposite outcomes**. For example, the outcome of the Eurovision Song Contest might be that the United Kingdom wins. The complementary outcome would therefore be that the United Kingdom does not win.

4.7 Consider the following examples of **complementary outcomes**.

A	B
It will rain this afternoon	It will *not* rain this afternoon
You will catch the bus on Monday morning	You will *not* catch the bus on Monday morning
The Rainbow Party will win the next general election	The Rainbow Party will *not* win the next general election

4.8 In the examples shown above, there are two outcomes, A and B. In general, the outcomes in column B are the opposite or negative of the outcomes in column A. We already know that the probabilities of all possible outcomes of a certain situation will total 100% or 1, therefore P(A) + P(B) must equal 100% or 1.

4.9 If we know the probability of one of the two complementary outcomes then we can deduce the probability of the other outcome.

(a) If there is a 50% chance of rain this afternoon, then there is a 50% (100% – 50%) chance that is will *not* rain this afternoon.

(b) If the probability of you catching the bus on Monday morning is 0.4. then the probability of you *not* catching the bus on Monday morning is 0.6 (1 – 0.4).

(c) Finally, if the odds of the Rainbow Party winning the next general election are 1 to 4, or 0.25, then the odds of the Rainbow Party *not* winning the next general election are 3 to 4 or 0.75.

4.10 Let us now return to the examination scenario. You are desperate to pass more of the examinations than your sworn enemy but, unlike you, he is more likely to pass the first examination if it is difficult. (He is very strange!!) What is the probability of the first examination being more suited to your enemy's requirements or in other words, what is the probability of a difficult examination?

4.11 There are two possible outcomes in our examination scenario. These are that there is an easy examination paper or that there is a difficult examination paper. We also know that the probabilities of these two outcomes must total 1.

Therefore P(easy examination) + P(difficult examination) = 1.

4.12 We also know that P(not easy examination) is the same as P(difficult examination).

$$
\begin{aligned}
\text{Since P(easy examination)} &= 1 - \text{P(not easy examination)} \\
\tfrac{1}{2}\text{(from par 4.3)} &= 1 - \text{P (not easy examination)} \\
\text{P(not easy examination)} &= \tfrac{1}{2}
\end{aligned}
$$

Since P(not easy examination) is the same as P(difficult examination), then the probability of the first examination being more suited to your enemy's requirements (i.e. difficult) is ½.

4.13 In general, **$P(\overline{X}) = 1 - P(X)$, where $\overline{X}$ is 'not X'.**

Example: complementary outcomes

4.14   If there is a 70 per cent chance of the you passing your driving test at the first attempt, use the law of complementary outcomes to calculate the probability of you *not* passing your driving test at the first attempt.

Solution

4.15   P(passing)   =   70% = 0.7
       P(not passing)   =   1 − P(passing) = 1 − 0.7 = 0.3

The simple addition or OR law

4.16   The time pressure in the second examination is enormous. The computer will produce a paper which will have between five and nine questions. You know that, easy or difficult, the examination must have six questions at the most for you to have any hope of passing it.

What is the probability of the computer producing an examination with six or fewer questions? In other words, what is the probability of an examination with five *or* six questions?

4.17   Don't panic. Let us start by using the basic principle.

$$P(5 \text{ questions}) = \frac{\text{Total number of ways of achieving a five-question examination}}{\text{Total number of possible outcomes } (= 5,6,7,8 \text{ or } 9 \text{ questions})}$$
$$= \ ^1/_5$$

Likewise P(6 questions) = $^1/_5$

Either five questions or six questions would be acceptable, so the probability of you passing the examination must be greater than if just five questions or just six questions (but not both) were acceptable. We therefore add the two probabilities together so that the probability of passing the examination has increased.

4.18   So P(5 or 6 questions)   =   P(5 questions) + P(6 questions)
       = $\frac{1}{5} + \frac{1}{5} = \frac{2}{5}$

In general, the **simple addition or OR law** is:

$$P(X \text{ or } Y \text{ or } Z) = P(X) + P(Y) + P(Z)$$

where X, Y and Z are **mutually exclusive outcomes**, which means that the occurrence of one of the outcomes excludes the possibility of any of the others happening. In the example the outcomes are mutually exclusive because it is impossible to have five questions *and* six questions in the same examination.

Venn diagram representation

4.19   You may find it useful to consider a **Venn diagram** representation of the simple addition/OR law.

4.20   In terms of a Venn diagram, mutually exclusive outcomes are presented as follows.

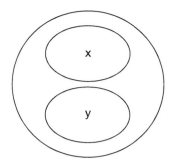

4.21 If outcomes are **mutually exclusive**, the probability that one of them will occur (and, by definition, it is not possible for more than one of them to occur) is the sum of their individual probabilities. In terms of a Venn diagram this is represented by the fact that the probability of the union (one outcome or the other outcome or both outcomes) of two non-overlapping outcomes is the sum of their individual probabilities. Thus if X and Y are mutually exclusive outcomes, we have $P(X \cup Y) = P(X) + P(Y)$.

This extends immediately to any number of outcomes.

Example: mutually exclusive outcomes

4.22 The delivery of an item of raw material from a supplier may take up to six weeks from the time the order is placed. The probabilities of various delivery times are as follows.

Delivery time	Probability
≤ 1 week	0.10
$> 1, \leq 2$ weeks	0.25
$> 2, \leq 3$ weeks	0.20
$> 3, \leq 4$ weeks	0.20
$> 4, \leq 5$ weeks	0.15
$> 5, \leq 6$ weeks	0.10
	1.00

What is the probability that a delivery will take the following times?

(a) Two weeks or less
(b) More than three weeks

Solution

4.23 (a) $P (\leq 1 \text{ or } > 1, \leq 2 \text{ weeks}) =$ $P (\leq 1 \text{ week}) + P (>1, \leq 2 \text{ weeks})$
  $=$ $0.10 + 0.25$
  $=$ 0.35

(b) $P (> 3, \leq 6 \text{ weeks})$ $=$ $P (> 3, \leq 4 \text{ weeks}) + P (> 4, \leq 5 \text{ weeks}) + P (> 5, \leq 6 \text{ weeks})$
  $=$ $0.20 + 0.15 + 0.10$
  $=$ 0.45

The simple multiplication or AND law

4.24 You still have three examinations to sit: astrophysics, geography of the moon and computer art. Stupidly, you forgot to revise for the astrophysics examination, which will have between 15 and 20 questions. You think that you may scrape through this paper if it is easy *and* if there are only 15 questions.

What is the probability that the paper the computer produces will exactly match your needs? Do not forget that there is no link between the standard of the examination and the number of questions.

4.25 The best way to approach this question is diagrammatically, showing all the possible outcomes.

	Number of questions					
	15	*16*	*17*	*18*	*19*	*20*
Type of paper						
Easy (E)	E and 15★	E and 16	E and 17	E and 18	E and 19	E and 20
Difficult (D)	D and 15	D and 16	D and 17	D and 18	D and 19	D and 20

The diagram shows us that, of the twelve possible outcomes, there is only one 'desired result' (which is asterisked). We can therefore calculate the probability as follows.

P(easy paper *and* 15 questions) = $\frac{1}{12}$

4.26 The answer can be found more easily as follows.

P(easy paper *and* 15 questions) = P(easy paper) × P(15 questions) = $\frac{1}{2} \times \frac{1}{6} = \frac{1}{12}$

4.27 In general, the **simple multiplication or AND law** is:

P(X and Y) = P(X) P(Y)

where X and Y are **independent events,** which means that the occurrence of one event in no way affects the outcome of the other events: whether it is an easy or difficult paper has no effect on the number of questions.

Example: independent events

4.28 A die is thrown and a coin is tossed simultaneously. What is the probability of throwing a 5 and getting heads on the coin?

Solution

4.29 The probability of throwing a 5 on a die is $\frac{1}{6}$.

The probability of a tossed coin coming up heads is $\frac{1}{2}$.

The probability of throwing a 5 and getting heads on a coin is $\frac{1}{2} \times \frac{1}{6} = \frac{1}{12}$.

The general rule of addition

4.30 The three examinations you still have to sit are placed face down in a line in front of you at the final examination sitting. There is an easy astrophysics paper, a difficult geography of the moon paper and a difficult computer art paper. Without turning over any of the papers you are told to choose one of them. What is the probability that the first paper that you select is difficult or is the geography of the moon paper?

4.31 Let us think about this carefully.

There are two difficult papers, so P(difficult) = $\frac{2}{3}$.

There is one geography of the moon paper, so P(geography of the moon) = $\frac{1}{3}$.

4.32 If we use the OR law and add the two probabilities then we will have double counted the difficult geography of the moon paper. It is included in the set of difficult papers and in the set of geography of the moon papers. In other words, we are *not* faced with mutually exclusive outcomes because the occurrence of a geography of the moon paper does not exclude the possibility of the occurrence of a difficult paper. We therefore need to take account of this double counting.

P(difficult paper or geography of the moon paper) = P(difficult paper) + P(geography of the moon paper) – P(difficult paper and geography of the moon paper).

Using the **AND law**, P(difficult paper or geography of the moon paper) = $\frac{2}{3} + \frac{1}{3} - (\frac{1}{3})$

= $\frac{2}{3}$

4.33　In general, the **general rule of addition** is:

P(X or Y) = P(X) + P(Y) – P(X and Y)

where the word 'or' is used in an inclusive sense: either X or Y or both. X and Y are therefore **not mutually exclusive**: it is *not* impossible to have an examination which is difficult *and* about the geography of the moon.

Venn diagram representation

4.34　Suppose we want to make a Venn diagram representation of the general addition law. We have the possibility that X and Y will both occur at the same time. If we were to add together the probability of the outcomes in X (difficult papers) with the probability of the outcomes in Y (geography of the moon paper) we shall have included twice over the probabilities of the outcomes common to both X and Y (difficult geography of the moon papers).

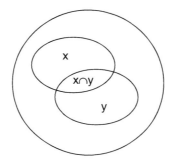

4.35　The probability of the **simultaneous occurrence** of an outcome in X and Y must therefore be subtracted out.

This gives P(X $\cup$ Y) = P(X) + P(Y) – P(X $\cap$ Y)

Note.　For union ($\cup$) read 'or', that is an outcome in X or Y or both.
For intersection ($\cap$) read 'and', that is an outcome in X and Y.

Exercise 2

If one card is drawn from a normal pack of 52 playing cards, what is the probability of getting an ace or a spade?

Solution

P(ace) = 4/52

P (spade) = 13/52

P(ace of spades) = 1/52

$\therefore$ P(ace or spades) = $\dfrac{4}{52} + \dfrac{13}{52} - \dfrac{1}{52} = \dfrac{16}{52} = \dfrac{4}{13}$

The general rule of multiplication

4.36 Computer art is your last examination. Understandably you are very tired and you are uncertain whether you will be able to stay awake. You believe that there is a 70% chance of your falling asleep if it becomes too hot and stuffy in the examination hall. It is well known that the air conditioning system serving the examination hall was installed in the 1990s and is therefore extremely unreliable. There is a 1 in 4 chance of it breaking down during the examination, thereby causing the temperature in the hall to rise. What is the likelihood that you will drop off?

4.37 The scenario in Paragraph 4.31 has led us to face what is known as **conditional probability**. We can rephrase the information provided as 'the probability that you will fall asleep, given that it is too hot and stuffy, is equal to 70%' and we can write this as follows.

P(fall asleep/too hot and stuffy) = 70%

4.38 Whether you fall asleep is conditional upon whether the hall becomes too hot and stuffy. The events are not, therefore, independent and so we cannot use **the simple multiplication law**. So:

P(it becomes too hot and stuffy and you fall asleep)

$$
\begin{aligned}
&= \quad \text{P(too hot and stuffy)} \times \text{P(fall asleep/too hot and stuffy)} \\
&= \quad 25\% \times 70\% = 0.25 \times 0.7 = 0.175 = 17^{1}/_{2}\%
\end{aligned}
$$

4.39 In general, if X and Y are two outcomes, then the probability that X and Y will occur is:

$$
\begin{aligned}
\text{P(X and Y)} &= \quad \text{P(X)} \times \text{P(Y/X)} \\
&= \quad \text{P(Y)} \times \text{P(X/Y)}
\end{aligned}
$$

where X and Y are **dependent events**.

4.40 We can rearrange the rule above as follows.

$$
\text{P(Y/X)} = \frac{\text{P(X and Y)}}{\text{P(X)}} = \frac{\text{P(Y) P(X / Y)}}{\text{P(X)}}
$$

This is called **Bayes' theorem**.

4.41 When X and Y are **independent events**, then P(Y/X) = P(Y) since, by definition, the occurrence of Y (and therefore P(Y)) does not depend upon the occurrence of X. Similarly P(X/Y) = P(X).

4.42 For example, suppose that a company plans to sell 12 new products next year, seven electrical products and five non-electrical products. Of the total of 12 products, two electrical and three non-electrical products are expected to make a profit.

If X is the event that the product is electrical and Y is the event that the product is profitable, then P(Y/X) is the probability that the product, given that it is electrical, is also profitable.

$$
\text{This is } \frac{\text{P(X and Y)}}{\text{P(X)}} = \frac{2/12}{7/12} = \frac{2}{7} = 0.286
$$

Example: conditional probabilities

4.43 The estimated probability that the labour force in a factory will improve its productivity over both of the next two years is 0.6. It is also thought that there is a 0.8 probability that productivity will improve in the first year.

Given that productivity does rise in the first year, what is the probability that productivity will also rise in the second year?

Solution

4.44   Let outcome X = an increase in productivity in Year 1
Let outcome Y = an increase in productivity in Year 2

$$P(Y/X) \quad = \quad \frac{P(X \text{ and} Y)}{P(X)}$$

$$= \quad \frac{0.6}{0.8}$$

$$= \quad 0.75$$

Venn diagram representation

4.45   The **general rule of multiplication** can also be built up using **Venn diagrams**.

4.46   Suppose are looking at the probability of event X, given that another event Y has occurred (P(X/Y)).

We know that event Y has occurred and given this fact, we want to know the probability of occurrence of event X. Because event Y has occurred, the only outcomes that can have occurred are those in event Y. Hence the only way X can occur is if the outcome is in both X and Y, that is an outcome in X ∩ Y.

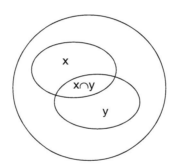

The chance of this happening is the chance of an X ∩ Y outcome as a proportion of all the possible Y outcomes which might have occurred. Hence the **conditional probability** of X given Y is P(X/Y) = P(X ∩ Y)/P(Y).

Since P(X ∩ Y) is P(X and Y) we can rearrange this to P(X and Y) = P(Y) P(X/Y).

Exercise 3

The independent probabilities that the three sections of a management accounting department will encounter one computer error in a week are respectively 0.1, 0.2 and 0.3. There is never more than one computer error encountered by any one section in a week. Calculate the probability that there will be the following number of errors encountered by the management accounting department next week.

(a)   At least one computer error
(b)   One and only one computer error

Solution

(a)   The probability of at least one computer error is 1 minus the probability of no error. The probability of no error is $0.9 \times 0.8 \times 0.7 = 0.504$.

(Since the probability of an error is 0.1, 0.2 and 0.3 in each section, the probability of no error in each section must be 0.9, 0.8 and 0.7 respectively.)

The probability of at least one error is $1 - 0.504 = 0.496$.

(b)   Y = yes, N = no

		Section 1	Section 2	Section 3
(i)	Error?	Y	N	N
(ii)	Error?	N	Y	N
(iii)	Error?	N	N	Y

			Probabilities
(i)	$0.1 \times 0.8 \times 0.7$ =		0.056
(ii)	$0.9 \times 0.2 \times 0.7$ =		0.126
(iii)	$0.9 \times 0.8 \times 0.3$ =		0.216
		Total	0.398

The probability of only one error only is 0.398.

Exercise 4

A glass bottle manufacturer has three inspection points: one for size, the second for colour and the third for flaws such as cracks and bubbles in the glass. The probability that each inspection point will incorrectly accept or reject a bottle is 0.02.

Required

Calculate the following probabilities.

(a)   A perfect bottle will be passed through all inspection points.
(b)   A bottle faulty in colour and with a crack will be passed through all inspection points.
(c)   A bottle faulty in size only will be passed through all inspection points.

Solution

The probability of incorrect testing is 0.02 at each stage, and so the probability of correct testing is 0.98.

(a)   A perfect bottle has a 98% probability of passing each stage, and so its probability of passing all three stages is $0.98 \times 0.98 \times 0.98 = 0.941192$.

(b)   A bottle faulty in colour and with a crack must pass three stages.

Size: probability 0.98
Colour: probability 0.02
Flaws: probability 0.02

Probability of passing = $0.98 \times 0.02 \times 0.02 = 0.000392$

(c)   A bottle faulty in size only must pass three stages.

Size: probability 0.02
Colour: probability 0.98
Flaws: probability 0.98

Probability of passing = $0.02 \times 0.98 \times 0.98 = 0.019208$

Exercise 5

Two accountants work together to prepare some costings for inclusion in a report to senior management. Both start work on the same day, and each has a different set of tasks to perform. The possible times required by each person to do his part of the job are as follows.

	Accountant X		Accountant Y	
Time	*Probability*		*Time*	*Probability*
Days			*Days*	
6	0.2		6	0.1
8	0.5		8	0.4
10	0.3		10	0.5

What is the probability that the total job will take the following number of days?

(a)   6 days
(b)   8 days
(c)   10 days

Solution

X Days		Y Days				
P(6	and	6)	=	0.2×0.1	=	0.02
P(6	and	8)	=	$0.2 \times 0.4 = 0.08$		
P(8	and	8)	=	$0.5 \times 0.4 = 0.20$	=	0.33
P(8	and	6)	=	$0.5 \times 0.1 = 0.05$		
P(10)			=	P(A = 10) + P(B = 10) −		
				P (A and B = 10)		
				$0.3 + 0.5 - (0.3 \times 0.5)$	=	0.65
						1.00

(a) The probability of 6 days is 2%
(b) The probability of 8 days is 33%
(c) The probability of 10 days is 65%

---

5 VENN DIAGRAMS

6/94, 6/95, 6/96, 12/97, 12/99

5.1 It is possible to use **Venn diagrams** to solve **probability problems**. For example if there are two outcomes they can be depicted by two overlapping circles, one for each outcome. The known probabilities can be filled in, then the unknown probabilities can be derived from the fact that **all the probabilities on the diagram must add up to 1**.

Example: Venn diagrams

5.2 Two outcomes are denoted by M and N. $\overline{M}$ (or M') denotes 'not M' and $\overline{N}$ denotes 'not N'. The following probabilities are given.

P(M) = 0.50   P(M and N) = 0.15   P($\overline{M}$ and $\overline{N}$) = 0.10

Required

Calculate P(N).

Solution

5.3 We can draw a Venn diagram with a circle for each outcome, M and N.

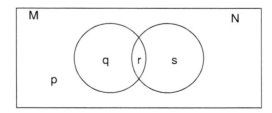

The given probabilities are as follows.

$$\begin{aligned} P(M) &= q + r = 0.50 \\ P(M \text{ and } \underline{N}) &= \quad r = 0.15 \\ P(\overline{M} \text{ and } \overline{N}) &= \quad p = 0.10 \end{aligned}$$

We want to know P(N), which is equal to r + s. We therefore need to deduce s.

$$\begin{aligned} p + (q + r) + s &= 1.00 \\ 0.10 + 0.50 + s &= 1.00 \\ s &= 1.00 - 0.10 - 0.50 = 0.40 \\ P(N) = r + s &= 0.15 + 0.40 \\ &= 0.55 \end{aligned}$$

Exercise 6

A food company is introducing a new flavour to its range of yoghurts and stops 120 customers at random in a supermarket and asks their opinions about three new flavours, strawberry (S), raspberry (R) and vanilla (V). It discovers the following.

Number who like S	49
Number who like V	25
Number who like R	67
Number who like S and R	12
Number who like S and V	15
Number who like R and V	13
Number who like all three	7

Determine the following probabilities.

(a) A customer who like exactly one flavour
(b) A customer who likes none of the flavours

Solution

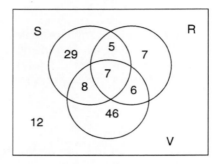

The figures are found by entering the 7 who like all three flavours first, then finding the numbers who like any two as balancing figures (for example, S, R not V = 12 − 7 = 5), then finding the number who like only one, and finally the number who like none.

(a) P(likes exactly one flavour) = $\dfrac{29+7+46}{120}$ = 0.683

(b) P(likes no flavour) = $\dfrac{(120-(29+5+7+8+7+6+46))}{120}$ = 0.1

6 EXPECTED VALUES

12/94

6.1 **An expected value (or EV) is a weighted average value, based on probabilities.**

6.2 **If the probability of an outcome of an event is p, then the expected number of times that this outcome will occur in n events (the expected value) is equal to n × p.**

For example, suppose that the probability that a transistor is defective is 0.02. How many defectives would we expect to find in a batch of 4,000 transistors?

EV = 4,000 × 0.02
= 80 defectives

Example: expected values

6.3 The daily sales of Product T may be as follows.

Units	Probability
1,000	0.2
2,000	0.3
3,000	0.4
4,000	0.1
	1.0

Required

Calculate the expected daily sales.

Solution

6.4 The EV of daily sales may be calculated by multiplying each possible outcome (volume of daily sales) by the probability that this outcome will occur.

Units	Probability	Expected value Units
1,000	0.2	200
2,000	0.3	600
3,000	0.4	1,200
4,000	0.1	400
	EV of daily sales	2,400

6.5 In the long run the expected value should be approximately the actual average, if the event occurs many times over. In the example above, we do not expect sales on any one day to equal 2,400 units, but in the long run, over a large number of days, average sales should equal 2,400 units a day.

Expected values and single events

6.6 The point made in the preceding paragraph is an important one. An expected value can be calculated when the event will only occur once or twice, but it will not be a true long-run average of what will actually happen, because there is no long run.

6.7 Suppose, for example, that a businessman is trying to decide whether to invest in a project. He estimates that there are three possible outcomes.

Outcome	Profit/(loss) £	Probability
Success	10,000	0.2
Moderate success	2,000	0.7
Failure	(4,000)	0.1

The expected value of profit may be calculated as follows.

Profit/(loss) £	Probability	Expected value £
10,000	0.2	2,000
2,000	0.7	1,400
(4,000)	0.1	(400)
	Expected value of profit	3,000

6.8 In this example, the project is a one-off event, and as far as we are aware, it will not be repeated. The actual profit or loss will be £10,000, £2,000 or £(4,000), and the average value of £3,000 will not actually happen. There is no long-run average of a single event.

6.9 Nevertheless, the expected value can be used to help the manager decide whether or not to invest in the project. All other things being equal **a project with a positive EV** (an expected value which is a profit) **should be accepted**, and **a project with a negative EV** (an expected value which is a loss) **should be rejected**.

6.10 Provided that we understand the limitations of using expected values for single events, they can offer a helpful guide for **management decisions**, and suggest to managers whether any particular decision is worth the risk of taking (subject, of course, to reasonable accuracy in the estimates of the probabilities themselves).

Exercise 7

A company manufactures and sells product D. The selling price of the product is £6 per unit, and estimates of demand and variable costs of sales are as follows.

Probability	Demand	Probability	Variable cost per unit
	Units		£
0.3	5,000	0.1	3.00
0.6	6,000	0.3	3.50
0.1	8,000	0.5	4.00
		0.1	4.50

The unit variable costs do not depend on the volume of sales.

Fixed costs will be £10,000.

Required

Calculate the expected profit.

Solution

The EV of demand is as follows.

Demand	Probability	Expected value
Units		Units
5,000	0.3	1,500
6,000	0.6	3,600
8,000	0.1	800
	EV of demand	5,900

The EV of the variable cost per unit is as follows.

Variable costs	Probability	Expected value
£		£
3.00	0.1	0.30
3.50	0.3	1.05
4.00	0.5	2.00
4.50	0.1	0.45
	EV of unit variable costs	3.80

		£
Sales	5,900 units × £6.00	35,400
Less variable costs	5,900 units × £3.80	22,420
Contribution		12,980
Less fixed costs		10,000
Expected profit		2,980

6.11 The expected value is summarised in equation form as follows.

$$E(x) = \Sigma x P(x)$$

This is read as **'the expected value of "x" is equal to the sum of the products of each value of x and the corresponding probability of that value of x occurring'.**

The expected value of a probability

6.12 You might be required to calculate a weighted average probability of an event occurring: an EV of a probability. Consider the following example.

Example: the expected value of a probability

6.13 A salesman has three small areas to cover, areas A, B and C. He never sells more than one item per day, and the probabilities of making a sale when he visits each area are as follows.

Area	Probability
A	30%
B	25%
C	10%

He visits only one area each day. He visits Area A as often as he visits Area B, but he only visits Area C half as often as he visits Area A.

Required

(a) Calculate the probability that on any day he will visit Area C.
(b) Calculate the probability that he will make a sale on any one day.
(c) Calculate the probability that if he does make a sale, it will be in Area A.

Solution

6.14 (a) The probabilities of visiting each area are obtained from the ratios in which he visits them.

Area	Ratio	Probability
A	2	0.4
B	2	0.4
C	$\underline{\dfrac{1}{5}}$	$\underline{\dfrac{0.2}{1.0}}$

The probability that he will visit Area C is 0.2.

(b) The probability of making a sale on any one day is found as follows.

Area	Probability of a sale	Probability of visiting area	EV of probability of a sale
	x	p	px
A	0.30	0.4	0.12
B	0.25	0.4	0.10
C	0.10	0.2	$\underline{\dfrac{0.02}{0.24}}$

The probability of making a sale is 0.24 or 24%.

(c) The probability of making a sale is 0.24 and the probability that the sale will be in Area A rather than B or C can be established as follows.

$$\frac{\text{EV of probability of sale in A}}{\text{EV of probability of sale in A, B or C}} = \frac{0.12}{0.24} = 0.5.$$

One half of all sales will be made in Area A.

7 PRIOR AND POSTERIOR PROBABILITIES

7.1 Consider a situation in which we are considering the sex and hair colour of people in a given group or population consisting of 70% men and 30% women. We have established the probabilities of hair colourings as follows.

	Men	*Women*
Brown	0.60	0.35
Blonde	0.35	0.55
Red	0.05	0.10

These probabilities of sex and hair colouring might be referred to as **prior probabilities**, to distinguish them from posterior probabilities.

Posterior probabilities consider the situation in reverse or retrospect, so that we can ask the question: 'Given that a person taken at random from the population is brown haired what is the probability that the person is male (or female)?'

BPP PUBLISHING

7.2   Posterior probabilities can be established by drawing a probability tree as follows.

The probability of being a man, given that a person is brown haired is

$$\frac{\text{Probability of being a man and brown haired}}{\text{Probability of being a man or woman and brown haired}} = \frac{0.42}{0.42 + 0.105} = \frac{0.42}{0.525} = 0.80$$

Example: posterior probabilities

7.3   As another example of the same type of computation, suppose that two machines produce the same product. The older machine produces 35% of the total output but eight units in every 100 are defective. The newer machine produces 65% of the total output but two units in every 100 are defective.

Determine the probability that a defective unit picked at random was produced by the older machine.

Solution

7.4   We want to establish the posterior probability that given a defective unit, it was produced by the older machine.

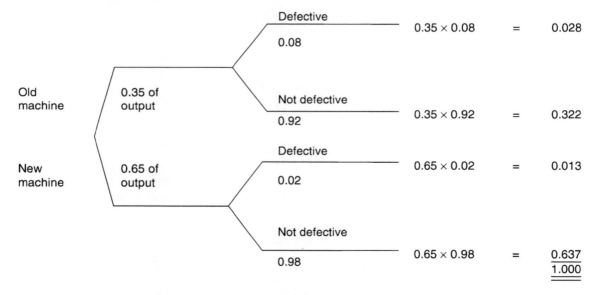

The probability of a defective unit being from the older machine is

$$\frac{0.028}{(0.028 + 0.013)} = 0.683$$

7.5   We could alternatively have used **Bayes' theorem** (see Paragraph 4.40), as follows.

Let X be a unit's being defective.
Let Y be a unit's having come from the older machine.
P(Y) = 0.35
P(X/Y) = 0.08
P(X) = (0.35 × 0.08) + (0.65 × 0.02) = 0.041

Then $P(Y/X) = \dfrac{P(Y)\,P(X/Y)}{P(X)} = \dfrac{0.35 \times 0.08}{0.041} = 0.683$

8   DECISION TREES

8.1   A probability problem such as 'what is the probability of throwing a six with one throw of a die?' is fairly straightforward and can be solved using the basic principles of probability.

More complex probability questions, although solvable using the basic principles, require a clear logical approach to ensure that all possible choices and outcomes of a decision are taken into consideration. Decision trees are a useful means of interpreting such probability problems.

8.2   Exactly how does the use of a decision tree permit a clear and logical approach?

- All the possible choices that can be made are shown as branches on the tree.
- All the possible outcomes of each choice are shown as subsidiary branches on the tree.

Constructing a decision tree

8.3   There are two stages in preparing a decision tree.

- Drawing the tree itself to show all the choices and outcomes
- Putting in the numbers (the probabilities, outcome values and EVs)

8.4   Every decision tree starts from a **decision point** with the decision options that are currently being considered.

(a)   It helps to identify the decision point, and any subsequent decision points in the tree, with a symbol. Here, we shall use a square shape.

(b)   There should be a line, or branch, for each option or alternative.

8.5   **It is conventional to draw decision trees from left to right**, and so a decision tree will start as follows.

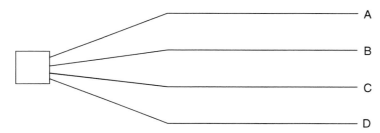

The square is the decision point, and A, B, C and D represent four alternatives from which a choice must be made (such as buy a new machine with cash, hire a machine, continue to use existing machine, raise a loan to buy a machine).

8.6   If the outcome from any choice is certain, the branch of the decision tree for that alternative is complete.

8.7   If, on the other hand, the outcome of a particular choice is uncertain, the various possible outcomes must be shown. We show this on a decision tree by inserting an outcome point on the branch of the tree. Each possible outcome is then shown as a subsidiary branch, coming out from the **outcome point**. The probability of each outcome occurring should be written on to the branch of the tree which represents that outcome.

8.8   To distinguish decision points from **outcome points**, a circle will be used as the symbol for an outcome point.

In the example above, there are two choices facing the decision-maker, A and B. The outcome if A is chosen is known with certainty, but if B is chosen, there are two possible outcomes, high sales (0.6 probability) or low sales (0.4 probability).

8.9   When several outcomes are possible, it is usually simpler to show two or more stages of outcome points on the decision tree.

8.10   Let us work through the following example. It will keep to clarify the rules about drawing decisions trees.

Example: several possible outcomes

8.11   A company can choose to launch a new product XYZ or not. If the product is launched, expected sales and expected unit costs might be as follows.

Sales		*Unit costs*	
Units	Probability	£	Probability
10,000	0.8	6	0.7
15,000	0.2	8	0.3

(a)   The decision tree could be drawn as follows.

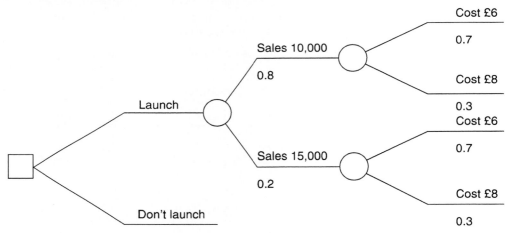

(b) The layout shown above will usually be easier to use than the alternative way of drawing the tree, which is as follows.

(c)

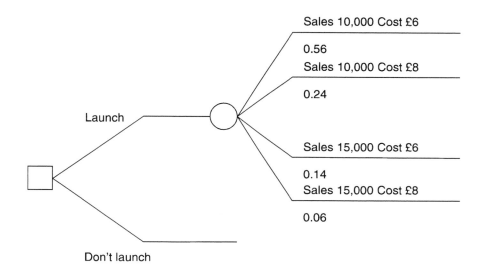

8.12 Sometimes, a decision taken now will lead to other decisions to be taken in the future. When this situation arises, the decision tree can be drawn as a two-stage tree, as follows.

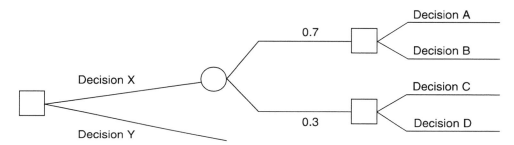

In this tree, either a choice between A and B or else a choice between C and D will be made, depending on the outcome which occurs after choosing X.

8.13 **The decision tree should be in chronological order from left to right. When there are two-stage decision trees, the first decision in time should be drawn on the left.**

Example: a decision tree

8.14 Beethoven Ltd has a new wonder product, the vylin, of which it expects great things. At the moment the company has two courses of action open to it, to test market the product or abandon it.

If the company test markets it, the cost will be £100,000 and the market response could be positive or negative with probabilities of 0.60 and 0.40.

If the response is positive the company could either abandon the product or market it full scale.

If it markets the vylin full scale, the outcome might be low, medium or high demand, and the respective net gains/(losses) would be (200), 200 or 1,000 in units of £1,000 (the result could range from a net loss of £200,000 to a gain of £1,000,000). These outcomes have probabilities of 0.20, 0.50 and 0.30 respectively.

If the result of the test marketing is negative and the company goes ahead and markets the product, estimated losses would be £600,000.

If, at any point, the company abandons the product, there would be a net gain of £50,000 from the sale of scrap. All the financial values have been discounted to the present.

(a) Draw a decision tree.

(b) Include figures for cost, loss or profit on the appropriate branches of the tree.

Solution

8.15 The starting point for the tree is to establish what decision has to be made now. What are the options?

(a) To test market
(b) To abandon

The outcome of the 'abandon' option is known with certainty. There are two possible outcomes of the option to test market, positive response and negative response.

Depending on the outcome of the test marketing, another decision will then be made, to abandon the product or to go ahead.

8.16 This is the decision tree.

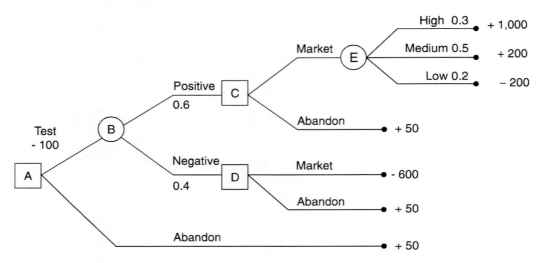

Evaluating the decision with a decision tree

8.17 The EV of each decision option can be evaluated, using the decision tree to help with keeping the logic properly sorted out.

The basic rules are as follows.

8.18 We start on the **right hand side** of the tree and **work back towards the left hand side** and the current decision under consideration. This is sometimes known as **the 'rollback' technique.**

8.19 Working from right to left, we calculate the **EV** of revenue, cost, contribution or profit at each outcome point on the tree.

8.20 In the above example, the right-hand-most outcome point is point E, and the EV is as follows.

	Profit	*Probability*	
	x	*p*	*px*
	£'000		£'000
High	1,000	0.3	300
Medium	200	0.5	100
Low	(200)	0.2	(40)
		EV	360

This is the EV of the decision to market the product if the test shows positive response. It may help you to write the EV on the decision tree itself, at the appropriate outcome point (point E).

8.21 (a) At decision point C, the choice is as follows.

   (i)   Market, EV = + 360 (the EV at point E)
   (ii)   Abandon, value = + 50

   The choice would be to market the product, and so the EV at decision point C is +360.

   (b) At decision point D, the choice is as follows.

   (i)   Market, value = - 600
   (ii)   Abandon, value = +50

   The choice would be to abandon, and so the EV at decision point D is +50.

The second stage decisions have therefore been made. If the original decision is to test market, the company will market the product if the test shows positive customer response, and will abandon the product if the test results are negative.

8.22 The evaluation of the decision tree is completed as follows.

   (a) Calculate the EV at outcome point B.

   $$0.6 \times 360 \quad \text{(EV at C)}$$
   $$+ \quad 0.4 \times 50 \quad \text{(EV at D)}$$
   $$= \quad 216 + 20 = 236.$$

   (b) Compare the options at point A, which are as follows.

   (i)   Test: EV = EV at B minus test marketing cost = 236 - 100 = 136
   (ii)   Abandon: Value = 50

The choice would be to test market the product, because it has a higher EV of profit.

Exercise 8

Interpret the following diagram in words and figures.

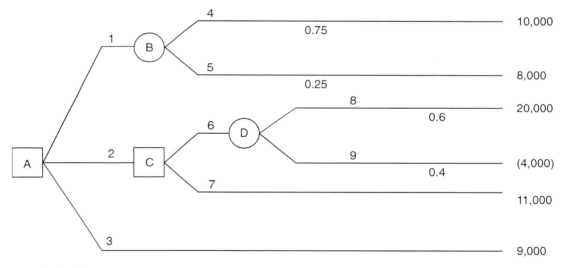

Solution

The square is a point at which a decision has to be made - here a choice between options 1, 2 and 3. A circle represents an event whose outcome is uncertain. Doubtful outcomes (4, 5, 8, 9) have probabilities assigned to them. To reach the decisions the various outcomes must be evaluated using expected values.

Point B: (0.75 × 10,000) + (0.25 × 8,000) = 9,500

Point D: (0.6 × 20,000) + (0.4 × (4,000)) = 10,400

Point C: Choice between 10,400 and 11,000

Point A: Choice between B (9,500), C (10,400 or 11,000) and choice 3 (9,000).

If we are trying to maximise the figure, option 2 and then option 7 are chosen to give 11,000.

If we are trying to minimise it, choice 3 is the one to go for.

Lose 20 marks if you only gave a single answer without stating a maximisation or minimisation assumption. Have 20 bonus marks if you recognised that different answers were possible.

8.23 **Evaluating decisions by using decision trees have a number of limitations.**

(a) The time value of money may not be taken into account.

(b) Decision trees are not very suitable for use in complex situations.

(c) The outcome with the highest EV may have the greatest risks attached to it. In practice therefore, managers may be reluctant to take risks which may result in the company making losses.

(d) The probabilities associated with different branches of the 'tree' are likely to be estimates, and possibly unreliable or inaccurate.

Chapter roundup

- In this chapter we introduced the concept of **uncertainty** in the business environment and explained that a knowledge of **probability** is vital if uncertainty is to be analysed.

- We introduced a number of terms and rules, which we have summarised below, and which you must be able to explain and use as appropriate.

- A **combination** is a set of items, selected from a larger collection of items, regardless of the order in which they are selected.

- A **permutation** is a set of items, selected from a larger group of items, in which the order of selection or arrangement is significant.

- **Mutually exclusive outcomes** are outcomes where the occurrence of one of the outcomes excludes the possibility of any of the others happening.

- **Independent events** are events where the occurrence of one event in no way affects the outcome of the other events.

- **Dependent** or **conditional events** are events where the occurrence of one event depends on the occurrence of the others.

- The **addition laws** for two events, X and Y, are as follows.

  $P(X \text{ or } Y)$ = $P(X) + P(Y)$ when X and Y are mutually exclusive outcomes.

  $P(X \text{ or } Y)$ = $P(X) + P(Y) - P(X \text{ and } Y)$ when X and Y are independent events.

  The **multiplication laws** for two events, X and Y, are as follows.

  $P(X \text{ and } Y)$ = 0 when X and Y are mutually exclusive outcomes.

  $P(X \text{ and } Y)$ = $P(X)\, P(Y)$ when X and Y are independent events.

  $P(X \text{ and } Y)$ = $P(X)\, P(Y/X)$

  = $P(Y)\, P(X/Y)$ when X and Y are dependent/conditional events.

- **Bayes' theorem** is used to calculate the conditional probability of an outcome.

- An **expected value (EV)** is a weighted average, based on probabilities.

- Ensure that you can differentiate between **prior** and **posterior probabilities**.

- **Decision trees** are a useful means of interpreting complex probability questions by showing all possible choices that can be made as branches on a tree, and by showing all possible outcomes of each choice as subsidiary branches on the tree.

- This chapter has introduced some important topics that underpin later chapters. Make sure you are happy with all the concepts before moving on.

Test your knowledge

1   What is the difference between a combination of items and a permutation of items? (see paras 3.3, 3.9)

2   State the formula for the number of combinations of x items from a set of n items. (3.10)

3   Define mutually exclusive outcomes, independent events and dependent events. (4.18, 4.27, 4.39)

4   What is the formula for the conditional probability of Y given X? (4.40)

5   How would you calculate the expected value of a probability distribution? (6.11)

6   What are the two stages in preparing a decision tree? (8.3)

Now try illustrative questions 21 to 23 at the end of the Study Text

BPP PUBLISHING

Chapter 10

PROBABILITY DISTRIBUTIONS

This chapter covers the following topics.

1   Probability distributions

2   The binomial distribution

3   The Poisson distribution

4   The normal distribution

Introduction

In Chapter 9 we looked at the calculation and interpretation of probability and uncertainty. This chapter begins by examining **probability distributions** in general. The importance of probability distributions is that they extend the areas to which probability can be applied and they provide a method of arriving at the probability of an event without having to go through all of the probability rules examined in the previous chapter. We will then turn our attention to three probability distributions and the ways in which they can be used in practice.

The **normal distribution**, one of the probability distributions examined in this chapter, is the basis for the topics looked at in Chapter 11.

1   PROBABILITY DISTRIBUTIONS

1.1   **A frequency distribution gives an analysis of the number of times each particular value occurs in a set of items. A probability distribution simply replaces actual numbers (frequencies) with proportions of the total.** For example, in a statistics test, the marks out of ten awarded to 50 students might be as follows.

Marks out of 10	Number of students (frequency distribution)	Proportion or probability (probability distribution)
0	0	0.00
1	0	0.00
2	1	0.02
3	2	0.04
4	4	0.08
5	10	0.20
6	15	0.30
7	10	0.20
8	6	0.12
9	2	0.04
10	0	0.00
	50	1.00

1.2   A graph of the probability distribution would be the same as the graph of the frequency distribution, but with the vertical axis marked in proportions rather than in numbers. In our example, this would be as follows.

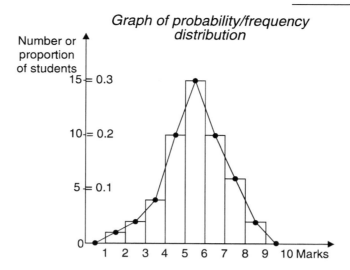

Graph of probability/frequency distribution

1.3 The area under the curve in the frequency distribution represents the total number of students whose marks have been recorded, 50 people. The **area under the curve in a probability distribution is 100%, or 1** (the total of all the probabilities).

1.4 In this chapter, we shall look at three types of distribution commonly found in business applications.

- The binomial distribution
- The Poisson distribution
- The normal distribution

1.5 The **binomial** and **Poisson** distributions describe the behaviour of **attributes** (success or failure, good or bad, black or white and so on) while the normal distribution describes the behaviour of variables. The **binomial** and **Poisson** are **discrete distributions** whereas the **normal distribution** is **continuous**.

2 THE BINOMIAL DISTRIBUTION

12/94, 6/95, 6/96, 12/96, 12/98, 12/99, 6/00

2.1 The **binomial distribution** can be derived from a situation which involves the **repetition of an event** which has **only two possible outcomes** such as success or failure, win or lose, late or not late and so on. Each repetition (or **trial**) must be **independent**. For example, whether a coin comes down heads or tails on a second toss is entirely independent of whether it was heads or tails on a first toss.

2.2 In n independent trials of an event (tossing a coin, rolling a die), each of which has the same probability of success, p, and the same probability of failure, q = 1 − p, a binomial distribution will indicate the probability that one of the results (either p or q depending on the situation in question) will occur a certain number of times within the total of n.

Example: a binomial distribution

2.3 Suppose, for example, that a coin is tossed twice. The probability of the coin coming down as heads is 0.5 on each throw, and the probability of tails is also 0.5. In two throws, the possible results will be as follows.

	First toss		*Second toss*		*Probability*
P	(Heads	and	Heads)	0.5×0.5	0.25
P	(Heads	and	Tails)	0.5×0.5	0.25
P	(Tails	and	Heads)	0.5×0.5	0.25
P	(Tails	and	Tails)	0.5×0.5	0.25
					$\overline{1.00}$

The probabilities are a binomial distribution for the toss of a coin twice.

Example: another binomial distribution

2.4 If a coin is tossed three times, the possible outcomes are as follows.

	First toss	Second toss	Third toss	Probability
3 'heads'	H	H	H	*0.125
2 'heads'	H	T	H	
	H	H	T	**0.375
	T	H	H	
1 'heads'	H	T	T	
	T	H	T	**0.375
	T	T	H	
0 'heads'	T	T	T	*0.125
				1.000

* $(0.5 \times 0.5 \times 0.5)$
** $3 \times (0.5 \times 0.5 \times 0.5)$

The right hand column gives the binomial distribution for three tosses of the coin.

2.5 If an experiment is performed n times then the probability of x successes is given by

$$P(x) = \frac{n!}{x!(n-x)!} \, p^x \, q^{n-x}$$

where   p = the probability of success in a single trial
         q = the probability of failure in a single trial
         q = 1 – p

The first part of the expression, $\dfrac{n!}{x!(n-x)!}$ is the formula for the number of combinations $_nC_x$.

The formula could therefore be re-written as $P(x) = {}_nC_x \, p^x \, (1-p)^{n-x}$

Example: tossing a coin

2.6 A coin is tossed five times. What are the various results which might occur (that is, x heads and (5 – x) tails) and what is the probability of each result?

Solution

2.7 Let P(x) = the probability that x heads occurs.

The probability of heads is 0.5 (= p) and the probability of tails is 0.5 (= q = 1 – p).

No of heads	No of tails			Probability
5	0	$P(0) = \dfrac{5!}{0!5!}(0.5)^5(0.5)^0$	=	0.03125
4	1	$P(1) = \dfrac{5!}{1!4!}(0.5)^4(0.5)^1$	=	0.15625
3	2	$P(2) = \dfrac{5!}{2!3!}(0.5)^3(0.5)^2$	=	0.31250
2	3	$P(3) = \dfrac{5!}{3!2!}(0.5)^2(0.5)^3$	=	0.31250
1	4	$P(4) = \dfrac{5!}{4!1!}(0.5)^1(0.5)^4$	=	0.15625
0	5	$P(5) = \dfrac{5!}{5!0!}(0.5)^0(0.5)^5$	=	0.03125
				$\overline{1.00000}$

Example: probabilities other than 0.5

2.8 A company is planning to sell a new product in four areas, North, South, East and West. The probability that the product will be successful in an area is 0.3. Success in one area will be independent of success or failure in the other areas.

Required

Calculate the probability of success in no area, one area, two areas, three areas or four areas.

Solution

2.9 The probabilities are p = 0.3 and q = 0.7. The number of areas, four, gives us our value for n.

Number of successes				Probability
P(0)	=	$\dfrac{4!}{0!4!}(0.3)^0(0.7)^4$	=	0.2401
P(1)	=	$\dfrac{4!}{1!3!}(0.3)^1(0.7)^3$	=	0.4116
P(2)	=	$\dfrac{4!}{2!2!}(0.3)^2(0.7)^2$	=	0.2646
P(3)	=	$\dfrac{4!}{3!1!}(0.3)^3(0.7)^1$	=	0.0756
P(4)	=	$\dfrac{4!}{4!0!}(0.3)^4(0.7)^0$	=	0.0081
				$\overline{1.0000}$

Exercise 1

The demand for an item of raw material is usually less than ten units per month, but there is a 10% probability that demand in one month will be ten units or more.

Calculate the following probabilities for a six-month period.

(a) Demand will equal or exceed ten units in two of the six months.
(b) Demand will equal or exceed ten units in three of the six months.
(c) Demand will equal or exceed ten units in at least two months.

Solution

(a) Let the probability of demand equalling or exceeding ten units be p, and the probability of demand being less than ten units be q.

$$p = 0.1, q = 0.9$$

$$P(2) = \frac{6!}{2!4!} (0.1)^2 (0.9)^4 = 0.0984$$

(b) $$P(3) = \frac{6!}{3!3!} (0.1)^3 (0.9)^3 = 0.01458$$

(c) $$P(\geq 2) = 1 - [P(0) + P(1)]$$

$$P(0) = \frac{6!}{0!6!} (0.1)^0 (0.9)^6 = 0.5314$$

$$P(1) = \frac{6!}{1!5!} (0.1)^1 (0.9)^5 = 0.3543$$

$$P(\geq 2) = 1 - 0.5314 - 0.3543 = 0.1143$$

The mean and the standard deviation of a binomial distribution

2.10 **The arithmetic mean of a binomial distribution is np.** (This is the same as the expected value, or EV).

The **standard deviation of a binomial distribution** $= \sqrt{npq} = \sqrt{np(1-p)}$

The **variance of a binomial distribution** is therefore $npq = np(1-p)$

Although the mean and standard deviation can be calculated using normal techniques, these formulae are considerably more convenient. The next paragraph shows that the two methods produce the same result.

2.11 Consider the example of three tosses of a coin (see Paragraph 2.4). If x is the number of 'heads' and f is the probability of the result occurring, the mean and the standard deviation could be calculated as follows.

No of heads	Probability		
x	*f*	*fx*	*fx*^{2}
0	0.125	0.000	0.000
1	0.375	0.375	0.375
2	0.375	0.750	1.500
3	0.125	0.375	1.125
	1.000	1.500	3.000

$$\bar{x} = \frac{\Sigma fx}{\Sigma f} = \frac{1.5}{1} = 1.5.$$ This is also the **expected value** of the number of heads.

$$s = \sqrt{[3.000/1 - 1.5^2]} = \sqrt{0.75} = 0.866$$

The mean is 1.5 heads in the three tosses of a coin, with a standard deviation of 0.866 heads.

2.12 The same results could have been obtained more quickly using the formulae.

Mean $= np = 3 \times 0.5 = 1.5$

Standard deviation $= \sqrt{npq} = \sqrt{3 \times 0.5 \times 0.5} = \sqrt{0.75} = 0.866.$

The binomial distribution and quality inspection schemes

2.13 Binomial distributions are quite commonly found, since they usefully describe any situation in which we are considering the likelihood of something either happening or else not happening. **Binomial distributions** are therefore often applied to **quality control sampling** for defectives and the next example is of this nature.

Example: quality inspection scheme

2.14 The quality control department of Woof Ltd checks 12 squeaky bones from each batch of 500 produced. The batch of bones is rejected if more than three defective bones are found. In fact, ten percent of all bones are defective.

Required

Calculate the probability that a batch of bones will be rejected.

Solution

2.15 A batch will be rejected if 4, 5, 6, 7, 8, 9, 10, 11 or 12 bones in the sample are defective.

One method of calculating the rejection probability is to find the probability of those numbers of defective bones and add the probabilities together.

A quicker method is to find the probabilities of 0, 1, 2 or 3 defectives, add them together and deduct the total probability from 1.

We are dealing with a binomial distribution with n = 12 and p = 0.10

$$P(3 \text{ defectives}) = \frac{12!}{3!9!}(0.1)^3(0.9)^9 = 0.085$$

$$P(2 \text{ defectives}) = \frac{12!}{2!10!}(0.1)^2(0.9)^{10} = 0.230$$

$$P(1 \text{ defective}) = \frac{12!}{1!11!}(0.1)^1(0.9)^{11} = 0.377$$

$$P(0 \text{ defectives}) = \frac{12!}{0!12!}(0.1)^0(0.9)^{12} = 0.282$$

$$\overline{\underline{0.974}}$$

Hence P(3 or less defectives) = P(0) + P(1) + P(2) + P(3) = 0.974

So P(batch rejected) = P(more than 3 defectives) = 1 – 0.974 = 0.026

Just 2.6% of the batches of squeaky bones can expect to be rejected by this sampling scheme.

Exercise 2

A product is tested in batches of 15 as it comes off a production line. It is estimated that 10% of the product is defective. Determine the probability that in a batch:

(a)   none are defective;
(b)   one is defective;
(c)   more than two are defective.

Solution

n = 15 p = 0.1

(a) $P(0) = \dfrac{15!}{0!15!} \, 0.1^0 \, 0.9^{15} = 0.21$

(b) $P(1) = \dfrac{15!}{1!14!} \, 0.1^1 \, 0.9^{14} = 0.34$

(c)   P(> 2) = 1 – P(0,1,2)

$$P(2) = \frac{15!}{2!13!} \; 0.1^2 \, 0.9^{13} = 0.27$$

∴ P(>2) = 1 – (0.21 + 0.34 + 0.27) = 0.18

---

3   THE POISSON DISTRIBUTION   *12/94, 6/96, 6/97, 6/98*

3.1   The Poisson distribution is used in the following situations.

(a)   **Where events occur randomly** (that is, they are independent of each other) within an interval, for example defects in a length of rope, or cars arriving at a junction in an hour

(b)   **As an approximation to the binomial distribution**, when n is large (say fifty or more) and p is small (say 0.1 or less). These conditions are, however, only a guide

3.2   Like the binomial distribution the **Poisson distribution** is **discrete:** when we estimate the probability P(x), the probability of an event happening no times at all, once, twice, or whatever, x must be a whole number.

3.3   There is a formula which can be used to calculate P(x).

$$P(x) = \frac{m^x}{x!} \; e^{-m}$$

where   P(x)   is the probability of an event occurring x times

m   is the expected, or average number of times an event occurs per unit of time (or space)

e   is a special constant whose value is approximately 2.71828. A table of e^{-x} is given in your examination and provided in the Appendix at the end of this Study Text.

x   = 0, 1, 2, 3, ...

The mean of a Poisson distribution is obviously m and the standard deviation is √m.

3.4   When a Poisson distribution is used to approximate a binomial distribution, m equals np, which is the mean of a binomial distribution.

Applications of the Poisson distribution

3.5   The examples and exercise that follow illustrate applications of the Poisson distribution. Remember, however, that the Poisson distribution only applies when **events occur randomly**.

Example: the occurrence of random events

3.6   The mean number of calls received on a telephone per hour is 1.6.

Required

Calculate the following probabilities.

(a)   Exactly two calls will be received in an hour
(b)   More than two calls will be received in an hour
(c)   Exactly five calls will be received in a three-hour period

Solution

3.7 (a) $P(2) = \dfrac{1.6^2}{2!}e^{-1.6} = 0.2584$

(b) $\begin{aligned}P(>2) &= 1 - (P(0) + P(1) + P(2))\\ &= 1 - (0.2019 + 0.3230 + 0.2584)\\ &= 1 - 0.7833\\ &= 0.2167\end{aligned}$

(c) P(5 in 3 hours)

If the mean per hour is 1.6, the mean per three hours is $3 \times 1.6 = 4.8$.

$$\dfrac{4.8^5}{5!}e^{-4.8} = \dfrac{2,548.0397}{120} \times \dfrac{1}{121.5104}$$

$$= 0.1747$$

Example: the Poisson distribution as an approximation to the binomial distribution

3.8 Transistors are packed in boxes of 1,000. On average 0.1% will be defective.

Required

Calculate the proportion of boxes which will contain the following number of defectives.

(a) 0 defectives
(b) 1 defective
(c) 2 defectives
(d) 3 or more defectives

Solution

3.9 The binomial distribution applies, with $n = 1,000$ and $np = 1,000 \times 0.001 = 1$.

Since n is large and p is small, the Poisson distribution will be used as an approximation to the binomial distribution. Any error will be small, and a lot of computational work will be saved.

(a) $P(0) = \dfrac{m^0}{0!}e^{-m} = \dfrac{1^0}{0!}e^{-1} = e^{-1} = 0.3679$

(b) $P(1) = \dfrac{1^1}{1!}e^{-1} \qquad = e^{-1} = 0.3679$

(c) $P(2) = \dfrac{1^2}{2!}e^{-1} \quad = \dfrac{1}{2}(0.36788) = 0.1839$

(d) $\begin{aligned}P(3 \text{ or more}) &= 1 - P(0) - P(1) - P(2)\\ &= 1 - 0.3679 - 0.3679 - 0.1839\\ &= 0.0803\end{aligned}$

Exercise 3

The mean number of invoices received by a company on any one day is 2.6. What is the probability that seven invoices will be received over a two-day period?

Solution

Mean per two days $= 2.6 \times 2 = 5.2$

P(7 over 2 days) $= \dfrac{5.2^7}{7!}e^{-5.2} = 0.1125$

Acceptance sampling and the Poisson distribution

3.10 **Acceptance sampling** is a **statistical method** of deciding whether or not to accept a batch of items received from an outside supplier. It is most appropriate to low cost components bought and used in large quantities, such as transistors, because n will be very large and the probability of defectives should be very small.

Example: acceptance sampling

3.11 Hitech Electronics buy transistors in huge quantities from Jap Components. From past experience they know that in an average batch of 100,000 transistors approximately 0.1% are defective. They wish to design a quality control procedure so that a batch with a higher percentage of defectives will be rejected and returned to Jap Components.

Suppose that a reasonable sample to test is 1,000 or 1%. The mean number of defectives in a sample of this size is $m = 1,000 \times 0.001 = 1$.

For $m = 1$, we have the following.

	Probabilities	*Cumulative probabilities*
P(0)	0.3679	0.3679
P(1)	0.3679	0.7358
P(2)	0.1839	0.9197
P(3)	0.0613	0.9810

3.12 From the cumulative probabilities it can be seen that the probability of finding three or fewer defectives is 0.9810 or 98.1%. Consequently the probability of finding four or more defectives is 1.9%. Hitech might well decide to adopt the rule, 'test 1,000 transistors and reject the delivery if four or more defectives are found'. This would, of course, mean rejecting 1.9% of deliveries which are satisfactory.

3.13 Now let us consider what would happen if a sub-standard batch with, say, 0.8% defectives was received. In this case $m = 1,000 \times 0.008 = 8$.

For $m = 8$, $e^{-m} = 0.0003354$ and we have the following probabilities.

	Probabilities	*Cumulative probabilities*
P(0)	0.0003	0.0003
P(1)	0.0027	0.0030
P(2)	0.0107	0.0137
P(3)	0.0286	0.0423

3.14 From the above figures it can be seen that there is only a 0.04 or 4% chance that a batch with 0.8% defectives will give three or fewer defectives in a sample of 1,000. In other words, only 4% of batches with this level of defectives will be accepted when they should have been returned to Jap Components.

Exercise 4

Sunnyday Travel Tours organise holiday excursions. One of their regular excursions is to Malta, but the number of places on each Malta excursion is restricted to 100 tourist class passengers and 50 luxury class passengers.

Because of cancellations after bookings are made, the tour company accepts up to 104 tourist class holiday bookings for the 100 places, but will not overbook luxury class places. If there are any vacancies in luxury class places, the spare berths can be filled with tourist class customers, if more than 100 places are booked and are not subsequently cancelled.

Over the past few years, the mean number of vacant luxury class places has been 2. The numbers of tourist class customers per excursion who did not subsequently cancel their bookings have followed the following distribution.

Numbers booked and not subsequently cancelled	Probability
100 or more	0.25
101 or more	0.15
102 or more	0.09
103 or more	0.06
104	0.01

Required

(a) Using the Poisson distribution, and ignoring the effect of excess tourist class passengers taking luxury class places, calculate the probability that on any excursion there will be the following number of vacant luxury class places.

(i) No vacant luxury class places
(ii) At least two vacant luxury class places

(b) Assuming a Poisson distribution for the number of vacant luxury class places, calculate the probability that all the tourist class customers who book and do not subsequently cancel can be fitted into a berth on the tour, using available vacant luxury class places.

Solution

(a) We have m = 2.

$$P(0) = \frac{2^0}{0!}e^{-2} = e^{-2} = \frac{1}{2.71828^2} = 0.1353$$

$$P(1) = \frac{2^1}{1!}e^{-2} = 2e^{-2} = 0.2707$$

$$\underline{0.4060}$$

P(2 or more) = balancing figure $\quad$ 0.5940

$$\underline{\underline{1.0000}}$$

(i) The probability of no vacant luxury class places is 0.1353.

(ii) The probability of at least two vacant places is 0.5940.

(b) We want to know the probability that the tour company will not end up with more customers than places because of overbooking. There will be too many customers when the following combinations occur.

Luxury class places		Tourist class places
50	+	101 or more
49	+	102 or more
48	+	103 or more
47	+	104

Luxury class places

Probability of 50 places and 0 vacancies = P(0) = 0.1353

49 places = P(1) = 0.2707

48 places = $P(2) = \dfrac{2^2}{2!}e^{-2} = 0.2707$

47 places = $P(3) = \dfrac{2^3}{3!}e^{-2} = 0.1804$

The probability distribution of tourist class numbers is given in the problem.

The probability of having too many customers is

$(0.1353 \times 0.15) + (0.2707 \times 0.09) + (0.2707 \times 0.06) + (0.1804 \times 0.01) = 0.0627$

The probability of being able to offer every customer a place is 1 − 0.0627 = 0.9373.

---

4 THE NORMAL DISTRIBUTION
12/94, 12/95, 6/96, 12/96, 6/98, 6/99, 6/00

4.1 The **normal distribution** is an **important probability distribution** of **continuous variables** that occurs frequently in practice. In other words, in calculating P(x), x can be any value, and does not have to be a whole number.

4.2 Examples of continuous variables include the following.

(a) The heights of people. The height of a person need not be an exact number of centimetres, but can be anything within a range of possible figures.

(b) The temperature of a room. It need not be an exact number or degrees, but can fall anywhere within a range of possible values.

4.3 **The normal distribution can also apply to discrete variables which can take many possible values.** For example, the volume of sales, in units, of a product might be any whole number in the range 100 – 5,000 units. There are so many possibilities within this range that the variable is for all practical purposes continuous.

4.4 The normal distribution can be drawn as a graph, and it would be a **bell-shaped curve**.

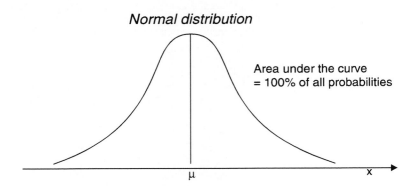

Normal distribution

Area under the curve
= 100% of all probabilities

4.5 **The normal curve is symmetrical.** The left hand side of the area under the curve to the left of μ is the mirror image of the right hand side.

μ is the mean, or average of the distribution.

Because it is a probability distribution, **the area under the curve totals exactly 1**.

4.6 The normal distribution is important because in the practical application of statistics, it has been found that many probability distributions are close enough to a normal distribution to be treated as one without any significant loss of accuracy.

The standard deviation and the normal distribution

4.7 For any normal distribution, the dispersion around the mean of the frequency of occurrences can be measured exactly in terms of the standard deviation.

4.8 **The entire frequency curve represents all the possible outcomes** and their frequencies of occurrence and the normal curve **is symmetrical**; therefore 50% of outcomes have a value greater than the mean value, and 50% of outcomes have a value less than the mean value.

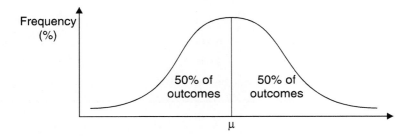

Frequency (%)

50% of outcomes

50% of outcomes

μ

4.9 **About 68% of frequencies have a value within one standard deviation either side of the mean.**

Thus if a normal distribution has a mean of 80 and a standard deviation of 3, 68% of the total outcomes would occur within the range ± one standard deviation from the mean, that is, within the range 77 – 83.

Since the curve is symmetrical, 34% of the values must fall in the range 77 – 80 and 34% in the range 80 – 83.

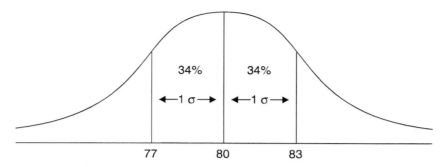

4.10 **95% of the frequencies in a normal distribution occur in the range ± 1.96 standard deviations from the mean.**

In our example, when $\mu = 80$, and $\sigma = 3$, 95% of the frequencies in the distribution would occur in the range

$$80 \pm 1.96\,(3)$$
$$= \quad 80 \pm 5.88 \text{ (the range 74.12 to 85.88)}$$

47½% of outcomes would be in the range 74.12 to 80 and 47½% would be in the range 80 to 85.88.

4.11 **99% of the frequencies occur in the range ± 2.58 standard deviations from the mean.**

In our example, 99% of frequencies in a normal distribution with $\mu = 80$ and $\sigma = 3$ would lie in the range

$$80 \pm 2.58\,(3)$$
$$= \quad 80 \pm 7.74$$
$$= \quad 72.26 \text{ to } 87.74.$$

Exercise 5

A normal distribution for daily output (in units) of workers in a factory has a mean of 50 and a standard deviation of 10. Within what range from 50 upwards would $47^{1}/2$ % of the frequencies fall?

Solution

Between 50 and 50 + (1.96 × 10) = 69.6. Thus $47^{1}/2$ % of workers would have daily outputs of between 50 and 69.6 units.

Normal distribution tables

4.12 Although there is an infinite number of normal distributions, depending on values of the mean μ and the standard deviation σ, **the relative dispersion of frequencies around the mean, measured as proportions of the total population, is exactly the same for all normal distributions**. In other words, whatever the normal distribution, 47½% (for example) of outcomes will always be in the range between the mean and 1.96 standard deviations below the mean.

4.13 **Normal distribution tables,** such as the ones shown at the end of this text show the area under the normal curve which is to the left of a given number of standard deviations. To use these tables, it is necessary to calculate the standardised deviate Z.

193

4.14   The **standardised deviate** Z is calculated as follows.

$$z = \left| \frac{x - \mu}{\sigma} \right|$$

where   z   =   the number of standard deviations above or below the mean
x   =   the value of the variable under consideration
μ   =   the mean
σ   =   the standard deviation

The parallel lines, in the above formula mean that we are only interested in the number of standard deviations calculated and not whether they are positive or negative.

Example: the normal distribution

4.15   A frequency distribution is normal, with a mean of 100 and a standard deviation of 10.

What proportion of the total frequencies will be:

(a)   above 80;
(b)   above 90;
(c)   above 100;
(d)   above 115;
(e)   below 85;
(f)   below 110;
(g)   in the range 80 - 110;
(h)   in the range 90 - 95?

Solution

4.16   (a)   80 is $\left| \frac{80 - 100}{10} \right|$ = 2 standard deviations **below** the mean. From the tables, where

z = 2 standard deviations **above** the mean, the area to the left of z is 0.9772. This is the answer, because the normal distribution is symmetrical so the area to the left of z standard deviations above the mean equals the area to the right of z standard deviations below the mean.

(b)   90 is $\left| \frac{90 - 100}{10} \right|$ = 1 standard deviation **below** the mean. From the tables, when z = 1

standard deviation below the mean, the proportion to the right is 0.8413 (using the same reasoning as in (a)).

(c)   100 is the mean. The proportion above this is 0.5, because the distribution is symmetrical.

(d)   115 is $\left| \frac{115 - 100}{10} \right|$ = 1.5 standard deviations **above** the mean. From the tables, where z

= 1.5 standard deviations above the mean, the proportion to the left is 0.9332. We want the proportion to the right (above 115), which is 1 – 0.9332 = 0.0668.

(e)   85 is $\left| \frac{85 - 100}{10} \right|$ = 1.5 standard deviations **below** the mean. The area to the right of a

point 1.5 standard deviations **above** the mean is 1 – 0.9332 = 0.0668. This is the same as the area to the left of a point 1.5 standard deviations below the mean and hence is the answer we require.

(f)   110 is $\left|\dfrac{110-100}{10}\right|$ = 1 standard deviation **above** the mean. The area to the left of this point = 0.8413.

(g)   The range 80 to 110 may be divided into two parts:

(i)   80 to 100 (the mean);
(ii)   100 to 110.

The proportion between 80 and 100 is that between two standard deviations below the mean and the mean itself. This is the same as the proportion between the mean and z = 2 standard deviations above the mean, which is 0.9772 – 0.5 = 0.4772.

The proportion in the range 100 to 110 is (1 standard deviation) 0.8413 – 0.5 = 0.3413

The proportion in the total range 80 to 110 is 0.4772 + 0.3413 = 0.8185.

(h)   The range 90 to 95 may be analysed as:

(i)   the proportion below 95
(ii)   minus the proportion below 90.

95 is 0.5 standard deviations **below** the mean, so the area to the left of 95 is the same as the area to the right of z = 0.5 standard deviations above the mean, which is 1 – the area to the left of z = 0.5 standard deviations above the mean = 1 – 0.6915 = 0.3085.

Similarly, the area to the left of 90 (one standard deviation below the mean) is 1 – 0.8413 = 0.1587.

Proportion below 95 (0.5 standard deviations)	0.3085
Less proportion below 90 (1 standard deviation)	0.1587
Proportion between 90 and 95	0.1498

Using the normal distribution

4.17   Many distributions of variables such as lengths, weights and times follow, at least approximately, normal distributions and hence you may be faced with any number of different scenarios involving this particular probability distribution. The example and exercise which follow are indicative of normal distribution problems.

Example: using the normal distribution

4.18   Your company requires a special type of inelastic rope which is available from only two suppliers. Supplier A's ropes have a mean breaking strength of 1,000 kg with a standard deviation of 100 kg. Supplier B's ropes have a mean breaking strength of 900 kg with a standard deviation of 75kg. The distribution of the breaking strengths of each type of rope is normal. Your company requires that the breaking strength of a rope must be not less than 750 kg.

Required

Decide which rope you should buy and why.

Solution

4.19   **Supplier A**. 750 kg lies 250 kg below the mean which is 250/100 = 2.5 standard deviations below the mean. From tables, the probability of the breaking strength being at least 750 kg is 0.9938.

Supplier B. 750 kg lies 150 kg below the mean, which is 150/75 = 2 standard deviations below the mean. From tables, the probability of the breaking strength being at least 750 kg is 0.9772.

If the company is most concerned about the breaking strength not being less than 750 kg (rather than with the mean breaking strength of each supplier's rope) it would be better to purchase supplier A's rope.

Exercise 6

The salaries of employees in an industry are normally distributed, with a mean of £14,000 and a standard deviation of £4,000.

(a) What proportion of employees earn less than £12,000?
(b) What proportion of employees earn between £11,000 and £19,000?

Solution

(a) £12,000 is (12,000 − 14,000)/4,000 = 0.50 standard deviations below the mean.

From tables, the proportion of the normal distribution more than 0.50 standard deviations below the mean is 1 − 0.6915 = 0.3085

(b) £11,000 is (11,000 − 14,000)/4,000 = 0.75 standard deviations below the mean.
£19,000 is (19,000 − 14,000)/4,000 = 1.25 standard deviations above the mean.

The proportion with earnings between £11,000 and £14,000 is 0.7734 − 0.5 = 0.2734
The proportion with earnings between £14,000 and £19,000 is 0.8944 − 0.5 = 0.3944
The required proportion is 0.2734 + 0.3944 = 0.6678

The normal distribution and measurement errors

4.20 One particular application of the normal distribution is the assessment of whether errors which have occurred in a process which provides standard measures (weight of jam in jars, volume of juice in bottles, width of individual components) are **acceptable**. The following example will illustrate the general approach to such problems.

Example: measurement errors

4.21 A machine is set to fill bags with 1 kg of flour. A member of the quality control department checks the filled bags for errors. These error recordings are known to have a normal distribution with a mean value of 0g and a standard deviation of 25g. The bags of flour are acceptable as long as the error lies between 62.5g too light and 75g too heavy.

Required

Calculate the chance that a bag of flour chosen at random is unacceptable.

Solution

4.22 The diagram below illustrates the scenario.

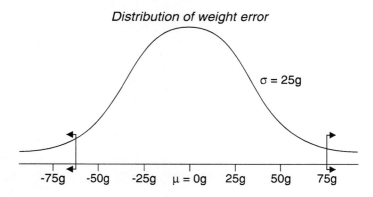

Distribution of weight error

(a) We need to calculate P(error < 62.5g)

−62.5g is 2.5 ((62.5 − 0)/25) standard deviations below the mean.

From the tables, when z = 2.5 standard deviations above the mean, the proportion to the left is 0.9938. We want the proportion to the right (the normal distribution is symmetrical, remember) which is 1 − 0.9938 = 0.0062.

(b) We now need to calculate P(error > 75g)

From the tables, for 3 standard deviations above the mean, the proportion to the left is 0.9987. The proportion we require is therefore 0.0013 (1 – 0.9987).

(c) Since the outcomes 'error < –62.5g' and 'error > 75g' are **mutually exclusive**, we can use the **additional law**:

P(error < –62.5g or > 75g) = P(error < –62.5g) + P(error > 75g) = 0.0062 + 0.0013 = 0.0075

There is therefore a 0.75% chance that a randomly chosen bag of flour will be unacceptable.

The normal distribution and the binomial distribution

4.23 **When n in a binomial distribution gets large, then so long as p is reasonably close to 0.5** (say 0.3 to 0.7) **a binomial distribution approximates closely to a normal distribution.** Since the binominal distribution is discrete and the normal distribution is continuous, we need to consider the **continuity correction**.

The continuity correction

4.24 **When normal distributions are used for discrete variables rather than continuous variables, it is appropriate to use a continuity correction when estimating probabilities.** Quite simply, what this means is that if values can only be whole numbers, 0, 1, 2, 3 and so on, then in the normal distribution, the value 0 should be represented by – 0.5 to + 0.5, 1 should be represented by 0.5 to 1.5, 2 by 1.5 to 2.5 and 3 by 2.5 to 3.5 and so on.

4.25 **When the range of values of the discrete variable we are interested in is large, the continuity correction can be ignored because it will be insignificant.** It ought to be used, however, when the range is small enough to make a difference of 0.5 potentially significant.

4.26 Suppose that we have a normal distribution for the number of players in a football team of 11 who have broken their leg at some time in the past, with a mean of 5.3 and a standard deviation of 1.2. Values are only whole numbers, since we cannot have a fraction of a player. What is the probability that in a particular football team, Mishap United, at least four players will have broken their leg at some time in the past?

4.27 We should apply the continuity correction, as follows.

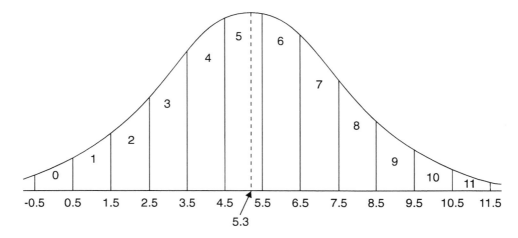

The possible number of players in the team who have suffered a broken leg will range between 0 and 11 and the values 0, 1, 2, 3, 4 and so on, are represented by the ranges shown in the diagram.

The probability of at least four is the probability of exceeding 3.5.

3.5 is $(5.3 - 3.5)/1.2 = 1.5$ standard deviations below the mean.

From the table, when z = 1.5, P = 0.9332, and so the probability of four or more players having broken a leg is 0.9332.

Example: the normal distribution as an approximation

4.28 The probability that a company secretary will make a mistake filling in a Companies House form is 0.3.

Required

Calculate the probability that fewer than 570 forms out of 2,000 will be in error.

Solution

4.29 Using a binomial distribution, we could make calculations as follows.

$$P(0) = \frac{2,000!}{0!\,2,000!}\ (0.7)^{2,000}\ (0.3)^0$$

$$P(1) = \frac{2,000!}{1!\,1,999!}\ (0.7)^{1,999}\ (0.3)^1$$

$$P(2) = ...$$

This would be a laborious process.

4.30 Instead, we can assume that the binomial distribution approximates closely to a normal distribution, with:

(a) a mean of np $= 2,000 \times 0.3 = 600$

(b) a standard deviation of $\sqrt{npq} = \sqrt{2,000 \times 0.3 \times 0.7} = 20.49$.

4.31 We need a cut-off point for 'fewer than 570'. Since we are using the normal distribution (continuous) as an approximation to the binominal distribution (discrete), we need to consider the continuity correction and establish our cut-off point as 569.5. This gives z = $(569.5 - 600)/20.49 = -1.49$, or about 1.5 standard deviations below the mean. We want the area to the left of this, which is the same as the area to the right of z = 1.5 standard deviations above the mean.

Normal distribution tables give us the required probability, $1 - 0.9332 = 0.0668$.

Exercise 7

An analysis of a college's student register shows that 62% of all students are female. A group of 200 of the students is randomly selected. Using a suitable normal distribution as an approximation, determine the probability that the number of male students is more than 86.

Solution

p = (100 − 62)% = 38% = 0.38

Mean = n × p =200 × 0.38 = 76

Standard deviation = $\sqrt{n \times p \times q}$ = √(200 × 0.38 × 0.62)

= 6.86

P(more than 86) = P(more than 86.5)

86.5 is (86.5 − 76)/6.86 = 1.53 standard deviations above the mean.

P(number of males > 86) $\triangleq$ 1 − 0.9332 = 0.0668

Chapter roundup

- We have covered three of the most important probability distributions in this chapter. It is not always easy to recognise when a binomial, a Poisson or a normal distribution applies. The following guidelines might help.

- **The binomial distribution**

  There are **two possible conditions** (good/bad, black/white, male/female, acceptable/not acceptable and so on).

  Outcomes have **discrete values** (0, 1, 2, 3) and **not continuous** values (1.257)

  A probability p is given for the likelihood that an item will have one of the conditions, so that the probability of an item having the other condition is 1 − p. (1 − p) is sometimes referred to as q so that p + q = 1.

  The **arithmetic mean** of a binomial distribution is **np** and the **standard deviation** is √**npq**

- **The Poisson distribution**

  This is similar to a binomial distribution (it is discrete), but is concerned with events occurring at random in an interval, or with rare events (small p). It can be used as **an approximation to the binomial** when n is large and p is small.

- **The normal distribution**

  This is the most commonly applied probability distribution. It applies to variables with a **continuous** range of possible values (**continuous variables**), such as distance and time. It provides a **good approximation for a binomial distribution** with large n and p fairly close to 0.5.

Test your knowledge

1 What is the formula for the binomial distribution? (see para 2.5)

2 What are the formulae for the mean and standard deviation of a binomial distribution? (2.10)

3 When is the Poisson distribution a good approximation to the binomial distribution? (3.1)

4 What is the formula for the Poisson distribution? (3.3)

5 What is the value of e to use in the Poisson formula? (3.3)

6 What is the value of the standard deviation of a Poisson distribution? (3.3)

7 When is the normal distribution a good approximation to the binomial distribution? (4.23)

8 Explain when the continuity correction should be used with the normal distribution. (4.24, 4.25)

Now try illustrative questions 24 and 25 at the end of the Study Text

Chapter 11

STATISTICAL INFERENCE

This chapter covers the following topics.

1. Statistical inference
2. Estimation of the population mean
3. Confidence intervals
4. Estimation of the population proportion
5. The size of a sample
6. Hypothesis testing
7. Two-sample hypothesis testing

Introduction

One of the probability distributions which we looked at in the previous chapter, the normal distribution, provides the basis for this chapter, which examines statistical inference.

Statistical inference is the process by which conclusions are drawn about some measure or attribute of a population based upon analysis of sample data. It can be divided into two types.

Estimation involves estimating **population characteristics** (such as the population mean and standard deviation) from **sample characteristics** (such as the sample mean and the sample standard deviation).

Hypothesis testing is concerned with setting up a theory or hypotheses about some characteristic of the population and then sampling in order to ascertain whether the hypothesis is supported or not.

---

1 STATISTICAL INFERENCE

1.1 During the run up to a general election we are bombarded with the results of countless opinion polls predicting who will be forming the next government, but have you ever wondered about the basis for these predictions? It would be almost physically impossible and financially undesirable to question the entire population of the country so small samples are taken and opinions gleaned from the samples. From these results the pollsters can then infer the opinions of the entire population.

1.2 This process by which conclusions are drawn about some measure or **attribute** of a population based upon **analysis of sample data** is known as **statistical inference**.

1.3 **Samples are taken and analysed in order to draw conclusions about the whole population** not only when public opinion (as described above) is sought, but also if the measurement or testing process may be destructive so that sampling is the only possible method. For example there would be little point in a battery manufacturer testing all batteries to destruction to discover the average life of the batteries.

1.4 **Sampling is quicker and cheaper than testing the entire population** and is often the only feasible method of obtaining information about the population. Look back at Chapter 1 (Sections 6 to 8) if you need reminding about sampling.

Understanding statistical inference

1.5 Three basis factors affect the results of statistical inference.

- The size of the sample
- The variability in the relevant population
- The level of confidence we wish to have in the results

The size of the sample

1.6 **Increases in sample size will generally make results more accurate** (that is, the sample results will be closer to results from testing the population) but note that there is not a linear relationship.

The variability in the relevant population

1.7 If there was no variation in the original population then a sample of one would be sufficient. We do not, however, live in such a homogeneous world, and there is likely to be a wide range of opinions on, for example, government policy. The design of the sample will therefore need to ensure that the full range of opinions is represented. Even items which are supposed to be exactly the same, such as items coming off the end of a production line, are unlikely to be so, due perhaps to machine wear, quality of raw materials, skills of operatives and so on.

The level of confidence

1.8 We can never be 100% certain that the results we glean from a sample are the same as those which would be produced if the population were tested. There will, therefore, always be a risk that we will be wrong. You may wish to be 99% certain that you have the correct answer, or maybe 95%, or 90%. The more certain you wish to be correct, the less exact the answer is going to be.

Statistical inference and decision making

1.9 **Statistical inference is a method of data analysis which can be used as a valuable aid to decision making.** Compare the following examples.

(a) A cosmetics company is considering the launch of a new perfume. They may test a sample of people to assess whether they like the fragrance. If the results are favourable and indicate that the population as a whole would like the fragrance, then the cosmetics company may decide to market the perfume.

(b) A political party may also test the opinion of a sample of voters on a controversial policy in their manifesto. If the sample results indicate that the population as a whole would act adversely if the policy were to be introduced, the party may drop the policy.

(c) A company which produces one litre bottles of orange juice has received complaints from a number of customers that the bottles contain less than one litre. The company may decide to test the volume of orange juice in a sample of bottles in order to decide whether or not the machine which fills the bottles with juice is performing correctly.

1.10 There are, of course, countless other examples of situations in which the results from a sample would aid decision making.

2 ESTIMATION OF THE POPULATION MEAN

2.1 In the previous chapter we looked at distributions occurring as a result of considering a population. We can also construct probability distributions, known as **sampling distributions**, for samples rather than populations and, when we start taking fairly large random samples (over 30) from a population and measuring the mean of those samples, we find an uncanny relationship with the normal distribution.

2.2 Suppose that we wish to estimate the mean of a population, say the average weight of a product made in a factory. A sample of, say, 100 units of the product might be taken, and the mean weight per unit of the sample might be, say, 5.8 kg.

Another sample of 100 units might then be taken and the mean weight might be, say, 6.3 kg.

A large number of samples might be taken and the mean of each sample calculated. These means will not all be the same and they can be plotted as a frequency distribution. This distribution is called a **sampling distribution of the mean**.

2.3 In our example, a frequency distribution of the mean weight per unit in each of 250 samples (of 100 units per sample) might be as follows.

Mean weight per unit kg	Mid-point of class interval	Frequency (No of samples)
5.45 and < 5.55	5.5	3
5.55 and < 5.65	5.6	7
5.65 and < 5.75	5.7	16
5.75 and < 5.85	5.8	30
5.85 and < 5.95	5.9	44
5.95 and < 6.05	6.0	50
6.05 and < 6.15	6.1	44
6.15 and < 6.25	6.2	30
6.25 and < 6.35	6.3	16
6.35 and < 6.45	6.4	7
6.45 and < 6.55	6.5	3
		250 samples

The mean weight per unit of 100 units in a sample might thus range from 5.45 to 6.55 kg. The **true mean of the population**, that is, the true mean weight of all units produced, presumably lies somewhere within this range.

2.4 **A sampling distribution of the mean has the following important properties**.

(a) **It is very close to being normally distributed.** This is true even if the distribution of the population from which the samples are drawn is fairly heavily skewed. The larger the sample the more closely will the sampling distribution approximate to a normal distribution. The statistical rule that a sampling distribution of sample means is normally distributed is known as the **central limit theorem**.

(b) The mean of the sampling distribution is the **same as the population mean, μ.**

(c) The sampling distribution has a standard deviation which is called the **standard error of the mean.**

2.5 In our example, the 250 samples give an estimate of the population mean. This distribution of sample means would be (approximately) **normally distributed**, with a mean of about 6 kg (weight per unit of product).

This mean of 6 kg would be the same as the population mean, μ, so that we would be able to state that the true population mean is about 6 kg.

The standard deviation of the sampling distribution (which could be calculated as 0.2 kg: workings not shown) **is the standard error (se).**

The standard error

2.6 **The size of the standard error depends on the size of the sample**. The larger the sample size chosen, the smaller the standard error will become. This is not surprising, because small samples are more likely to be unrepresentative of the population as a whole.

2.7 **The standard error is also related to the standard deviation of the population**. The larger the dispersion of values in the population, the more likely it will be that the mean of a sample will vary from the true mean of the population.

2.8 Combining the points made in the last two paragraphs, it can be shown that the **standard error of the mean** is

$$se = \sigma/\sqrt{n}$$

where n is the size of each sample and σ is the standard deviation of the population. This formula is provided in the examination.

2.9 The standard error is given by $\sigma/\sqrt{n}$, but σ is the standard deviation of the whole population and is normally not known. To overcome this problem the standard deviation of a sample is taken as the best estimate of the standard deviation of the whole population, so that

se = sample standard deviation/$\sqrt{n}$ = s/$\sqrt{n}$.

This formula is provided in the examination.

3 CONFIDENCE INTERVALS

3.1 From our knowledge of the properties of a normal distribution, together with the rule that sample means are normally distributed around the true population mean, with a standard deviation equal to the standard error, we can predict (using normal distribution tables) the following.

- 68% of all sample means will be within one standard error of the population mean.
- 95% of all sample means will be within 1.96 standard errors of the population mean.
- 99% of all sample means will be within 2.58 standard errors of the population mean.

3.2 Let us look at it another way.

(a) With **68% probability**, the population mean lies within the range: **sample mean ± one standard error.**

(b) With **95% probability**, the population mean lies within the range: **sample mean ± 1.96 standard errors**.

(c) With **99% probability**, the population mean lies within the range: **sample mean ± 2.58 standard errors**.

These degrees of certainty (such as 95%) are known as **confidence levels**, and the ends of the ranges (such as sample mean + 2.58 standard errors) around the sample mean are called **confidence limits**. The ranges (such as sample mean ± one standard error) are called **confidence intervals**.

3.3 **Confidence intervals** can therefore be calculated as

$\bar{x} \pm z\sigma/\sqrt{n}$ or $\bar{x} \pm zse,$

where z is the number of standard errors.

Example: confidence intervals

3.4 From a random sample of 576 of a company's 20,000 employees, it was found that the average number of days each person was absent from work due to illness was eight days a year, with a standard deviation of 3.6 days.

What are the confidence limits for the average number of days absence a year through sickness per employee for the company as a whole at the following confidence levels?

(a) 95%
(b) 99%

Solution

3.5   We must first calculate the standard error, which is estimated as $s/\sqrt{n}$ (because we do not know the standard deviation of the entire population).

$$se = 3.6/\sqrt{576} = 0.15.$$

(a)   At the 95% level of confidence $z = 1.96$ and therefore the true average number of days absence a year is in the range $8 \pm (1.96 \times 0.15)$

$$= \quad 8 \pm 0.294$$
$$= \quad 7.706 \text{ days to } 8.294 \text{ days, say } 7.7 \text{ days to } 8.3 \text{ days.}$$

(b)   At the 99% level of confidence $z = 2.58$ and therefore the true average number of days absence a year is in the range $8 \pm (2.58 \times 0.15)$

$$= \quad 8 \pm 0.387$$
$$7.613 \text{ days to } 8.387 \text{ days, say } 7.6 \text{ days to } 8.4 \text{ days.}$$

3.6   Why is it necessary to calculate confidence limits? If the sample mean was eight days would it not be sufficient to use eight days as a point estimate of the population mean?

3.7   In practice, a **sample mean** might indeed be used as a '**point estimate**' of the population mean. However, we could not be sure how reliable the estimate might be, without first considering the size of the standard error. The sample mean might be above or below the true population mean, but we can say with 95% confidence that the sample mean is no more than 1.96 standard errors above or below the true population mean. We are therefore 95% confident that the average number of days absence a year through sickness per employee is in the range 7.7 days to 8.3 days.

3.8   If the confidence limits cover a wide range of values, a point estimate of the population mean from the sample would not be reliable. On the other hand, if the confidence limits cover a narrow range of values, a point estimate of the population mean, using the sample mean, would be reliable.

Exercise 1

The cost of assembling an item of equipment has been estimated by obtaining a sample of 144 jobs. The average cost of assembly derived from the sample was £4,000 with a standard deviation of £1,500.

Required

Estimate confidence limits for the true average cost of assembly. Use the 95% level of confidence.

Solution

The standard error is estimated as $1,500/\sqrt{144} = £125$.

At the 95% level of confidence, the population mean is in the range $£(4,000 \pm (1.96 \times 125)) = £(4,000 \pm 245)$, that is, £3,755 to £4,245.

---

4   ESTIMATION OF THE POPULATION PROPORTION

4.1   The arithmetic mean is a very important statistic, and sampling is often concerned with estimating the **mean of a population**. Many surveys, however, especially those concerned with attitudes or opinions about an issue or the percentage of times an event occurs (for example, the proportion of faulty items out of the total number of items produced in a manufacturing department) attempt to estimate a **proportion** rather than an arithmetic mean.

Suppose for example, that we wished to know what proportion of an electorate intends to vote for the Jacobin party at the forthcoming general election. Several samples might be obtained, and the proportion of pro-Jacobin voters in a sample might vary, say from 37% to 45%. The central limit theorem would apply, and the proportion of pro-Jacobin voters in each sample could be arranged into a sampling distribution (the **sampling distribution** of a proportion) with the following features.

- It is normally distributed.
- It has a mean equal to the proportion of pro-Jacobin voters in the population.
- It has a standard deviation equal to the standard error of a proportion.

The formula for the standard error of a proportion is $\sqrt{[pq/n]} = \sqrt{(p(1-p)/n)}$

where p is the proportion in the population
       q is $1-p$
       n is the size of the sample.

The formula is provided in the examination.

We use the sample proportion p as an estimate of the population proportion.

Example: a confidence interval for a proportion

4.2   In a random sample of 500 out of 100,000 employees, 320 were members of a trade union. Estimate the proportion of trade union members in the entire organisation at the 95% confidence level.

Solution

4.3   The sample proportion is $320/500 = 0.64$.

$$\text{Standard error} = \sqrt{\frac{0.64 \times (1 - 0.64)}{500}} = = \sqrt{\frac{0.64 \times 0.36}{500}} = 0.0215$$

An estimate of the population proportion at the 95% confidence level ($z = 1.96$) is the sample proportion ± 1.96 standard errors.

The confidence interval for the population proportion is $0.64 \pm (1.96 \times 0.0215) = 0.64 \pm 0.04$. The percentage of employees who are trade union members is between 60% and 68% at the 95% level of confidence.

Exercise 2

A researcher wishes to know the proportion of people who regularly travel by bus. Of a sample of 400 people, 285 said they did so. Estimate the population proportion with 99% confidence.

Solution

The sample proportion is $285/400 = 0.7125$.

The standard error is $\sqrt{\frac{0.7125 \times (1 - 0.7125)}{400}} = 0.0226$

The 99% confidence interval for the population proportion is

$0.7125 \pm (2.58 \times 0.0226)$
= 0.7125 ± 0.0583
= 0.6542 to 0.7708

---

5   THE SIZE OF A SAMPLE

5.1   Suppose that we require a sample mean to provide an estimate of the population mean, to a **specified degree of accuracy**, say $\pm$ r units from the true mean, at a **given level of confidence** (say at the 95% level of confidence).

We would know that the range of possible values for a population mean μ would be given (at the 95% confidence level) by $\bar{x} \pm 1.96$ se (where $\bar{x}$ is the sample mean).

5.2 If we require $\bar{x}$ to be within r units of the true mean μ, then we require

$$r \quad = \quad 1.96 \text{ se}$$
$$= \quad 1.96 \; \sigma/\sqrt{n}$$
$$\text{Therefore } \sqrt{n} \quad = \quad 1.96 \; \sigma/r$$
$$n \quad = \quad (1.96 \; \sigma/r)^2$$

5.3 This formula gives us the **size of sample** required in order to obtain a **sufficient degree of accuracy** at the **given level of confidence**. Note that an estimate must be provided for σ even before the sample is collected. At the 99% confidence level, 1.96 is replaced by 2.58.

Example: sample sizes

5.4 The management of a company making a certain type of car component wish to ascertain the average number of components per hour produced by the workers. Based on a previous sample, it is estimated that the average number produced by each employee every hour is 100, with a standard deviation of 25. The management now wish to know the true average to within two units. Calculate the sample size at the following confidence levels.

(a) 95% confidence
(b) 99% confidence

Solution

5.5 (a) At a 95% level of confidence, $n = [1.96 \times 25/2]^2 = 24.5^2$

$$= \quad 600.25 \text{ workers, say } 601.$$

The sample size must be 601 workers to provide an accurate estimate of the population mean to within two units, at the 95% level of confidence. Note that we need to **round up.**

(b) At a 99% level of confidence, $n = [2.58 \times 25/2]^2 = 32.25^2$

$$= \quad 1{,}040.06 \text{ workers, say } 1{,}041.$$

To have 99% confidence about the accuracy of the sample mean as an estimate of the population mean to within two units, the sample size would need to be 1,041 workers.

Selecting a sample size in order to estimate a proportion

5.6 The considerations relating to the size of sample required in order to calculate the arithmetic mean of a population with sufficient accuracy also apply to the problem of deciding a sample size to obtain the proportion of a population with sufficient accuracy.

5.7 Let r be the degree of accuracy required, expressed as units of the population proportion. Thus if we require an estimate of the proportion which is accurate to within 3%, r would be 0.03.

We know that, at the 95% level of confidence:

$$r \quad = \quad 1.96 \text{ se}$$
$$= \quad 1.96 \; \sqrt{[pq/n]}$$
$$r^2 \quad = \quad \frac{1.96^2 \times pq}{n}$$
$$n \quad = \quad \frac{1.96^2 \times pq}{r^2}$$

At the 99% confidence level, 1.96 is replaced by 2.58.

Example: sample sizes for estimating proportions

5.8 A manufacturer wishes to estimate the proportion of defective components. He would be satisfied if he obtained an estimate within 0.5% of the true proportion, and was 99% confident of his result. An initial (large) sample indicated that p = 0.02. What size of sample should he examine?

Solution

5.9   p   =   0.02, therefore q = 1 – p = 0.98
      r   =   0.5% = 0.005

At a 99% level of confidence

$$n \quad = \quad \frac{2.58^2 \times 0.02 \times 0.98}{0.005^2}$$

     =   5,218.6 units, say 5,219 units

The sample would need to consist of 5,219 units.

5.10 If we have no initial idea of the population proportion, we work out a required sample size using p = 0.5, as this gives the largest possible value for p(1 – p), and hence the largest possible value for n. We will thus at least achieve the required accuracy.

6   HYPOTHESIS TESTING   6/94

6.1   Hypothesis testing is the process of setting up a theory or hypothesis about some characteristic of the population and then sampling in order to ascertain whether the hypothesis is supported or not.

6.2   The procedure for hypothesis testing is as follows.

     (a)   We establish a hypothesis about the population, for example that the mean value of all a company's invoices is £200. This is the **null hypothesis** (H_0). We also state an **alternative hypothesis**(H_1), for example that the mean value is not £200.

     (b)   We test the hypothesis by examining a sample. Are the sample results near enough what we would expect to get if the null hypothesis were true? To test the null hypothesis, we must select a **significance level**. This is the chance we take of wrongly rejecting the null hypothesis.

     (c)   Having tested the hypothesis, we draw a conclusion.

Example: hypothesis testing (1)

6.3   A company's management accountant has estimated that the average direct cost of providing a certain service to a customer is £40.

A sample has been taken, consisting of 150 service provisions, and the mean direct cost for the sample was £45 with a standard deviation of £10.

Required

Assess whether the sample is consistent with the estimate of an average cost of £40.

Solution

6.4   To apply a hypothesis test, we begin by stating the **null hypothesis** that the average direct cost per unit of service is £40. The alternative hypothesis will be that it is *not* £40.

6.5   Next, we select a **significance level**. Here, we will use 5%. 5% is a common choice. The lower the significance level, the lower the probability of wrongly rejecting the null hypothesis, but the higher the probability of wrongly accepting it. However, the probability of wrongly accepting the null hypothesis is *not* (100 - significance level) %. You do not need to know how to compute this probability.

6.6   Our choice of 5% means that we shall assume that the sample mean (£45) is consistent with our estimated population mean (£40) provided that the sample mean is within what would be a 100% – 5% = 95% confidence interval around a mean equal to the mean given by H_0.

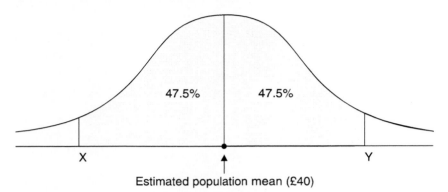

You may prefer to think of this in terms of the diagram above. If the sample mean of £45 is within the range from X to Y ($\pm$ 1.96 standard errors from the mean), we will conclude that our null hypothesis is acceptable.

6.7   From our sample, we can calculate the standard error as $s/\sqrt{n} = 10/\sqrt{150} = 0.816$.

6.8   We can now **test the hypothesis**. The sample mean is £5 higher than our hypothesised population mean, and this is $5/0.816 = 6.1$ standard errors above the mean.

6.9   At the 5% level of significance we would expect the sample mean to be within 1.96 standard errors of the hypothesised mean. It is not, and so at this level of significance, we reject the null hypothesis.

Conclusion. The average direct cost per unit of service is not £40, and the management accountant is wrong.

Exercise 3

It is thought that the mean number of times a person uses a credit card in a year is 180, neither more nor less. To test this hypothesis, a sample of 55 people is taken. The sample mean is 192 uses and the sample standard deviation is 50 uses. What conclusion should be reached at 5% significance?

Solution

H_0 is that $\mu = 180$, and H_1 is that $\mu \neq 180$.

The standard error is $50/\sqrt{55} = 6.74$

The sample mean is $192 - 180 = 12$ higher than the hypothesised mean, and is $12/6.74 = 1.78$ standard errors above the mean.

As this is within 1.96 standard errors, the null hypothesis (that the population mean is 180 uses) cannot be rejected.

Example: hypothesis testing (2)

6.10   In a manufacturing operation, the standard level of scrapped units is 8% of input.

During one week, 18,400 units were input to the operation of which 1,580 were scrapped.

Required

Assess whether the level of rejects appears to exceed the expected level. Test at the 5% level of significance.

Solution

6.11   We begin by **establishing a null hypothesis** (H_0) that the true level of rejects is 8% or 0.08.

We also need an **alternative hypothesis** (H_1) so that if the null hypothesis is rejected, we will accept the alternative hypothesis instead. In this example, H_1 will be that the level of scrapped units is *over* 8%.

6.12   The actual level of rejects is 1,580/18,400 = 0.08587.

6.13   We must establish a limit for the number of units scrapped, so as to ensure that there is only a 5% probability of the number of rejects in the sample exceeding the limit, if the average rejection rate for the population is in fact 8%. This may be shown in a diagram as follows.

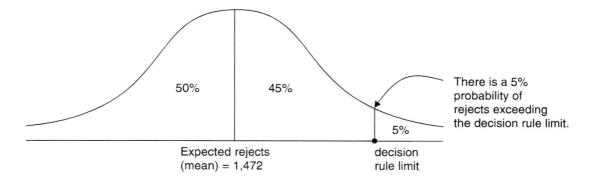

6.14   The decision rule limit (as shown in the diagram) must be such that there is only a 5% probability of the actual scrapped units in the sample being a greater amount. This means that 95% of the frequency distribution must lie to the left hand side of the limit. From normal distribution tables, 0.05 of the distribution lies more than 1.65 standard errors above the mean.

6.15   The standard error of the proportion, calculated from the proportion in the null hypothesis, is $\sqrt{[pq/n]} = \sqrt{[0.08 \times 0.92/18,400]} = 0.002$.

6.16   The actual level of rejects is 0.00587 above the expected level. This represents 0.00587/0.002 = 2.935 standard errors.

6.17   At the 5% level of significance, we would expect the sample proportion to be not more than 1.65 standard errors above the hypothesised mean. It is not since it is 2.935 standard errors above the hypothesised mean. We therefore **reject the null hypothesis** and conclude that the level of rejects is higher than 8% (at the 5% level of significance).

One-tail tests and two-tail tests

6.18   There are two different types of hypothesis test, known as **one-tail** (one-sided) or **two-tail** (two-sided) tests.

6.19   The first example above (Paragraph 6.3) was of a two-tail test, because the alternative hypothesis was of the form '... **does not equal** ...'. In the diagram we wanted 5% of the area in both tails taken together, hence our limits of ± 1.96 standard errors. For 1% significance, we would have used ± 2.58 standard errors.

6.20 **A one-tail test is used to determine, at a given level of significance, whether the results from a sample differ from expected results in one 'direction' only.** The second example (Paragraph 6.10) was of a one-tail test, because the alternative hypothesis was of the form '... is greater than ...'. Where the alternative hypothesis is of the form '... **is less than** ...' we also have a **one-tail test**. In the diagram, we wanted 5% of the area in one tail only, hence our use of 1.65 (2.33 for 1% significance).

Exercise 4

It is thought that the mean net weight of bags of sugar produced by a machine is at least 1.03 kg. A sample of 230 bags had a mean net weight of 1.02 kg, with a standard deviation of weights of 0.02 kg.

Required

Test the hypothesis that the population mean is at least 1.03 kg at the 1% significance level.

Solution

H_0 : $\mu \geq 1.03$ kg
H_1 : $\mu < 1.03$ kg

This is a one-tail test, so the critical value for 1% significance is -2.33. (The minus sign is put in because we will reject H_0 if the sample mean is more than 2.33 standard errors *below* the hypothesised mean.)

Standard error = $0.02/\sqrt{230}$ = 0.00132

$(1.02 - 1.03)/0.00132 = -7.58$.

H_0 should be rejected. There is clear evidence that the population mean weight is below 1.03 kg.

---

7 TWO-SAMPLE HYPOTHESIS TESTING

6/94, 6/97

Differences between means

7.1 We may compare the means of two different samples. In such a comparison, we might want to learn whether the mean of one population equals that of the other, or whether there appears to be a difference between them. Hypothesis tests can be made in such cases.

7.2 The **standard error of the difference between two means** is given by the formula

$$\sqrt{\frac{\sigma_1^2}{n_1} + \frac{\sigma_2^2}{n_2}}$$

where σ_1^2 is the population variance estimated from the first sample

      n_1 is the size of the first sample

      σ_2^2 is the population variance estimated from the second sample

      n_2 is the size of the second sample

Example: differences between means

7.3 Sample I might be a sample of the productivity of 160 employees at Factory A on day 1, which shows that the mean productivity index is 106 with a standard deviation of 8. Sample II might be a sample of 150 employees at Factory A on day 2 which shows a mean productivity index of 103 with a standard deviation of 6.

Required

Assess whether it is probable that there has been a change in the productivity index at Factory A between day 1 and day 2.

Solution

7.4 The standard error of the difference between the two sample means would be calculated as follows.

Sample I Standard deviation $\quad\quad\quad\quad\quad s = 8$
Variance $\quad\quad\quad\quad\quad\quad\quad\quad\quad s^2 = 64$
Estimate of population variance $\quad \sigma_1^2 = 64$

Sample II Standard deviation $\quad\quad\quad\quad s = 6$
Variance $\quad\quad\quad\quad\quad\quad\quad\quad\quad s^2 = 36$
Estimate of population variance $\quad \sigma_2^2 = 36$

$$\text{Standard error of the difference between the means} = \sqrt{\frac{64}{160} + \frac{36}{150}}$$
$$= \sqrt{(0.4 + 0.24)}$$
$$= 0.8$$

The mean productivity index on day 1 was 106 and on day 2 it was 103. The difference between the means was 3. A difference of 3 is $3/0.8 = 3.75$ standard errors.

7.5 The **null hypothesis** is that there is no difference between the two population means. The **alternative hypothesis** is that there is a difference.

7.6 We will test the null hypothesis with a **two-tail test** at the 5% level of significance. The null hypothesis would be accepted if the actual difference between the sample means did not exceed 1.96 standard errors. However, because the difference is 3.75 standard errors, the null hypothesis would be rejected at the 5% level of significance, and management would assume that average productivity on day 2 was different from that on day 1, because 3.75 standard errors is over 1.96.

Exercise 5

The analysis of sales for two sales areas for 20X6 based on random samples was as follows.

	Number of customers	
Annual sales by customer turnover	Midland	South
< £10	1	1
£10 and < £20	10	1
£20 and < £30	12	8
£30 and < £40	10	14
£40 and < £50	6	17
£50 and < £60	8	16
£60 and < £70	8	20
£70 and < £80	4	12
£80 and < £90	5	4
£90 and < £100	6	5
£100 and < £300	30	2
	100	100
Σfx	9,330	5,770
Σfx^2	1,404,950	411,250

Required

Test the hypothesis that there is no difference in the average annual sales per customer between the two areas.

Solution

The mean of the midland sample is $\dfrac{\Sigma fx}{n} = \dfrac{9,330}{100} = 93.3$

The variance of the midland sample is $\dfrac{\Sigma fx^2}{n} - \dfrac{(\Sigma fx)^2}{n}$

$$= \dfrac{1,404,950}{100} - 93.3^2$$

$$= 5,344.61$$

Similarly, the mean of the south sample is $\dfrac{5,770}{100} = 57.7$

The variance of the sample is $\dfrac{411,250}{100} - 57.7^2$

$$= 783.21$$

The **null hypothesis H_0** is that there is no difference between the means of the two areas.

The **alternative hypothesis H_1** is that there is a difference.

The **standard error of the difference between the two means** is

$$\sqrt{\dfrac{5,344.61}{100} + \dfrac{783.21}{100}} = 7.83$$

The actual difference between the sample means is $93.3 - 57.7 = 35.6$

This is $35.6/7.83 = 4.55$ standard errors.

The difference is significant at the 1% level of significance and therefore the null hypothesis is rejected, and it may be concluded that the average annual sales per customer differs between the two areas.

Differences between proportions

7.7 Another form of significance test involves the difference between **proportions** taken from two samples. The standard error of the difference between two proportions is given by the following formula.

Standard error of the difference between two proportions $= \sqrt{\dfrac{p_1 q_1}{n_1} + \dfrac{p_2 q_2}{n_2}}$

Example: the difference between two proportions

7.8 In 20X7, the Government carried out an intensive advertising campaign to encourage car drivers to use their rear seat belts. A sample investigation was carried out in London and Bournemouth with a view to determining the percentage of car owners who use their rear seat belts. 1,000 people were interviewed in London and 260 of them used rear seat belts. In Bournemouth, 100 out of the 500 car drivers interviewed used these belts.

Required

Assess whether there is any significant difference between the habits of drivers in London and Bournemouth.

Solution

7.9 In London $\qquad p = 0.26, \qquad q = 0.74$

In Bournemouth $\quad p = \dfrac{100}{500} = 0.2, \quad q = 0.8$

The standard error of the difference between the sample proportions is:

$$\sqrt{\frac{0.26 \times 0.74}{1,000} + \frac{0.2 \times 0.8}{500}}$$

$$= \sqrt{0.00051}$$

$$= 0.023$$

The null hypothesis is that there is no significant difference between the proportions in the two samples.

The actual difference between the two samples is $0.26 - 0.2 = 0.06$.

This is $\frac{0.06}{0.023} = 2.61$ standard errors.

At the 1% level of significance (± 2.58 standard errors) we would reject the null hypothesis, but only just, and conclude that there is a difference between drivers in London and Bournemouth.

Chapter roundup

- **Statistical inference** is the process by which conclusions are drawn about some measure or attribute of a population based upon analysis of sample data. It can be divided into two types, **estimation** and **hypothesis testing**.

- According to the **central limit theorem**, if a large number of samples are taken from the population, their means calculated and the means plotted as a frequency distribution, this distribution (the sampling distribution of the mean) will be very close to being **normally distributed**.

- The mean of this sampling distribution is the same as the **population mean**, μ. The standard deviation of the distribution is called the **standard error of the mean** (se) and is estimated using the standard deviation, s, of a sample.

- Armed with knowledge of the central limit theorem and properties of the sampling distribution of the mean, we can estimate, with a certain level of confidence and using sample data, the range within which the true population mean falls.

- The chapter also looked at the **sampling distribution of a proportion** which is normally distributed, has a mean equal to the population proportion and has a standard deviation called the **standard error of a proportion**. Ensure that you are able to estimate, with a certain level of confidence and using sample data, the range within which the true population proportion falls.

- We encountered a number of symbols in the chapter. Students often get these symbols muddled up and consequently find the whole topic of statistical inference confusing. Ensure that you know what all of the following symbols mean.

    $\bar{x}$ is the mean of the population

    μ (mu) is the mean of the population

    s   is the standard deviation of a sample

    σ (sigma) is the standard deviation of a population

    se   the standard error of the mean, is the standard deviation of the sampling distribution of the mean

- The chapter then focused on hypothesis testing, which looks at whether or not a belief about a population is supported by sample values. Note the differences between **null** and **alternative hypotheses**, and **one-** and **two-tail tests**.

- We can also use hypothesis testing to compare means/proportions of two different samples to assess whether there are differences between the two populations for which the samples are taken.

- In both estimation and hypothesis testing, we can never know whether our estimates are 100% accurate or whether differences between sample data and the hypothesis are attributable to chance or are due to the falsity of the hypothesis. All we can do is make decisions in a scientific manner so that we have a reasonable chance of reaching the correct conclusions.

Test your knowledge

1 What is the sampling distribution of the mean? (see para 2.2)

2 What is the standard error of the mean? (2.4)

3 What is the statistical rule covered by the central limit theorem? (2.4)

4 What is the formula for the standard error of the mean? (2.8)

5 What is used as the best estimate of the standard deviation of the whole population when calculating the standard error? (2.9)

6 Define confidence intervals, confidence levels and confidence limits. (3.2)

7 What are the features of a sampling distribution of a proportion? (4.1)

8 What is the formula for the standard error of a proportion? (4.1)

9 What is the procedure for hypothesis testing? (6.2)

10 What is a one-tail test? (6.20)

11 What is the formula for the standard error of the difference between two sample means? (7.2)

Now try illustrative questions 26 and 27 at the end of the Study Text

Part F
The representation of business situations using models

Chapter 12

EQUATIONS

This chapter covers the following topics.

1   Linear equations

2   Linear equations and graphs

3   Simultaneous linear equations

4   Non-linear equations

5   Quadratic equations

6   Graphs and maximum and minimum values

Introduction

This part of the Study Text looks at the ways in which business situations can be represented using models. A model is basically a representation of a 'real-world' situation.

The models in which we are interested are built using **equations** and hence this chapter takes you through both the structure and the methods of solution of various types of equation and looks at how equations can be represented on **graphs**.

Once you have worked through and understood this chapter you will be ready to tackle Chapter 13, which covers **breakeven analysis**.

---

1   LINEAR EQUATIONS

1.1   You are over the moon. You have just been awarded a £1,000 pay rise. If the man on the Clapham omnibus asks you to explain your new salary in terms of your old salary, what would you say? You might say something like 'my new salary equals my old salary plus £1,000'. Easy. What would you say, on the other hand, to the mathematics professor who asks you to give a mathematical equation which describes your new salary in terms of your old salary? Like many students, you may be perfectly capable of answering the man on the omnibus, but not the professor.

1.2   Your reply to the professor should be something like '$y = x + 1,000$' but many students get completely confused when they have to deal with mathematical symbols and letters instead of simple words. There is, however, no need to worry about equations: they are simply a shorthand method of expressing words. Work through this chapter and it should help to make things clearer.

Structure

1.3   **An equation is an expression of the relationship between variables**. We will begin by looking at one of the more common types of equation which involve **two variables**, the **linear equation**.

BPP PUBLISHING

1.4 **A linear equation has the general form y = a + bx**

where y is the dependent variable, depending for its value on the value of x;

x is the independent variable whose value helps to determine the corresponding value of y;

a is a constant, that is, a fixed amount;

b is also a constant, being the coefficient of x (that is, the number by which the value of x should be multiplied to derive the value of y).

1.5 Let us establish some basic linear equations. Suppose that it takes Joe Bloggs 15 minutes to walk one mile. How long does it take Joe to walk two miles? Obviously it takes him 30 minutes. How did you calculate the time? You probably thought that if the distance is doubled then the time must be doubled. How do you explain (in words) the relationships between the distance walked and the time taken? One explanation would be that every mile walked takes 15 minutes.

1.6 That is an explanation in words. Can you explain the relationship with an equation?

1.7 First you must decide which is the **dependent variable** and which is the **independent variable.** In other words, does the time taken depend on the number of miles walked or does the number of miles walked depend on the time it takes to walk a mile? Obviously the time depends on the distance. We can therefore let y be the dependent variable (time taken in minutes) and x be the independent variable (distance walked in miles).

1.8 We now need to determine the **constants** a and b. There is no fixed amount so a = 0. To ascertain b, we need to establish the number of times by which the value of x should be multiplied to derive the value of y. Obviously $y = 15x$ where y is in minutes. If y were in hours then $y = {}^x\!/_4$.

Example: deriving a linear equation

1.9 A salesman's weekly wage is made up of a basic weekly wage of £100 and commission of £5 for every item he sells.

Required

Derive an equation which describes this scenario.

Solution

1.10
x	=	number of items sold
y	=	weekly wage
a	=	£100
b	=	£5
∴ y	=	5x + 100

1.11 Note that the letters used in an equation do not have to be x and y. It may be sensible to use other letters, for example we could use p and q if we are describing the relationship between the price of an item and the quantity demanded.

2 LINEAR EQUATIONS AND GRAPHS

2.1 One of the clearest ways of presenting the relationship between two variables is by plotting a linear equation as a **straight line** on a graph.

The rules for drawing graphs

2.2 **A graph has a horizontal axis, the x axis and a vertical axis, the y axis.** The x axis is used to represent the independent variable and the y axis is used to represent the dependent variable.

2.3 If calendar time is one variable, it is always treated as the independent variable. When time is represented on the x axis of a graph, we have a **time series**.

2.4 (a) If the data to be plotted are derived from calculations, rather than given in the question, make sure that there is a **neat table in your working papers**.

(b) The scales on each axis should be selected so as to use as much of the graph paper as possible. Do not cramp a graph into one corner.

(c) In some cases it is best not to start a scale at zero so as to avoid having a large area of wasted paper. This is perfectly acceptable as long as the scale adopted is clearly shown on the axis. One way of avoiding confusion is to **break the axis** concerned, as follows.

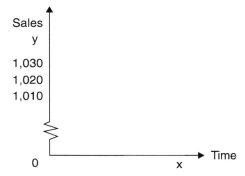

(d) The **scales** on the x axis and the y axis should be **marked**. For example, if the y axis relates to amounts of money, the axis should be marked at every £1, or £100 or £1,000 interval or at whatever other interval is appropriate. The axes must be marked with values to give the reader an idea of how big the values on the graph are.

(e) A graph should **not be overcrowded** with too many lines. Graphs should always give a clear, neat impression.

(f) A graph must always be given a **title**, and where appropriate, a reference should be made to the **source of data**.

Example: drawing graphs

2.5 Plot the graph for the relationship $y = 4x + 5$. Consider the range of values from $x = 0$ to $x = 10$.

Solution

2.6 The first step is to draw up a table. Although the problem mentions $x = 0$ to $x = 10$, it is not necessary to calculate values of y for $x = 1, 2, 3$ etc. A graph of a linear equation can actually be drawn from just two (x, y) values but it is always best to calculate a number of values in case you make an arithmetical error. We have calculated five values. You could settle for three or four.

x	0	2	4	6	8	10
y	5	13	21	29	37	45

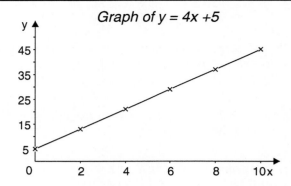

Graph of $y = 4x + 5$

The equation $y = 4x + 5$ gives a straight line. This is true of all equations of the type $y = a + bx$.

The intercept and the slope

2.7 The graph of a linear equation is determined by two things, the **gradient** (or slope) of the straight line and the point at which the straight line crosses the y axis.

2.8 The point at which the straight line crosses the y axis is known as the **intercept**. Look back at Paragraph 2.6. The intercept of $y = 4x + 5$ is $(0, 5)$. It is no coincidence that the intercept is the same as the constant represented by a in the general form of the equation **y = a + bx**. a is the value y takes when $x = 0$, in other words a **constant**, and so is represented on a graph by the point $(0, a)$.

2.9 The gradient of the graph of a linear equation is $(y_2 - y_1)/(x_2 - x_1)$ where (x_1, y_1) and (x_2, y_2) are two points on the straight line.

The slope of $y = 4x + 5 = (21 - 13)/(4 - 2) = 8/2 = 4$ where $(x_1, y_1) = (2, 13)$ and $(x_2, y_2) = (4, 21)$

Exercise 1

Find the gradient of $y = 10 - x$

Solution

Gradient $= -1$

2.10 Note that the gradient of $y = 4x + 5$ is positive whereas the gradient of $y = 10 - x$ is negative. A **positive gradient** slopes **upwards** from **left to right** whereas a **negative** gradient slopes **downwards** from **left to right**. The greater the value of the gradient, the steeper the slope.

2.11 Just as the intercept can be found by inspection of the linear equation, so can the gradient. It is represented by the coefficient of x (b in the general form of the equation). The slope of the graph $y = 7x - 3$ is therefore 7 and the slope of the graph $y = 3,597 - 263x$ is -263.

Exercise 2

Find the intercept and slope of the graph $4y = 16x - 12$

Solution

$4y = 16x - 12$

Equation must be form $y = a + bx$

$y = -\dfrac{12}{4} + \dfrac{16}{4}x = -3 + 4x$

Intercept = a = –3 ie (0, –3)

Slope = 4

Equations of trend lines

2.12 We saw in Chapters 6 and 7 how a line of best fit can be drawn through the points on a **scattergraph** to produce a **trend line**. We are now in a position to determine the equation of that trend line.

2.13 Here is an example of a scattergraph with a trend line added.

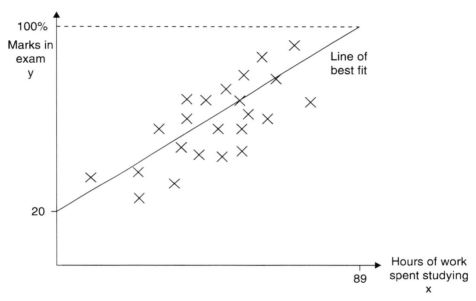

The line passes through the point x = 0, y = 20, so if its equation is y = a + bx, we have a = 20. The line also passes through x = 89, y = 100, so 100 = 20 + b × 89, and b = (100 – 20)/89 = 0.9. The line is y = 20 + 0.9x.

3   SIMULTANEOUS LINEAR EQUATIONS

3.1 **Simultaneous equations are two or more equations which are satisfied by the same variable values**. For example, we might have the following two linear equations.

$y = 3x + 16$

$2y = x + 72$

3.2 There are two unknown values, x and y, and there are two different equations which both involve x and y. There are as many equations as there are unknowns and so we can find the values of x and y.

Graphical solution

3.3 One way of finding a solution is by a graph. If both equations are satisfied together, the values of x and y must be those where the straight line graphs of the two equations intersect.

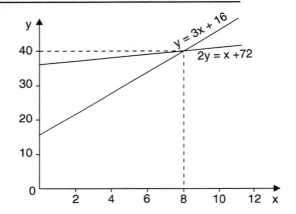

Since both equations are satisfied, the values of x and y must lie on both the lines. Since this happens only once, at the intersection of the lines, the value of x must be 8, and of y 40.

Algebraic solution

3.4 A more common method of solving simultaneous equations is by **algebra**.

(a) Returning to the original equations, we have:

$$y = 3x + 16 \qquad (1)$$
$$2y = x + 72 \qquad (2)$$

(b) Rearranging these, we have:

$$y - 3x = 16 \qquad (3)$$
$$2y - x = 72 \qquad (4)$$

(c) If we now multiply equation (4) by 3, so that the coefficient for x becomes the same as in equation (3) we get:

$$6y - 3x = 216 \qquad (5)$$
$$y - 3x = 16 \qquad (3)$$

(d) Subtracting (3) from (5) we get:

$$5y = 200$$
$$y = 40$$

(e) Substituting 40 for y in any equation, we can derive a value for x. Thus substituting in equation (4) we get:

$$2(40) - x = 72$$
$$80 - 72 = x$$
$$8 = x$$

(f) The solution is $y = 40, x = 8$.

Example: simultaneous equations

3.5 Solve the following simultaneous equations using algebra.

$$5x + 2y = 34$$
$$x + 3y = 25$$

Solution

3.6
$$
\begin{array}{lll}
5x + 2y = 34 & (1) & \\
x + 3y = 25 & (2) & \\
5x + 15y = 125 & (3) & 5 \times (2) \\
13y = 91 & (4) & (3) - (1) \\
y = 7 & & \\
x + 21 = 25 & & \text{Substitute into (2)} \\
x = 25 - 21 & & \\
x = 4 & & \\
\end{array}
$$

The solution is $x = 4, y = 7$.

Exercise 3

Solve the following simultaneous equations to derive values for x and y.

$$4x + 3y = 23 \qquad (1)$$
$$5x - 4y = -10 \qquad (2)$$

Solution

If we multiply equation (1) by 4 and equation (2) by 3, we will obtain coefficients of +12 and −12 for y in our two products.

$$16x + 12y = 92 \qquad (3)$$
$$15x - 12y = -30 \qquad (4)$$

Add (3) and (4).

$$31x = 62$$
$$x = 2$$

Substitute x = 2 into (1)

$$4(2) + 3y \quad = 23$$
$$3y \quad = 23 - 8 = 15$$
$$y \quad = 5$$

The solution is x = 2, y = 5.

Simultaneous equations with three unknowns

3.7 **If there are three unknowns, we can find a value for each unknown provided that we have three different simultaneous equations.**

Example: three unknowns

3.8 $x + y + z = 3 \qquad (1)$
      $2x - y + 3z = 15 \qquad (2)$
      $-x - 2y + 2z = 8 \qquad (3)$

Required

Find the values of x, y and z.

Solution

3.9   **The algebraic method of solution is to use one equation to derive an expression for one of the unknowns in terms of the other two.**

(a) Using equation (1), we could express x in terms of y and z as $x = 3 - y - z$.

(b) This value for x can now be substituted in equations (2) and (3).

$$2(3 - y - z) - y + 3z \quad = 15, \text{ that is,}$$
$$6 - 2y - 2z - y + 3z \quad = 15, \text{ that is,}$$
$$-3y + z = 9 \qquad\qquad\qquad (4)$$

$$-(3 - y - z) - 2y + 2z \quad = 8, \text{ that is,}$$
$$-3 + y + z - 2y + 2z \quad = 8, \text{ that is,}$$
$$-y + 3z = 11 \qquad\qquad\qquad (5)$$

(c) Multiply equation (4) by 3, to raise the coefficient of z to 3.

$$-9y + 3z = 27 \qquad\qquad\qquad (6)$$

(d) Subtract equation (6) from equation (5).

$$8y = -16$$
$$y = -2$$

BPP PUBLISHING

(e)   Substitute –2 for y in equation (5).

$$-(-2) + 3z = 11$$
$$3z = 9$$
$$z = 3$$

(f)   Substitute –2 for y and 3 for z in equation (1).

$$x + (-2) + 3 = 3$$
$$x + 1 = 3$$
$$x = 2$$

(g)   The solution is x = 2, y = –2, z = 3.

4   NON-LINEAR EQUATIONS

4.1   In the previous sections we have been looking at equations in which the highest power of the unknown variable(s) is one (that is, the equation contains x, y but not x^2, y^3 and so on).

4.2   We are now going to turn our attention to **non-linear equations** in which **one variable varies with the nth power of another**, where n > 1. The following are examples of non-linear equations.

$$y = x^2$$
$$y = 3x^3 + 2$$
$$2y = 5x^4 - 6$$
$$y = -x^{12} + 3$$

4.3   It is common for a non-linear equation to include a number of terms, all to different powers. Here are some examples.

$$y = x^2 + 6x + 10$$
$$2y = 3x^3 - 4x^2 - 8x + 10$$
$$y = -12x^9 + 3x^6 + 6x^3 + 3x^2 - 1$$
$$3y = 22x^8 + 7x^7 + 3x^4 - 12$$

4.4   Non-linear equations can be expressed in the form

$$y = ax^n + bx^{n-1} + cx^{n-2} + dx^{n-3} + ... + \text{constant. Consider the following equation.}$$

$$y = -12x^9 + 3x^6 + 6x^3 + 2x^2 - 1$$

In this equation a = –12, b = 0, c = 0, d = 3, e = 0, f = 0, g = 6, h = 2, i = 0, constant = –1 and n = 9.

Solving such equations is outside the scope of your syllabus.

Graphing non-linear equations

4.5   The graph of a **linear equation**, as we saw earlier, is a **straight line**. The graph of a **non-linear equation**, on the other hand, is **not a straight line**. Let us consider an example.

Example: graphing non-linear equations

4.6   Graph the equation $y = -2x^3 + x^2 - 2x + 10$.

Solution

4.7   The graph of this equation can be plotted in the same way as the graph of a linear equation is plotted. Take a selection of values of x, calculate the corresponding values of y, plot the pairs of values and join the points together. The joining must be done using as smooth a curve as possible.

x	-3	-2	-1	0	1	2	3
$-2x$	6	4	2	0	-2	-4	-6
x^2	9	4	1	0	1	4	9
$-2x^3$	54	16	2	0	-2	-16	-54
10	10	10	10	10	10	10	10
y	79	34	15	10	7	-6	-41

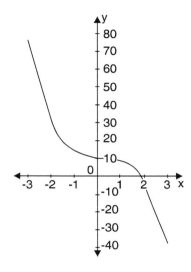

5 QUADRATIC EQUATIONS

12/99

5.1 **Quadratic equations are a type of non-linear equation in which one variable varies with the square (or second power) of the other variable.** The following equations are all quadratic equations.

$$y = x^2$$
$$y = 5x^2 + 7$$
$$2y = -2x^2 - 3$$
$$y = -x^2 + 3$$

5.2 A quadratic equation may include both a term involving the square and also a term involving the first power of a variable. Here are some examples.

$$y = x^2 + 6x + 10$$
$$2y = 3x^2 - 4x - 8$$
$$y = 2x^2 + 3x + 6$$

5.3 **All quadratic equations can be expressed in the form y = ax² + bx + c.** For instance, in the equation $y = 3x^2 + 2x - 6$, $a = 3$, $b = 2$, $c = -6$.

Graphing a quadratic equation

5.4 The graph of a quadratic equation can be plotted using the same method as that illustrated in Paragraph 4.7.

Example: graphing a quadratic equation

5.5 Graph the equation $y = -2x^2 + x - 3$.

Solution

5.6

x	−3	−2	−1	0	1	2	3
$-2x^2$	−18	−8	−2	0	−2	−8	−18
−3	−3	−3	−3	−3	−3	−3	−3
y	$\underline{\underline{-24}}$	$\underline{\underline{-13}}$	$\underline{\underline{-6}}$	$\underline{\underline{-3}}$	$\underline{\underline{-4}}$	$\underline{\underline{-9}}$	$\underline{\underline{-18}}$

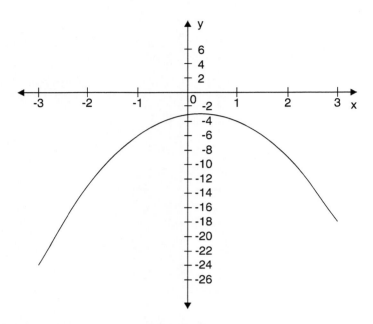

5.7 Graphs shaped like that in Paragraph 5.6 are sometimes referred to as **parabolas** and illustrate a number of points about the graph of the equation $y = ax^2 + bx + c$.

(a) The constant term 'c' determines the value of y at the point where the curve crosses the y axis (the intercept). In the graph above c = −3 and the curve crosses the y axis at y = −3.

(b) The sign of 'a' determines the way up the curve appears. If a is **positive**, the curve is **shaped like a ditch**, but if a is **negative**, as in Paragraph 5.6, the curve is **shaped like a bell**.

A ditch-shaped curve is said to have a **minimum point** whereas a bell-shaped curve is said to have a **maximum point**.

(c) The graph enables us to find the values of x when y = 0 (if there are any). In other words the graph allows us to solve the quadratic equation $0 = ax^2 + bx + c$.

For the curve in Paragraph 5.6 we see that there are no such values (that is, $0 = -2x^2 + x - 3$ cannot be solved)

Solving quadratic equations

5.8 There are many situations in business mathematics which call for the solution to a quadratic equation and the graphical method is not, in practice, the most efficient way to determine the solution.

5.9 Many quadratic equations have two values of x (called 'solutions for x' or ' roots of the equation') which satisfy the equation for any particular value of y. These values can be found using the following formula.

If, $ax^2 + bx + c = 0$ then $x = \dfrac{-b \pm \sqrt{(b^2 - 4ac)}}{2a}$

Example: quadratic equations

5.10   Solve $x^2 + x - 2 = 0$.

Solution

5.11 $x = \dfrac{-1 \pm \sqrt{(1^2 - (4 \times 1 \times (-2)))}}{2 \times 1}$

$x = \dfrac{-1 \pm \sqrt{(1 + 8)}}{2}$

$x = \dfrac{-1 \pm 3}{2}$

$= \dfrac{-4}{2}$ or $\dfrac{2}{2}$

So $x = -2$ or $x = 1$

Quadratic equations with a single value for x

5.12   Sometimes, $b^2 - 4ac = 0$, and so there is only one solution to the quadratic equation. Let us solve $x^2 + 2x + 1 = 0$.

$x = \dfrac{-2 \pm \sqrt{(2^2 - (4 \times 1 \times 1))}}{2}$

$x = \dfrac{-2 \pm 0}{2} = -1$

This quadratic equation can only be solved by one value of x.

Simultaneous quadratic equations

5.13   When there are **simultaneous quadratic equations**, values for x and y can be found by:

(a)   **eliminating y from the equations** by means of multiplication and addition or subtraction of the equations (in the manner previously described for linear simultaneous equations);

(b)   **solving the remaining quadratic equation** to derive two values for x;

(c)   **substituting each value for x in one of the original equations** to derive two corresponding values for y.

Example: simultaneous quadratic equations

5.14   Solve the following simultaneous equations to find the values of x and y.

$\begin{aligned} y &= x^2 + 4x + 33 & (1) \\ 2y &= 3x^2 - x + 30 & (2) \end{aligned}$

Solution

5.15   (a)   Multiply equation (1) by 2 so that the coefficient for y is the same as in equation (2).

$2y = 2x^2 + 8x + 66$ (3)

(b)   Subtract equation (3) from equation (2).

$0 = x^2 - 9x - 36$ (4)

(c)   Solve quadratic equation (4).

BPP
PUBLISHING

$$x = \frac{-(-9) \pm \sqrt{[81 - (4 \times 1 \times (-36))]}}{2} = \frac{9 \pm \sqrt{225}}{2}$$

$$= \frac{9+15}{2} \text{ or } \frac{9-15}{2} = 12 \text{ or } -3$$

(d) Substitute x = 12 in equation (1): y = 144 + 48 + 33 = 225.

(e) Substitute x = –3 in equation (1): y = 9 – 12 + 33 = 30.

Solution: either x = 12, y = 225
or x = –3, y = 30

6   GRAPHS AND MAXIMUM AND MINIMUM VALUES

6.1 Graphs can be used to find the **maximum** or **minimum** value of the **dependent variable**. For example, if sales turnover is being plotted against time, we can find the month in which sales turnover was at a maximum or minimum.

The **maximum value** is shown on a graph where the curve reaches a **peak**.

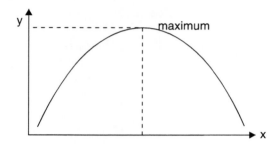

Similarly, a **minimum value** is where the curve reaches its **lowest point**.

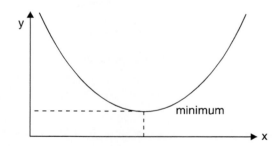

The maximum or minimum value can be read off the graph, and we can also read off the corresponding value of the independent variable, x.

Example: finding a maximum

6.2 On a bus route, when the fare is reduced from its original value of £1 by x%, the number of passengers increases by 2x% so that the new total revenue is the original total revenue multiplied by:

$(1 - 0.01x)(1 + 0.02x) = 1 + 0.01x - 0.0002x^2$

Required

Using a graph, find the value of x which produces the maximum revenue, and hence calculate the percentage increase in revenue which this would bring.

Solution

6.3 We begin by tabulating a variety of values for x and y in order to plot a graph for $y = 1 + 0.01x - 0.0002x^2$

228

x	y
0	1.000
10	1.080
20	1.120
30	1.120
40	1.080
50	1.000
25★	1.125

★Since the value of y is the same for x = 20 and x = 30, it clearly makes sense to calculate another value for y between these points.

The graph shows that a 12½% increase in revenue is the maximum which can be achieved, with a 25% reduction in the original fare.

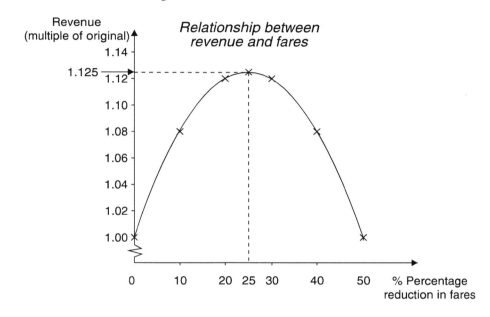

Chapter roundup

- A **linear equation** has the general form **y = a + bx**, where x is the **independent** variable and y the dependent variable, and a and b are fixed amounts.

- Make sure that you are aware of the rules for drawing graphs.

- The graph of a **linear equation** is a **straight line**. The intercept of the line on the y axis is a in **y = a + bx** and the slope of the line is b.

- **Simultaneous equations** are two or more equations which are satisfied by the same variable values. They can be solved **graphically** or **algebraically**. They can prove to be a quicker method for apportioning service department overheads than the repeated distribution method.

- In **non-linear equations**, one variable varies with the nth power of another, where n> 1. The graph of a non-linear equation is **not a straight line**.

- **Quadratic equations** are **non-linear equations** in which one variable varies with the square of the other variable. The graphs of **quadratic equations** are **parabolas**, the sign of c in the general form of the quadratic equation (y = ax2 + bx + c) determining the way up the curve appears.

- Quadratic equations can be solved by the formula $x = \dfrac{-b \pm \sqrt{(b^2 - 4ac)}}{2a}$

- Graphs can be used to find the **maximum** or **minimum value** of the dependent variable.

Test your knowledge

1   What is the general form of a linear equation? (see para 1.4)

2   On which axis of a graph is the independent variable represented? (2.2)

3   What are the rules for drawing graphs? (2.2 - 2.4)

4   What is the intercept? (2.8)

5   In which direction does a positive gradient slope? (2.10)

6   What are simultaneous equations? (3.1)

7   If the graph of a quadratic curve has a minimum point, is 'a' positive or negative? (5.7)

8   What is the formula for solving a quadratic equation? (5.9)

Now try illustrative questions 28 and 29 at the end of the Study Text

Chapter 13

BREAKEVEN ANALYSIS

This chapter covers the following topics.

1 An introduction to breakeven analysis

2 Constructing algebraic breakeven analysis models

3 Breakeven analysis and non-linear relationships

Introduction

The knowledge gained from Chapter 12 on equations is used in this chapter to enable us to construct breakeven analysis models. **Breakeven analysis** attempts to represent the behaviour of total costs and revenues and so provide information about profit levels, breakeven points and so on.

Chapters 14 and 15 examine another type of modelling which uses equations, **linear programming**.

---

1 AN INTRODUCTION TO BREAKEVEN ANALYSIS

6/95

1.1 Managers like to be able to assess and plan their future profits (profit planning), so they need to be able to **forecast future costs** and **revenues**.

1.2 One way of presenting information about expected future costs and revenues for management decision making is **breakeven analysis**. Breakeven analysis is sometimes called **CVP** or **cost-volume-profit analysis**. It uses **marginal costing**.

1.3 The basic idea of **marginal costing** is that if one extra unit is produced, then the costs which vary with production will all go up slightly. It therefore makes sense to identify those costs as the costs of production, the **marginal costs**. On the other hand, overheads such as rent, rates and heating will remain the same even if an extra unit is produced. They are **fixed costs**, and are not linked directly to the level of production.

1.4 The **marginal cost per unit** of production of an item will consist of the following.

- Direct materials
- Direct labour
- Variable production overheads, such as power costs

Contribution

1.5 **Contribution is the difference between sales value and the marginal cost of sales.**

For instance, if a stock item has a **marginal cost** of £10 a unit, and is sold for £12 a unit, each sale generates a **contribution** of £2. This contribution will go towards covering the fixed overheads of the business, and once these have been covered, the excess is profit. If the business has fixed overheads of £10,000 a year, the first 5,000 units sold will generate enough contribution to pay the fixed overheads of the year, and any further sales contribute £2 a unit clear profit. In any business, the total contribution from all sales during a period can be compared with the fixed costs for that period; any excess of contribution over fixed costs or of fixed costs over contribution represents the profit or loss respectively for the period.

The breakeven point

1.6 The management of an organisation usually wishes to know not only the profit likely to be made if the aimed-for production and sales for the year are achieved, but **also the point at which neither profit nor loss occurs (the breakeven point)**, and the amount by which actual sales can fall below anticipated sales without a loss being incurred.

The breakeven point can be calculated arithmetically. The number of units which must be sold in order to break even will be the total fixed costs divided by the contribution per unit. This is because the contribution required to break even must be an amount which exactly equals the amount of fixed costs.

Example: the breakeven point

1.7
Expected sales	10,000 units at £8 = £80,000
Variable cost	£5 a unit
Fixed costs	£21,000

Required

Compute the breakeven point.

Solution

1.8 The contribution per unit is £ (8 – 5) = £3
Breakeven point (BEP) = £21,000 ÷ £3
= 7,000 units
In revenue, BEP = 7,000 × £8 = £56,000

Sales above £56,000 will result in profit of £3 for each unit of additional sales and sales below £56,000 will mean a loss of (7,000 units – actual units sold) × £3.

	Sales	
	7,000 units	*7,001 units*
	£	£
Revenue	56,000	56,008
Less variable costs	35,000	35,005
Contribution	21,000	21,003
Less fixed costs	21,000	21,000
Profit	0	3

The margin of safety

1.9 **The margin of safety is the difference in units between budgeted sales volume and breakeven sales volume,** and it is sometimes expressed as a percentage of the budgeted sales volume. It may also be expressed as the difference between the budgeted sales revenue and breakeven sales revenue, expressed as a percentage of the budgeted sales revenue.

2   CONSTRUCTING ALGEBRAIC BREAKEVEN ANALYSIS MODELS   *6/95, 6/98, 12/99*

2.1 Before we begin our examination of the construction of algebraic breakeven analysis models, we need to set out the assumptions upon which breakeven analysis is based.

(a) **It is assumed that fixed costs are the same in total and variable costs are the same per unit at all levels of output**. This assumption is a great simplification.

(b) **It is assumed that selling prices will be constant at all levels of activity.** This may not be true, especially at high volumes of output, where the price may have to be reduced to win extra sales.

(c) **Production and sales are assumed to be the same**; therefore the consequences of any increases in stock levels (when production exceeds sales) or de-stocking (when sales exceed production) are ignored.

2.2   Although these assumptions limit the extent to which breakeven analysis reflects reality, we can still use the technique to enable us to build up formulae which explain, in simplified general terms, how costs and revenues behave.

The total revenue formula

2.3   **We assume that the selling price is constant at all levels of activity.** Total revenue is therefore equal to the selling price per unit multiplied by the quantity sold.

We can write this as $R = pq$

where R = total revenue
        p = selling price per unit
        q = sales volume or quantity sold

The total cost formula

2.4   **Total costs are made up of fixed costs and variable costs.** Since we are assuming that fixed costs are the same in total and variable cost per unit remain the same whatever the level of output, we can write

$$C = F + vq$$

where C = total costs
        F = fixed costs
        v = variable cost per unit
        q = quantity sold

The total profit formula

2.5   **Total profit (P) is the difference between total revenue and total cost and so we can write**

$$P = R - C$$

We can, however, substitute our formulae for R and C into the formula for P.

$$\begin{aligned} P &= R - C \\ &= pq - (F + vq) \\ &= (p - v)q - F \end{aligned}$$

The total contribution formula

2.6   **Contribution per unit**, as we have already seen, **is the difference between the selling price per unit and the variable cost per unit** (or marginal cost). We can therefore write

$$k = (p - v)$$

where k = contribution per unit

The formula for total contribution, K, can therefore be written as

$$K = (p - v)q$$

2.7   A comparison of the formulae for total contribution and total profit reveals that the difference between them is, obviously, F, fixed costs. If you cannot see why the difference had to be F, reread the explanation of contribution at the beginning of the chapter.

What happens at the breakeven point

2.8 We have now established the formulae necessary to solve any breakeven analysis problem. Before we tackle a few questions, let us just consider what happens to the formulae at breakeven point.

2.9 **At the breakeven point neither profit nor loss occurs** and so P = 0.

We know that P = R − C

If P = 0 then 0 = R − C and so R = C, that is, total revenue equals total costs.

If R = pq and C = F + vq, at the breakeven point pq = F + vq and so (p − v)q = F

Remember that K = (p − v)q and so, at the breakeven point, K = F.

Example: using the formulae

2.10 The budgeted annual output of a factory is 120,000 units. The fixed overheads amount to £40,000 and the variable costs are 50p a unit. The selling price is £1 a unit.

Required

(a) Calculate the budgeted profit.

(b) Ascertain the breakeven point.

(c) Determine the margin of safety in units and as a percentage of budgeted sales revenue.

Solution

2.11 (a) **Budget**

	£
Sales (120,000 units)	120,000
Less variable costs	60,000
Contribution	60,000
Less fixed costs	40,000
Profit	20,000

(b) F = £40,000
 v = £0.50
 p = £1
 q = breakeven quantity

At the breakeven point K = F
 but K = (p − v)q
 and so (p − v)q = F

Substituting in the values given we find

(1 − 0.5)q = 40,000
and so q = 80,000

(c) **Margin of safety** = (120,000 − 80,000) units
 = 40,000 units = £40,000 of revenue
 = $33^1/_3$ % of expected revenue

Example: the formulae approach again

2.12 Butterfingers Ltd makes a product which has a variable cost of £7 a unit. Fixed costs are £63,000 a year.

Required

Calculate the selling price per unit if the company wishes both to break even and to sell 12,000 units of the product.

Solution

2.13 Required contribution to break even = K = F   = £63,000
      Volume of sales   = 12,000 units   £

Required contribution per unit	= £63,000 ÷ 12,000 =	5.25
Variable cost per unit		7.00
Required selling price per unit		12.25

Target profits

2.14 A similar approach may be applied where a company wishes to achieve a certain profit during a period. To achieve this profit, **sales must cover all costs and leave the required profit**.

$$R = C + P$$

We can rewrite this as $pq = F + vq + P$

Subtracting vq from each side of the equation, we get the following.

$$pq - vq = F + P$$
$$(p - v)q = F + P$$

Total contribution required = F + P

Example: a required profit

2.15 Riding Breeches Ltd makes and sells a single product, for which variable costs are as follows.

	£
Direct materials	10
Direct labour	8
Variable production overhead	4
Variable sales overhead	2
	24

The selling price is £30 a unit, and fixed costs are £68,000 a year. The company wishes to make a profit of £16,000 a year.

Required

Calculate the sales required to achieve this profit.

Solution

2.16 Required contribution = F + P

                             = £68,000 + £16,000 = £84,000

$$\frac{\text{Required contribution}}{\text{Contribution per unit}} = \frac{£84,000}{£(30 - 24)}$$

                             = 14,000 units = £420,000 in revenue.

Exercise 1

Seven League Boots Ltd wishes to sell 14,000 units of its product, which has a variable cost of £15. Fixed costs are £47,000 and the required profit is £23,000.

Required

Calculate the required price per unit.

Solution

Required contribution	=	F + P	
	=	£47,000 + £23,000	
	=	£70,000	
Required sales	=	14,000 units	

			£
Required contribution per unit sold	=	£70,000 ÷ 14,000 =	5
Variable cost per unit, v			15
Required price per unit, p			20

Exercise 2

(a)   A company manufactures a product and finds that the fixed costs are £10,000, the labour costs are £6 per unit and other variable costs are £14 per unit. The selling price is fixed at £40.

Required

Find the following levels of sales.

(i)   At breakeven point
(ii)   To produce a profit of £2,200

(b)   The company can purchase a new machine for £2,100 (this would increase the fixed costs by this amount). The new machine would mean that labour costs could be reduced by a third. Assume that other costs and the selling price remain unchanged.

Required

(i)   Find the following levels of sales.

(1)   At breakeven point
(2)   To produce a profit of £2,200

(ii)   Advise the company on the level of output at which it would be economic to purchase the new machine.

Solution

(a)   Let q = quantity sold.

$$\text{Then profit} = \text{revenue} - \text{costs}$$
$$= 40q - (6q + 14q + 10,000)$$
$$= 20q - 10,000$$

(i)   At breakeven point, profit = 0

20q − 10,000	=	0
20q	=	10,000
q	=	500

(ii)   At a profit of £2,200,

20q − 10,000	=	2,200
20q	=	12,200
q	=	610

(b)   Fixed costs will rise to £12,100, and labour costs per unit will fall to £6 × $^2/_3$ = £4.

$$\text{Then profit} = 40q - (4q + 14q + 12,100)$$
$$= 22q - 12,100$$

(i)   (1)   At breakeven point,

profit	=	0
22q − 12,100	=	0
22q	=	12,100
q	=	550

(2)   At a profit of £2,200

22q − 12,100	=	2,200
22q	=	14,300
q	=	650

(ii) The machine is clearly worth purchasing so long as quantity produced is above some critical level, since the machine increases fixed costs but decreases variable costs. This level will be that at which profits both with and without the machine are equal. This will be at:

$$20q - 10,000 = 22q - 12,100$$
$$2,100 = 2q$$
$$q = 1,050$$

The machine should be bought if output will exceed 1,050 units. At precisely 1,050 units, profit will be the same both with and without the machine.

---

3 BREAKEVEN ANALYSIS AND NON-LINEAR RELATIONSHIPS   6/95, 6/98

3.1 In the problems we have looked at so far, the relationships have been linear. In other words, the variables in the formulae were all to the power of one.

3.2 You may, however, be asked to deal with **non-linear relationships**. The basic principles still hold (for example total revenue equals the product of the selling price and quantity sold) but you may be provided with algebraic expressions for the components of the original formulae. Do not worry, it sounds a lot more complicated than it actually is.

3.3 Such questions often involve **plotting a graph** and **extracting information** from that graph. The method is perhaps best illustrated with a comprehensive example.

Example: non-linear relationships

3.4 A company manufactures a product. The total fixed costs are £75 and the variable cost per unit is £5. The total revenue function is given by $R = (25 - q)q$, where q is the quantity sold.

Required

(a) Find an expression for total costs in terms of q, the quantity produced.

(b) The unit selling price function is in the form $p = a + bq$, where q is the quantity sold. Calculate the values of a and b.

(c) Plot on the same axes the revenue function and the total cost function found in part (a). Shade the region where profits are made.

(d) Using the graph, or otherwise, obtain the output levels where total revenue equals total costs. For these output levels find the corresponding price.

(e) Calculate the profit-maximising level of output and the profit at this output level.

Solution

3.5 (a) Let C = total costs
          C = total variable costs + total fixed costs
          C = 5q + 75

(b) We are given that $R = (25 - q)q$.

We know that $R = pq$ and hence $pq = (25 - q)q$.

Dividing both sides by q gives $p = 25 - q$.

If $p = a + bq$, a = 25 and b = −1.

BPP PUBLISHING

(c) *Workings for graph*

q	C 5q + 75	R (25 – q)q
0	75	0
3		66
6		114
9		144
12		156
15		150
18		126
21		84
24		24
25	200	0

Note that as the **total cost function** is a **straight line** (it is a linear function of q), only two points are needed. On the other hand, $R = (25 - q)q = 25q - q^2$, which is non-linear and so several points are needed.

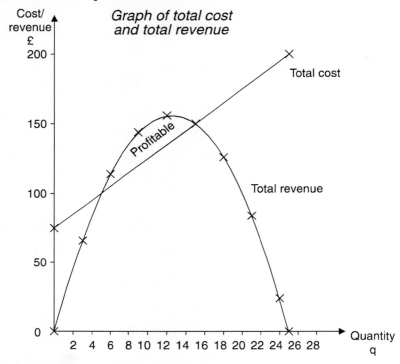

(d) **Total revenue = total costs at the point where the total costs line crosses the total revenue curve**. The coordinates of these two points may be found approximately from the graph, or may be found by solving the following equation:

$C = R$
$5q + 75 = (25 - q)q$
$5q + 75 = 25q - q^2$
$q^2 - 20q + 75 = 0$

This is a **quadratic equation** of the form $ax^2 + bx + c = 0$. We can solve the equation as follows.

$$q = 20 \pm \frac{\sqrt{(20^2 - (4 \times 1 \times 75))}}{2 \times 1}$$

$$q = \frac{20 \pm 10}{2}$$

$q = 5$ or 15

Using p = 25 − q, we have the following two points

Quantity	Price
	£
5	20
15	10

(e) **Profit = total revenue − total costs**. Profit is therefore represented by the vertical gap between the total revenue curve and the total cost line on the graph. This gap is maximised at q = 10.

The profit at this level is $((25 - 10) \times 10) - ((5 \times 10) + 75) = £25$.

3.6 This question has covered the majority of techniques which are likely to come up in a breakeven analysis question dealing with non-linear relationships. Ensure that you attempt the illustrative question recommended at the end of this chapter as it too covers non-linear relationships.

Exercise 3

(a) A company manufactures a product. For the accounting period, the total costs are £1,050 when the output is 20 units and £1,850 when the output is 40 units. Assuming linearity, find an expression for total costs in terms of q, the quantity of output.

(b) When the price is £20, the demand in the accounting period is 40 units. If the price is reduced to £10, the demand increases to 45 units. Assuming linearity, obtain the relationship between price and demand (q).

(c) Obtain an expression for the revenue function and hence show that the profit function is

$P = -2q^2 + 60q - 250$

By a graphical method or otherwise find the output which maximises profits.

Solution

(a) When q rises by 20 units (from 20 units to 40 units) total costs rise by £800 (from £1,050 to £1,850). This is a rise of £800/20 = £40 a unit, so variable costs are £40 a unit. At 20 units, we have:

Fixed costs + 20 × £40 = £1,050

Fixed costs = £1,050 − £800 = £250

The required expression for total costs is therefore T = 250 + 40q.

(b) Let p = price, and assume that p = a + bq

Then	20	= a + 40b	(1)
	10	= a + 45b	(2)
	10	= −5b	(3) (subtract (2) from (1))
	b	= −2	(4)
	20	= a −80	(5) (from (1))
	a	= 100	(6)

The required relationship is p = 100 − 2q.

(c) Revenue $= pq = q(100 - 2q) = 100q - 2q^2$
Profit $= P$ = revenue − costs
$= 100q - 2q^2 - (250 + 40q)$
$= -2q^2 + 60q - 250$

A graph may be plotted using the following values.

q	$-2q^2 + 60q - 250$
5	0
10	150
15	200
20	150
25	0

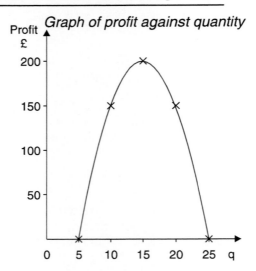

Graph of profit against quantity

We can see from the graph that profit is maximised at q = 15. At this point, profit = £200.

Chapter roundup

- **Breakeven analysis** has a number of purposes: to provide information to management about cost behaviour for routine planning and 'one-off' decision making; to determine what volume of sales is needed at any given budgeted sales price in order to break even; to identify the 'risk' in the budget by measuring the margin of safety; to calculate the effects on profit of changes in variable costs, sales price and so on.

- The **algebraic approach** to breakeven analysis relies on three principal equations.

  R = pq

  C = F + vq

  P = R – C

- At the **breakeven point**, P = 0 and R = C.

- The **margin of safety** is the difference between budgeted sales volume/revenue and breakeven sales volume/revenue.

- As well as dealing with linear relationships, you might also have to tackle problems which involve **non-linear relationships**. Such questions often involve plotting a graph of the total cost and total revenue functions and extracting information from the graph.

Test your knowledge

1   What is contribution? (see para 1.5)

2   At the breakeven point, will total contribution equal fixed costs? (1.6)

3   What are the assumptions upon which breakeven analysis is based? (2.1)

4   What is the total revenue formula? (2.3)

5   What is the total cost formula? (2.4)

6   How is profit represented on the graph of a total revenue curve and total cost line? (3.5)

Now try illustrative question 30 at the end of the Study Text

Chapter 14

LINEAR PROGRAMMING: THE GRAPHICAL APPROACH

This chapter covers the following topics.

1   Formulating the problem

2   Graphing the model

3   Finding the best solution

4   Sensitivity analysis

Introduction

This chapter continues our look at the way in which business situations can be represented by models.

As with Chapter 13, Chapter 12 provides the foundations for this chapter, which introduces **linear programming** and explains the **graphical approach**. Chapter 15 will cover the other approach to linear programming, the **Simplex method**.

But what is linear programming?

Suppose that Jack Russell is the production manager of Barkers Ltd, a small company which manufactures dog kennels. The company produces a number of different types of kennel but has a flexible workforce that can be switched easily from one production line to another. Much of the machinery is used in the production of more than one type of kennel, as are many of the raw materials, wood, paint, fleece and fur (for lining the kennels), plastic (for water and food bowls inside the kennels) and so on. Profit earned depends on the type of kennel sold. Pooch's Parlour (a model for small breeds such as poodles) does not generate as much profit as the Penthouse (centrally heated, and suitable for the most pampered of pets). The time taken to produce a kennel and the potential market also depend on the type of kennel in question.

Jack Russell's problem is to decide how the company should divide up its production among the various types of kennel it manufactures in order to obtain the maximum possible profit, taking the factors mentioned above into account. In other words, he cannot simply produce as many as possible of each model of kennel because there will be limitations or constraints within which the production must operate. Such constraints could be limited quantities of raw materials available, a fixed number of man-hours per week for each type of worker, limited machine hours and so on. Moreover, since the profits generated by each model of kennel vary, it may be better not to produce any of a less profitable line, but to concentrate all resources on producing the more profitable ones. On the other hand limitations in market demand could mean that all those kennels produced may not be sold.

You can see from this brief outline of the problem that the chances of Jack Russell arriving at the '**best solution**' (the one giving **maximum possible profits**) by simply thinking about it are minimal. What Jack needs is a systematic way of tackling the problem which guarantees that he will end up with the most profitable solution and ensures that the company operates within the constraints of man hours, machine hours, quantities of raw materials and so on.

Linear programming is a technique for solving problems of profit maximisation (or cost minimisation) and resource allocation, such as the one faced by Jack.

1   FORMULATING THE PROBLEM   6/94 - 6/00

1.1   In common with many quantitative methods, we need a rather simple example to illustrate the basic linear programming techniques. Let us imagine that Barkers Ltd makes just two models, the Super and the Deluxe, and that the only constraint faced by the company is that monthly machine capacity is restricted to 400 hours. The Super requires 5 hours of machine time per unit and the Deluxe 1.5 hours. Government restrictions mean that the maximum number of kennels that can be sold each month is 150, that number being made up of any combination of the Super and the Deluxe.

1.2   Let us now work through the steps involved in setting up a linear programming model.

Step one: define variables

1.3   What are the quantities that the company can vary? Obviously not the number of machine hours or the maximum sales, which are fixed by external circumstances beyond the company's control. The only things which it can determine are the number of each type of kennel to manufacture. It is these numbers which Jack Russell has to determine in such a way as to get the maximum possible profit. Our variables will therefore be as follows.

Let x = the number of units of the Super kennel manufactured.
Let y = the number of units of the Deluxe kennel manufactured.

Step two: establish constraints

1.4   Having defined these two variables we can now translate the **two constraints** into inequalities involving the variables.

1.5   Let us first consider the machine hours constraint. Each Super requires 5 hours of machine time. Producing five Supers therefore requires $5 \times 5 = 25$ hours of machine time and, more generally producing x Supers will require 5x hours. Likewise producing y Deluxes will require 1.5y hours. The total machine hours needed to make x Supers and y Deluxes is 5x + 1.5y. We know that this cannot be greater than 400 hours so we arrive at the following **inequality**.

$$5x + 1.5y \leq 400$$

1.6   We can obtain the other inequality more easily. The total number of Supers and Deluxes made each month is x + y but this has to be less than 150 due to government restrictions. The **sales order constraint** is therefore as follows.

$$x + y \leq 150$$

1.7   The variables in linear programming models should usually be **non-negative** in value. In this example, for instance, you cannot make a negative number of kennels and so we need the following constraints.

$$x \geq 0; y \geq 0$$

Do not forget these **non-negativity constraints** when formulating a linear programming model.

Step 3: establish objective function

1.8   We have yet to introduce the question of profits. Let us assume that the profit on each type of kennel is as follows.

	£
Super	100
Deluxe	200

1.9   The objective of Barkers Ltd is to maximise profit and so the objective function to be maximised is as follows.

$$\text{Profit (P)} = 100x + 200y$$

Note that another organisation might have, for example, the minimisation of costs or the maximisation of contribution as its objective.

1.10 The problem has now been reduced to the following four inequalities and one equation.

$$5x + 1.5y \leq 400$$
$$x + y \leq 150$$
$$x \geq 0$$
$$y \geq 0$$
$$P = 100x + 200y$$

1.11 Before we progress to the next step, let us look at an example which involves formulating a linear programming model which involves three variables.

Example: formulating a problem

1.12 Maxim Wise Ltd makes three products, A, B and C. Each product is made by the same grades of labour, and the time required to make one unit of each product is as follows.

	A	*B*	*C*
Skilled labour	3 hours	4 hours	1 hour
Unskilled labour	2.5 hours	2 hours	6 hours

The variable costs per unit of A, B and C are £28, £30 and £26 respectively. The products sell for £40, £40 and £34 respectively.

In March 20X3 the company expects to have only 600 hours of skilled labour and 2,000 hours of unskilled labour available. There is a minimum requirement for 40 units of B and 120 units of C in the month.

Monthly fixed costs are £1,500.

Required

Formulate a linear programming problem.

Solution

1.13 The variables are the products A, B and C. We want to decide how many of each to produce in the month.

Let the number of units of product A made be a.
Let the number of units of product B made be b.
Let the number of units of product C made be c.

The objective is to maximise the monthly profit. Since fixed costs are a constant value of £1,500, which will be incurred regardless of which production plan is selected, these are irrelevant to the objective function, which can be stated as **'to maximise profit by maximising contribution'**. The contribution per unit is £12 for A, £10 for B and £8 for C.

The objective is therefore to maximise 12a + 10b + 8c (contribution).

There are constraints relating to the availability of skilled labour and unskilled labour, and the minimum requirements for B and C. In addition, there are the constraints that A, B and C cannot have negative values, but since B and C must exceed 40 and 120 respectively, the non-negativity constraints are redundant for these two variables.

The programme may therefore be formulated as follows.

Objective: maximise 12a + 10b + 8c (contribution)
subject to the constraints:

3a + 4b + c	≤	600	(skilled labour)
2.5a + 2b + 6c	≤	2,000	(unskilled labour)
b	≥	40	(requirement for B)
c	≥	120	(requirement for C)
a	≥	0	

2   GRAPHING THE MODEL   6/94 - 6/00

2.1   In the previous section we looked at how to **formulate** a linear programming problem. We shall now look at the steps involved in **solving** a linear programming problem by using graphs.

2.2   It is important to note that **linear programming problems may only be solved graphically when there are two variables in the problem**. One variable is represented by the x axis and one by the y axis of the graph. Since non-negative values are not usually allowed, the graph shows only zero and positive values of x and y. It would therefore not be possible to solve the problem in paragraph 1.12 by graphing the model since there are three variables.

2.3   If when formulating a linear programming problem we establish the constraint y ≤ 6, how would we go about showing this on a graph?

The answer is that we would draw y ≤ 6 as y = 6 on a graph, as follows.

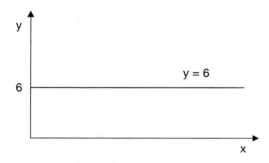

As the problem includes the constraint that y cannot exceed 6, the **inequality** y ≤ 6 would be represented by the shaded area of the graph as follows.

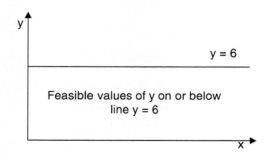

2.4   Similarly, if we establish the constraint 4x + 3y ≤ 24, when formulating our linear programming problem, we would draw the line 4x + 3y = 24 as a straight line on the graph. To draw any straight line, we need only to plot two points and join them up. The easiest points to plot are the following.

(a)   x = 0 (in this example, if x = 0, 3y = 24, y = 8)
(b)   y = 0 (in this example, if y = 0, 4x = 24, x = 6)

By plotting the points, (0, 8) and (6, 0) on a graph, and joining them up, we have the line for 4x + 3y = 24.

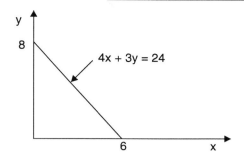

2.5 As we have the constraint $4x + 3y \leq 24$, any combined value of x and y within the shaded area below (on or below the line) would satisfy the constraint.

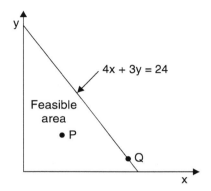

For example, at point P where $(x = 2, y = 2)$ $4x + 3y = 14$ which is less than 24; and at point Q where $x = 5.5$, $y = 2/3$, $4x + 3y = 24$. Both P and Q lie within the **feasible area** (the area where the inequality is satisfied, also called the **feasible region**). A **feasible area** enclosed on all sides may also be called a **feasible polygon**.

2.6 The inequalities $y \geq 6$, $x \geq 6$ and $4x + 3y \geq 24$, would therefore be shown graphically as follows.

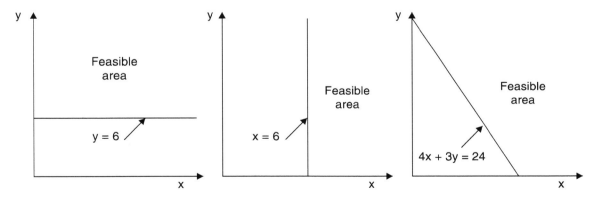

2.7 When there are several constraints, the feasible area of combinations of values of x and y must be an area where all the inequalities are satisfied.

Thus, if $y \leq 6$ *and* $4x + 3y \leq 24$ the feasible area would be the shaded area in the following graph.

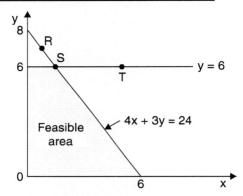

(a) **Point R** (x = 0.75, y = 7) is not in the feasible area because although it satisfies the inequality 4x + 3y ≤ 24, it does not satisfy y ≤ 6.

(b) **Point T** (x = 5, y = 6) is not in the feasible area, because although it satisfies the inequality y ≤ 6, it does not satisfy 4x + 3y ≤ 24.

(c) **Point S** (x = 1.5, y = 6) satisfies both inequalities and lies just on the boundary of the feasible area since y = 6 exactly, and 4x + 3y = 24. Point S is thus at the intersection of the two equation lines.

2.8 Similarly, if y ≥ 6 and 4x + 3y ≥ 24 but x ≤ 6, the feasible area would therefore be the shaded area in the graph below.

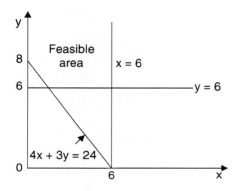

2.9 Have you noticed how all of the inequalities drawn so far are straight lines, and that all of the inequalities we have met are linear expressions (of the form y = a + bx)? This is because linear programming requires that all factors in the problem have linear relationships.

2.10 Obviously not all business decision involve factors which are linear. Linear programming is however best suited to those that are. The next step in the graphical approach to linear programming is to **find the best solution**.

Exercise 1

Draw the feasible region which arises from the constraints facing Barkers.

Solution

If 5x + 1.5y = 400, then if x = 0, y = 267 and if y = 0, x = 80.
If x + y = 150, then if x = 0, y = 150 and if y = 0, x = 150.

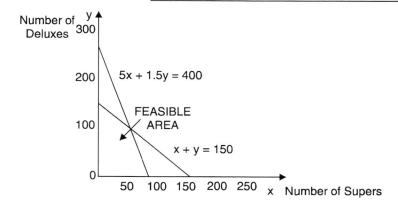

Exercise 2

Draw the feasible area for the following inequalities.

$$2x + 3y \leq 12$$
$$y \geq 2x$$
$$x \geq 0, y \geq 0$$

Solution

The new problem here is the inequality $y \geq 2x$. The equation $y = 2x$ is a straight line, and you need to plot two points to draw it, for example:

(a)   when $x = 0$, $y = 0$
(b)   when $x = 2$, $y = 4$

Since $y \geq 2x$, feasible combinations of x and y lie above this line (if $x = 2$, y must be 4 or more).

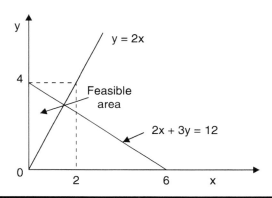

---

3   FINDING THE BEST SOLUTION   6/94 - 6/00

3.1   Having found the **feasible region** (which includes **all the possible solutions to the problem**) we need to find which of these possible solutions is 'best' in the sense that it yields the **maximum possible profit**. We could do this by finding out what profit each of the possible solutions would give, and then choosing as our 'best' combination the one for which the profit is greatest.

3.2   Consider, however, the feasible region of the problem faced by Barkers Ltd (see the solution to Exercise 1). Even in such a simple problem as this, there are a great many possible solution points within the feasible area. Even to write them all down would be a time consuming process and also an unnecessary one, as we shall see.

3.3   Let us look again at the graph of Barker's problem.

BPP
PUBLISHING

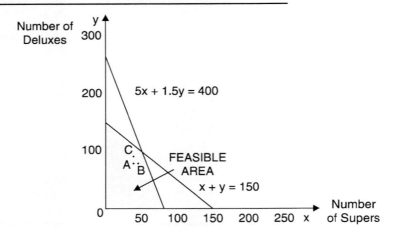

Consider, for example, the point A at which 40 Supers and 80 Deluxes are being manufactured. This will yield a profit of $((40 \times 100) + (80 \times 200)) = £20,000$. We would clearly get more profit at point B, where the same number of Deluxes are being manufactured but where the number of Supers being manufactured has increased by five, or from point C where the same number of Supers but 10 more Deluxes are manufactured. This argument suggests that the 'best' solution is going to be a point on the edge of the feasible area rather than in the middle of it.

3.4   This still leaves us with quite a few points to look at but there is a way we can narrow down the candidates for the best solution still further. Suppose that Barkers wish to make a profit of £10,000. The company could sell the following combinations of Supers and Deluxes.

(a)   100 Super, no Deluxe

(b)   No Super, 50 Deluxe

(c)   A proportionate mix of Super and Deluxe, such as 80 Super and 10 Deluxe or 50 Super and 25 Deluxe

3.5   The possible combinations of Supers and Deluxes required to earn a profit of £10,000 could be shown by the straight line $100x + 200y = 10,000$.

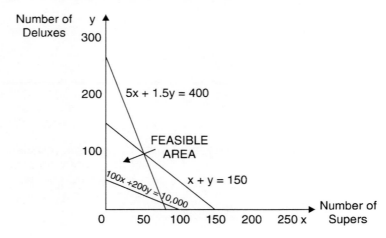

3.6   For a total profit of £15,000, a similar line $100x + 200y = 15,000$ could be drawn to show the various combinations of Supers and Deluxes which would achieve the total of £15,000.

Similarly a line $100x + 200y = 8,000$ would show the various combinations of Supers and Deluxes which would earn a total profit of £8,000.

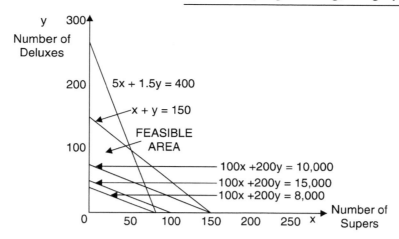

3.7   These profit lines are all parallel. (They are called **iso-profit lines**, 'iso' meaning equal.) A similar line drawn for any other total profit would also be parallel to the three lines shown here. This means that if we wish to know the slope or gradient of the profit line, for any value of total profit, we can simply draw one line for any convenient value of profit, and we will know that all the other lines will be parallel to the one drawn: they will have the same slope.

3.8   **Bigger profits are shown by lines further from the origin** (100x + 200y = 15,000), smaller profits by lines closer to the origin (100x + 200y = 8,000). As Barkers try to increase possible profit we need to slide the profit line outwards from the origin, while always keeping it parallel to the other profit lines.

3.9   As we do this there will come a point at which, if we were to move the profit line out any further, it would cease to lie in the feasible region and therefore larger profits could not be achieved in practice because of the constraints. In our example concerning Barkers this will happen, as you should test for yourself, where the profit line is just passing through the intersection of x + y = 150 with the y axis (at (0, 150)). The point (0, 150) will therefore give us the best production combination of the Super and the Deluxe, that is, to produce 150 Deluxe models and no Super models.

Example: a maximisation problem

3.10   Brunel Ltd manufactures plastic-covered steel fencing in two qualities, standard and heavy gauge. Both products pass through the same processes, involving steel-forming and plastic bonding.

Standard gauge fencing sells at £18 a roll and heavy gauge fencing at £24 a roll. Variable costs per roll are £16 and £21 respectively. There is an unlimited market for the standard gauge, but demand for the heavy gauge is limited to 1,300 rolls a year. Factory operations are limited to 2,400 hours a year in each of the two production processes.

	Processing hours per roll	
Gauge	*Steel-forming*	*Plastic-bonding*
Standard	0.6	0.4
Heavy	0.8	1.2

Required

Determine the production mix which will maximise total contribution. Calculate the total contribution.

Solution

3.11   Let S be the number of standard gauge rolls per year.
Let H be the number of heavy gauge rolls per year.

The objective is to maximise 2S + 3H (contribution) subject to the following constraints.

$$0.6S + 0.8H \leq 2,400 \quad \text{(steel-forming hours)}$$
$$0.4S + 1.2H \leq 2,400 \quad \text{(plastic-bonding hours)}$$
$$H \leq 1,300 \quad \text{(sales demand)}$$
$$S, H \geq 0$$

Note that the constraints are *inequalities*, and are not equations. There is no requirement to use up the total hours available in each process, nor to satisfy all the demand for heavy gauge rolls.

3.12 If we take the production constraint of 2,400 hours in the steel-forming process

$$0.6S + 0.8H \leq 2,400$$

it means that since there are only 2,400 hours available in the process, output must be limited to a maximum of:

(a) $\dfrac{2,400}{0.6}$ = 4,000 rolls of standard gauge;

(b) $\dfrac{2,400}{0.8}$ = 3,000 rolls of heavy gauge; or

(c) a proportionate combination of each.

This maximum output represents the boundary line of the constraint, where the inequality becomes the equation

$$0.6S + 0.8H = 2,400.$$

3.13 The line for this equation may be drawn on a graph by joining up two points on the line (such as S = 0, H = 3,000; H = 0, S = 4,000).

3.14 The other constraints may be drawn in a similar way with lines for the following equations.

$$0.4S + 1.2H = 2,400 \quad \text{(plastic-bonding)}$$
$$H = 1,300 \quad \text{(sales demand)}$$

3.15

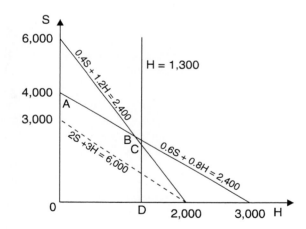

To satisfy all the constraints simultaneously, the values of S and H must lie on or below each constraint line. The outer limits of the feasible polygon are the lines, but all combined values of S and H within the shaded area are feasible solutions.

3.16 The next step is to find the optimal solution, which maximises the objective function. Since the objective is to maximise contribution, the solution to the problem must involve relatively high values (within the feasible polygon) for S, or H or a combination of both.

If, as is likely, there is only one combination of S and H which provides the optimal solution, this combination will be one of the outer corners of the feasible polygon. There are four such corners, A, B, C and D. However, it is possible that any combination of values for S and H on the boundary line between two of these corners might provide solutions with the same total contribution.

3.17 To solve the problem we establish the slope of the iso-contribution lines, by drawing a line for any one level of contribution. In our solution, a line $2S + 3H = 6,000$ has been drawn. (6,000 was chosen as a convenient multiple of 2 and 3). This line has no significance except to indicate the slope, or gradient, of every iso-contribution line for $2S + 3H$.

Using a ruler to judge at which corner of the feasible polygon we can draw an iso-contribution line which is as far to the right as possible, (away from the origin) but which still touches the feasible polygon.

3.18 This occurs at corner B where the constraint line $0.4S + 1.2H = 2,400$ crosses with the constraint line $0.6S + 0.8H = 2,400$. At this point, there are simultaneous equations, from which the exact values of S and H may be calculated.

$$
\begin{array}{llll}
0.4S + & 1.2H & = & 2,400 & (1) \\
0.6S + & 0.8H & = & 2,400 & (2) \\
1.2S + & 3.6H & = & 7,200 & (3)\,((1) \times 3) \\
1.2S + & 1.6H & = & 4,800 & (4)\,((2) \times 2) \\
 & 2H & = & 2,400 & (5)\,((3) - (4)) \\
 & H & = & 1,200 & (6)
\end{array}
$$

Substituting 1,200 for H in either equation, we can calculate that $S = 2,400$.

The contribution is maximised where $H = 1,200$, and $S = 2,400$.

	Units	Contribution per unit £	Total contribution £
Standard gauge	2,400	2	4,800
Heavy gauge	1,200	3	3,600
			8,400

Exercise 3

The Dervish Chemical Company operates a small plant. Operating the plant requires two raw materials, A and B, which cost £5 and £8 per litre respectively. The maximum available supply per week is 2,700 litres of A and 2,000 litres of B.

The plant can operate using either of two processes, which have differing contributions and raw materials requirements, as follows.

Process	Raw materials consumed (litres per processing hour)		Contribution per hour £
	A	B	
1	20	10	70
2	30	20	60

The plant can run for 120 hours a week in total, but for safety reasons, process 2 cannot be operated for more than 80 hours a week.

Required

Formulate a linear programming model, and then solve it, to determine how many hours process 1 should be operated each week and how many hours process 2 should be operated each week.

Solution

The decision variables are processing hours in each process. If we let the processing hours per week for process 1 be P_1 and the processing hours per week for process 2 be P_2 we can formulate an objective and constraints as follows.

The objective is to maximise $70P_1 + 60P_2$, subject to the following constraints.

$$
\begin{array}{llll}
20P_1 + 30P_2 & \leq & 2,700 & \text{(material A supply)} \\
10P_1 + 20P_2 & \leq & 2,000 & \text{(material B supply)}
\end{array}
$$

P_2	$\leq$	80	(maximum time for P_2)
$P_1 + P_2$	$\leq$	120	(total maximum time)
P_1, P_2	$\geq$	0	

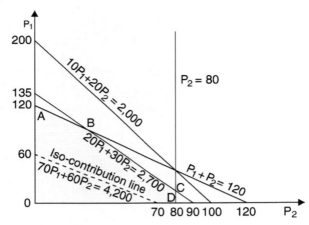

The feasible area is ABCDO.

The optimal solution, found by moving the iso-contribution line outwards, is at point A, where $P_1 = 120$ and $P_2 = 0$.

Total contribution would be $120 \times 70 = £8,400$ a week.

Minimisation problems in linear programming

3.19 Although decision problems with limiting factors usually involve the maximisation of contribution, there may be a requirement to **minimise costs**. A graphical solution, involving two variables, is very similar to that for a maximisation problem, with the exception that **instead of finding a contribution line touching the feasible area as far away from the origin as possible, we look for a total cost line touching the feasible area as close to the origin as possible**.

Example: a minimisation problem

3.20 Bilton Sandys Ltd has undertaken a contract to supply a customer with at least 260 units in total of two products, X and Y, during the next month. At least 50% of the total output must be units of X. The products are each made by two grades of labour, as follows.

	X	Y
	Hours	*Hours*
Grade A labour	4	6
Grade B labour	4	2
Total	$\overline{\underline{8}}$	$\overline{\underline{8}}$

Although additional labour can be made available at short notice, the company wishes to make use of 1,200 hours of Grade A labour and 800 hours of Grade B labour which has already been assigned to working on the contract next month. The total variable cost per unit is £120 for X and £100 for Y.

Bilton Sandys Ltd wishes to minimise expenditure on the contract next month.

Required

Calculate how much of X and Y should be supplied in order to meet the terms of the contract.

Solution

3.21 Let the number of units of X supplied be x, and the number of units of Y supplied be y.

We have introduced a new type of constraint into this example: 'At least 50% of the total output must be units of X'. We can express total output in terms of x and y as follows.

Total output = x + y

If at least 50% (or 0.5) of the total output is x, then x is greater than or equal to 50% of the total output.

This can be expressed as follows.

$x \geq 0.5(x + y)$

The objective is therefore to minimise $120x + 100y$ (costs), subject to the following constraints.

x + y	≥	260	(supply total)
x	≥	0.5 (x + y)	(proportion of x in total)
4x + 6y	≥	1,200	(Grade A labour)
4x + 2y	≥	800	(Grade B labour)
x, y	≥	0	

The constraint $x \geq 0.5 (x + y)$ needs simplifying further.

x	≥ 0.5 (x + y)
2x	≥ x + y
x	≥ y

In a graphical solution, the line will be x = y. Check this carefully in the following diagram.

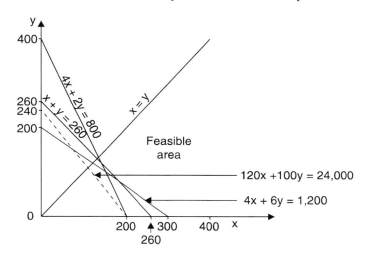

3.22 The cost line $120x + 100y = 24,000$ has been drawn to show the slope of every cost line $120x + 100y$. Costs are minimised where a cost line touches the feasible area as close as possible to the origin of the graph. This occurs where the constraint line $4x + 2y = 800$ crosses the constraint line $x + y = 260$. This point is found as follows.

x + y	=	260	(1)
4x + 2y	=	800	(2)
2x + y	=	400	(3) ((2) × 2)
x	=	140	(4) ((3) - (1))
y	=	120	(5)

BPP PUBLISHING

3.23 **Costs will be minimised by supplying the following.**

	Unit cost £	Total cost £
140 units of X	120	16,800
120 units of Y	100	12,000
		28,800

The proportion of units of X in the total would exceed 50%, and demand for Grade A labour would exceed the 1,200 hours minimum.

3.24 Another format of the cost minimisation problem incorporates quality requirements. An example will serve to illustrate this type of problem.

Example: quality requirements

3.25 J Farms Ltd can buy two types of fertiliser which contain the following percentages of chemicals.

	Nitrates	Phosphates	Potash
Type X	18	5	2
Type Y	3	2	5

For a certain crop the following minimum quantities (kg) are required.

Nitrates 100   Phosphates 50   Potash 40

Type X costs £10 per kg and Type Y costs £5 per kg. J Farms Ltd currently buys 1,000 kg of each type and wishes to minimise its expenditure on fertilisers.

Required

Recommend the quantity of each type of fertiliser which should be bought and the cost of these amounts.

Solution

3.26 **Define variables**

Let the company buy x kg of Type X fertiliser.
Let the company buy y kg of Type Y fertiliser.

Establish constraints

$$0.18x + 0.03y \geq 100 \quad \text{(nitrates)}$$
$$0.05x + 0.02y \geq 50 \quad \text{(phosphates)}$$
$$0.02x + 0.05y \geq 40 \quad \text{(potash)}$$
$$x, y \geq 0 \quad \text{(non-negativity)}$$

Establish objective function

The objective is to minimise the expenditure on fertilisers.

Minimise 10x + 5y

Graph the model (see following page)

Determine optimal solution

If we move a ruler up the graph parallel to the objective function, the first point reached in the feasible region is point A. We find the co-ordinates of this point by solving the simultaneous equations below.

$0.05x + 0.02y = 50$	(1)	
$0.02x + 0.05y = 40$	(2)	
$0.05x + 0.125y = 100$	(3) $((2) \times 2.5)$	
$0.105y = 50$	(4) $((3) - (1))$	
$y = 476.2$		

$$0.05x + (0.02 \times 476.2) = 50 \qquad \text{(5) (Substitute in (1))}$$

$$0.05x + 9.52 \quad = 50$$
$$0.05x \quad\quad\quad = 40.48$$
$$x \quad\quad\quad\quad = 809.5$$

So the company should buy 809.5 kg of Type X fertiliser and 476.2 kg of Type Y fertiliser.

The total cost is $(10 \times 809.5) + (5 \times 476.2) = £10,476$.

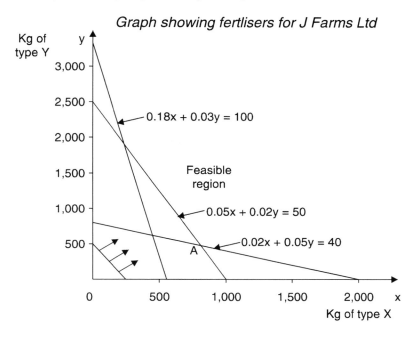

Graph showing fertlisers for J Farms Ltd

The use of simultaneous equations

3.27 You might think that a lot of time could be saved if we started by solving the simultaneous equations in a linear programming problem and did not bother to draw the graph. Certainly, this procedure may give the right answer, but in general (unless the example is very straightforward) it is *not* recommended until you have shown graphically which constraints are effective in determining the optimal solution. (In particular, if a question requires 'the graphical method', you *must* draw a graph.) To illustrate this point, consider the graph below.

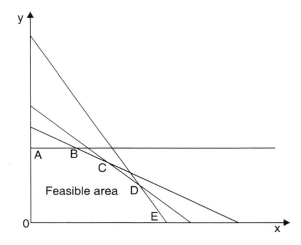

3.28 No figures have been given on the graph but the feasible area is OABCDE. When solving this problem, we would know that the optimum solution would be at one of the corners of the feasible area. We need to work out the profit at each of the corners of the feasible area and pick the one where the profit is greatest.

Once the optimum point has been determined graphically, simultaneous equations can be applied to find the exact values of x and y at this point.

Exercise 4

Given the following constraints and objective function, determine the optimal production level of product X and product Y.

Constraints

$$Y \leq -X/2 + 5 \quad (1)$$
$$Y \leq 2X \quad (2)$$
$$X \geq 0 \quad (3)$$
$$Y \geq 0 \quad (4)$$

Objective function

$$\text{Profit} = 3X + 4Y$$

Solution

Feasible solutions are at the intersection of the constraints:

(1) and (2)	*(1) and (3)*	*(1) and (4)*	*(2) and (3) (2) and (4) (3) and (4)*
X = 2, Y = 4	X = 0, Y = 5	X = 10, Y = 0	X = 0, Y = 0
Profit = 22	Profit = 20	Profit = 30	Profit = 0

Profit is maximised when 10 units of product X and no units of product Y are produced.

---

4 SENSITIVITY ANALYSIS

6/95, 12/96, 12/97, 12/99

4.1 In setting up the linear programming model we had to assume that we had adequate information about the amounts of the various resources by which production is constrained and about the profits which would be generated by the sale of the products. In practice, of course, these can be quite difficult to estimate, particularly when planning production not just for a week or two in advance, but for a whole year ahead. We may expect to be able to use a certain machine for 400 hours a month, only to find that, due to breakdowns, the figure is closer to 350 hours. We may hope to sell the Super at a price which will give us a profit of £100 per kennel, and then discover that a competitor has put a cheap new alternative on the market and we must cut our profit margins if we are to maintain our market share.

4.2 These circumstances could result in an optimal solution, worked out for a set of assumptions that are no longer valid, no longer being the optimal solution.

4.3 To examine this topic further a new example will be introduced.

Example: sensitivity analysis

4.4 Dual Ltd makes two products, X and Y, which have the following selling prices and costs.

	X		Y	
	£	£	£	£
Unit selling price		14		15
Costs				
Materials (at £1 per kg)	3		2	
Labour (at £3 per hr)	6		9	
		9		11
Unit profit		5		4

What production plan would maximise profit in the next period, given that the supply of materials will be restricted to 600 kg, only 450 labour hours will be available, and a minimum demand for 150 units of product X must be met?

How would changes in the selling prices affect the solution?

Solution

4.5   The problem could be solved graphically, as follows.

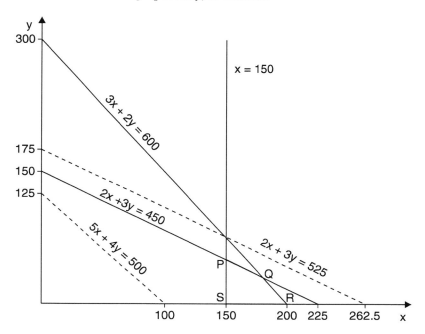

The feasible polygon is PQRS, and profit would be maximised at point Q, where

3x + 2y = 600
2x + 3y = 450

Therefore x = 180, y = 30, and total profit is £1,020.

The optimum will shift to point R (x = 200, y = 0) if X becomes sufficiently more profitable. It will shift when the iso-profit line becomes steeper than the line 3x + 2y = 600. That line's gradient is –1.5, and the iso-profit line's gradient is

$$\frac{- \text{ unit profit from X}}{\text{unit profit from Y}}$$

Thus the optimum will shift to R if the unit profit from Y remains at £4 but the unit profit from X increases to more than £6, corresponding to an increase in the unit selling price of more than £1 to more than £15.

Exercise 5

In the above example, if the unit profit from X remains at £5, what would the unit profit from Y have to increase to in order to shift the optimum to point P? What unit selling price of Y does this new profit correspond to?

Solution

The gradient of 2x + 3y = 450 is –2/3. We therefore need:

5/unit profit from Y < 2/3
Unit profit from Y > £7.50
Unit selling price of Y > £18.50

4.6   **The point of sensitivity analysis is that it indicates the risk of our selecting the wrong solution.** If small changes in prices would lead to a different optimum applying, there is a high risk of our selecting the wrong solution. If, on the other hand, large changes in prices would leave the optimum unchanged, errors in predicting prices are unlikely to lead to our selecting the wrong solution.

Dual prices

4.7 The **dual price** (also called the **shadow price**) of a resource which is fully used at the optimum is the amount by which:

(a) total profit would fall if the company were deprived of one unit of the resource;

(b) total profit would rise if the company were able to obtain one extra unit of the scarce resource, **provided that** the resource remains an effective constraint on production and **provided also** that the extra unit of the resource can be obtained at its normal unit cost. The dual price is therefore the maximum amount which should be paid **in excess of the normal rate** for each extra unit of the resource.

The dual price is calculated on the assumption that there is a change in the availability of one resource, but with the availability of other resources being held constant.

4.8 In the above example (Dual Ltd), both materials and labour hours are used up fully in the planned production mix. Let us therefore calculate the effect on total profit if the company were deprived of one unit of materials, so that only 599 kg were available (but labour hours available remain at 450).

The new optimal production mix would be at the intersection point of the two constraint lines:

$3x + 2y = 599$
$2x + 3y = 450$

Solving the simultaneous equations, $x = 179.4$ units and $y = 30.4$ units:

Product	Units	Profit
		£
X	179.4 (× £5)	897.00
Y	30.4 (× £4)	121.60
		1,018.60
Profit in original problem		1,020.00
Reduction in profit from loss of 1 kg of materials		1.40

The dual price of materials is therefore £1.40 per kg.

4.9 Suppose that materials available are 600 kg, but that the labour supply is reduced by 20 hours to 430 hours. **The optimal production mix occurs at the intersection of the two constraints:**

$2x + 3y = 430;$
$3x + 2y = 600.$

Solving the simultaneous equations, $x = 188$ units and $y = 18$ units.

Product	Units	Profit
		£
X	188 (× £5)	940
Y	18 (× £4)	72
		1,012
Profit in original problem		1,020
Reduction in profit from loss of 20 labour hours		8

The dual price of labour is therefore 8/20 = £0.40 an hour.

4.10 **The dual price of a resource also shows by how much profit would increase if an additional unit of the resource were made available.** In our example, if the materials available were 600 kg but the labour supply were raised to 451 hours, the optimum production mix would be 179.6 units of X and 30.6 units of Y.

Product	Units	Profit £
X	179.6 (× £5)	898.00
Y	30.6 (× £4)	122.40
		1,020.40
Profit in original problem		1,020.00
Increase in profit from one extra unit of labour		0.40

Once again, the dual price of labour is £0.40 an hour.

4.11 The increase in contribution of £0.40 per extra labour hour is calculated on the assumption that the extra labour hour would be paid for at the normal variable cost, which is £3 an hour in the problem.

(a) The management of the company should be prepared to pay up to £0.40 extra per extra hour of labour in order to obtain more labour hours (perhaps through overtime working: the maximum value of overtime premium would then be £0.40 per hour). We assume that the existing 450 hours of labour are still paid only £3 an hour.

(b) This value of labour only applies as long as labour remains fully used. If more and more labour hours are made available, there will eventually be so much labour that it is no longer a scarce resource. In our problem, this will occur when the third constraint, $x \geq 150$, prevents a further reduction in the output of X in order to increase output of Y.

4.12 We can calculate how many hours must be available before labour ceases to be fully used. This will happen when the new labour constraint passes through the intersection of $x = 150$ and $y = 75$, so that the constraint for labour $2x + 3y$ would be

$2x + 3y = ?$

If $x = 150$ and $y = 75$, $2x + 3y = (2 \times 150) + (3 \times 75) = 525$

This is shown as the upper right dotted line on the graph in Paragraph 4.5.

The dual price of labour is £0.40 per hour in the initial problem, but only up to a maximum supply of 525 labour hours (75 hours more than the original 450 hours). Extra labour above 525 hours would not have any use, and the two limiting factors would now be materials and the minimum demand for x. Beyond 525 hours, labour would have a dual price of zero. Once the labour constraint ceases to matter in this way, it becomes an **ineffective, non-binding** or **non-critical constraint**.

Any resource which is not fully used has a dual price of zero: losing one unit will not matter, and there is no point in paying over the normal rate for extra units.

Exercise 6

A linear programming problem is as follows.

Maximise profit, 4x + 2y, subject to the following constraints.

3x + 6y ≤ 12,000 (hours of labour)
5x + 2y ≤ 10,000 (hours of machine time)
x,y   ≥ 0

The optimum is at the intersection of the labour constraint and the machine time constraint. What is the dual price per hour of machine time?

Solution

The optimum is at the following point.

```
 3x + 6y  =  12,000
 5x + 2y  =  10,000
15x + 6y  =  30,000
     12x  =  18,000
       x  =   1,500
       y  =   1,250
```

BPP PUBLISHING

Profit = (1,500 x 4) + (1,250 × 2) = £8,500.

With one extra machine hour, the optimum would be as follows.

$$
\begin{aligned}
3x + 6y &= 12,000 \\
5x + 2y &= 10,001 \\
15x + 6y &= 30,003 \\
12x &= 18,003 \\
x &= 1,500.25 \\
y &= 1,249.875
\end{aligned}
$$

Profit = (1,500.25 × 4) + (1,249.875 × 2) = £8,500.75.

The dual price per machine hour is £(8,500.75 − 8,500.00) = £0.75

Chapter roundup

- **Linear programming**, at least at this fairly simple level, is a technique that can be carried out in a fairly 'handle-turning' manner once you have got the basic ideas sorted out. The steps in that technique are as follows.

  Step 1. Define variables

  Step 2. Establish constraints (including non-negativity)

  Step 3. Construct objective function

  Step 4. Draw a graph of the constraints

  Step 5. Establish the feasible region

  Step 6. Add an iso-profit/contribution line

  Step 7. Determine optimal solution

  The apparent simplicity of the technique should not, however, allow you to disregard the following **practical limitations** of linear programming.

- In all practical situations there are likely to be substantial problems involved in estimating the total quantities of scarce resources available. Furthermore, the **final estimates** used are likely to be subject to considerable **uncertainty**.

- **There is an assumption of linearity**. Each extra unit of a given product is supposed to change the contribution and the consumption of resources by the same amount. In practice, this assumption may be invalid except over small ranges. For example, in a profit maximisation problem, it may well be found that there are substantial changes in unit variable costs arising from increasing or decreasing returns to scale.

- The linear programming model is essentially **static** and is therefore **not really suitable for analysing in detail the effects of changes over time**.

- In some circumstances, a solution derived from a linear programming model may be of **limited use** if, for example, the variables may only take on integer values. A solution can be found by a combination of rounding up or down and trial and error, but this sort of approach is not really suitable for large-scale practical problems.

- **The graphical method can only cope with two variables**, whereas many companies have more than two products competing for the same resources. You will discover how to deal with this type of situation in the next chapter.

Test your knowledge

1 What is meant by an objective function? (see para 1.9)

2 What would the inequality $4x + 3y \leq 24$ look like when drawn on a graph? (2.5)

3 What is the feasible region? (2.5)

4 What is an iso-profit line? (3.7)

5 How does the graphical solution of minimisation problems differ from that of maximisation problems? (3.19)

6 Define the dual price of a resource. (4.7)

Now try illustrative questions 31 and 32 at the end of the Study Text

Chapter 15

LINEAR PROGRAMMING: THE SIMPLEX METHOD

> ## This chapter covers the following topics.
>
> 1　Formulating the problem
>
> 2　The initial tableau
>
> 3　Interpreting the final tableau and objective function
>
> 4　Sensitivity analysis
>
> ## Introduction
>
> The linear programming problems in the previous chapter included only **two decision variables**. In practice, few problems will be this simple. A method of solving linear programming problems with two or more decision variables is called the **Simplex method**.
>
> The formulation of the linear programming problem is identical whether it is the Simplex method or the graphical approach which is being used. It is in the solution of the problem that the difference lies. The Simplex method is a **repetitive step by step process** (and therefore an ideal computer application) that tests a number of **feasible solutions** in turn. If the manual process is used this is done in the form of a **tableau** (or table or matrix) of figures.
>
> The chapter is the last in the series which look at the **representation of business situations using models**. In the next, and last, section of the Study Text we turn our attention to **financial mathematics**.

1　FORMULATING THE PROBLEM

1.1　Rather than explaining in words what is involved, the Simplex method is best illustrated by an example.

1.2　Shore Toffer Lott Ltd produces and sells two products, X and Y. Products X and Y require the following resources.

	Materials Units	Labour Hours	Machine time Hours	Contribution per unit £
X, per unit	5	1	3	20
Y, per unit	2	3	2	16
Total available, each week	3,000 units	1,750 hours	2,100 hours	

Although we have just two decision variables, we can still use the Simplex method to solve the problem. We begin by formulating the problem in the usual way.

Define variables　Let x = the number of units of X that should be produced and sold

Let y = the number of units of Y that should be produced and sold

BPP PUBLISHING

Establish constraints	Materials	$5x + 2y \leq 3{,}000$
	Labour	$x + 3y \leq 1{,}750$
	Machine time	$3x + 2y \leq 2{,}100$
	Non-negativity	$x \geq 0, \quad y \geq 0$

Establish objective function   Maximise contribution $(C) = 20x + 16y$

Now we change our approach and introduce the **Simplex method**.

Slack variables

1.3 Using the **Simplex technique**, we begin by **turning each constraint** (ignoring the non-negativity constraints now) **into an equation**. This is done by introducing **slack variables**. A slack variable represents the amount of a constraining resource or item that is unused.

Let   a   be the quantity of unused materials
      b   be the number of unused labour hours
      c   be the number of unused machine hours

1.4 We can now express the original constraints as equations.

$$5x + 2y + a = 3{,}000$$
$$x + 3y + b = 1{,}750$$
$$3x + 2y + c = 2{,}100$$

1.5 The slack variables a, b and c will be equal to 0 in the final solution only if the combined production of X and Y uses up all the available materials (a), labour hours (b) and machine hours (c).

1.6 If there are **n constraints**, there will be **n variables** with a value greater than 0 in any feasible solution. In this example, there are five variables (x, y, a, b and c) in the problem and three equations. In any feasible solution that is tested, three variables will therefore have a non-negative value (since there are three equations) which means that two variables will have a value of zero.

1.7 It is also usual to express the objective function as an **equation** with the **right hand side equal to zero**. In order to keep the problem consistent, the **slack** (or surplus) **variables** are **inserted into the objective function equation**, but as the quantities they represent should have no effect on the objective function they are given zero coefficients. In our example, the objective function will be expressed as follows.

Maximise contribution (C) given by $C - 20x - 16y + 0a + 0b + 0c = 0$.

2   THE INITIAL TABLEAU

2.1 The first feasible solution that we test has a **zero value** for all of the **decision variables** and a **non-negative value** for all the **slack variables**. Obviously this will not be the optimal solution but it gives us a starting point from which we can develop other feasible solutions.

2.2 Simplex tableaux can be drawn in several different ways but the general rules of construction are as follows.

(a) There should be a **column for each variable** (decision and slack). In our example there should be five columns.

(b) There should also be a **solution column** (on the right).

(c) It helps to add a further column the left, to indicate the **variable in the solution** (the non-negative value variables) to which the corresponding value in the solution column relates. In our example there will be three non-negative value variables.

(d) There is a **row for each equation** in the problem. Our example will therefore have three rows (for the three constraints).

(e) There is also a **solution row**.

2.3 The initial tableau for the Shore Toffer Lott Ltd problem is therefore as follows.

Variable in solution	*x*	*y*	*a*	*b*	*c*	*Solution*
a	5	2	1	0	0	3,000
b	1	3	0	1	0	1,750
c	3	2	0	0	1	2,100
Solution	−20	−16	0	0	0	0

2.4 Let us look at how this tableau was put together.

(a) The figures in each row correspond with the **coefficients of the variables** in each of the revised constraints. The bottom row or solution row holds the **coefficients of the revised objective function**. For example the materials constraint $5x + 2y + a = 3,000$ gives us the first row, 5 (number of xs), 2 (number of ys), 1 (number of as) then zeros in the b and c columns (since these do not feature in the constraint equation) and finally 3,000 in the solution column.

(b) The variables in the solution are a, b and c (as indicated by the left hand column).

(i) The value of each variable is shown in the solution column.

(ii) The **column values** for each **variable in the solution** are as follows.

- 1 in the variable's own solution row
- 0 in every other row, including the solution row

(c) The **contribution per unit** obtainable from x and y are given in the solution row. These are called the **shadow prices** or **dual values** of the products X and Y. The minus signs are of no particular significance. An **optimal solution** has been reached when all the elements of the solution row have become positive.

Interpretation of the tableau

2.5 Interpreting the tableau, we can see that the solution is testing a = 3,000, b = 1,750 and c = 2,100, contribution = 0.

2.6 The **shadow prices** in the initial solution (tableau) indicate the following.

(a) The profit would be increased by £20 for every extra unit x produced (because the shadow price of x is £20 per unit).

(b) Similarly, the profit would be increased by £16 for every extra unit of y produced (because its shadow price is £16).

2.7 Since the solution is **not optimal**, the contribution may be improved by introducing either x or y into the solution.

Exercise 1

D Electronics produces three models of satellite dishes - Alpha, Beta and Gamma - which have contributions per unit of £400, £200 and £100 respectively.

There is a two-stage production process and the number of hours per unit for each process are as follows.

	Alpha	Beta	Gamma
Process 1	2	3	2.5
Process 2	3	2	2.0

There is an upper limit on process hours of 1,920 per period for Process 1 and 2,200 for Process 2.

The Alpha dish was designed for a low-power satellite which is now fading and the sales manager thinks that sales will be no more than 200 per period.

Fixed costs are £40,000 per period.

Required

(a)   Formulate these data into a linear programming model using the following notation.

x_1: number of Alphas
x_2: number of Betas
x_3: number of Gammas

(b)   Formulate (but do not attempt to solve) the initial simplex tableau using:

x_4 as slack for Process 1
x_5 as slack for Process 2
x_6 as slack for any sales limit

and describe the meaning of slack.

Solution

(a)   **Define variables**

Let x_1 be the number of Alphas produced/sold per period
Let x_2 be the number of Betas produced/sold per period
Let x_3 be the number of Gammas purchased/sold per period.

Establish constraints

$2x_1 + 3x_2 + 2.5x_3$	$\leq 1,920$	(Process 1)
$3x_1 + 2x_2 + 2x_3$	$\leq 2,200$	(Process 2)
$0 \leq x_1$	≤ 200	(Sales)
x_2 , x_3	≥ 0	(Non-negativity)

Establish objective functions

Maximise $C = 400x_1 + 200x_2 + 100x_3$ (Contribution)

To prepare the initial tableau we need to introduce slack variables.

Let x_4 = quantity of unused process 1 hours
Let x_5 = quantity of unused process 2 hours
Let x_6 = quantity of unused units of Alpha

The revised constraints are as follows.

$2x_1 + 3x_2 + 2.5x_3 + x_4 = 1,920$

$3x_1 + 2x_2 + 2x_3 + x_5 = 2,200$

$x_1 + x_6 = 200$

The objective function can be redefined as

$C - 400x_1 - 200x_2 - 100x_3 + 0x_4 + 0x_5 + 0x_6 = 0$

(b)   The **initial Simplex tabulation** is as follows.

Variable in solution	x_1	x_2	x_3	x_4	x_5	x_6	Solution
x_4	2	3	2.5	1	0	0	1,920
x_5	3	2	2	0	1	0	2,200
x_6	1	0	0	0	0	1	200
Solution	−400	−200	−100	0	0	0	0

3   INTERPRETING THE FINAL TABLEAU AND OBJECTIVE FUNCTION

6/94, 12/94, 6/96, 12/97

3.1   The following tableau is the final solution to the problem introduced in Paragraph 1.2.

Variable in solution	*x*	*y*	*a*	*b*	*c*	*Solution*
x	1	0	0	−0.2857	0.4286	400
a	0	0	1	0.5714	−1.8571	100
y	0	1	0	0.4286	−0.1429	450
Solution	0	0	0	1.1428	6.2858	15,200

3.2   The solution in this tableau is the **optimal** one because the **shadow prices** on the bottom row are **all positive**. The optimal solution is to make and sell 400 units of X and 450 units of Y, to earn a contribution of £15,200. The solution will leave 100 units of materials unused, but will use up all available labour and machine time.

The values in the solution row indicate the shadow price (or dual value) of the variables.

The shadow price of labour time (b) is £1.1428 per hour (bottom of column (b)), which indicates the amount by which contribution would increase/decrease if more/less labour time could be made available at its normal variable cost.

The shadow price of machine time (c) is £6.2858 per hour (bottom of column (c)), which indicates the amount by which contribution would increase/decrease if more/less machine time could be made available, at its normal variable cost.

The shadow price of materials is nil (bottom of column (a)) because there are 100 units of unused materials in the solution and therefore the materials constraint is not critical. Note, however, that if either x or y had a shadow price, this would indicate the amount by which the overall contribution would decrease if one more unit of x or y were produced.

3.3   **In an examination you will probably be asked to interpret the final objective function rather than the final tableau.**

3.4   The final objective function of our example is

CONTRIBUTION = 15,200 − 1.1428 (slack labour time) − 6.2858 (slack machine time)

Exercise 2

When solved by the Simplex method, the final objective function of the problem set out in Exercise 1 is:

CONTRIBUTION = 181,333.3 − 66.67 (Gammas) − 66.67 (slack process 1) − 266.7 (slack sales limit)

Discuss the information contained in this equation.

Solution

Overall contribution = £181,333.30.

Since this is the optimal solution, contribution will *fall* by £66.67 per unit of Gamma produced. (If it were to rise, the solution would not be optimal.)

If the number of Process 1 hours were reduced/increased by one, contribution would fall/rise by £66.67.

If the upper limit on sales of Alpha were reduced/increased by one, contribution would fall/rise by £266.7.

---

4 SENSITIVITY ANALYSIS

4.1 We looked at sensitivity analysis in Chapter 14. You might also be required to carry out some **sensitivity analysis** on the solution to a problem solved by the Simplex method. You might have to work out how the value of the **objective function** might change if there were either more or less of a **scarce resource**. Alternatively you might have to test whether it would be worthwhile to obtain more of a scarce resource by paying a premium for the additional resources, for example by paying an overtime premium for extra labour hours, or by paying a supplier a higher price for extra raw materials.

4.2 Let us go back to our original example and the objective function of the optimal solution:

CONTRIBUTION = 15,200 – 1.1428 (slack labour time) – 6.2858 (slack machine time)

The effect of having more or less of a scarce resource

4.3 **The objective function gives us information about the effect on contribution if additional labour hours or machine time becomes available.** For example, if three additional labour hours became available, contribution would increase by $3 \times £1.1428 = £3.4284$. Note, however, that if extra materials become available contribution would be unaffected because materials availability is not a critical constraint.

4.4 There must be a limit to the number of extra labour hours that would earn an extra £1.1428 towards contribution. As we saw in the previous chapter, there will be a point when there is so much labour available that it is no longer a scarce resource. You can use the same process as set out in Chapter 14 to determine this point.

Exercise 3

Draw a graph of the linear programming problem facing Short Toffer Lott Ltd and determine the number of additional labour hours (over and above the original 1,750 hours) over which the shadow price of £1.1428 per hour is valid.

Solution

The shadow price of £1.1428 per hour is valid for about 1,400 *extra* labour hours.

Obtaining extra resources at a premium on cost

4.5 **The shadow price, or dual price, of a scarce resource indicates the amount by which the value of the objective function would change if more or less units of the scarce resource were available at their normal variable cost per unit.** It follows that if more units of a scarce resource were available at a premium over their normal variable cost, we can decide whether it would be worthwhile paying the premium in order to obtain the extra units.

4.6 Returning for the last time to the example of Shore Toffer Lott Ltd, we are given the following information.

(a) The normal variable cost of labour hours is £4 per hour, but extra labour hours could be worked in overtime, when the rate of pay would be time-and-a-half.

(b) The normal variable cost of machine time is £1.50 per hour, but some extra machine time could be made available by renting another machine for 40 hours per week, at a rental cost of £160. Variable running costs of this machine would be £1.50 per hour.

4.7 We know that the shadow price of labour hours is £1.1428 and of machine hours, £6.2858. We can therefore deduce the following.

(a) Paying an overtime premium of £2 per hour for labour would not be worthwhile, because the extra contribution of £1.1428 per hour would be more than offset by the cost of the premium, leaving the company worse off by £0.0572 per hour worked in overtime.

(b) Renting the extra machine would be worthwhile, but only by £91.43 (which is perhaps too small an amount to bother with).

	£
Extra contribution from 40 hours of machine time ($\times$ £6.2858)	251.43
Rental cost	160.00
Net increase in profit	91.43

Note that the variable running costs do not enter into this calculation since they are identical to the normal variable costs of machine time. We are concerned here only with the **additional costs**.

Exercise 4

A company manufactures three products, tanks, trays and tubs, each of which passes through three processes, X, Y and Z.

	Process hours per unit			Total process
Process	Tanks	Trays	Tubs	hours available
X	5	2	4	12,000
Y	4	5	6	24,000
Z	3	5	4	18,000

The contribution to profit of each product are £2 for each tank, £3 per tray and £4 per tub.

Required

(a) Formulate these data into a linear programming model using the following notation.

Let a   be the number of units of tanks produced
     b   be the number of units of trays produced
     c   be the number of units of tubs produced

(b) Formulate the initial Simplex tableau using the slack variables x, y and z to represent the number of unused hours in processes X, Y and Z respectively.

(c) When the problem is solved by the Simplex method, the final objective function is found to be:

CONTRIBUTION = 14,000 – 2.33 (tanks) – 0.667 (slack Process X) – 0.333 (Slack Process Z)

(i) Discuss the information contained in this equation.

(ii) What would happen to budgeted contribution if an order were received for 300 units of tanks which the company felt that it had to accept, because of the importance of the customer?

Solution

(a) The objective function is to:

Maximise   2a + 3b + 4c (contribution)
Subject to the constraints   5a + 2b + 4c $\leq$ 12,000 (process X hours)
                              4a + 5b + 6c $\leq$ 24,000 (process Y hours)
                              3a + 5b + 4c $\leq$ 18,000 (process Z hours)
                              a, b, c $\geq$ 0

(b) Initial tableau

Variables in the solution	a	b	c	x	y	z	Solution
x	5	2	4	1	0	0	12,000
y	4	5	6	0	1	0	24,000
z	3	5	4	0	0	1	18,000
Solution	–2	–3	–4	0	0	0	0

(c) (i) The maximum contribution available is £14,000

Contribution would fall by £2.33 for every tank produced.

If the number of hours in Process X were reduced/increased by one, contribution would fall/rise by £0.667.

If the number of hours in Process Z were reduced/increased by one, contribution would fall/rise by £0.333.

Process Z hours would be fully utilised in the optimal solution.

(ii) If an order were to be received for 300 tanks and they were produced, contribution would fall by $300 \times £2.333 = £700$.

Chapter roundup

- This chapter has described how to solve a linear programming problem using the **Simplex method**. The method can be used with any number of decision variables, whereas the graphical method can only be applied to problems involving two decision variables.

- For your examination you must be able to **formulate the linear programming problem** and then set up an **initial tableau**. The method for setting up this tableau is as follows.

  ° Turn each constraint (ignoring non-negativity constraints) into an equation by introducing slack variables (which represent the amount of constraining resource or item that is unused).

  ° Express the objective function as an equation with the right hand side equal to zero. Insert the slack variables into the equation, giving them zero coefficients.

  ° The initial feasible solution tested is that all the decision variables have a zero value but all the slack variables have a non-negative value.

  ° There should be a column for each variable and also a solution column.

  ° There is a row for each equation in the problem (which correspond with the coefficients of the variables in each of the revised constraints), and a solution row which holds the coefficients of the revised objective function.

- The final solution is reached when the **shadow prices** on the solution row are all positive. The shadow price indicates the amount by which contribution/profit would increase/decrease if more/less of the resource could be made available at its normal variable cost.

- **Sensitivity analysis** allows you to test the effect of having more or less of a scarce resource or of obtaining extra resources at a premium on cost.

Test your knowledge

1 What is a slack variable? (see para 1.3)

2 How is it possible to differentiate the final tableau from other tableaux? (2.4)

3 What is a shadow price? (2.4)

4 What is involved in doing sensitivity analysis with the Simplex method? (4.1)

Now try illustrative question 33 at the end of the Study Text

Part G
Compound interest and investment appraisal

Chapter 16

INTEREST

This chapter covers the following topics.

1 Simple interest

2 Compound interest

3 Effective and nominal rates of interest

4 Sinking funds

5 Regular investments

Introduction

The previous chapters introduced a variety of quantitative methods relevant to business analysis. This chapter and the next look at aspects of **financial analysis** typically undertaken in a business organisation.

Financial mathematics deals with problems of **investing money**, or **capital**. If a company (or an individual investor) puts some capital into an investment, a **financial return** will be expected.

(a) If Arthur puts £1,000 into an account with a building society, he will expect a return in the form of interest, which will be added to the original investment in his account.

(b) If Newbegin Ltd invests £10,000 in an item of equipment, the company will expect to make a profit out of the item over its working life.

Investors may wish to know the following.

(a) How much return will be obtained by investing money now for a given period, say n years.

(b) How much return will be obtained in n years time by investing some money every year for n years.

Time is an important element in investment decisions. The longer an investment continues, the greater will be the return required by the investor. For example, if a bank lends £20,000 to a company, it would expect bigger interest payments in total if the loan lasted for two years than if it lasted for only one year.

This time factor in investment decisions is not solely to do with **inflation** and the **declining value of money over time**. The required total return would increase the longer an investment lasted even if inflation did not exist. The effect of inflation is simply to **increase** the size of the return required by the investor over **any period of time**.

The two major techniques of financial mathematics are **compounding** and **discounting**. These techniques are very closely related to each other. This chapter will describe compounding and the next will introduce discounting.

---

1 SIMPLE INTEREST

1.1 **Interest is the amount of money which an investment earns over time.**

Simple interest is interest which is earned in equal amounts every year (or month) and which is a given proportion of the original investment (the principal).

1.2 If a sum of money is invested for a period of time, then the amount of simple interest which accrues is equal to the number of periods × the interest rate × the amount invested.

$$P_n = P_o(1 + ni)$$

where P_o = the original sum invested
i = the interest rate (expressed as a proportion, so 10% = 0.1)
n = the number of periods (normally years)
P_n = the sum invested after n periods, consisting of the original capital (P) plus interest earned.

Example: simple interest

1.3 How much will an investor have after five years if he invests £1,000 at 10% simple interest per annum?

Solution

1.4 P_n = £1,000 (1 + (5 × 0.1))
= £1,500

1.5 If, for example, the sum of money is invested for 3 months and the interest rate is a rate per annum, then $n = {}^3/_{12} = {}^1/_4$. If the investment period is 197 days and the rate is an annual rate, then $n = {}^{197}/_{365}$.

2 COMPOUND INTEREST

6/94

2.1 **Interest is normally calculated by means of compounding.**

If a sum of money, the principal, is invested at a fixed rate of interest such that the interest is added to the principal and no withdrawals are made, then the amount invested will grow by an increasing number of pounds in each successive time period, because interest earned in earlier periods will itself earn interest in later periods.

2.2 Suppose, for example, that £2,000 is invested to earn 10% interest. After one year, the original principal plus interest will amount to £2,200.

	£
Original investment	2,000
Interest in the first year (10%)	200
Total investment at the end of one year	2,200

(a) After two years the total investment will be £2,420.

	£
Investment at end of one year	2,200
Interest in the second year (10%)	220
Total investment at the end of two years	2,420

The second year interest of £220 represents 10% of the original investment, and 10% of the interest earned in the first year.

(b) Similarly, after three years, the total investment will be £2,662.

	£
Investment at the end of two years	2,420
Interest in the third year (10%)	242
Total investment at the end of three years	2,662

2.3 **The basic formula for compound interest is $P_n = P_o (1 + i)^n$**

where P_o = the original sum invested
i = the interest rate, expressed as a proportion (so 5% = 0.05)
n = the number of periods
P_n = the sum invested after n periods.

This formula is provided in the examination.

2.4 In the previous example, £2,000 invested at 10% per annum for three years would increase in value to

$$£2,000 \times 1.10^3$$
$$= £2,000 \times 1.331$$
$$= £2,662.$$

The interest earned over three years is £662.

Exercise 1

(a) What would be the total value of £5,000 invested now:

    (i) after three years, if the interest rate is 20% per annum;
    (ii) after four years, if the interest rate is 15% per annum;
    (iii) after three years, if the interest rate is 6% per annum?

(b) At what annual rate of compound interest will £2,000 grow to £2,721 after four years?

Solution

(a) (i) $£5,000 \times 1.20^3 = £8,640$
    (ii) $£5,000 \times 1.15^4 = £8,745.03$
    (iii) $£5,000 \times 1.06^3 = £5,955.08$

(b) $2,721 = 2,000 \times (1 + r)^4$
    $(1 + r)^4 = 2,721/2,000 = 1.3605$
    $1 + r = \sqrt[4]{1.3605} = 1.08$
    $r = 0.08 = 8\%$

Inflation

2.5 The same compounding formula can be used to **predict future prices** after allowing for inflation. For example, if we wish to predict the salary of an employee in five years time, given that he earns £8,000 now and wage inflation is expected to be 10% per annum, the formula would be applied as follows.

$$P_n = P_o (1 + i)^n$$
$$= £8,000 \times 1.10^5$$
$$= £12,884.08$$
$$\text{say,} \quad £12,900.$$

Withdrawals of capital or interest

2.6 If an investor takes money out of an investment, it will cease to earn interest. Thus, if an investor puts £3,000 into a bank deposit account which pays interest at 8% per annum, and makes no withdrawals except at the end of year 2, when he takes out £1,000, what would be the balance in his account after four years?

	£
Original investment	3,000.00
Interest in year 1 (8%)	240.00
Investment at end of year 1	3,240.00
Interest in year 2 (8%)	259.20
Investment at end of year 2	3,499.20
Less withdrawal	1,000.00
Net investment at start of year 3	2,499.20
Interest in year 3 (8%)	199.94
Investment at end of year 3	2,699.14
Interest in year 4 (8%)	215.93
Investment at end of year 4	2,915.07

2.7 A quicker approach would be as follows.

	£
£3,000 invested for 2 years at 8% would increase in value to £3,000 × 1.08^2 =	3,499.20
Less withdrawal	1,000.00
	2,499.20

£2,499.20 invested for a further two years at 8% would increase in value to
£2,499.20 × 1.08^2 = £2,915.07

Changes in the rate of interest

2.8 **If the rate of interest changes during the period of an investment, the compounding formula must be amended slightly,** as follows.

$$P_n = P_o (1 + i_1)^x (1 + i_2)^{n-x}$$

where
i_1 = the initial rate of interest
x = the number of years in which the interest rate r_1 applies
i_2 = the next rate of interest
n – x = the (balancing) number of years in which the interest rate r_2 applies.

Exercise 2

(a) If £8,000 is invested now, to earn 10% interest for three years and 8% thereafter, what would be the size of the total investment at the end of five years?

(b) An investor puts £10,000 into an investment for ten years. The annual rate of interest earned is 15% for the first four years, 12% for the next four years and 9% for the final two years. How much will the investment be worth at the end of ten years?

(c) An item of equipment costs £6,000 now. The annual rates of inflation over the next four years are expected to be 16%, 20%, 15% and 10%. How much would the equipment cost after four years?

Solution

(a) £8,000 × 1.10^3 × 1.08^2 = £12,419.83

(b) £10,000 × 1.15^4 × 1.12^4 × 1.09^2 = £32,697.64

(c) £6,000 × 1.16 × 1.20 × 1.15 × 1.10   = £10,565.28

---

3 EFFECTIVE AND NOMINAL RATES OF INTEREST   *6/94, 12/95*

Effective annual rate of interest

3.1 In the previous examples, interest has been calculated **annually**, but this need not be the case. Interest may be compounded **daily**, **weekly**, **monthly** or **quarterly**.

The **equivalent annual rate of interest**, when interest is compounded at shorter intervals, may be calculated as follows. This is known as an **effective annual rate of interest**.

$$\textbf{Effective Annual Rate} = [(1+i)^{\frac{12}{n}} - 1] \text{ or } [(1+i)^{\frac{365}{x}} - 1]$$

where   i is the rate of interest for each time period
n is the number of months in the time period
x is the number of days in the time period.

Example: the effective annual rate of interest

3.2 Calculate the effective annual rate of interest of:

(a) 1.5% per month, compound;
(b) 4.5% per quarter, compound;
(c) 9% per half year, compound.

Solution

3.3   (a) $(1.015)^{12} - 1 \;= 0.1956 = 19.56\%$
     (b) $(1.045)^{4} - 1 \;= 0.1925 = 19.25\%$
     (c) $(1.09)^{2} - 1 \;= 0.1881 = 18.81\%$

Nominal rates of interest and the annual percentage rate

3.4   Most interest rates are expressed as **per annum figures** even when the interest is compounded over periods of less than one year. In such cases, the given interest rate is called a **nominal rate**. We can, however, work out the **effective rate**. It is this effective rate (shortened to one decimal place) which is quoted in advertisements as the **annual percentage rate (APR)**, sometimes called the **compound annual rate (CAR)**.

Depending on whether the compounding is done daily, weekly, monthly, quarterly or six monthly, the APR will vary by differing amounts from the nominal rate.

Example: nominal and effective rates of interest

3.5   A building society may offer investors 10% per annum interest payable half-yearly. If the 10% is a nominal rate of interest, the building society would in fact pay 5% every six months, compounded so that the effective annual rate of interest would be

$$[(1.05)^{2} - 1] = 0.1025 = 10.25\% \text{ per annum.}$$

3.6   Similarly, if a bank offers depositors a nominal 12% per annum, with interest payable quarterly, the effective rate of interest would be 3% compound every three months, which is

$$[(1.03)^{4} - 1] = 0.1255 = 12.55\% \text{ per annum.}$$

Exercise 3

Calculate the effective annual rate of interest of:

(a)   15% nominal per annum compounded quarterly;

(b)   24% nominal per annum compounded monthly.

Solution

(a)   15% per annum (nominal rate) is 3.75% per quarter. The effective annual rate of interest is

      $[1.0375^{4} - 1] = 0.1587 = 15.87\%$

(b)   24% per annum (nominal rate) is 2% per month. The effective annual rate of interest is

      $[1.02^{12} - 1] = 0.2682 = 26.82\%$

---

4   SINKING FUNDS   *12/94, 12/95, 6/96, 12/97, 6/99*

4.1   **A sinking fund is an investment into which equal annual instalments are paid in order to earn interest, so that by the end of a given number of years, the investment is large enough to pay off a known commitment at that time.**

4.2   Thus, if Arthur needs £5,000 in three years time, he could make an annual payment into a sinking fund, so that after three years, the total investment (payments into the fund plus interest earned) equals £5,000.

4.3   **Sinking funds are commonly used for the repayment of debt.** Another common known future commitment is the need to replace an asset at the end of its life. To ensure that the money is available to buy a replacement, a company might decide to invest cash in a sinking fund during the course of the life of the existing asset.

Example: sinking funds

4.4　A company has just bought an asset with a life of four years. At the end of four years, a replacement asset will cost £12,000, and the company has decided to provide for this future commitment by setting up a sinking fund into which equal annual investments will be made, starting at year 1 (one year from now). The fund is expected to earn interest at the rate of 12% per annum.

4.5　The total value of an investment (fund) at the end of n years is given by the formula:

$$= \frac{a[(1+i)^n - 1]}{i}$$

where a is the annual investment and i is the rate of interest earned, expressed as a proportion.

4.6　In the examination you are provided with the following general formula of the value of an investment of £1 per annum over n years at a rate of interest of i per annum:

$$S_n = \frac{(1+i)^n - 1}{i}$$

4.7　Let us go back to our example. Since the fund must equal £12,000 by year 4,

$$12,000 = \frac{a \times (1.12^4 - 1)}{1.12 - 1}$$

$$12,000 = \frac{0.5735193a}{0.12}$$

$$a = £2,510.81$$

Four investments, each of £2,510.81, should therefore be enough to allow the company to replace the asset.

Sinking fund schedules

4.8　A schedule can be written out to show the **growth of a sinking fund**, with a column for the interest earned, a column for the total increase in the fund each year (the interest plus the regular payment), and a column for the value of the fund.

Example: sinking fund schedules

4.9　A company has decided to set up a sinking fund to replace an asset in six years time. The value of the fund after six years must be £80,000 and the fund is expected to earn interest at the rate of 8% per annum.

Required

(a)　Calculate the annual payment into the fund, commencing at year 1 and with a final payment at year 6.

(b)　Prepare a schedule showing the growth of the fund.

Solution

4.10 (a) $80,000 = a\left(\dfrac{1.08^6 - 1}{0.08}\right)$

$80,000 = \dfrac{0.5868743a}{0.08}$

a $= £10,905.23.$

(b)

Year	Interest on fund £	Increase in fund £	Value of fund £
0	0	0	0
1	0	10,905.23	10,905.23
2	872.42	11,777.65	22,682.88
3	1,814.63	12,719.86	35,402.74
4	2,832.22	13,737.45	49,140.19
5	3,931.22	14,836.45	63,976.64
6	5,118.13	16,023.36	80,000.00

Exercise 4

A company has set up a sinking fund into which equal annual instalments will be paid to provide for the replacement of an asset in five years time. It is anticipated that the asset will cost £20,000. The funds are expected to earn interest at 15% per annum.

Required

(a) Calculate the annual payment, commencing at year 1 and ending in year 5.
(b) Prepare a schedule showing the growth of the fund.

Solution

(a) $20,000 = \dfrac{a(1.15^5 - 1)}{0.15}$

∴ a = £2,966.31

(b)

Year	Interest on fund £	Increase in fund £	Value of fund £
1	0	2,966.31	2,966.31
2	444.95	3,411.26	6,377.57
3	956.64	3,922.95	10,300.52
4	1,545.08	4,511.39	14,811.91
5	2,221.79	5,188.10	20,000.01

Example: a sinking fund to repay a loan

4.11 Submerged Ltd intends to purchase new equipment costing £30,000. The funds to buy the equipment are being provided as a loan by the managing director. The agreed rate of interest is 12%, and the loan will be repayable in full with interest at the end of the four-year term.

To provide for this eventual repayment, the board of directors of Submerged Ltd decide to put an equal annual amount at the end of each year into a sinking fund, which will earn 15% per annum interest.

Required

Calculate the annual payment into the sinking fund which will repay the loan after four years.

Solution

4.12 Let the annual payments into the sinking fund be £S.

The cash flows are as follows.

Year		Cash flow
1	Payment into sinking fund	S
2	Payment into sinking fund	S
3	Payment into sinking fund	S
4	Payment into sinking fund	S
4	Repay loan	$30,000 \times 1.12^4$

By year 4, the value of the sinking fund must have risen to $£30,000 \times 1.12^4 = £47,205.58$ to enable the company to repay the loan in full with interest at 12%.

4.13 $S\left[\dfrac{(1.15)^4 - 1}{0.15}\right]$ has to equal $£30,000 \times (1.12)^4$

$$\therefore 4.993375S = £47,3205.58$$
$$S = £9,453.64$$

4.14 Annual payments into a sinking fund of £9,453.58 at the end of each year will therefore create a fund large enough, earning 15% per annum, to repay a loan at the end of four years, where the original loan is £30,000 and interest on the loan is at 12%.

Sinking funds and mortgages

4.15 **Repayments against a repayment mortgage can also be seen as payments into a sinking fund**. The total of the constant annual payments (which are usually paid in equal monthly instalments) plus the interest they earn over the term of the mortgage must be sufficient to pay off the initial loan plus accrued interest, interest being added to the loan retrospectively at the end of each year.

Example: mortgage

4.16 Sam has taken out a £30,000 mortgage over 25 years. Interest is to be charged at 10% per annum. Calculate the monthly repayment assuming that the repayments will earn interest at 13% per annum.

Solution

4.17 $S = £30,000 \times (1.10)^{25} = £325,041$

$$\therefore £325,041 = \frac{a((1.13)^{25} - 1)}{0.13}$$

Annual repayment = £2,089

$\therefore$ Monthly repayment = £174.08

Sinking funds and debt

4.18 The sinking fund schedule drawn up when a sinking fund is used to repay debt is slightly different to those we have encountered so far.

Example: sinking funds and debt

4.19 Suppose a company borrows £40,000, which is compounded at 10%. The debt will be discharged at the end of four years with regular annual payments into a sinking fund which pays 8%. Calculate the annual payment into the fund and construct a schedule, assuming the first payment into the fund is made a year from now.

Solution

4.20 In four year's time the debt $= £40,000 \times (1.1)^4$
$= £58,564$

$$£58,564 = \frac{a((1.08)^4 - 1)}{0.08}$$

$\therefore a = £12,996.57$

Sinking fund schedule

Year	Debt at start of year £	Interest £	Debt at end of year £	Amount in fund at start of year £	Interest earned £	Payments into fund £	Amount in in fund at at year end £
1	40,000	4,000	44,000	-	-	12,996.57	12,996.57
2	44,000	4,400	48,400	12,996.57	1,039.73	12,996.57	27,032.87
3	48,400	4,840	53,240	27,032.87	2,162.63	12,996.57	42,192.07
4	53,240	5,324	58,564	42,192.07	3,375.36	12,996.57	58,564.00

5 REGULAR INVESTMENTS
12/95

5.1 An investor may decide to add to his investment from time to time, and you may be asked to calculate the **final value** (or **terminal value**) of an investment to which equal annual amounts will be added. An example might be an individual or a company making annual payments into a pension fund: we may wish to know the value of the fund after n years.

Example: regular investments at the beginning of each year

5.2 A person invests £400 now, and a further £400 each year for three more years.

Required

Calculate how much the total investment would be worth after four years, if interest is earned at the rate of 10% per annum.

Solution

5.3 In problems such as this, we call now 'Year 0', the time one year from now 'Year 1' and so on.

			£
(Year 0)	The first year's investment will grow to £400 $(1.10)^4$	=	585.64
(Year 1)	The second year's investment will grow to £400 $(1.10)^3$	=	532.40
(Year 2)	The third year's investment will grow to £400 $(1.10)^2$	=	484.00
(Year 3)	The fourth year's investment will grow to £400 (1.10)	=	440.00
			2,042.04

5.4 You may be able to identify a **geometric progression** here. The solution is

$$(400 \times 1.1) + (400 \times 1.1^2) + (400 \times 1.1^3) + (400 \times 1.1^4)$$

(with the values placed in reverse order, for convenience).

The formula for the sum of such a progression is

$$S_n = \frac{a(r^n - 1)}{(r - 1)}$$

where a is the initial expression in the series
       r is the common ratio between the expressions
       n is the number of expressions

$$S_4 = \frac{400 \times 1.1 \times (1.1^4 - 1)}{1.1 - 1} = \frac{440 \times 0.4641}{0.1} = \text{£2,042.04}$$

A general formula is given in your examination in the form

$$S_n = \frac{(1 + i)^n - 1}{i}$$

Example: regular investments at the end of each year

5.5 If, in the previous example, the investments had been made at the end of each of the first, second, third and fourth years, so that the last £400 invested had no time to earn interest, the value of the fund after four years would have been

$$400 + (400 \times 1.1) + (400 \times 1.1^2) + (400 \times 1.1^3)$$

$$= \frac{400 \times (1.1^4 - 1)}{1.1 - 1} = \text{£1,856.40}$$

5.6 If our investor made investments as in Paragraph 5.5, but also put in a £2,500 lump sum one year from now, the value of the fund after four years would be

$$\text{£1,856.40} + \text{£2,500} \times 1.1^3$$

$$= \text{£1,856.40} + \text{£3,327.50} = \text{£5,183.90}$$

That is, we can compound parts of investments separately, and add up the results.

Tables for compounding

5.7 In your examination, you will be provided with financial tables, as reproduced at the end of this book. You should now look at the first table (**compound interest**) and the third table (**the future value of an annuity**), and follow the following example of their use. (**An annuity is a series of annual payments.**)

Example: the use of tables

5.8 (a) £1,000 is invested at 10% per annum compound interest. How much will the investment have grown to after six years?

(b) £600 is invested at 5% per annum compound interest for three years, and the interest rate is then increased to 10% for two years. £200 is then withdrawn, and the remaining investment earns 15% interest for four years. What is the total investment at the end of that time?

(c) An investor puts £400 into a fund each year for four years, making the first investment at the end of the first year. The fund earns compound interest at 10% per annum. What will be the value of the fund at the end of the four years?

(d) An investor puts £700 into a fund each year for five years, making the first investment at the start of the first year. The fund earns compound interest at 15% per annum. What will be the value of the fund at the end of the five years?

Solution

5.9 (a) In the first table, in the column for 10% and the row for six years, we find 1.77156.

The answer is £1,000 × 1.77156 = £1,771.56.

(b) £600 × 1.15763 = £694.58
£694.58 × 1.21 = £840.44
£840.44 − £200 = £640.44
£640.44 × 1.74901 = £1,120.14
The final balance is £1,120.14.

(c) In the third table, in the column for 10% and the row for four years, we find 4.64100.

The answer is £400 × 4.64100 = £1,856.40

(d) **The table for the future value of an annuity assumes payments are made at the end of each year.** If payments are made in advance, that is, at the beginning of each year, we need to add one year's interest on the total value of the fund, as follows.

£700 × 6.74238 × 1.15 = £5,427.62.

Exercise 5

What annual payment must be made into a sinking fund to replace an asset which will cost £73,500 in three years' time, if the investments will earn interest at 10% per annum and the first investment will be a year from now? Use tables.

Solution

£73,500 = 3.31 × a

∴a = £22,205.44

Chapter roundup

- **Simple interest** is interest which is earned in equal amounts every year (or month) and which is a given proportion of the principal. The simple interest formula is $Pn = Po (1 + ni)$.

- **Compounding** means that, as interest is earned, it is added to the original investment and starts to earn interest itself. The basic formula for compound interest is $Pn = Po (1 + i)n$.

- If the rate of interest changes during the period of an investment, the compounding formula must be amended slightly to $Pn = Po (1 + i1)x (1 + i2)n-x$.

- If interest is compounded at shorter intervals than a year, an **effective annual rate of interest** can be calculated.

- Most interest rates are expressed as per annum figures even when the interest is compounded over periods of less than one year. In such cases, the given interest rate is called a **nominal rate**. The **annual percentage rate (APR)** is the rate of interest an investment would earn if the interest were calculated only once a year.

- A **sinking fund** is an investment into which equal annual instalments are paid in order to earn interest, so that by the end of a given number of years, the investment is large enough to pay off a known commitment at that time.

- The **terminal value** of regular investments can be calculated using a geometric progression formula.

Test your knowledge

1   If a sum P is invested earning a simple annual interest rate of r, how much will the investor have after n years? (see para 1.2)

2   If a sum P is invested earning a compound annual interest rate of r, how much will the investor have after n years? (2.3)

3   How should withdrawals of money be dealt with in compound interest calculations? (2.6, 2.7)

4   How should changes in the rate of interest be dealt with in compound interest calculations? (2.8)

5   What is meant by an effective annual rate of interest? (3.1)

6   What is a sinking fund? (4.1)

7   What is an annuity? (5.7)

Now try illustrative questions 34 and 35 at the end of the Study Text

Chapter 17

DISCOUNTING

This chapter covers the following topics.

1   The concept of discounting

2   The net present value (NPV) method

3   Annuities

4   The internal rate of return (IRR) method

Introduction

Discounting is the reverse of compounding, the topic of the previous chapter. Its major application in business is in **investment appraisal**, to decide whether investments offer a satisfactory return to the investor.

---

1   THE CONCEPT OF DISCOUNTING

The basic principles of discounting

1.1   The basic principle of compounding is that if we invest £P now for n years at i% interest per annum, we should obtain $£P_o (1 + i)^n$ in n years time (where i is expressed as a proportion).

1.2   Thus if we invest £10,000 now for four years at 10% interest per annum, we will have a total investment worth $£10,000 \times 1.10^4 = £14,641$ at the end of four years (that is, at year 4 if it is now year 0).

1.3   **The basic principle of discounting is that if we wish to have £S in n years' time, we need to invest a certain sum now (year 0) at an interest rate of i% in order to obtain the required sum of money in the future.**

1.4   For example, if we wish to have £14,641 in four years time, how much money would we need to invest now at 10% interest per annum? This is the reverse of the situation described in Paragraph 1.2.

Let P_o be the amount of money invested now.

$$£14,641 = P_o \times 1.10^4$$
$$P_o = £14,641 \times \frac{1}{1.10^4} = £10,000$$

1.5   £10,000 now, with the capacity to earn a return of 10% per annum, is the equivalent in value of £14,641 after four years. We can therefore say that £10,000 is the *present value* of £14,641 at year 4, at an interest rate of 10%.

Present value

1.6   The term 'present value' (PV) simply means the amount of money which must be invested now (P_o) for n years at an interest rate of i%, to earn a given future sum of money (P_n) at the time it will be due.

The formula for discounting

1.7   The **discounting formula** is

$$PV = P_n \times \frac{1}{(1+i)^n}$$

where P_n is the sum to be received after n time periods
            PV   is the present value of that sum
            i   is the interest rate, expressed as a proportion
            n   is the number of time periods (usually years).

The rate i is sometimes called the **rate of return** (that is, the return (as a proportion) that can be obtained on an investment)

Example: discounting

1.8   (a)   Calculate the present value of £60,000 at year 6, if an interest rate (or a return) of 15% per annum is obtainable.

        (b)   Calculate the present value of £100,000 at year 5, if an interest rate (or a return) of 6% per annum is obtainable.

        (c)   How much would a person need to invest now at 12% to earn £4,000 at year 2 and £4,000 at year 3?

Solution

1.9   (a)   PV $= 60,000 \times \dfrac{1}{1.15^6}$

                    $= 60,000 \times 0.43233$
                    $=$ £25,939.80

        (b)   PV $= 100,000 \times \dfrac{1}{1.06^5}$

                    $= 100,000 \times 0.74726$
                    $=$ £74,726

        (c)   PV $= (4,000 \times \dfrac{1}{1.12^2}) + (4,000 \times \dfrac{1}{1.12^3})$

                    $= 4,000 \times (0.79719 + 0.71178)$
                    $=$ £6,035.88

This calculation can be checked as follows.

	£
Year 0	6,035.88
Interest for the first year (12%)	724.31
	6,760.19
Interest for the second year (12%)	811.22
	7,571.41
Less withdrawal	(4,000.00)
	3,571.41
Interest for the third year (12%)	428.57
	3,999.98
Less withdrawal	(4,000.00)
Rounding error	0.02

Exercise 1

What is the present value at 7% interest of £16,000 at year 12?

Solution

$$PV = £16,000 \times \frac{1}{1.07^{12}} = £7,104$$

Investment appraisal

1.10 **Discounted cash flow techniques can be used to evaluate capital expenditure proposals (investments).**

1.11 Discounted cash flow (DCF) involves the application of discounting arithmetic to the estimated future cash flows (receipts and expenditures) from a project in order to decide whether the project is expected to earn a satisfactory rate of return.

There are two methods of using DCF techniques.

- The **net present value** (NPV) method
- The **internal rate of return** (IRR) method

2 THE NET PRESENT VALUE (NPV) METHOD   *6/94, 12/98*

2.1 The **net present value (NPV) method** works out the **present values** of all items of income and expenditure related to an investment at a given rate of return, and then works out a net total. If it is **positive**, the investment is considered to be **acceptable**. If it is **negative**, the investment is considered to be **unacceptable**.

Example: the net present value of a project

2.2 Dog Ltd is considering whether to spend £5,000 on an item of equipment. The 'cash profits', the excess of income over cash expenditure, from the project would be £3,000 in the first year and £4,000 in the second year.

The company will not invest in any project unless it offers a return in excess of 15% per annum.

Required

Assess whether the investment is worthwhile, or 'viable'.

Solution

2.3 In this example, an outlay of £5,000 now promises a return of £3,000 *during* the first year and £4,000 *during* the second year. It is a convention in DCF, however, that cash flows spread over a year are assumed to occur *at the end of the year*, so that the cash flows of the project are as follows.

	£
Year 0 (now)	(5,000)
Year 1 (at the end of the year)	3,000
Year 2 (at the end of the year)	4,000

2.4 The NPV method takes the following approach.

(a) The project offers £3,000 at year 1 and £4,000 at year 2, for an outlay of £5,000 now.

(b) The company might invest elsewhere to earn a return of 15% per annum.

(c) If the company did invest at exactly 15% per annum, how much would it need to invest now, at 15%, to earn £3,000 at the end of year 1 plus £4,000 at the end of year 2?

(d) Is it cheaper to invest £5,000 in the project, or to invest elsewhere at 15%, in order to obtain these future cash flows?

2.5 If the company did invest elsewhere at 15% per annum, the amount required to earn £3,000 in year 1 and £4,000 in year 2 would be as follows.

Year	Cash flow £	Discount factor 15%	Present value £
1	3,000	$\dfrac{1}{1.15} = 0.86957$	2,608.71
2	4,000	$\dfrac{1}{(1.15)^2} = 0.75614$	3,024.56
			5,633.27

2.6 The choice is to invest £5,000 in the project, or £5,633.27 elsewhere at 15%, in order to obtain these future cash flows. We can therefore reach the following conclusion.

(a) It is cheaper to invest in the project, by £633.27.
(b) The project offers a return of over 15% per annum.

2.7 The net present value is the difference between the present value of cash inflows from the project (£5,633.27) and the present value of future cash outflows (in this example, £5,000 × $1/1.15^0$ = £5,000).

2.8 An NPV statement could be drawn up as follows.

Year	Cash flow £	Discount factor 15%	Present value £
0	(5,000)	1.00000	(5,000.00)
1	3,000	$\dfrac{1}{1.15} = 0.86957$	2,608.71
2	4,000	$\dfrac{1}{(1.15)^2} = 0.75614$	3,024.56
		Net present value	+633.27

The project has a positive net present value, so it is acceptable.

Exercise 2

A company is wondering whether to spend £18,000 on an item of equipment, in order to obtain cash profits as follows.

Year	£
1	6,000
2	8,000
3	5,000
4	1,000

The company requires a return of 10% per annum.

Required

Use the NPV method to assess whether the project is viable.

Solution

	Cash flow £	Discount factor 10%	Present value £
0	(18,000)	1.00000	(18,000.00)
1	6,000	$\dfrac{1}{1.10} = 0.90909$	5,454.54
2	8,000	$\dfrac{1}{1.10^2} = 0.82645$	6,611.60
3	5,000	$\dfrac{1}{1.10^3} = 0.75131$	3,756.55
4	1,000	$\dfrac{1}{1.10^4} = 0.68301$	683.01
		Net present value	(1,494.30)

The NPV is negative. We can therefore draw the following conclusions.

(a) It is cheaper to invest elsewhere at 10% than to invest in the project.
(b) The project would earn a return of less than 10%.
(c) The project is not viable.

Discount tables

2.9 Assuming that money earns, say, 10% per annum:

(a) the PV (present value) of £1 at year 1 is $£1 \times \dfrac{1}{1.10}$ $= £1 \times 0.90909$;

(b) similarly, the PV of £1 at year 2 is $£1 \times \dfrac{1}{(1.10)^2}$ $= £1 \times 0.82645$;

(c) the PV of £1 at year 3 is $£1 \times \dfrac{1}{(1.10)^3}$ $= £1 \times 0.75131$.

Discount tables show the value of $1/(1 + i)^n$ for different values of i and n. The 10% discount factors of 0.90909, 0.82645 and 0.75131 are shown in the discount tables at the end of this Study Text in the column for 10%. (You will be given discount tables in your examination.)

Exercise 3

Daisy Ltd is considering whether to make an investment costing £28,000 which would earn £8,000 cash per annum for five years. The company expects to make a return of at least 15% per annum.

Required

Assess whether the project is viable.

Solution

Year	Cash flow £	Discount factor 15%	Present value £
0	(28,000)	1.00000	(28,000.00)
1	8,000	0.86957	6,956.56
2	8,000	0.75614	6,049.12
3	8,000	0.65752	5,260.16
4	8,000	0.57175	4,574.00
5	8,000	0.49718	3,977.44
		NPV	(1,182.72)

The NPV is negative, therefore the project is not viable because it earns less than 15% per annum.

3   ANNUITIES

3.1   **An annuity is a constant sum of money each year for a given number of years**.

In the exercise at the end of Section 2, there was a constant annual cash flow of £8,000 for five years, years 1 to 5.

Annuity tables

3.2   To calculate the present value of a constant annual cash flow, or annuity, we can multiply the annual cash flows by **cumulative present value factors** or **annuity factors**. There are tables for **annuity factors**, which are shown at the end of this text (table 4: present value of an annuity). For example, the **cumulative present value factor** of £1 per annum for five years at 15% per annum is in the column for 15% and the year 5 row, and is 3.35216. The present value in Exercise 3 could have been calculated as £8,000 × 3.35216 – £28,000 = – £1,182.72.

Example: the present value of an annuity

3.3   (a)   The PV of £100 earned each year from years 3 to 6 when the required return is 5% per annum is found as follows.

PV of £1 per annum for years 1 to 6 at 5%	5.07569
Less PV of £1 per annum for years 1 to 2 at 5%	1.85941
PV of £1 per annum for years 3 to 6 at 5%	3.21628

£100 × 3.21628 = £321.63

(b)   Hannah U Witty Ltd is considering a project which would cost £10,500 now and earn £3,000 per annum in years 1 to 4 and £2,000 per annum in years 5 and 6. The appropriate discount rate is 10%. Is the project viable?

PV of £1 per annum at 10%, years 1 to 6	4.35526
Less PV of £1 per annum at 10%, years 1 to 4	3.16987
PV of £1 per annum at 10%, years 5 to 6	1.18539

Years	Cash flow £	Discount factor 10%	Present value £
0	(10,500)	1.00000	(10,500.00)
1 - 4	3,000	3.16987	9,509.61
5 - 6	2,000	1.18539	2,370.78
		Net present value	1,380.39

The project has a **positive NPV** and is therefore **viable** because it will earn more than 10% per annum.

The formula for the present value of an annuity

3.4   You may be expected to use a formula to calculate the **present value of an annuity**. The formula is a development of the formula for the **sum of a geometric progression**.

The **present value of an annuity** of £a starting a year from now is as follows.

$$PV = \frac{a}{1+r} + \frac{a}{(1+r)^2} + \frac{a}{1(+r)^3} + \cdots + \frac{a}{(1+r)^n}$$

3.5   This is a **geometric progression** with a first term of $\frac{a}{(1+r)}$ and a common ratio between expressions of $\frac{1}{(1+r)}$. The formula for the sum is $a\left[\dfrac{1-(\frac{1}{1+r})^n}{r}\right]$

3.6 This formula is given in your examination, with 'a' taken to be 1 and therefore omitted, with i for r and with $\left(\dfrac{1}{1+i}\right)^{n}$ written as $(1+i)^{-n}$. The formula given is

$$a_n = \frac{1-(1+i)^{-n}}{i}$$

Example: the formula for the present value of an annuity

3.7 What is the present value of £4,000 per annum for years 1 to 4, at a discount rate of 10% per annum?

Solution

3.8 $PV = \dfrac{4,000(1-(\frac{1}{1.10})^{4})}{0.1}$

$\quad = \dfrac{4,000 \times (1-0.68301)}{0.1} = £12,679.60$

This can be checked from the annuity tables: the PV for years 1 to 4 is £4,000 × 3.16987 = £12,679.48, so there is a small rounding error.

Exercise 4

What is the present value of £4,000 per annum for four years, years 2 to 5, at a discount rate of 10% per annum? Use the formula and not tables.

Solution

The formula gives the present value at the year preceding the first annuity cash flow. Using the formula will thus give us the present value at one year before year 2 (the year of the first annuity cash flow), ie year 1.

We therefore have to discount the solution further, from a year 1 value to a year 0 value.

$$PV = \frac{4,000(1-(\frac{1}{1.10})^{4})}{0.1} \times \frac{1}{1.10}$$

$$= £12,679.60 \times \frac{1}{1.10}$$

$$= £11,526.90$$

Calculating a required annuity

3.9 If $PV = \dfrac{a\left(1-\left(\dfrac{1}{1+r}\right)^{n}\right)}{r}$

then $a = \dfrac{PV \times r}{\left(1-\left(\dfrac{1}{1+r}\right)^{n}\right)}$

This enables us to calculate the annuity required to yield a given rate of return (r) on a given investment.

Example: calculating a required annuity

3.10 A building society grants a £3,000 mortgage at 10% per annum. The borrower is to repay the loan in six annual instalments. How much must he pay each year?

Solution

3.11 $\quad a \quad = \dfrac{3,000 \times 0.10}{(1 - \frac{1}{1.10^6})}$

$\qquad = \dfrac{300}{1 - 0.56447}$

$\qquad = \dfrac{300}{0.43553} = £688.82$ per annum

The use of annuity tables to calculate a required annuity

3.12 Just as the formula can be used to calculate an annuity, so too can the tables. Since the present value of an annuity is **PV = a × annuity factor** from the tables, we have

$\qquad a \quad = \dfrac{PV}{\text{annuity factor}}$

3.13 In the previous example, the annual repayment on the mortgage would be

$$\frac{£3,000}{\text{PV factor of £1 per annum at 10\% for 6 years}}$$

$\qquad = \dfrac{£3,000}{4.35526}$

$\qquad = £688.82$

Perpetuities

3.14 **A perpetuity is an annuity which lasts for ever, instead of stopping after n years.**

3.15 The **present value of a perpetuity is PV = a/r** where r is the cost of capital as a proportion.

Example: a perpetuity

3.16 Mostly Ltd is considering a project which would cost £50,000 now and yield £9,000 per annum every year in perpetuity, starting a year from now. The cost of capital is 15%.

Required

Assess whether the project is viable.

Solution

3.17

Year	Cash flow £	Discount factor 15%	Present value £
0	(50,000)	1.0	(50,000)
1 - ∞	9,000	1/0.15	60,000
		NPV	10,000

The project is **viable** because it has a **positive net present value** when discounted at 15%.

The timing of cash flows

3.18 Note that both annuity tables and our formulae **assume that the first payment or receipt is a year from now**. Always check examination questions for when the first payment falls.

For example, if there are four equal payments starting now, and the interest rate is 5%, we should use a factor of 1 (for today's payment) + 2.72325 (for the other three payments) = 3.72325.

4 THE INTERNAL RATE OF RETURN (IRR) METHOD   *6/94, 6/96, 12/98*

4.1 **The internal rate of return (IRR) method of evaluating investments is an alternative to the NPV method.**

4.2 The NPV method of discounted cash flow determines whether an investment earns a positive or a negative NPV when discounted at a given rate of interest. If the NPV is zero (that is, the present values of costs and benefits are equal) the return from the project would be exactly the rate used for discounting.

4.3 **The IRR method of discounted cash flow is to determine the rate of interest (the internal rate of return) at which the NPV is 0. The internal rate of return is therefore the rate of return on an investment.**

4.4 The IRR method will indicate that a project is **viable** if the **IRR exceeds the minimum acceptable rate of return**. Thus if the company expects a minimum return of, say, 15%, a project would be viable if its IRR is more than 15%.

Example: the IRR method over one year

4.5 If £500 is invested today and generates £600 in one year's time, the internal rate of return (r) can be calculated as follows.

PV of cost $=$ PV of benefits

$$500 = \frac{600}{(1+r)}$$

$$500(1+r) = 600$$

$$1+r = \frac{600}{500} = 1.2$$

$$r = 0.2 = 20\%$$

Example: the internal rate of return (2)

4.6 If £1,000 is invested today and generates £700 in the first year and £600 in the second year the internal rate of return can be calculated as follows.

PV of cost = PV of benefits

$$1,000 = \frac{700}{(1+r)} + \frac{600}{(1+r)^2}$$

Multiply both sides by $(1 + r)^2$

$1,000 (1 + r)^2 = 700 \times (1 + r) + 600$

$1,000 + 2,000r + 1,000r^2 = 700 + 700r + 600$

$1,000r^2 + 1,300r - 300 = 0$

$10r^2 + 13r - 3 = 0$

$$r = \frac{-13 \pm \sqrt{[169 - (4 \times 10 \times (-3))]}}{20}$$

$$= \frac{-13-17}{20} \text{ or } \frac{-13+17}{20}$$

$$= -1.5 \text{ or } +0.2$$

$$= -150\% \text{ or } 20\%$$

Since high negative returns are not a practical proposition, r = 20%.

4.7 **The IRR method will indicate that a project is viable if the IRR exceeds the minimum acceptable rate of return**. Thus if the company expects a minimum return of, say, 15%, a project would be viable if its IRR is more than 15%.

4.8 The arithmetic for calculating the IRR is more complicated for investments and cash flows extending over a period of time longer than one year. A technique known as the **interpolation method** can be used to calculate an approximate IRR.

Example: interpolation

4.9 A project costing £800 in year 0 is expected to earn £400 in year 1, £300 in year 2 and £200 in year 3.

Required

Calculate the internal rate of return.

Solution

4.10 The IRR is calculated by first of all finding **the NPV at each of two interest rates**. Ideally, one interest rate should give a small positive NPV and the other a small negative NPV. The IRR would then be somewhere between these two interest rates: above the rate where the NPV is positive, but below the rate where the NPV is negative.

4.11 A very rough guideline for estimating at what interest rate the NPV might be close to zero, is to take

$$\tfrac{2}{3} \times (\frac{\text{profit}}{\text{cost of the project}})$$

In our example, the total profit over three years is £(400 + 300 + 200 − 800) = £100. An approximate IRR is therefore calculated as:

$$\tfrac{2}{3} \times \frac{100}{800} = 0.08 \text{ approx.}$$

A starting point is to try 8%.

(a) Try 8%

Year	Cash flow £	Discount factor 8%	Present value £
0	(800)	1.00000	(800)
1	400	0.92593	370
2	300	0.85734	257
3	200	0.79383	159
		NPV	(14)

The NPV is negative, therefore the project fails to earn 8% and the IRR must be less than 8%.

(b) Try 6%

Year	Cash flow £	Discount factor 6%	Present value £
0	(800)	1.00000	(800)
1	400	0.94340	377
2	300	0.89000	267
3	200	0.83962	168
		NPV	12

The NPV is positive, therefore the project earns more than 6% and less than 8%.

4.12 The IRR is now calculated by **interpolation**. The result will **not be exact**, but it will be a **close approximation. Interpolation assumes that the NPV falls in a straight line** from +12 at 6% to −14 at 8%.

Graph to show IRR calculation by interpolation

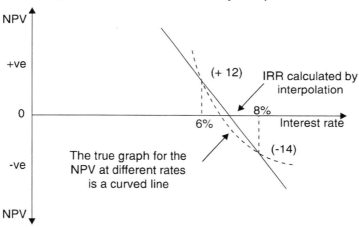

4.13 The IRR, where the NPV is zero, can be calculated as:

$$a\% + \left[\frac{A}{A-B} \times (b-a)\right]\% \text{ where}$$

a is one interest rate
b is the other interest rate
A is the NPV at rate a
B is the NPV at rate b

$$\text{IRR} = 6\% + \left[\frac{12}{(12+14)} \times (8-6)\right]\%$$

$$= 6\% + 0.92\%$$

$$= 6.92\% \text{ approx}$$

4.14 The answer is only an **approximation** because the NPV falls in a **slightly curved line** and not a straight line between +12 and −14. Provided that NPVs close to zero are used, the **linear assumption** used in the interpolation method is nevertheless fairly accurate.

4.15 Note that the formula will still work if A and B are **both positive**, or **both negative**, and even if a and b are a long way from the true IRR, but the results will be less accurate.

4.16 The graph in Paragraph 4.12 indicates that the IRR is approximately 7% (the point where the straight line crosses the horizontal axis). Using a graph rather interpolation may be perfectly acceptable in certain questions. Read examination questions carefully for phrases such as 'using a graph, determine the IRR'.

Chapter roundup

- **Discounting** is the reverse of compounding. The discounting formula is $P = Sn \times 1/(1+r)n$.

- The concept of present value can be thought of in two ways.
    - It is the value today of an amount to be received some time in the future.
    - It is the amount which would have to be invested today to produce a given amount at some future date.

- **Discounted cash flow techniques** can be used to evaluate capital expenditure projects. There are two methods: the **NPV method** and the **IRR method**.

- The **NPV method** works out the present values of all items of income and expenditure related to an investment at a given rate of return, and then works out a net total. If it is **positive**, the investment is considered to be **acceptable**. If it is **negative**, the investment is considered to be **unacceptable**.

- An **annuity** is a constant sum of money each year for a given number of years.

- A **perpetuity** is an annuity which lasts forever, instead of stopping after n years.

- The **IRR method** is to determine the rate of interest (the IRR) at which the NPV is 0. Interpolation, using the following formula, is often necessary. The project is viable if the IRR exceeds the minimum acceptable return.

$$\text{IRR} = a\% + \left[\frac{A}{A-B} \times (b-a) \right]\%$$

- Ensure that you are aware of all of the points above and can use the formulae correctly.

Test your knowledge

1 What is the meaning of the term 'present value'? (see para 1.6)

2 What is the present value of a sum of money P_n in n years time, given an interest rate of r? (1.7)

3 What are the two usual methods of capital expenditure appraisal using DCF techniques? (1.11)

4 What is an annuity? (3.1)

5 What is the formula for the present value of an annuity? (3.4)

6 What is a perpetuity? (3.14)

7 What is the formula for a present value of a perpetuity? (3.15)

8 What is the internal rate of return of an investment? (4.3)

9 How would you determine the internal rate of return of a series of cash flows using interpolation? (4.10 - 4.13)

Now try illustrative questions 36 and 37 at the end of the Study Text

Appendix: Tables and formulae

TABLES AND FORMULAE

FINANCIAL TABLES

1 Compound interest

Year	5%	10%	15%	20%
0	1.00000	1.00000	1.00000	1.00000
1	1.05000	1.10000	1.15000	1.20000
2	1.10250	1.21000	1.32250	1.44000
3	1.15763	1.33100	1.52088	1.72800
4	1.21551	1.46410	1.74901	2.07360
5	1.27628	1.61051	2.01136	2.48832
6	1.34010	1.77156	2.31306	2.98598
8	1.47746	2.14359	3.05902	4.29982
10	1.62890	2.59374	4.04556	6.19174

2 Discount factors

Year	5%	10%	15%	20%
0	1.00000	1.00000	1.00000	1.00000
1	0.95238	0.90909	0.86957	0.83333
2	0.90703	0.82645	0.75614	0.69444
3	0.86384	0.75131	0.65752	0.57870
4	0.82270	0.68301	0.57175	0.48225
5	0.78353	0.62092	0.49718	0.40188
6	0.74622	0.56447	0.43233	0.33490
8	0.67684	0.46651	0.32690	0.23257
10	0.61391	0.38554	0.24719	0.16151

3 s_n = Future Value of an Annuity

Year	5%	10%	15%	20%
1	1.00000	1.00000	1.00000	1.00000
2	2.05000	2.10000	2.15000	2.20000
3	3.15250	3.31000	3.47250	3.64000
4	4.31013	4.64100	4.99338	5.36800
5	5.52563	6.10510	6.74238	7.44160
6	6.80191	7.71561	8.75374	9.92992
8	9.54911	11.43589	13.72682	16.49908
10	12.57789	15.93742	20.30372	25.95868

4 a_n = Present Value of an Annuity

Year	5%	10%	15%	20%
1	0.95238	0.90909	0.86957	0.83333
2	1.85941	1.73554	1.62571	1.52778
3	2.72325	2.48685	2.28323	2.10648
4	3.54595	3.16987	2.85498	2.58873
5	4.32948	3.79079	3.35216	2.99061
6	5.07569	4.35526	3.78448	3.32551
8	6.46321	5.33493	4.48732	3.83716
10	7.72174	6.14457	5.01877	4.19247

Table of Areas of the Normal Distribution

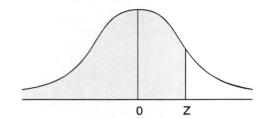

Standardised Deviate Z	Area to left of Z	Standardised Deviate Z	Area to left of Z
0.00	0.5000	1.96	0.9750
0.25	0.5987	2.00	0.9772
0.50	0.6915	2.25	0.9878
0.67	0.7486	2.33	0.9901
0.75	0.7734	2.50	0.9938
1.00	0.8413	2.58	0.9951
1.25	0.8944	2.75	0.9970
1.50	0.9332	3.00	0.9987
1.64	0.9495	3.09	0.9990
1.75	0.9599		

VALUE OF NEGATIVE EXPONENTIAL FUNCTION

x	e^{-x}	x	e^{-x}
0	1.00000	5	0.00674
1	0.36788	6	0.00248
2	0.13534	7	0.00091
3	0.04979	8	0.00034
4	0.01832	9	0.00012

BASIC FORMULAE

These formula are supplied for assistance only. Their use is *not* compulsory.

Arithmetic mean and standard deviation

$$\bar{x} = \frac{\Sigma fx}{\Sigma f} \qquad s = \sqrt{\frac{\Sigma fx^2}{\Sigma f} - \frac{(\Sigma fx)^2}{(\Sigma f)^2}}$$

Quartile deviation $= \dfrac{Q_3 - Q_1}{2}$

Skewness

Quartile measure $= \dfrac{Q_3 + Q_1 - 2(\text{Median})}{Q_3 - Q_1}$

Pearson measure $= \dfrac{3(\bar{x} - \text{Median})}{s}$

Coefficient of variation $= \dfrac{100s}{\bar{x}}$

Spearman rank correlation coefficient

$$r_s = 1 - \frac{6\Sigma d^2}{n(n^2-1)}$$

Product moment correlation coefficient

$$r = \frac{n\Sigma xy - \Sigma x \Sigma y}{\sqrt{(n\Sigma x^2 - (\Sigma x)^2)(n\Sigma y^2 - (\Sigma y)^2)}}$$

Regression.

Regression line of y on x: $y = a + bx$

$$b = \frac{n\Sigma xy - \Sigma x \Sigma y}{n\Sigma x^2 - (\Sigma x)^2} \qquad a = \frac{\Sigma y}{n} - \frac{b\Sigma x}{n}$$

Standard error of a sample mean

$$= \frac{\sigma}{\sqrt{n}} \text{ or } \frac{s}{\sqrt{n}} \text{ when } \sigma \text{ is unknown.}$$

Standard error of a sample proportion

$$= \sqrt{\frac{\pi(1-\pi)}{n}} \text{ or } \sqrt{\frac{p(1-p)}{n}} \text{ when } \pi \text{ is unknown.}$$

Index numbers

$\dfrac{\Sigma wI}{\Sigma w}$ where w = Weight; I = Price relative

	Price	*Quantity*
Laspeyre	$\dfrac{\Sigma P_n Q_0}{\Sigma P_0 Q_0} \times 100$	$\dfrac{\Sigma P_0 Q_n}{\Sigma P_0 Q_0} \times 100$
Paasche	$\dfrac{\Sigma P_n Q_n}{\Sigma P_0 Q_n} \times 100$	$\dfrac{\Sigma P_n Q_n}{\Sigma P_n Q_0} \times 100$
Fisher's ideal	$\sqrt{\text{Laspeyre} \times \text{Paasche}}$	

Compound interest $Pn = Po(1 + i)^n$

Present value of an annuity : $a_{n\rceil} = \dfrac{1-(1+i)^{-n}}{i}$

Sinking fund or future value of an annuity: $s_{n\rceil} = \dfrac{(1+i)^n - 1}{i}$

Discounted values

$$\frac{A_1}{(1+r)} + \frac{A_2}{(1+r)^2} + \frac{A_3}{(1+r)^3} + \dots \frac{A_n}{(1+r)^n}$$

Illustrative questions

Exam standard questions have mark and time allocations.

1 KILBURN LTD

(a) Explain the importance of careful planning for a statistical survey, and list the matters which should be considered.

(b) Kilburn Ltd is planning to survey its regular customers, by sending each of them a questionnaire asking about delivery times, the quality of goods and payment terms.

Outline the problems which may arise with the survey, and suggest how they might be overcome.

2 COLLECTING DATA (25 marks) *45 mins*

(a) Compare and contrast the interview and the postal questionnaire as methods of collecting data.

(9 marks)

(b) Compare quota sampling and random sampling as survey methods. (9 marks)

(c) The major survey conducted by most countries is a population census. Outline the main reasons why population censuses are usually conducted only every ten years. (7 marks)

3 SAMPLING METHODS

(a) Sampling methods are frequently used for the collection of data. Explain the terms simple random sampling, stratified random sampling and sampling frame.

(b) Suggest a suitable sampling frame for each of the following in which statistical data will be collected.

(i) An investigation into the reactions of workers in a large factory to new proposals for shift working

(ii) A survey of students at a college about the relevance and quality of the teaching for their **professional examinations**

(iii) An enquiry into the use of home computers by school children in a large city

(c) Explain briefly, with reasons, the type of sampling method you would recommend in each of the three situations given above.

4 MODERNISATION (25 marks) *45 mins*

The head office of a company is situated in Central London. The building is in urgent need of modernisation and refurbishment. The lease on the head office is due to run out in 4 years time. The company has a number of options.

(a) Apply to have the lease extended.
(b) Search for an up-to-date office accommodation in Central London.
(c) Move out of London into a new purpose-built office block.

The advantage of option (c) is that the cost of office space is much cheaper outside London. Staff would be easier to recruit and rates of pay outside London are much lower. It is expected that some office staff would wish to move outside London since house prices are cheaper and travelling time and travelling expenses are much lower. Relocation expenses (removal costs, all expenses in buying and selling a property, new carpets and curtains etc) would be met. However, it is thought that the majority of staff would accept redundancy payments which would be more generous than those under the Government scheme.

The company decides to send a questionnaire together with a short explanatory letter to all the London employees to find out their views on the possibility of a move out of London.

Required

Draft the explanatory letter and the questionnaire.

5   THE SOYUZ INSURANCE COMPANY (25 marks)   *45 mins*

(a)   By 20X9, the Soyuz Insurance Company had been in business for nine years. It now employs 20,770 people, of whom the largest group (36%) were sales staff, the next largest group (21%) were accountants and the third largest group (18%) were actuaries. Other groups of employees made up the rest of the staff.

Things had been very different when the company first began operations in 20X0. Then, it had just 4,200 employees, of whom the 1,260 actuaries were the biggest group; there were 1,176 sales staff and just 840 accountants.

By 20X3, the company had nearly doubled in size, employing 7,650 people, of whom 2,448 were actuaries, 2,372 were sales staff and 1,607 were accountants.

By 20X6, the company employed 12,740 people, and the growth in numbers had been most noticeable amongst sales staff, of whom there were 4,840. There were 3,185 actuaries. Accountants had increased substantially in number to 2,550.

The company's managing director has been very pleased with the growth in business over the past nine years, but has tried to limit the growth in the numbers of staff who are not sales staff, actuaries or accountants.

Required

Present the data above in tabular form.

Explain whether there are any comments you would make about what the information in the table should tell the managing director of the company.   (9 marks)

(b)   The management of Tell Hall Ltd wish to present some information about results to employees. It has been decided that a visual form of display would be the best way to communicate the information.

The relevant data are as follows.

	20X5 £'000	20X4 £'000	20X3 £'000	20X2 £'000	20X1 £'000
Sales	5.2	5.1	4.8	4.0	3.5
Costs					
Direct materials	1.5	1.4	1.2	1.0	0.8
Direct wages	2.3	1.8	1.6	1.3	1.0
Production overhead	0.7	0.7	0.6	0.5	0.4
Other overhead	0.6	0.5	0.4	0.3	0.2
Taxation	0.0	0.3	0.4	0.3	0.3
Profit	0.1	0.4	0.6	0.6	0.8

Product groups, as a percentage of total sales.

Product group	20X5 %	20X4 %	20X3 %	20X2 %	20X1 %
W	33	36	38	30	25
X	5	10	12	18	25
Y	46	36	30	30	25
Z	16	18	20	22	25
	100	100	100	100	100

Required

Prepare two different visual displays to show the following.

(i)   Sales by product group   (8 marks)

(ii)   A comparison of 20X4 with 20X5, analysing total sales into costs, taxation and profit, with particular emphasis on direct wages   (8 marks)

6   GRADES OF EMPLOYEE

(a)   The following table shows the salary, in pounds, of various grades of computing employee in four regions of a country.

	Region of the country			
Job title	North	South	East	West
Manager	17,000	18,000	21,000	23,000
Project leader	15,000	19,000	17,000	17,000
Analyst	14,000	14,000	16,000	14,000

Required

Using a suitable form of bar chart, display this information graphically.

(b) A survey produced the following data on the number of terminals on 315 company sites.

Number of terminals	Number of sites
1 - 5	100
6 - 10	90
11 - 20	60
21 - 50	45
51 - 100	20
	315

Required

Draw a histogram of the above data.

(c) Briefly explain the differences between a bar chart and a histogram.

7 COMPONENT BAR CHART (25 marks) *45 mins*

(a) Your company is preparing its published accounts and the chairman has requested that the assets of the company be compared in a component bar chart for the last five years. The data are contained in the following table.

Asset	20X3 £'000	20X4 £'000	20X5 £'000	20X6 £'000	20X7 £'000
Property	59	59	65	70	74
Plant and machinery	176	179	195	210	200
Stock and work in progress	409	409	448	516	479
Debtors	330	313	384	374	479
Cash	7	60	29	74	74

Required

(i) Construct the necessary component bar chart.
(ii) Comment upon the movements in the assets over the five-year period. (12 marks)

(b) The company has a Canadian subsidiary. During this year the Finance Director has monitored weekly the exchange rate of the Canadian dollar to the pound, after each Monday's trading. His findings are summarised in the following table.

Rate of Exchange Canadian dollars to £1	Number of weeks
1.80 but less than 1.85	1
1.85 but less than 1.90	8
1.90 but less than 1.95	2
1.95 but less than 2.00	6
2.00 but less than 2.05	3
2.05 but less than 2.10	5
2.10 but less than 2.15	6
2.15 but less than 2.20	10
2.20 but less than 2.25	10
2.25 but less than 2.30	1

Required

(i) Plot an ogive from these data.
(ii) Determine the median exchange rate from the ogive.
(iii) Determine the lower and upper quartiles of the exchange rate using the ogive.

(13 marks)

---

8   GRUFF DRAWERS LTD (25 marks)   *45 mins*

(a)   Gruff Drawers Ltd has five factories, and output at each factory for the last five years has been as follows (in thousands of standard hours).

			Factories		
Year	*A*	*B*	*C*	*D*	*E*
20X1	250	608	326	563	294
20X2	258	638	339	597	323
20X3	271	670	353	627	333
20X4	290	704	381	645	363
20X5	316	746	419	652	370

Required

(i)   Convert these figures to a basis which enables the changes in output to be readily compared.

(ii)   Plot your findings on a graph.   (12 marks)

(b)   The following figures relate to the distribution of wealth in Utopia in the years 20X0 and 20X9.

Net wealth per household		*20X0*		*20X9*	
		No. of household s	*Total wealth of households in wealth class*	*No. of household s*	*Total wealth of households*
Over	*Not over*				
Dollars	*Dollars*	*('000)*	*('000m dollars)*	*('000)*	*('000m dollars)*
-	1,000	5,200	2.6	3,500	2.0
1,000	3,000	5,400	8.6	4,900	7.4
3,000	5,000	3,100	14.0	2,900	13.1
5,000	8,000	2,200	14.3	3,800	24.9
8,000	12,000	1,200	11.8	1,500	14.7
12,000	16,000	600	8.4	700	9.9
16,000	25,000	300	6.0	500	11.2
25,000	50,000	100	3.8	200	7.4
50,000	100,000	100	7.5	100	7.5
100,000	-	100	1.5	0	0
		18,300	78.5	18,100	98.1

Required

Present the information in the form of a Lorenz curve and comment on the results.   (13 marks)

---

9   PRODCO LTD

The manufacturing costs of Prodco Ltd for the period from January 20X6 to December 20X7 are displayed in the table below.

Month 20X6	*Manufacturing costs £'000*	*Month 20X7*	*Manufacturing costs £'000*
January	35.8	January	43.9
February	33.6	February	40.1
March	35.5	March	46.0
April	37.5	April	48.7
May	37.2	May	48.9
June	34.6	June	46.0
July	36.3	July	48.3
August	36.0	August	47.9
September	35.4	September	48.2
October	30.4	October	47.0
November	36.1	November	49.4
December	37.5	December	51.6

Required

(a)   Draw a Z chart using the above data.

(b)   Describe the purpose of such a chart. Use the diagram that you have just drawn to illustrate your answer.

10   HANDLING COSTS (25 marks)   *45 mins*

(a)   The cost accountant of Ware Howser Ltd has calculated standard costs for handling items of stock in a warehouse. The costs are based on the labour time required to deal with stock movements, and are as follows.

Time required for job of handling stock Minutes	Standard cost £
Less than 10	9
≥ 10 and up to 20	11
≥ 20 and up to 40	13
≥ 40 and up to 60	15
≥ 60 and up to 90	23
≥ 90 and up to 120	29
≥ 120 and up to 180	38

The warehouse operates a working day of seven hours, and a five day week. There are 12 people employed.

An examination of the time sheets for a typical week showed that the following costs had been incurred.

Standard cost £	Frequency
9	240
11	340
13	150
15	120
23	20
29	20
38	10

Required

(i)   Estimate the mean handling time for a stock movement.   (6 marks)

(ii)   Estimate the total number of hours in the week spent moving items of stock.

(2 marks)

(iii) Calculate the percentage capacity utilisation of the labour force in the warehouse.

(2 marks)

(iv) Calculate the average number of jobs handled by each employee each week if each individual job is dealt with by one person.   (2 marks)

(b)   The following figures were published by the National Gardeners Association.

Earnings in 20X2		
At least £	Not more than £	Number of gardeners
0	500	1
500	1,000	4
1,000	1,500	6
1,500	2,000	12
2,000	2,500	9
2,500	3,000	7
3,000	3,500	5
3,500	4,000	3
4,000	4,500	2
4,500	5,000	1

Illustrative questions

Required

(i)	Calculate the modal earnings.	(3 marks)
(ii)	Calculate the median earnings.	(5 marks)
(iii)	Calculate the arithmetic mean earnings.	(5 marks)

11   JOURNEY TIMES

(a)   Set out the advantages and disadvantages of the mean, median, and mode as measures of central tendency.

(b)   Journey times to work of employees of a company are as follows.

Time Minutes	No of employees
less than 10	14
10 but less than 20	26
20 but less than 30	64
30 but less than 40	46
40 but less than 50	28
50 but less than 60	16
60 but less than 80	8
80 but less than 100	4

Required

(i)   Obtain the mean, median and mode of travel time to work.

(ii)   Negotiations are under consideration for payment for average travelling time to work. State, giving reasons, which measure of central tendency you would use if you are (1) the employer, and (2) a trade union representing the employees.

12   AVERAGES AND DISPERSION (25 marks)   *45 mins*

(a)   From the figures given below, calculate:

(i)   the range;
(ii)   the arithmetic mean;
(iii)   the median;
(iv)   the lower quartile;
(v)   the upper quartile;
(vi)   the mean deviation;
(vii)   the standard deviation.

3	14	24	33	42
6	17	25	37	48
9	18	27	38	51
10	21	31	40	56
12	61	63	65	74

(8 marks)

(b)   Explain the term 'measure of dispersion' and briefly list the advantages and disadvantages of using:

(i)   the range;
(ii)   the quartile deviation;
(iii)   the mean deviation;
(iv)   the standard deviation.

(6 marks)

(c)   On the Monday morning of each week, a supervisor gives her 14 employees their work schedules for the next five days. She speaks to each employee separately, and goes over any points of detail which may need to be cleared up and answers any questions about the individual's schedule.

The time required to deal with each employee varies. As soon as she has finished with one employee, the supervisor is free to see the next. There are periods when employees are queuing to see her, and there are periods when she is free.

The following data are for the interview times on one Monday morning.

Employee No.	Arrival time Starts interview	Completion time Ends interview
1	9.00	9.03
2	9.03	9.07
3	9.07	9.09
4	9.11	9.16
5	9.16	9.19
6	9.22	9.24
7	9.24	9.27
8	9.27	9.28
9	9.30	9.34
10	9.34	9.36
11	9.36	9.40
12	9.42	9.45
13	9.45	9.50
14	9.50	9.52

Required

(i) Illustrate the variability of interview times by preparing a frequency distribution. Calculate the mean interview time for this distribution. (4 marks)

(ii) Calculate the standard deviation of the interview times for this distribution. (4 marks)

(iii) Each employee is given a certain number of tasks for the week. Over a year, the mean weekly number of tasks for one employee is 27, with a standard deviation of 4.2 tasks. Calculate the mean and standard deviation for the number of tasks performed by that employee over a six-week period. State any assumption you make. (3 marks)

13 EARNINGS (25 marks)   *45 mins*

(a) The following data on earnings in a company are supplied.

Daily earnings £ £	Number of employees
≥ 40 and <50	2
≥ 50 and <60	15
≥ 60 and <70	21
≥ 70 and <80	30
≥ 80 and <90	20
≥ 90 and <100	9
≥ 100 and <110	3

(i) Calculate the following from these data.

(1) The mean
(2) The standard deviation
(3) The coefficient of variation
(4) The median (7 marks)

(ii) Since the mean and the median can be the same number, explain the different interpretations of the data to be derived from each. (3 marks)

(iii) Define and explain the use of:

(1) the standard deviation;
(2) the coefficient of variation. (3 marks)

(b)

Average weekly hours of work of full time employees
in non-manual occupations in 20X6

Hours	Men %	Women %
under 34	5.0	10.2
34 but under 36	18.6	23.9
36 but under 40	56.7	58.9
40 but under 44	9.7	4.6
44 but under 48	4.7	1.4
48 but under 50	1.5	0.4
50 and over	3.8	0.6

Source: New Earnings Survey 20X6

Required

(i)   Compare the two distributions by finding the median, lower quartile, upper quartile and quartile deviation.   (7 marks)

(ii)   Write a brief report on the data and your findings.   (5 marks)

14   **REGRESSION LINE**

You are given the following values for pairs of data, x and y.

x	y
9	16
11	20
14	25
17	28
20	34
21	35
25	44

Required

(a)   Calculate the correlation coefficient.

(b)   Use the least squares method to determine the equation of the straight line which best fits the data.

(c)   Draw a scattergraph of the data, and plot the least squares regression line on this graph.

15   **GILBERT LTD (25 marks)**   *45 mins*

(a)   Gilbert Ltd employs a large number of sales staff who submit quarterly claims for travel. A random sample of ten of these staff have submitted claims stating the number of miles (in hundreds) that they drove on company business during January - March, quarter 1, and April - June, quarter 2. Over these periods the company pays 17.5 pence per mile travelled.

Salesperson	Miles travelled in quarter 1 ('00)	Miles travelled in quarter 2 ('00)
A	28	45
B	26	54
C	35	49
D	20	36
E	30	50
F	16	32
G	40	64
H	36	56
I	24	44
J	25	50

Required

(i)   Without using the data for quarter 1, obtain an estimate for the average travel expenses per sales person to be paid in quarter 2.

(ii)   (1)   Determine the least squares regression line that predicts the miles travelled in the second quarter of the year based on the miles travelled in the first quarter.

        (2)   The average distance travelled by all the company's sales staff in quarter 1 is known to be 3,000 miles.

                Use the regression equation in (1) to obtain an estimate for the average travel expenses per sales person in quarter 2.

(iii)   Assess the strength of correlation between the sample mileage figures for the two quarters.   (9 marks)

(b)   Give an example of a pair of variables you would expect to be positively correlated and an example of a pair of variables you would expect to be negatively correlated.   (3 marks)

(c)   A large manufacturing company is investigating the cost of sickness amongst production workers who have been employed by the company for more than one year. The following regression equation, based on a random sample of 50 such production workers, was derived for 20X5.

$$y = 15.6 - 1.2x$$

y represents the number of days absent because of sickness and x represents the number of years employment with the company. The coefficient of determination, r^2, was 0.9.

Required

(i)   State the value of the correlation coefficient.

(ii)   State the meaning of the coefficients in the equation.

(iii)   Predict the number of days absence through sickness to be expected of an employee who has been with the company for eight years.

(iv)   Draw a scatter diagram, including the regression line, to illustrate approximately the situation in this manufacturing company.

(v)   List any limitations or problems of using this equation in practice.   (13 marks)

16   RANK CORRELATION

(a)   Describe the difference between the product moment and the rank coefficients of correlation and explain the circumstances in which one might prefer to use each of them.

(b)   Research has been conducted into the percentage recall of advertising material amongst a panel of readers of daily newspapers. Members of the panel have also been asked to indicate their liking for each newspaper by placing them in order of preference. From the summary data that follow calculate the rank coefficient of correlation and comment upon the result.

Newspaper	Order of preference	% recall of advertisements
A	9	7.2
B	3	9.8
C	10	6.8
D	1	11.5
E	6	9.3
F	4	10.3
G	12	4.6
H	2	10.7
I	7	6.4
J	11	5.3
K	5	8.7
L	8	7.2

17 MOVING AVERAGE

The output of a factory, in standard hours, over a period of 16 months, has been as follows.

20X3	Output '000s of standard hours	20X4	Output '000s of standard hours
May	40.6	January	37.9
June	33.3	February	36.4
July	29.5	March	43.7
August	34.8	April	40.0
September	36.1	May	38.2
October	42.2	June	32.2
November	40.5	July	34.6
December	31.1	August	35.8

Required

(a) Round the output figures to the nearest whole thousand standard hours.

(b) Calculate a four-month moving average of the rounded series. Do not round your averages.

(c) Plot the actual and moving average series on a graph, from July 20X3 to June 20X4.

18 HOPWOOD TRENDS LTD

The quarterly sales of Hopwood Trends Ltd in recent years have been as follows.

	Quarter			
	1	2	3	4
	Units	Units	Units	Units
20X2	200	110	320	240
20X3	214	118	334	260
20X4	220	124	340	278

Required

(a) Calculate a moving average of quarterly sales.

(b) Calculate the average seasonal variations.

(c) Use the results of (a) and (b) to predict sales in the third quarter of 20X5.

19 PRICE RELATIVES

A company wishes to construct a price index for three commodities, A, B and C. The prices in 20X0 were £2, £3 and £5 respectively and quantities consumed in the same period were 5,000, 6,000 and 3,000 respectively. The prices for 20X1 and 20X2 are given as percentages of 20X0 prices.

	20X1	20X2
A	100	110
B	108	115
C	90	100

Required

Construct a price index using 20X0 as a base year.

20 PRICE AND QUANTITY (25 marks)　　　　　　　　　　　　　　　　*45 mins*

(a) Compute a price index at 1 July 20X6 for the following basket of items (using the Laspeyre method) taking 1 July 20X2 as the base date.

Items	Quantity used per week 1 July 20X2 Units	Quantity used per week 1 July 20X6 Units	Cost of the item 1 July 20X2 £ per unit	Cost of the item 1 July 20X6 £ per unit
Widgets	18	19	8	6
Fidgets	12	11	7	8
Splodgets	24	27	2	4
Tudgets	15	11	6	7
Ringlets	8	12	10	9

(4 marks)

(b) A factory makes three products, hocks, nocks and socks. The factory manager wishes to establish a productivity index by which to measure changes in productivity from month to month. Each product has a different work content, and is therefore given a weighting. The weightings to be used are as follows.

Hocks	9
Nocks	4
Socks	5

In addition, some months contain more working days than others, and the index must be designed so as to offset the effects of this.

Data for October, November and December 20X3 were as follows.

	October	November	December
Working days	22	20	16
Output (units)			
Hocks	30	25	24
Nocks	24	28	20
Socks	18	20	16

October 20X3 has been selected as the base month, with a productivity index of 100.

Required

(i) Calculate productivity index values for November and December 20X3. (5 marks)

(ii) Suppose that at the beginning of January 20X4, a new weight is required for socks, to reflect changes in the work content in its production. Production data for the second and third weeks of January, when productivity was judged about equal, were as follows.

	Week 2 (5 days)	Week 3 (5 days)
Hocks	7	6
Nocks	7	10
Socks	6	5

If there is no change in the weighting of hocks and nocks, use these data to recommend a new weighting for socks. (4 marks)

(c) La Passion Spares Ltd has been in business for ten years, and now has four independent divisions operating in four different product markets. Results for the ten years have been as follows.

	Division A		Division B		Division C		Division D	
	Sales volume '000 units	Value £m	Sales volume '000 units	Value £m	Sales volume '000 units	Value £m	Sales volume '000 units	Value £m
20X0	3.0	0.30	-	-	-	-	-	-
20X1	3.2	0.32	-	-	-	-	-	-
20X2	3.5	0.37	1.0	0.20	-	-	-	-
20X3	3.6	0.40	1.4	0.29	-	-	-	-
20X4	3.8	0.44	1.5	0.32	0.8	0.08	-	-
20X5	3.9	0.47	1.8	0.43	1.0	0.11	4.0	0.25
20X6	4.0	0.52	2.1	0.51	1.2	0.14	4.3	0.30
20X7	4.2	0.57	2.2	0.55	1.3	0.16	4.2	0.32
20X8	4.0	0.56	2.4	0.67	1.5	0.20	4.4	0.35
20X9	3.0	0.33	2.5	0.75	1.0	0.14	4.6	0.41

The company wishes to establish an index to measure changes in the volume of the business. 20X5 is to be the base year.

Required

(i)   Calculate the index figure for 20X9 using:

(1)   the Laspeyre method;
(2)   the Paasche method.   (6 marks)

Note that you should first calculate unit selling prices.

(ii)   Explain why 20X5, and not 20X0 (the year the company began operations) was chosen as the base year.   (2 marks)

(iii) Explain why the Paasche index might be preferable in this example to the Laspeyre index.

(2 marks)

(iv)   The sales in 20X5 totalled £1,260,000 and in 20X9 £1,630,000. This is an increase of £370,000 or 29%. Explain why your solutions in (a) did not give an index value of 129 in 20X9.   (2 marks)

21   PROBABILITIES

(a)   Probability theory is a branch of statistics which attempts to predict the likelihood of a particular event occurring out of a large population of events. Explain and elaborate on this statement

(b)   Here are some data.

	Number surviving at each age	
Age in years	Male	Female
0	100,000	100,000
10	89,023	91,083
25	85,824	88,133
50	74,794	78,958
80	16,199	24,869

Required

Calculate for each sex the probability:

(i)   at birth of reaching the age of 80 years;
(ii)   that a person aged 25 years will *not* survive to the age of 50;
(iii) that a new born baby will survive the first ten years of life;
(iv)   that a person aged 50 will *not* survive to the age of 80.

Comment on your results.

22   PERRY WINKLE LTD (25 marks)   *45 mins*

The directors and senior managers of Perry Winkle Ltd have met to consider three subjects.

(a)   There is a proposal to move the head office of the company from London to Liverpool, and the current state of opinion appears to be as follows.

	In favour	Opposed	Undecided	Total
Executive directors	4	1	2	7
Non-executive directors	2	3	3	8
Senior managers	7	12	2	21
	13	16	7	36

Required

Calculate the probability that a person at the meeting, selected at random, will be:

(i)   an executive director in favour of the proposal;
(ii)   opposed to the proposal;
(iii)   either a senior manager or undecided about the proposal.   (5 marks)

(b)   Two independent major installations of new equipment are about to take place. The time to complete each installation is uncertain, but the following probabilities have been estimated.

Installation A		*Installation B*	
Duration	*Probability*	*Duration*	*Probability*
Months		Months	
1	0.1	2	0.6
2	0.2	3	0.2
3	0.6	4	0.2
4	0.1		

Required

(i)   Calculate the probability that:

(1)   both installations are completed within three months;
(2)   both installations are completed within three months, but not within two months;
(3)   both installations are completed at the same time;
(4)   installation A is completed before installation B.

(ii)   Decide which installation has the shorter expected completion time.   (10 marks)

(c)   The company manufactures and sells a single product, the Clam. Estimated sales, costs and selling prices for the coming year are as follows.

Sales	*Probability*	*Selling price per unit*	*Probability*
Units		£	
10,000	0.4	8.00	0.3
15,000	0.4	7.50	0.6
20,000	0.2	7.00	0.1

Variable cost per unit	*Probability*	*Fixed costs for the year*	*Probability*
£		£	
5.00	0.1	12,000	0.4
5.50	0.2	15,000	0.6
5.80	0.5		
6.00	0.2		

The outcome for each item (selling price, sales, variable and fixed costs) is in no way dependent on the outcome of any other item.

Required

(i)   Calculate the expected annual profit.

(ii)   Calculate the worst possible result for the coming year, and the probability that this will occur.   (10 marks)

23 THREE MACHINES

A factory has a machine shop in which three machines (A, B and C) each produce 100cm aluminium tubes. An inspector is equally likely to sample tubes from A and B and three times as likely to select from C as he is from B. The defective rates from the three machines are

A 10%   B 10%   C 20%

Required

Calculate the probability that a tube selected by the inspector:

(a)   is from machine A;
(b)   is defective;
(c)   comes from machine A, given that it is defective.

24 ONE IN A MILLION LTD (25 marks)   *45 mins*

(a)   The management of One In A Million Ltd are very keen on punctuality and there is a bonus scheme for prompt attendance. Under the rules of the scheme, if an employee is late more than three times in any two-week period (ten working days) he will forfeit his bonus at the end of that period.

The probability that an employee will be late on any one day is 0.15.

The number of employees in the factory is 1,800.

Required

(i)   Find the mean number of times an average employee will be late in a two-week period.

(ii)   Find the number of employees you would expect to lose their bonuses at the end of the period.   (8 marks)

(b)   (i)   In the stores department of the factory, consignments of component A are received. In a large consignment, 5% of the components are defective.

Calculate the probability that a random sample of 20 items selected from the consignment will contain fewer than three defectives.

(ii)   Of a number of consignments which are to be inspected, one third have 5% defectives, the rest have 10% defectives. If a consignment is rejected when a random sample of 20 contains more than two defective components, find the proportion of consignments rejected.   (9 marks)

(c)   1% of widgets produced by a company is known to be defective. If a random sample of 50 widgets is selected for inspection, calculate the probability of getting no defectives by using the following.

(i)   The binomial distribution   (4 marks)
(ii)   The Poisson distribution   (4 marks)

25 BATTERIES

A company produces batteries whose lifetimes are normally distributed with a mean of 100 hours. It is known that 96% of the batteries last at least 40 hours.

Required

(a)   Estimate the standard deviation lifetime.
(b)   Calculate the percentage of batteries that will last less than 57 hours.

26 NIGER LTD (25 marks)   *45 mins*

(a)   Niger Ltd manufactures large numbers of a component called a tridget in batches of 1,000. The component must be produced to a high standard of accuracy. Finished tridgets may be tested to discover whether they are defective at a cost of £1.25 a unit; defective units may then be put in good order at a cost of £5 per unit. If tridgets are not tested, any defects would become apparent later when they are incorporated in a final product. At that stage, however, it would cost £10 a unit to put the components in good order.

A random sample of 100 tridgets from a recently completed batch has just been tested. 20% of the units in the sample are defective.

Required

(i)   Prepare a calculation showing the minimum proportion of defective units in a batch such that it would be cheaper to test all the components rather than none of them.

(5 marks)

(ii)   Calculate a 95% confidence interval for the proportion of defective units in the batch from which a sample has just been tested.   (5 marks)

(iii) Calculate the sample size required to indicate with 95% confidence that the proportion of defective units in the population is less than 25%, assuming that the sample continues to indicate 20% defective.   (5 marks)

(b)   A random sample of 100 sales invoices has been classified by sales value into the following frequency distribution.

Value	Number of invoices
£	
0 and <100	20
100 and <200	18
200 and <300	22
300 and <400	15
400 and <500	9
500 and <600	8
600 and <700	4
700 and <800	2
800 and <900	2
	100

Required

(i)   Calculate the mean and the standard deviation of the sample.   (5 marks)

(ii)   Place confidence limits on the mean value of all sales invoices at:

(1)   the 95% confidence level;
(2)   the 99% confidence level.   (5 marks)

27   DRY GULCH LTD

The factory manager of Dry Gulch Ltd maintains that the average time required to make one unit of a product, the sloon, is not more than 48 minutes.

In one sample of 49 trials taken in January 20X3, the average time was 50 minutes, with a standard deviation of two minutes.

Required

(a)   Test the manager's claim, at the 1% level of significance.
(b)   Place 95% confidence limits on the mean production time per unit of sloon.

28   SOLVE

(a)   Solve the following simultaneous equations.

$2x + y - 4z = -20$
$x - 2y + 3z = -5$
$3x - 3y - z = -37$

(b)   The sum of the squares of two positive numbers is 890, and the difference between the two numbers is 4. Calculate the two numbers.

(c)   A rectangle has a perimeter of 44 metres and an area of 112 square metres. Calculate the length and breadth of the rectangle.

29   QUADRATIC EQUATIONS (25 marks)   *45 mins*

(a)   Solve the following quadratic equations.

   (i) $x^2 - 1.28x - 5.16 = 0$

   (ii) $4x^2 + 33x + 68 = 0$

   (iii) $-3x^2 + 6x + 30 = 6$

   (iv) $x^2 - 4.8x + 5.76 = 0$ (6 marks)

(b)   If q units of a product are sold at a price of p pounds a unit, then p = 600 − 0.15q. q cannot exceed 4,000. Calculate the value or values of q that will give total revenue of £450,000.

                                                                                                       (4 marks)

(c)   The management of Landslide Ltd have received a market research report in which it is stated that there appears to be a linear relationship between the demand and the unit price of its product over the price range £12.80 to £16.40 a unit.

   As we would expect, demand falls as price rises. At the two extremes of this price range, demand would be as follows.

   (i)   24,200 units at a price of £12.80 a unit
   (ii)   16,100 units at a price of £16.40 a unit

   Required

   (i)   Find the values of a and b which could complete the linear equation y = ax + b, where y is the demand and x is the selling price per unit.

            The equation is to be valid over the price range £12.80 to £16.40.   (5 marks)

   (ii)   If total costs are £40,000 + £8 per unit, derive the formula for profit at any level of selling price in that range.   (5 marks)

   (iii)   Calculate the combination of price and demand that would give a total profit of £89,000.

                                                                                                       (5 marks)

30   REVENUES AND COSTS (25 marks)   *45 mins*

A company manufactures a product. The fixed costs per accounting period are £1,200 and the variable costs per unit are £60. When the price is £120, the demand per accounting period is 20 units. If the price is reduced to £100, the demand increases to 30 units. You may assume that the cost and demand functions are linear.

Required

(a)   Find an expression for the total costs in terms of q, the quantity produced.   (3 marks)

(b)   Show that demand (q) and price (p) are related by the following expression: (5 marks)

      p = 160 − 2q

(c)   Obtain an expression for the revenue function in terms of q. Graph on the same axes, the revenue function and the total cost function found in part (a). You may assume that the maximum output per accounting period is 80 units.   (10 marks)

(d)   Using the graph, read off the breakeven points. Verify the graphical results for the breakeven points by an algebraic method.   (7 marks)

31   BRASS LTD

Brass Ltd produces two products, the Masso and the Russo. Budgeted data relating to these products on a unit basis for August 20X2 are as follows.

	Masso	*Russo*
	£	£
Selling price	150	100
Materials	80	30
Sales staff's commission	30	20

Each unit of product incurs costs of machining and assembly. The total capacity available in August 20X2 is budgeted to be 700 hours of machining and 1,000 hours of assembly, the cost of this capacity being fixed at £7,000 and £10,000 respectively for the month, whatever the use made of it.

The number of hours required in each of these departments to complete one unit of output is as follows.

	Masso	Russo
Machining	1.0	2.0
Assembly	2.5	2.0

Selling prices are fixed by the government and the maximum permitted output of any one product in August is 400 units. At the present controlled selling prices the demand for the products exceeds this considerably.

Required

(a) Calculate Brass Ltd's optimal production plan for August 20X2, and the profit earned and indicate graphically the breakeven position.

(b) State the principal assumptions underlying your calculations in (a) above, and assess their general significance.

32 WALLOP LTD

Wallop Ltd manufactures two similar products, hakes and panes, using the same labour force and machines for each. Information about the selling price and costs of each product is as follows.

	Hake		Pane	
	£	£	£	£
Selling price		116		120
Variable costs				
Direct materials	43		36	
Direct labour	32		24	
Machining	25		40	
		100		100
Contribution		16		20

The cost of direct labour is £4 an hour and the variable cost of machining is £5 an hour.

In any one month, direct labour hours are restricted to 9,600 hours and machine hours are restricted to 8,125 hours.

There is a maximum monthly demand for hakes of 1,000 units.

Required

(a) Formulate the linear programming problem to determine the monthly production levels of each product.

(b) Solve the problem graphically.

33 HITECH (25 marks)   *45 mins*

(a) Hitech, a division of Sunrise plc, produces and sells three products, HT01, HT02 and HT03.

The following details of prices and product costs have been extracted from Hitech's cost accounting records.

	Product		
	HT01	HT02	HT03
Prices per unit	£150	£200	£220
Costs per unit			
Direct labour at £4/hr	£100	£120	£132
Direct material at £20/kg	£20	£40	£40

Direct labour is regarded as a variable product cost.

A regression analysis has been carried out in order to estimate the relationship between overhead costs and production of the three products. Expressed in weekly terms the results of the analysis show:

$$y = 4,000 + 0.5x_1 + 0.7x_2 + 0.8x_3$$

where y = total overhead cost per week
x_1 = HT01, weekly direct labour hours
x_2 = HT02, weekly direct labour hours
x_3 = HT03, weekly direct labour hours

The company operates a 46-week year.

Required

Compute the total variable product costs for each of HT01, HT02 and HT03. (6 marks)

(b) The material used by Hitech is also used in a wide variety of other applications and is in relatively limited supply. As business conditions improve in general, there will be pressure for the price of this material to rise, but strong competition in Hitech's sector of the market would make it unlikely that increased material costs can be passed on to customers in higher product prices. The position on material supplies is that Hitech can obtain 20,000 kgs at current prices.

Further, reductions in the skilled labour force made during the recession mean that the number of available direct labour hours is estimated at no more than 257,600 hours for the next year.

Demand for each product over the year is forecast to be as follows.

HT01	16,000 units
HT02	10,000 units
HT03	6,000 units

Required

Formulate a linear programme from the above data in order to obtain the annual production/sales plan which will maximise Hitech's contribution earnings and profit. (You are not required to solve the problem.) (11 marks)

(c) The final objective function is

CONTRIBUTION = 180,320 – 2.0 (HT02) – 1.5 (HT03) – 0.7 (slack labour)

Discuss the information contained in this equation. (8 marks)

34 HOUND CAMPING LTD

(a) The treasurer of Hound Camping Ltd had to invest some surplus cash. He decided on the following investments.

(i) £8,000 was placed in a bank deposit account for three years. The expected annual rate of interest is 11%, calculated yearly.

(ii) £15,000 was placed in a savings account for five years, with interest added yearly at 14%.

(iii) £6,000 was placed in an account for four years where the annual interest rate is expected to be 10% for the first two years and 15% in years 3 and 4, with interest added at the end of each year.

Required

Calculate the interest that will be earned in total from the three investments.

(b) The treasurer is also aware of three other investments.

(i) Investment A would last for three years, and pay interest at a nominal rate of 10.5%. Interest would be added every half year, compound.

(ii) Investment B would last for five years, with a nominal interest rate of 12%, payable monthly.

(iii) Investment C would last for four years, with a nominal interest rate of 12%, payable quarterly.

Required

Compare investments A, B and C with the investments in (a)(i), (a)(ii) and (a)(iii) respectively, and decide which is the better investment, A or (a)(i), B or (a)(ii), and C or (a)(iii).

35   WILFRED AND MABEL (25 marks)   *45 mins*

(a)   Your rich Uncle Wilfred dies and leaves you £5,000 invested in unit trusts. Your accountant advises you that the value of your investment can be expected to grow by 8% per annum compound. Estimate the value of the investment after six years.   (2 marks)

(b)   You now decide to increase the value of the investment, and instruct your bank manager to invest £1,000 annually in unit trusts. If the first purchase is made 12 months after the death of your uncle, estimate the total value of your investment six years after his death.   (3 marks)

(c)   Your Aunt Mabel has also decided to invest some money on your behalf. She has made an initial investment (at year 0) of £2,000 and will add a further £1,500 each year until the end of year 5 (starting a year from now), when the entire investment will be handed over to you. Calculate what it will be worth at this time if interest is earned at 10% per annum.   (5 marks)

(d)   Aunt Mabel has an investment of £300,000. The investment is expected to earn interest of 10% per annum for two more years, and 8% per annum for the two years after that. She expects to withdraw £40,000 from the investment at the end of each year, beginning at the   year 1. (It is now year 0.) Calculate the value of her investment at year 4.   (5 marks)

(e)   Sunk Fun Ltd wishes to set up a sinking fund which will realise £100,000 at the end of five years. Payments into the fund occur at the end of each of the five years, and investments in the fund earn interest at 14% per annum. Calculate the annual payment which must be made.

(5 marks)

(f)   Sunk Fun Ltd has another sinking fund in operation into which the final payment of £10,000 has just been made. The fund was originally set up six years ago and payments were made at the end of each of the six years (including the payment just made). The fund has earned interest of 8% per annum compound. Calculate the worth of the fund now.   (5 marks)

36   WITCHES CHEEPER LTD

Witches Cheeper Ltd is about to borrow a sum of money, at an interest rate of 3% per quarter. The lender has offered two alternative schemes of repayment.

(a)   The company could pay £1,680.45 at the end of each quarter for five years.
(b)   The company could pay £1,081.60 at the end of each quarter for ten years.

Required

Calculate the size of the loan. Use both repayment schemes, and calculate two answers, one for each scheme.

Do not use discount tables.

37   DAISY HOOF LTD

(a)   Daisy Hoof Ltd is considering a project to purchase some equipment which would have the following cash flows.

Year	Cash flow
	£
0	(50,000)
1	18,000
2	25,000
3	15,000
4	10,000

The estimated trade-in value of the equipment, which is £2,000, has not been included in the cash flows above.

The company has a cost of capital of 16%.

Required

Without using discount tables, calculate the following.

(i)   The NPV of the project
(ii)   The IRR of the project

(b)   Assuming that the company decides to go ahead with the project, there are three ways in which the necessary finance could be raised.

   (i)   The company could use a bank loan for the full £50,000, repayable at the end of four years and with interest at 12% payable at the end of each year.

   (ii)   The company could use the machine for four years at an annual rental of £16,000 payable at the end of each year.

   (iii) The company could use hire purchase, which would involve an initial payment of £15,000 and then four annual payments of £15,000.

Required

Select the cheapest method of finance, comparing the methods by using a discount rate of 12% per annum. Do not use discount tables.

Suggested answers

1 KILBURN LTD

(a) A statistical survey needs to be carefully planned, because otherwise the data collected may not fulfil the purpose of the survey. All surveys should have **clearly defined purposes**, and those purposes should be borne in mind at all times. Otherwise, the results may not be useful for any one purpose, or they may only be good for purposes which are irrelevant to the goals of the person for whom the survey is made.

For example, a company might be interested in the potential market for a new product. The goal is to **make profits**, so the immediate purpose of the survey is to find out whether there would be **sufficient demand**, at a high enough price, for the new product to be profitable. If this purpose is not made central to the planning of the survey, the person carrying out the survey might ask people in general (instead of potential customers) whether they like the idea of a product of the same type (instead of how much they would pay for the specific product).

The following matters should be considered in planning a survey.

- The objectives of the survey
- The units of measurement
- The accuracy of data required
- The definition of the population
- The depth of enquiry
- Cost effectiveness

(b) Problems which may arise, and possible remedies, are as follows.

(i) **Respondents may place differing interpretations on the questions**. This may be overcome by careful testing of questions, asking several people to write down all the interpretations of each question they can think of and then amending questions accordingly.

(ii) **Respondents may give answers which are hard to interpret**. If someone writes that the quality of goods is 'occasionally below standard', does he mean that some goods are unacceptable to him, or that all are acceptable but some are of lower than normal quality? The remedy is to ask questions in multiple choice form, where respondents have to choose one from a list of (unambiguous) answers.

(iii) **Respondents may give the answers which they feel are in their interests, rather than honest answers**. For example, some customers may complain not because they are really dissatisfied but because they hope that things will then get even better. It may help to ask respondents who state that Kilburn Ltd's performance is poor to give their reasons. Respondents might then refrain from stating that the company's performance is poor if they cannot give specific reasons.

(iv) **Many questionnaires may not be returned**. Some incentive to return questionnaires, such as entry in a prize draw, could be offered.

2 COLLECTING DATA

(a) The interview can be compared with the postal questionnaire as a method of collecting data under the following headings.

(i) **Cost**

Interviewing is likely to prove a more expensive method, since trained staff must carry out the interview process, to avoid the possibility of interview bias arising. Provided that the postal questionnaire is well designed, sending out the forms and collecting the returned data should be simple and inexpensive.

(ii) **Time requirement**

The interview process will take a longer period of employee time, since one-to-one interviewing is required. The interviewer's time and the lost interviewee time must both be taken into account. Postal questionnaires do not require so much time.

(iii) **Response expected**

Interviews will produce a 100% response rate of those people interviewed. The number of interviews to be conducted can be chosen by management. Postal questionnaires are a more uncertain business. Typically only a small minority (around 10-15%) of those receiving such a questionnaire will bother to fill it in and return it. This proportion cannot be ascertained for certain in advance.

(iv) **Sample size**

Sample sizes for interviews tend to be smaller than for postal questionnaires, for the reasons stated above.

(v) **Possibility of misunderstanding questions**

This should be rare in personal interviews, since the interviewer is in a position to explain each question fully. Questions are more likely to be misunderstood by a respondent filling out a questionnaire by himself.

(vi) **Possibility of deep questioning**

Interviews are more suitable for deep or detailed questions to be asked, since the interviewer can take the time required with each interviewee to explain the implications of the question. Postal questionnaires do not offer the possibility of spending longer with certain respondents to probe their feelings more deeply.

(b) (i) **Quota sampling**

In quota sampling, investigators are told to interview all the people they meet up to a certain quota. A large degree of bias can be introduced. For example, an interviewer may fill his quota by only meeting housewives out shopping. In practice, this problem is partially overcome by sub-dividing the quota into different types of people, eg on the basis of age, sex and social class. For example, if the numbers of students attending the four courses at a college are as follows:

	Male	Female
Course I	30	20
Course II	40	10
Course III	60	10
Course IV	50	30

and a quota sample of 25 students was required, an investigator's quota would be:

	Male	Female	Total
Course I	3	2	5
Course II	4	1	5
Course III	6	1	7
Course IV	5	3	8
			25

Using quota sampling, the investigator would interview the first three males he met from Course I, the first two females he met from Course I etc. One major advantage of quota sampling is that, although a fairly detailed knowledge of the characteristics of a population is required, it is not necessary to establish a sampling frame. In many practical situations, it will be either impossible or prohibitively expensive to compile a complete list of the population under study.

(ii) **Random sampling**

A random sample is one selected in such a way that every item in the population has an equal chance of being included.

Before selecting a random sample, an investigator should try to establish a sampling frame. This is simply a list of all the items in the population. In some situations, it is obviously quite impractical to compile such a list and true random sampling is then impossible. A random sample can be selected from the sampling frame by two main methods.

(1) **The lottery method**, such as picking numbers out of a hat.

(2) **The use of random number tables**. This method is to be preferred as it provides a high guarantee against bias.

Quota sampling is therefore a method of non-random sampling. If further statistical inferences are to be made from the characteristics of sample data, it is important that the sample was originally selected randomly.

(c) **A population census involves collecting data from every member of the population of a country covering information such as age, employment, ethnic origin etc.** This is a massive exercise. In the UK the census forms are first delivered by hand, then follow up visits are made to collect the filled up forms by census staff after a few days. These census staff are each responsible for small geographical areas of the country.

Time and expense are the major constraints on the exercise. Planning, running and then interpreting the results of the census takes many months or even years from start to finish. Carrying out all this more regularly than every ten years is not a practicable proposition. The exercise is also expensive. The census staff must all be fully trained so that they can help citizens to fill out their forms, for example if they are illiterate or if English is not their native language. The results of each form must be properly processed on receipt - another major task.

It is not worthwhile carrying out any task if the expected benefits are outweighed by the expected costs. Most national authorities take the view that the surplus of benefits over costs is maximised when the census is carried out every ten years.

3   SAMPLING METHODS

(a)   **Simple random sampling** means that the sample is selected in such a way that every item in the population has an equal chance of being included in the sample.

Stratified random sampling means that the population is first divided into strata (ie layers, eg by income level) and then simple random sampling is applied to each stratum. The advantage is that at least some representative items will be selected from each section.

A **sampling frame** is simply a list of all the items in a population.

(b)   (i)   The sampling frame should be a list of all workers who will be affected by the new proposals. The personnel or wages departments should be able to provide such a list.

(ii)   The college registration department should be able to provide a list of all students attending courses to prepare them for their professional examinations.

(iii)   The Education department of the local authority should be able to provide a school roll, ie a list of all schoolchildren in the City. If not, the Health department may be able to help.

(c)   In the large factory, the recommended type of sampling method will depend on whether the workers affected by the new proposals are homogeneous, or whether they can be classified by level of seniority, department, etc. In the former case, **simple random sampling** would be appropriate. In the latter case, **stratified random sampling** would be appropriate.

In the college it is likely that the different years of each course would be given separate tuition which was more or less relevant to the professional examinations. **Stratified random sampling** should therefore be performed, the strata being the years of each course.

In the large city, each of **simple random sampling** and **stratified random sampling** would be prohibitively expensive to carry out. A system such as **multi-stage sampling** would be more appropriate, in which a **random sample** is taken from a random selection of schools from throughout the city.

4   MODERNISATION

XYZ Equipment Ltd

4 High Street, London SW1
Telephone: 0207-XXX XXXX   Fax: 0207-XXX XXXX

Directors:	Registered Office:
A Smith	4 High Street
B Smith	London SW1
C Jones	Registered No XXXXXXX
D Jones	Registered in England

Our ref IW/EE   7th June 20XX

JM Bloggs Esq
1 The Cottages
London E3

Dear Mr Bloggs

Possible Company Relocation out of London

You may be aware that the lease on our head office building is due to run out in four years' time. I am writing to let you know of the possibilities that we are considering to deal with this situation, and to ask you to fill in the enclosed questionnaire.

Several staff members have expressed an interest in the company relocating out of Central London. The main benefits of this course of action are that house prices would be much cheaper for you out of London, and that travelling time and costs would be lower. The company would pay you all reasonable relocation expenses (removal costs, expenses in buying and selling properties, new carpets and curtains and so on) to help with any move that may be required.

The other option would be for the company to stay in Central London, either in our existing building (which we would refurbish once we knew we were going to stay) or in another suitable building.

I would be grateful if you would fill in your opinions on the enclosed questionnaire, and return the form to me in Room 413 by X June 20XX.

Please contact me if you have any problems filling in the questionnaire, or if you want any more information about the matters in this letter.

Yours sincerely,

I M Wright

Personnel Director

Enc.

QUESTIONNAIRE

FOR OFFICE
USE ONLY

Please fill in the details below.

Your name _

Your employee number _

PLEASE TICK AS APPROPRIATE

	No	Undecided	Yes	
1. Do you like the idea of relocating the company out of London?	☐	☐	☐	1 2 3
2. If the company were to relocate out of London, would you be prepared to stay with the company?	☐	☐	☐	4 5 6

(**Note**: The company would offer redundancy terms more generous than the Government scheme.)

	No	Undecided	Yes	
3. If the company were to relocate and you did stay with the company, would you seek relocation expenses?	☐	☐	☐	7 8 9

Please return this questionnaire to Ian Wright in Room 413 by X June 20XX. Thank you for your time.

---

5 THE SOYUZ INSURANCE COMPANY

(a) The two dimensions of the table should be years and each group of employees, including a category for 'others'.

It would also be possible to include percentage growth with the years.

The entries in the 'cells' of the table could be actual numbers of employees, percentages of the total work force or both.

Analysis of employee groups at the Soyuz Insurance Company

	20X0		20X3			20X6			20X9		
	Number empl'd	% of total	Number empl'd	% of total	% growth in total	Number empl'd	% of total	% growth in total	Number empl'd	% of total	% growth in total
Sales staff	1,176	28	2,372	31	102	4,840	38	104	7,477	36	54
Actuaries	1,260	30	2,448	32	94	3,185	25	30	4,362	21	37
Accountants	840	20	1,607	21	91	2,550	20	59	3,739	18	47
Other groups	924	22	1,223	16	32	2,165	17	77	5,192	25	140
Total	4,200	100	7,650	100	82	12,740	100	67	20,770	100	63

The table shows that there has been a substantial increase in the number of sales staff over the years, with the percentage of employees who are sales staff rising from under 30% in 20X0 to over 36% in

20X9. There has been a decrease in the proportion of employees who are actuaries, and a small decrease in the proportion who are accountants. The managing director's concern about the rapid growth in other groups of employees might be justified. The percentage increase in their numbers between 20X6 and 20X9 suggests that efforts to control their numbers have not yet had much success.

(b) (i)

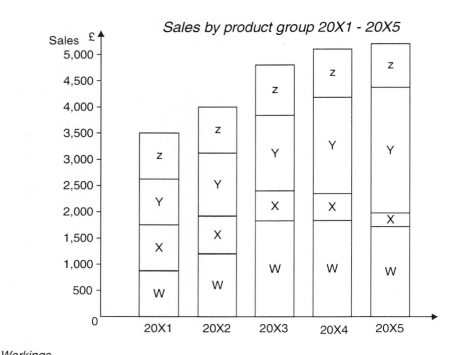

Sales by product group 20X1 - 20X5

Workings

Product group	20X1		20X2		20X3		20X4		20X5	
	%	£'000	%	£'000	%	£'000	%	£'000	%	£'000
W	25	0.875	30	1.20	38	1.824	36	1.836	33	1.716
X	25	0.875	18	0.72	12	0.576	10	0.510	5	0.260
Y	25	0.875	30	1.20	30	1.440	36	1.836	46	2.392
Z	25	0.875	22	0.88	20	0.960	18	0.918	16	0.832
	100	3.500	100	4.00	100	4.800	100	5.100	100	5.200

(ii)

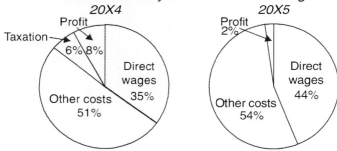

Where the money from sales revenue goes

Workings

	20X4		20X5	
	£'000	%	£'000	%
Direct wages	1.8	35	2.3	44
Other costs	2.6	51	2.8	54
Taxation	0.3	6	0.0	0
Profit	0.4	8	0.1	2
	5.1	100	5.2	100

6 GRADES OF EMPLOYEE

(a)

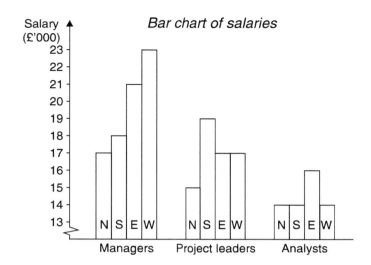

Bar chart of salaries

(b)

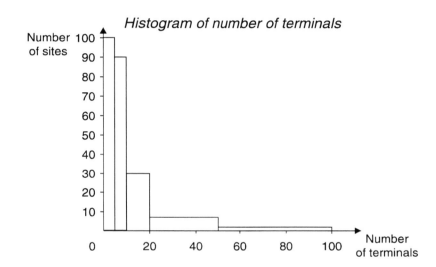

Histogram of number of terminals

(c) **A histogram is used to represent a grouped frequency distribution**. Each column corresponds to a group, and the area of the column is proportional to the group's frequency. Thus if one group covers twice the range of the variable as another, but its frequency is the same, the wider group's column will be only half the height of the narrower group's column.

A bar chart can also be used to represent a grouped frequency distribution, but it is not suitable where the groups do not all have the same width. Bar charts are more commonly used where the groups correspond to, for example, regions or products, rather than ranges of a variable. They can also break down data to a greater extent than can histograms, by using clusters of bars (as in part (a)), or bars divided into components.

7 COMPONENT BAR CHART

(a) (i)   Acceptable bar charts could be drawn vertically or horizontally.

Suggested answers

Asset breakdown 20X3 to 20X7

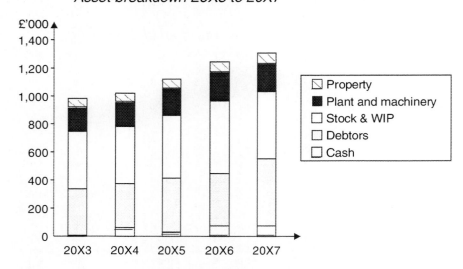

(ii) The bar chart clearly shows that total assets have risen steadily over the five year period. Property remained static from 20X3 to 20X4, and showed only small increases from then on. Plant and machinery and stocks and work in progress both rose slowly from 20X3 to 20X4 and more steeply from 20X4 to 20X6, and then declined from 20X6 to 20X7. Debtors have behaved unevenly but with an increasing trend: total assets rose from 20X6 to 20X7 only because of the large increase in debtors over this period. Cash balances have also behaved unevenly but they exhibit an increasing trend over the five year period.

(b) (i)

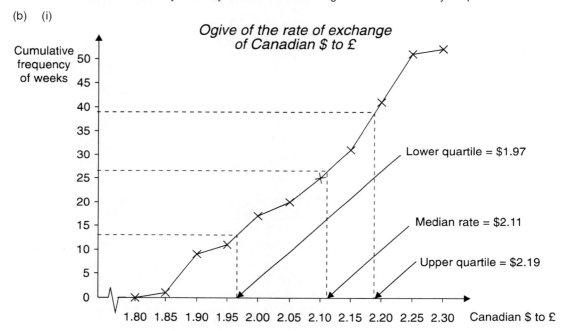

Workings

Rates	Frequency	Cumulative frequency
≥ 1.80 but < 1.85	1	1
≥ 1.85 but < 1.90	8	9
≥ 1.90 but < 1.95	2	11
≥ 1.95 but < 2.00	6	17
≥ 2.00 but < 2.05	3	20
≥ 2.05 but < 2.10	5	25
≥ 2.10 but < 2.15	6	31
≥ 2.15 but < 2.20	10	41
≥ 2.20 but < 2.25	10	51
≥ 2.25 but < 2.30	1	52

(ii)   The median exchange rate is determined by reading across to the graph from a cumulative frequency of 52/2 = 26 weeks, and then reading down to the rate scale. The median is $2.11 to £1.

(iii)   We find the quartiles in the same way.

- The **lower quartile**, at 52/4 = 13 weeks, is $1.97 to £1.
- The **upper quartile**, at 52 × 3/4 = 39 weeks, is $2.19 to £1.

8   GRUFF DRAWERS LTD

(a) (i)   A useful method of comparing changes in output at the factories would be to measure the rate of annual growth in total output, as a percentage of the previous year's output.

| | Factory A | | Factory B | | Factory C | | Factory D | | Factory E | |
Year	Output	Growth	Output	Growth	Output	Growth	Output	Growth	Output	Growth
20X1	250	-	608	-	326	-	563	-	294	-
20X2	258	3%	638	5%	339	4%	579	6%	323	10%
20X3	271	5%	670	5%	353	4%	627	5%	333	3%
20X4	290	7%	704	5%	381	8%	645	3%	363	9%
20X5	316	9%	746	6%	419	10%	652	1%	370	2%

Notes

(1)   Growth rates are rounded to the nearest whole per cent.

(2)   Annual growth is calculated as

$$\frac{\text{Current year's output - previous year's output}}{\text{Previous year's output}} \times 100\%$$

(ii)

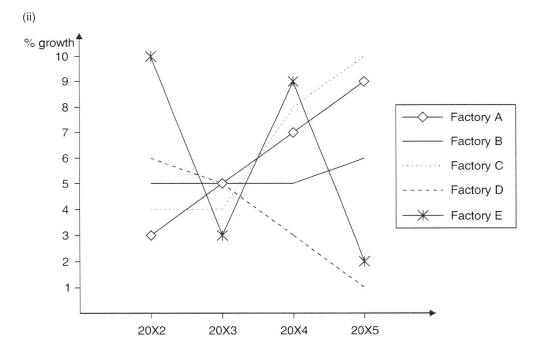

BPP PUBLISHING

Suggested answers

(b) *Workings*

		20X0					20X9			
	No. of households			*Wealth*		*households*			*No. of Wealth*	
Not over	%	Cum %	%	Cum %	%	Cum %	%	Cum %
1,000	28.0	28.0	3	3	19	19	2	2
3,000	30.0	58.0	11	14	27	46	8	10
5,000	17.0	75.0	18	32	16	62	13	23
8,000	12.0	87.0	18	50	21	83	25	48
12,000	7.0	94.0	15	65	8	91	15	63
16,000	3.0	97.0	11	76	4	95	10	73
25,000	1.5	98.5	8	84	3	98	11	84
50,000	0.5	99.0	5	89	1	99	8	92
100,000	0.5	99.5	9	98	1	100	8	100
Open	0.5	100.0	2	100	0	100	0	100
	100.0		100		100		100	

The number of households is here taken as the x axis.

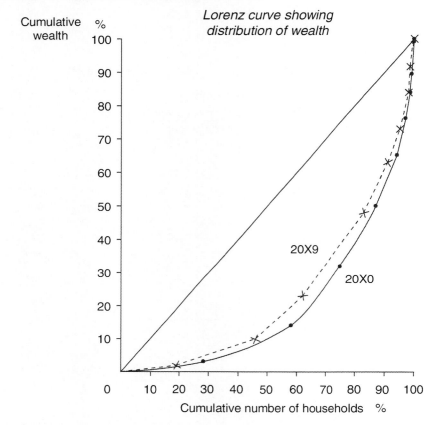

There has been some shift in the distribution of wealth between 20X0 and 20X9. The total wealth of the country was more evenly spread in 20X9, but there is still considerable inequality in the distribution.

Note

If your x axis was the cumulative wealth, your curves would have been shaped as follows.

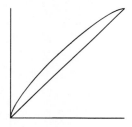

Your comments should, however, have been the same.

9   **PRODCO LTD**

(a)   The data required to draw a Z chart are as follows.

Month	Costs 20X6 £'000	Costs 20X7 £'000	Cumulative costs 20X7 £'000	Annual moving total £'000
January	35.8	43.9	43.9	434.0
February	33.6	40.1	84.0	440.5
March	35.5	46.0	130.0	451.0
April	37.5	48.7	178.7	462.2
May	37.2	48.9	227.6	473.9
June	34.6	46.0	273.6	485.3
July	36.3	48.3	321.9	497.3
August	36.0	47.9	369.8	509.2
September	35.4	48.2	418.0	522.0
October	30.4	47.0	465.0	538.6
November	36.1	49.4	514.4	551.9
December	37.5	51.6	566.0	566.0
	425.9			

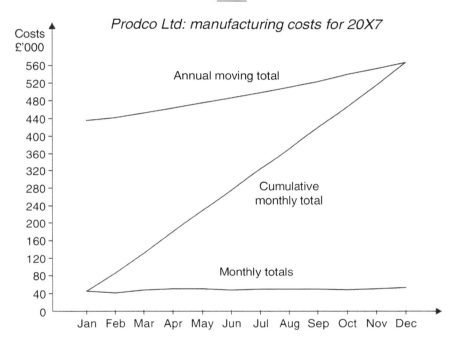

Prodco Ltd: manufacturing costs for 20X7

(b)   The purpose of a Z chart is to display simultaneously:

(i)   **monthly totals** which show the monthly results together with any seasonal variations;

(ii)   **cumulative totals** which show the performance for the year to date, and can be easily compared with planned or budgeted performance by superimposing a budget line;

(iii) **annual moving totals** which compare the current levels of performance with those of the previous year and disclose any long-term trend.

The graph drawn in part (a) shows a fairly stable pattern of monthly costs. The annual moving total line shows a significant increase in monthly costs for 20X7 as compared to 20X6.

10   HANDLING COSTS

(a)   (i)   The frequency distribution of stock movements per week is given below.

Handling time		Mid point		
At least	*Less than*	*x*	*f*	*fx*
-	10	5	240	1,200
10	20	15	340	5,100
20	40	30	150	4,500
40	60	50	120	6,000
60	90	75	20	1,500
90	120	105	20	2,100
120	180	150	10	1,500
			900	21,900

Mean = 21,900/900 = 24.33 minutes.

(ii)   Using the mid-points of the class intervals, the estimated total time spent each week in moving items of stock is 21,900 minutes = 365 hours.

(iii)   The **capacity per week** is 5 days × 7 hours × 12 employees = 420 person hours.

The **percentage capacity utilisation** is $\dfrac{365}{420}$ × 100% = 86.9%.

(iv)   The **average number of jobs handled** by each employee each week is 900/12 = 75.

(b)   (i)   The class with the highest frequency is £1,500 – £2,000. This is the **modal class**. The mode is estimated by using the formula.

$$\textbf{Mode} = L + \frac{(F_1 - F_0)}{2F_1 - F_0 - F_2} \times c = £1,500 + \frac{12-6}{2\times12-6-9} \times 500 = £1,833$$

More gardeners earn an estimated £1,833 than any other amount.

(ii)   In order to work out the median, we need the cumulative frequency distribution.

Earnings in 20X2

At least	*Not more than*	*Number of gardeners*	*Cumulative frequency*
£	*£*		
0	500	1	1
500	1,000	4	5
1,000	1,500	6	11
1,500	2,000	12	23
2,000	2,500	9	32
2,500	3,000	7	39
3,000	3,500	5	44
3,500	4,000	3	47
4,000	4,500	2	49
4,500	5,000	1	50

There are 50 gardeners, so the median will be the earnings of the 25th gardener, which will be somewhere in the range £2,000 – £2,500. The **estimated median** is:

Value of lower limit of median class interval + $\dfrac{R}{f}$ × c

$$= £2,000 + \frac{25-23}{9} \times (£2,500 - £2,000)$$

$$= £2,000 + \frac{2}{9} \times £500 = £2,111.11$$

(iii)

	Earnings in 20X2	Mid-point of		
At least	Not more than	range	Frequency	
£	£	x	f	fx
0	500	250	1	250
500	1,000	750	4	3,000
1,000	1,500	1,250	6	7,500
1,500	2,000	1,750	12	21,000
2,000	2,500	2,250	9	20,250
2,500	3,000	2,750	7	19,250
3,000	3,500	3,250	5	16,250
3,500	4,000	3,750	3	11,250
4,000	4,500	4,250	2	8,500
4,500	5,000	4,750	1	4,750
			50	112,000

So the arithmetic mean earnings are

$$\frac{\Sigma fx}{\Sigma f} = \frac{112,000}{50} = £2,240.$$

11 JOURNEY TIMES

(a) (i) **The mean**

The mean has the following **advantages**.

- It is widely understood.
- It uses every value in its computation.
- It gives a unique value.

It does, however, have two major **disadvantages**.

- It may give an impossible value (eg 2.2 children).
- It may be distorted by extremely high/low values.

(ii) **The mode**

Advantages of the mode are as follows.

- It is an actual value.
- It is not distorted by extreme values.

It has the following **disadvantages**.

- It may not be unique.
- It ignores dispersion about the modal value.
- It does not take every value into account.

(iii) **The median**

The median has the following **advantage**.

- It is not distorted by extreme values.

There is a **disadvantage** to the median.

- It does not take every value into account.

(b) (i)

Times	Midpoint	Frequency	
	x	f	fx
0 - 10	5	14	70
10 - 20	15	26	390
20 - 30	25	64	1,600
30 - 40	35	46	1,610
40 - 50	45	28	1,260
50 - 60	55	16	880
60 - 80	70	8	560
80 - 100	90	4	360
		206	6,730

$$\text{Mean } \overline{x} = \frac{\Sigma fx}{\Sigma f} = \frac{6,730}{206} = 32.67 \text{ minutes}$$

Median = 103 rd item in the ranking

$$= 20 + \left(\frac{103 - 40}{64} \times 10\right)$$

$$= 20 + 9.84 = 29.84 \text{ minutes}$$

$$\text{Mode} = L + \left[\frac{F_1 - F_0}{2F_1 - F_0 - F_2} \times c\right]$$

$$= 20 + \left[\frac{64 - 26}{2 \times 64 - 26 - 46} \times 10\right]$$

$$= 20 + 6.79 = 26.79 \text{ minutes.}$$

(ii) (1) The employer would seek to minimise the amount paid for travelling time. He should therefore choose the mode, perhaps arguing that the **modal time** is the **most representative** because the largest number of employees take that long to come to work.

(2) The trade union would seek to maximise the amount paid for travelling time. It should therefore choose the mean, perhaps arguing that the mean time is the only average which takes into account the travelling times of *all* employees.

12   AVERAGES AND DISPERSION

(a)

x	$\lvert x - \overline{x} \rvert$	$(x - \overline{x})^2$
3	30	900
6	27	729
9	24	576
10	23	529
12	21	441
14	19	361
17	16	256
18	15	225
21	12	144
24	9	81
25	8	64
27	6	36
31	2	4
33	0	0
37	4	16
38	5	25
40	7	49
42	9	81
48	15	225
51	18	324
56	23	529
61	28	784
63	30	900
65	32	1,024
74	41	1,681
825	424	9,984

There are 25 items in the array.

(i) The **range** is 74 – 3 = 71 units.
(ii) The **arithmetic mean** is 825/25 = 33 units.
(iii) The **median** is the 13th item, 31 units.
(iv) The **lower quartile** is the mean of the 6th and 7th items, 15½ units.
(v) The **upper quartile** is the mean of the 19th and 20th items, 49½ units.
(vi) The **mean deviation** is 424/25 = 16.96 units.
(vii) The **standard deviation** is √(9,984/25) = 19.98 units.

(b) A **measure of dispersion** is a quantification of the spread of values of a variable around the average value.

   (i) The **range** is simple and easily understood. It is the difference between the lowest value and the highest value in the distribution. However, it fails to give an indication of how the bulk of the frequencies are dispersed, since it is only concerned with extreme values.

   (ii) The **quartile deviation** is one half of the inter-quartile range, which is the range of the middle 50% of items in the distribution. It therefore attempts to measure the dispersion of the central part of the distribution and ignores extremes of the range. This is both an advantage and a disadvantage, since the two extreme portions, although perhaps less significant, are nevertheless an important feature in the dispersion of a distribution.

   (iii) The **mean deviation** is the average difference between an item in the distribution and the mean of the distribution (ignoring plus or minus signs). It has the advantages of taking every item in the distribution into account, of being fairly easy to calculate, and of being fairly easy to understand. It has little value, however in advanced statistical analysis.

   (iv) The **standard deviation** also takes every item in the distribution into account, but it is more difficult to calculate and to understand. Nevertheless, it is of great value in advanced statistical analysis and it is therefore the most valuable measure of dispersion.

(c) (i)

Interview time x (Minutes)	(Tally)	Frequency f	fx	x^2	fx^2
1	/	1	1	1	1
2	////	4	8	4	16
3	////	4	12	9	36
4	///	3	12	16	48
5	//	2	10	25	50
		14	43		151

Mean interview time = 43/14 = 3.07 minutes

   (ii)

$$s = \sqrt{\frac{\Sigma fx^2}{n} - \left(\frac{\Sigma fx}{\Sigma f}\right)^2}$$

$$= \sqrt{\frac{151}{14} - \left(\frac{43}{14}\right)^2}$$

$$= \sqrt{(10.7857 - 9.4337)}$$

$$= \sqrt{1.352}$$

$$= 1.16 \text{ minutes}$$

The standard deviation of the interview times is 1.16 minutes.

   (iii) We must assume that the number of tasks given to an employee in any one week is independent of the number of tasks given to the employee in any other week.

     (1) **Mean** over six weeks = $27 \times 6 = 162$ tasks.

     (2) **Standard deviation** over six weeks = $\sqrt{(4.2^2 \times 6)} = 10.29$ tasks.

13   EARNINGS

(a) (i)

Daily earnings

At least £	Less than £	Mid-point x	Frequency f	fx	fx²
40	50	45	2	90	4,050
50	60	55	15	825	45,375
60	70	65	21	1,365	88,725
70	80	75	30	2,250	168,750
80	90	85	20	1,700	144,500
90	100	95	9	855	81,225
100	110	105	3	315	33,075
			100	7,400	565,700

(1) **Mean** = £7,400/400 = £74.

(2) **Standard deviation** =

$$\sqrt{\frac{\Sigma fx^2}{\Sigma f} - \left(\frac{\Sigma fx}{\Sigma f}\right)^2}$$

$$= \sqrt{\frac{565,700}{100} - \left(\frac{7,400}{100}\right)^2}$$

$$= \sqrt{181}$$

$$= £13.45$$

(3) **The coefficient of variation** is £13.45/£74 = 0.182.

(4) The **median** is the daily earnings of the 50th employee. 38 employees earn less than £70, and the earnings of the median employee are therefore approximately

$$£70 + \frac{50 - 38}{30} \times £(80 - 70) = £74.$$

(ii)   **The mean gives an average earnings figure, taking into account the earnings of every employee in the sample data**. If there had been one employee or a few employees with very high earnings compared to everyone else, the mean would have been increased by the influence of these extreme earnings.

The median tells us that one half of the employees earn less than a certain amount and one half earn more. It does not tell us how much less or how much more employees might earn so that in an extreme case, if the median earnings were £74, the minimum earnings might be close to £74 (perhaps £70) but the maximum earnings might be well in excess of £74 (perhaps £300).

(iii)   (1) **The standard deviation is a measure of dispersion**. It is calculated from data by taking the square root of the average of the squared differences between the mean and actual data.

(2) **The coefficient of variation expresses the standard deviation as a proportion of the mean**. This facilitates comparisons between distributions. For example, the mean weekly wage in one industry might be £200, and that in another industry might be £300. If the standard deviations are £40 and £50 respectively, then taking account of the average level of wages we would say that wages are less variable in the second industry than in the first, with a coefficient of variation in the second industry of 50/300 = 0.17 as against 40/200 = 0.20 in the first industry.

(b) (i)   **Summary of results**

	Men	Women
Median	37.860	37.08
Lower quartile	36.100	35.24
Upper quartile	39.630	38.78
Quartile deviation	1.765	1.77

Workings

Median = lower limit of class interval + $\left[\dfrac{R}{f} \times c\right]$

where   R   =   difference between median member and frequency up to the start of the class interval

           f   =   frequency of the class interval

           c   =   size of the class interval

For men, median $= 36 + \left[\dfrac{50 - 23.6}{56.7} \times 4\right]$

                              $= 36 + 1.86 = 37.86$ hours

For women, median $= 36 + \left[\dfrac{50 - 34.1}{58.9} \times 4\right]$

                              $= 36 + 1.08 = 37.08$ hours

Similar formulae can be used to find the lower and upper quartiles.

For men, lower quartile $= 36 + \left[\dfrac{25 - 23.6}{56.7} \times 4\right]$

                              $= 36 + 0.10 = 36.10$ hours

For women, lower quartile $= 34 + \left[\dfrac{25 - 10.2}{23.9} \times 2\right]$

                              $= 34 + 1.24 = 35.24$ hours

For men, upper quartile $= 36 + \left[\dfrac{75 - 23.6}{56.7} \times 4\right]$

                              $= 36 + 3.63 = 39.63$ hours

For women, upper quartile $= 36 + \left[\dfrac{75 - 34.1}{58.9} \times 4\right]$

                              $= 36 + 2.78 = 38.78$ hours

Quartile deviation $= \dfrac{Q_3 - Q_1}{2}$

For men, quartile deviation $= \dfrac{39.63 - 36.10}{2} = 1.765$ hours

For women, quartile deviation $= \dfrac{38.78 - 35.24}{2} = 1.77$ hours

(ii)   REPORT

To: A. Mann
From: The company secretary
Date: 01.02.20X7
Subject: Comparison of the weekly hours worked by full time non-manual male and female employees in 20X6.

It is clear from the data calculated in part (i) above that each of the median, lower quartile and upper quartile is slightly higher for men than for women. So on average men work slightly longer hours than women in full time non-manual employment.

However, **the quartile deviation measures the dispersion of data about the median**, and the quartile deviation for men is almost identical to the quartile deviation for women. Therefore the dispersion about the median of period of time worked is very similar for men and women.

14   REGRESSION LINE

Workings

x	y	xy	x^2	y^2
9	16	144	81	256
11	20	220	121	400
14	25	350	196	625
17	28	476	289	784
20	34	680	400	1,156
21	35	735	441	1,225
25	44	1,100	625	1,936
117	202	3,705	2,153	6,382

$n = 7$

(a) $r = \dfrac{(7 \times 3,705) - (117 \times 202)}{\sqrt{[(7 \times 2,153) - 117^2] \times [(7 \times 6,382) - 202^2]}}$

$= \dfrac{25,935 - 23,634}{\sqrt{(15,071 - 13,689) \times (44,674 - 40,804)}}$

$= \dfrac{2,301}{\sqrt{1,382 \times 3,870}} = \dfrac{2,301}{2,312.65} = 0.995$

(b) If $y = a + bx$

$b = \dfrac{(7 \times 3,705) - (117 \times 202)}{(7 \times 2,153) - 117^2} = \dfrac{2,301}{1,382} = 1.665$

$a = \dfrac{202}{7} - \dfrac{1.665 \times 117}{7} = 1.028$

$y = 1.028 + 1.665x$

(c)

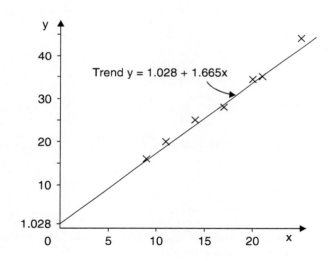

15 GILBERT LTD

(a) *Workings*

Quarter 1 x	Quarter 2 y	x^2	y^2	xy
28	45	784	2,025	1,260
26	54	676	2,916	1,404
35	49	1,225	2,401	1,715
20	36	400	1,296	720
30	50	900	2,500	1,500
16	32	256	1,024	512
40	64	1,600	4,096	2,560
36	56	1,296	3,136	2,016
24	44	576	1,936	1,056
25	50	625	2,500	1,250
280	480	8,338	23,830	13,993

(i) An estimate for average travel expenses for quarter 2 is $\dfrac{48,000}{10} \times 17.5\text{p} = £840$.

(ii) (1) If the **regression line is y = a + bx**, then

$$b = \frac{10 \times 13,993 - 280 \times 480}{10 \times 8,338 - 280^2} = 1.11$$

$$a = \frac{480}{10} - 1.11 \times \frac{280}{10} = 16.92$$

The line is y = 16.92 + 1.11x.

Note that x and y are both in hundreds of miles.

(2) Predicted quarter 2 average travel expenses are

$100 \times (16.92 + 1.11 \times 30) \times £0.175 = £878.85 \triangleq £879$.

(iii) The mileage figures for each sales person for the two quarters are fairly well correlated.

$$r = \frac{10 \times 13,993 - 280 \times 480}{\sqrt{(10 \times 8,338 - 280^2) \times (10 \times 23,830 - 480^2)}} = 0.88$$

(b) Variables expected to be **positively correlated** are those which either depend one on the other, or which both depend on some third factor, where low values of one variable are associated with low values of the other, and high values of one variable are associated with high values of the other.

An example would be the cost of fixed assets in the balance sheet and the depreciation charge in the profit and loss account. Another would be the value of sales and the value of cost of sales in the profit and loss account.

Monthly retail sales of cocoa and monthly retail sales of ice cream are likely to be negatively correlated.

(c) (i) We have **negative correlation** here, as shown by the **negative coefficient of x** in the regression line. That is, as the number of years employed with the company rises, so the number of days absent through sickness falls.

Correlation coefficient $= -\sqrt{0.9} = -0.95$.

(ii) y = 15.6 − 1.2x

The 15.6 represents the numbers of days absence through sickness that an employee with zero years service is expected to suffer, so it is the number of days that an employee will need off through sickness in their first year of employment. The −1.2 represents the **gradient of the regression line**, meaning that for each extra year's service with the company, an employee will take 1.2 fewer days off sick per year.

(iii) y = 15.6 − 1.2 × 8 = 15.6 − 9.6 = 6 days.

An employee who has been with the company for eight years is expected to require six days sick leave per year.

(iv)

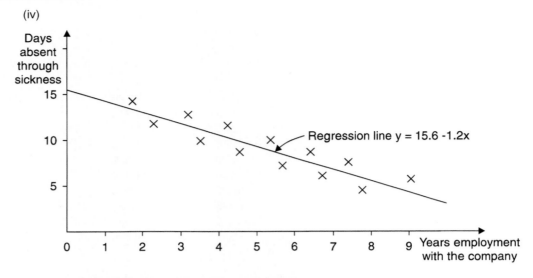

(v) **Limitations and problems in using this equation in practice**

(1) The regression line approach **presupposes that there is a linear relationship** between the two variables: a sample of 50 workers has given us quite strong correlation, but still a **strict linear relationship** seems unlikely.

(2) A **linear relationship** may hold good within a **small relevant range of data** within which the equation may be useful in practice. But extrapolating outside this range will lead to serious inaccuracies. Thus the equation would predict that an employee with more than $15.6/1.2 = 13$ years' service would have less than zero sick leave.

(3) If we use the equation to **predict the future**, we will use **historical data** to forecast the future, which is always risky.

(4) The **regression line** shows the **expected number of days sick** for a given employment period. But it is unlikely that all categories of workers will experience the same sickness pattern. The equation would be most useful if there were many employees all doing the same job in the same work conditions.

16 RANK CORRELATION

(a) (i) Both **correlation coefficients** measure the **strength of the linear relationship** between two variables and both show whether the variables increase together or whether one decreases as the other increases.

(ii) The **product moment correlation coefficient** uses the actual values whilst the rank coefficient measures only the relationship between the rankings of those values.

(iii) The circumstances in which each should be used are as follows.

(1) For **ranked data** r_S should often be used since it is easier to compute than r.

(2) For **unranked data**, in general r should be used since information is lost about the actual values when we rank data and so r gives a better measure of the relationship than does r_S.

(3) If the linearity of the actual values is important, as it is when we find the equation of the **line of best fit** and use it to make estimates, r must be used.

(4) If linearity is not important in that you want to investigate the relationship between the variables but have no interest in whether it is linear or curved, it might be easier to deliberately rank the data and calculate r_S.

(b)

Newspaper	Order of preference	Ranked % recall	|d|	d^2
A	9	7.5	1.5	2.25
B	3	4.0	1.0	1.00
C	10	9.0	1.0	1.00
D	1	1.0	0.0	0.00
E	6	5.0	1.0	1.00
F	4	3.0	1.0	1.00
G	12	12.0	0.0	0.00
H	2	2.0	0.0	0.00
I	7	10.0	3.0	9.00
J	11	11.0	0.0	0.00
K	5	6.0	1.0	1.00
L	8	7.5	0.5	0.25
				16.50

Tutorial note. You will see that we have ranked the largest percentage recall number 1 and the smallest number 12. This is because, where preference is concerned, the convention is to rank the biggest score as number one. In an exam it would be perfectly acceptable to rank according to numerical magnitude but r_S would then be negative. The interpretation would be the same, namely that preference and percentage recall are strongly linked and increase together. The negative would arise from the allocation of the lowest numerical rank to the most preferred newspaper.

Note also that A and L have **tied rankings**. If they had been different they would have been 7th and 8th so we rank them both 7.5.

$$r_S = 1 - \frac{6\Sigma d^2}{n(n^2 - 1)} \quad n = 12 \quad \Sigma d^2 = 16.5$$

$$= 1 - \frac{6 \times 16.5}{12 \times 143}$$

$$= 1 - \frac{99}{1,716} = 1 = 0.06$$

$$= 0.94$$

The value of r_S indicates that there is a **very strong relationship** between ability to recall advertising material and preference for a newspaper. As preference increases, so does % recall.

17 MOVING AVERAGE

Year	Month	Output (000s)	Rounded values (000s) (A)	Moving 4 month total (000s)	Moving 8 month total (000s)	Moving Average (÷ 8) (000s) (B)
20X3	May	40.6	41			
	June	33.3	33			
	July	29.5	30	139	273	34.125
	August	34.8	35	134	277	34.625
	September	36.1	36	143	297	37.125
	October	42.2	42	154	304	38.000
	November	40.5	41	150	302	37.750
	December	31.1	31	152	298	37.250
20X4	January	37.9	38	146	295	36.875
	February	36.4	36	149	307	38.375
	March	43.7	44	158	316	39.500
	April	40.0	40	158	312	39.000
	May	38.2	38	154	299	37.375
	June	32.2	32	145	286	35.750
	July	34.6	35	141		
	August	35.8	36			

Suggested answers

(a) The solution to (a) is column (A) above.

(b) The solution to (b) is column (B) above.

(c)

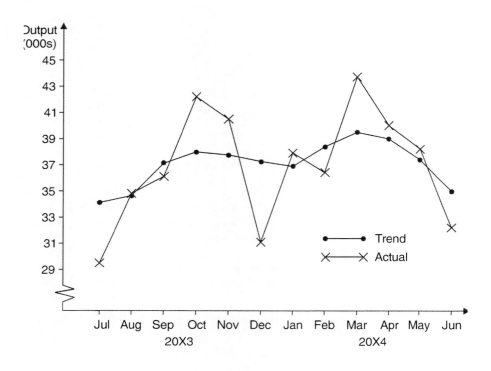

18   HOPWOOD TRENDS LTD

(a)

Year	Quarter	Sales	Moving total of 4 quarters sales	Moving 8 quarter total	Moving average(÷ 8) (solution)	Variation
20X2	1	200				
	2	110				
			870			
	3	320		1,754	219	+101
			884			
	4	240		1,776	222	+18
			892			
20X3	1	214		1,798	225	-11
			906			
	2	118		1,832	229	-111
			926			
	3	334		1,858	232	+102
			932			
	4	260		1,870	234	+26
			938			
20X4	1	220		1,882	235	-15
			944			
	2	124		1,906	238	-114
			962			
	3	340				
	4	278				

(b)

Year	Quarter 1	2	3	4	Total
20X2			+101.0	+18.0	
20X3	-11.0	-111.0	+102.0	+26.0	
20X4	-15.0	-114.0			
Unadjusted average	-13.0	-112.5	+101.5	+22.0	-2
Adjustment	+0.5	+0.5	+0.5	+ 0.5	+2
Adjusted average	-12.5	-112.0	+102.0	+22.5	0

(c) The average quarterly rise in the trend is $(238 - 219)/7 = 2.7$ units.

The predicted sales for the third quarter of 20X5 are therefore $238 + (5 \times 2.7) + 102 = 353.5$, or 354 units to the nearest unit.

19 PRICE RELATIVES

The values of items consumed in the base period are:

A   £10,000
B   £18,000
C   £15,000

These can be divided by 1,000 to give weights of 10, 18 and 15 (total 43).

	Price relative × weight			
Period	*A*	*B*	*C*	*Total*
20X0	1,000	1,800	1,500	4,300
20X1	1,000	1,944	1,350	4,294
20X2	1,100	2,070	1,500	4,670

Price index for 20X1 $= \dfrac{4,294}{4,300} \times 100 = 99.8$

Price index for 20X2 $= \dfrac{4,670}{4,300} \times 100 = 108.6$

20 PRICE AND QUANTITY

(a)

Item	Quantity Q_o	Price 1.7.X2 P_o £	Price 1.7.X6 P_n £	P_oQ_o	P_nQ_o
Widgets	18	8	6	144	108
Fidgets	12	7	8	84	96
Splodgets	24	2	4	48	96
Tudgets	15	6	7	90	105
Ringlets	8	10	9	80	72
				446	477

Index at 1.7.X6 $= \dfrac{477}{446} \times 100 = 107$

(b) (i) The base month is October 20X3.

Item	Quantity	Weighting	Q_0w
Hocks	30	9	270
Nocks	24	4	96
Socks	18	5	90
			456

Suggested answers

To remove differences in the number of days worked, we should calculate a daily rate of output in October 20X3.

$$\frac{456}{22 \text{ days}} = 20.727 \text{ weighted units per day}$$

Item	Quantity Nov 20X3 Q_1	Quantity Dec 20X3 Q_2	Weighting w	$Q_1 w$	$Q_2 w$
Hocks	25	24	9	225	216
Nocks	28	20	4	112	80
Socks	20	16	5	100	80
				437	376

Days in month	20	16
Weighted units per day	21.85	23.5

Productivity index numbers are as follows.

November 20X3 $\dfrac{21.85}{20.727} \times 100 = 105.4$

December 20X3 $\dfrac{23.5}{20.727} \times 100 = 113.4$

(ii) Since productivity in week 2 and week 3 are about the same, and the number of days in each week is the same, $\Sigma Q_2 w = \Sigma Q_3 w$

where Q_2 is the quantity of each item in week 2
          Q_3 is the quantity of each item in week 3
          w is the weighting

Let the new weighting for Socks be X.

$$(9 \times 7) + (4 \times 7) + (6 \times X) = (9 \times 6) + (4 \times 10) + (5 \times X)$$
$$63 + 28 + 6X = 54 + 40 + 5X$$
$$X = 3$$

The new weighting for Socks should be 3.

(c) (i)

	20X5 P_o £	Q_o '000s	20X9 P_n £	Q_n '000s	$P_o Q_n$	$P_o Q_o$	$P_n Q_n$	$P_n Q_o$
A	120.51	3.9	110.00	3.0	361.53	469.99	330.00	429.00
B	238.89	1.8	300.00	2.5	597.22	430.00	750.00	540.00
C	110.00	1.0	140.00	1.0	110.00	110.00	140.00	140.00
D	62.50	4.0	89.13	4.6	287.50	250.00	410.00	356.52
					1,356.25	1,259.99	1,630.00	1,465.52

(1) **The Laspeyre volume index for**

20X9 based on 20X5 $= \dfrac{\Sigma P_o Q_n}{\Sigma P_o Q_o} \times 100 = \dfrac{1,356.25}{1,259.99} \times 100 = 107.64$

(2) **The Paasche volume index for**

20X9 based on 20X5 $= \dfrac{\Sigma P_n Q_n}{\Sigma P_n Q_o} \times 100 = \dfrac{1,630.00}{1,465.52} \times 100 = 111.22$

(ii) 20X5 was chosen as the **base year** because it was the first year in which all divisions were operating. An earlier year would therefore have been an unrepresentative base for an index.

(iii) There was a substantial fall in sales volume in division A between 20X5 and 20X9, so an index based on 20X5 quantities will not properly reflect current sales. The Paasche index, using 20X9 volumes, is likely to be preferable in this case to a Laspeyre index because it reflects the new distribution of sales between the divisions.

(iv) The revenue increased by 29%, but prices also changed. A volume index cannot be based on revenues alone, but it must also take account of differing prices from year to year. This is done by preparing an index with constant prices (either P_0 in the Laspeyre index or P_n in the Paasche index). An index of 129 would be obtained using

$$\frac{\Sigma P_n Q_n}{\Sigma P_0 Q_0}$$

which gives a turnover index, but not a price index.

21 PROBABILITIES

(a) **The probability of an outcome is the likelihood or chance of it happening**. It is usually expressed as a **proportion**: for example, the probability of a tossed coin coming up heads is ½. The sum of the probabilities of all the (**mutually exclusive**) outcomes which could happen is always 1: for example, P(heads) + P(tails) = ½ + ½ = 1. If the probability of something is 1, then it **must happen**. On the other hand, if the probability of something is 0, then it **cannot happen**.

Probability theory uses formulae to compute the probabilities of various combinations of outcomes occurring. The appropriate formula depends on the relationships between events and between their outcomes. Here are some examples.

(i) Two outcomes are **mutually exclusive** when one of them cannot occur if the other occurs. Several outcomes are mutually exclusive if the occurrence of any one of them excludes the possibility of any of the others occurring.

(ii) Events are said to be **independent** if the outcome of one of them in no way affects the probabilities of the various outcomes of the others.

If several outcomes, X, Y and Z are mutually exclusive, then the probability that one of X, Y and Z will occur is given by the special **rule of addition**.

P (X, Y or Z) = P(X) + P(Y) + P(Z)

A more general **rule of addition** must be applied when outcomes are **not mutually exclusive**. If A and B are two possible outcomes then we apply the following rule.

P(A or B) = P(A) + P(B) − P(A and B)

The probability of outcomes A and B of two **independent events** both occurring is given by the special **rule of multiplication**.

P(A and B) = P(A) × P(B)

If the probability of one outcome occurring is affected by whether another outcome occurs, then the probability that both outcomes will occur is given by the **general rule of multiplication**.

P(A and B) = P(A) × P(B|A) = P(B) × P(A|B)

where P(B|A) means the probability of B occurring given that A occurs.

(b) (i) P(male reaching age of 80) = $\dfrac{16,199}{100,000}$ = 0.16199

P(female reaching age of 80) = $\dfrac{24,869}{100,000}$ = 0.24869

(ii) P(male of 25 not reaching age of 50)

$= \dfrac{85,824 - 74,794}{85,824} = \dfrac{11,030}{85,824} = 0.1285$

P(female of 25 not reaching age of 50)

$= \dfrac{88,133 - 78,958}{88,133} = \dfrac{9,175}{88,133} = 0.1041$

(iii) P(new born male survives until 10)

$= \dfrac{89,023}{100,000} = 0.89023$

P(new born female survives until 10)

$= \dfrac{91,083}{100,000} = 0.91083$

BPP
PUBLISHING

(iv) P(male of 50 not reaching age of 80)

$$= \frac{74,794 - 16,199}{74,794} = \frac{58.595}{74,794} = 0.7834$$

P(female of 50 not reaching age of 80)

$$= \frac{78,958 - 24,869}{78,958} = \frac{54,089}{78,958} = 0.6850$$

A glance at the table of figures shows that females are likely to live longer than males. The probability calculations confirm that conclusion. Such data are used by life assurance companies, which use the statistics on the large numbers of people taking out life assurance policies to determine premiums. Note that reliable statistics can only be compiled on the basis of large samples, and that life assurance companies can only use them appropriately if they write many policies. If only one person has a policy, and he or she dies early, the assurer would suffer a loss even if that person had been 'likely' to live to a great age

22   PERRY WINKLE LTD

(a) (i)   Probability $= \dfrac{4}{36} = 0.111$

(ii)   Probability $= \dfrac{16}{36} = 0.444$

(iii)   Probability $= \dfrac{21 + 7 - 2}{36} = \dfrac{26}{36} = 0.722$

(b) (i)   (1)   Probability that A will be completed within 3 months = 0.9

Probability that B will be completed within 3 months = 0.8

The probability that both will be completed in this time is $0.9 \times 0.8 = 0.72$

(2)   Similarly, the probability that both will be completed within two months is

$(0.1 + 0.2) \times 0.6 = 0.18$.

The probability of completion of both within three months but not within two months is $0.72 - 0.18 = 0.54$.

To answer parts (3) and (4) it might be helpful to construct a grid of completion times and joint probabilities.

			Installation A			
			1 month	2 months	3 months	4 months
			0.1	0.2	0.6	0.1
	2 months	0.6	0.06	0.12	0.36	0.06
Installation B	3 months	0.2	0.02	0.04	0.12	0.02
	4 months	0.2	0.02	0.04	0.12	0.02

(3)   A and B both completed in 2 months   0.12
A and B both completed in 3 months   0.12
A and B both completed in 4 months   0.02
Probability of completion at the same time   0.26

(4)   A takes 1 month, B takes longer (0.06 + 0.02 + 0.02)   0.10
A takes 2 months, B takes 3 months   0.04
A takes 2 months, B takes 4 months   0.04
A takes 3 months, B takes 4 months   0.12
Probability that A is completed before B   0.30

(ii)   Expected completion times are as follows.

	A			B	
Duration Months	Probability	Expected duration Months	Duration Months	Probability	Expected duration Months
1	0.1	0.1	2	0.6	1.2
2	0.2	0.4	3	0.2	0.6
3	0.6	1.8	4	0.2	0.8
4	0.1	0.4			
Expected duration		2.7			2.6

Installation B has a slightly shorter expected duration.

(c)

Sales Units	Probability	Expected quantity	Selling price Units	Probability £	Expected value £
10,000	0.4	4,000	8.00	0.3	2.40
15,000	0.4	6,000	7.50	0.6	4.50
20,000	0.2	4,000	7.00	0.1	0.70
		EV = 14,000			EV = 7.60

Variable cost £	Probability	Expected value £	Fixed costs £	Probability	Expected value £
5.00	0.1	0.50	12,000	0.4	4,800
5.50	0.2	1.10	15,000	0.6	9,000
5.80	0.5	2.90			
6.00	0.2	1.20			
		EV = 5.70			EV = 13,800

(i)
	£
Expected sales revenue (14,000 × £7.60)	106,400
Less variable costs (14,000 × £5.70)	79,800
Contribution	26,600
Less fixed costs	13,800
Expected profit	12,800

(ii)   The worst possible outcome is as follows.
Sales of 10,000 units (probability 0.4)
Selling price of £7 (probability 0.1)
Variable cost per unit of £6 (probability 0.2)
Fixed costs of £15,000 (probability 0.6)

	£
Revenue (10,000 × £7)	70,000
Less variable costs	60,000
Contribution	10,000
Less fixed costs	15,000
Loss	(5,000)

The probability that a loss of £5,000 will occur is 0.4 × 0.1 × 0.2 × 0.6 = 0.0048.

23   THREE MACHINES

(a)
Machine	Ratio of inspection	Probability
A	1	0.2
B	1	0.2
C	3	0.6
	5	1.0

There is a 0.2 probability that a tube selected for inspection comes from machine A.

(b) The probability of a tube being defective can be calculated as an **expected value**.

Machine	Probability of selection for inspection	Probability of tube being defective	EV of probability of being defective
A	0.2	0.1	0.02
B	0.2	0.1	0.02
C	0.6	0.2	0.12
			0.16

The probability of a tube being defective is 0.16.

(c) The probability that a tube found to be defective comes from machine A

$$= \frac{\text{EV of probability of defective from A}}{\text{EV of probability of defective from A, B or C}}$$

$$= \frac{0.02}{0.16} = 0.125.$$

24 ONE IN A MILLION LTD

(a) $n = 10$ and the probability of being late on any day is $p = 0.15$. The distribution is binomial.

    (i)   The mean number of times an average employee will be late is $np = 10 \times 0.15 = 1.5$ times.

    (ii)   An individual employee will lose his bonus if he is late more than three times in a ten day period.

$$P(4 \text{ or more times}) = 1 - (P(0) + P(1) + P(2) + P(3))$$

$$P(0) = \frac{10!}{0!10!}(0.15)^0(0.85)^{10} = 0.1969$$

$$P(1) = \frac{10!}{1!9!}(0.15)^1(0.85)^9 = 10(0.15)(0.2316) = 0.3474$$

$$P(2) = \frac{10!}{2!8!}(0.15)^2(0.85)^8 = 45(0.0225)(0.2725) = 0.2759$$

$$P(3) = \frac{10!}{3!7!}(0.15)^3(0.85)^7 = 120(0.0034)(0.3206) = 0.1308$$

P(0)	0.1969
P(1)	0.3474
P(2)	0.2759
P(3)	0.1308
P(0 to 3)	0.9510
	1.0000
P(4 or more)	0.0490

The probability that a single employee will lose his bonus is 0.049, therefore in a workforce of 1,800 employees, the expected number to lose their bonus will be $0.049 \times 1,800 = 88.2$, say 88 people in each two week period.

(b) (i) $n = 20$, the probability of a defective is 0.05 and the probability of no defectives is 0.95.

$$P\text{ (less than 3)} = P(0) + P(1) + P(2)$$

$$P(0) = \frac{20!}{0!20!}(0.05)^0(0.95)^{20} = 0.3585$$

$$P(1) = \frac{20!}{1!19!}(0.05)^1(0.95)^{19} = 20(0.05)(0.3774) = 0.3774$$

$$P(2) = \frac{20!}{2!18!}(0.05)^2(0.95)^{18} = 190(0.0025)(0.3972) = 0.1887$$

P(0)	0.3585
P(1)	0.3774
P(2)	0.1887
P (up to 2)	0.9246

(ii)   The probability of a consignment with 5% defectives being rejected is $1 - 0.9246 = 0.0754$.

The probability of a batch with 10% defectives being rejected can be calculated as follows.

$$P(0) = \frac{20!}{0!\,20!}\ (0.1)^0\,(0.9)^{20} \quad = \qquad\qquad 0.1216$$

$$P(1) = \frac{20!}{1!\,19!}\ (0.1)^1\,(0.9)^{19} \quad = 20(0.1)(0.1351) = \qquad 0.2702$$

$$P(2) = \frac{20!}{2!\,18!}\ (0.1)^2\,(0.9)^{18} \quad = 190(0.01)(0.1501) = \qquad 0.2852$$

P (up to 2)   0.6770

Probability of rejection if 10% defectives = $1 - 0.6770$ =   0.3230

Therefore the proportion of consignments rejected is

$^1/3 \times 0.0754 + {}^2/3 \times 0.3230 = 0.2405$.

24.5% of consignments are likely to be rejected.

(c)   (i)   **Binomial distribution**

$n = 50$, $p = 0.01$, $q = 0.99$

The probability of no defectives is:

$$P(0) \quad = \frac{50!}{0!\,50!}\ (0.01)^0\,(0.99)^{50}$$

$$= \quad 1 \times 1 \times 0.99^{50}$$

$$= \quad 0.99^{50}$$

$$= \quad 0.605$$

(ii)   **Poisson distribution**

Mean = $np = 50 \times 0.01 = 0.5$

$$P(0) = \frac{0.5^0}{0!}\ e^{-0.5} = \frac{1}{e^{0.5}}$$

$e^{0.5}$ is the square root of e, which is:

$\sqrt{2.71828} = 1.64872$

$$P(0) = \frac{1}{1.64872} = 0.607$$

This is very close to the exact result obtained by using the binomial distribution.

25   BATTERIES

(a)   96% of batteries have a life exceeding 40 hours. From normal distribution tables, 96% of the area under the normal curve lies to the left of $z = 1.75$ standard deviations above the mean, so 96% of the area lies to the right of 1.75 standard deviations below the mean.

Therefore 100 hours - 40 hours = 1.75 standard deviations

Standard deviation $= \dfrac{60 \text{ hours}}{1.75} = 34.3$ hours

(b)   The probability of a battery's life being less than 57 hours is represented by the area to the left of $(100 - 57)/34.3 = 1.25$ standard deviations below the mean, which is $1 - 0.8944 = 0.1056$. The required percentage is therefore 10.56%.

26   NIGER LTD

(a)   (i)   The cost of testing a batch of tridgets is $1{,}000 \times £1.25 + 1{,}000p \times £5$,

where p is the proportion of defective units in a batch.

The cost of rectifying the finished product is $1{,}000p \times £10$.

It would be cheaper to test all the tridgets rather than none of them if the former cost is less than the latter.

$1{,}000 \times £1.25 + 1{,}000p \times £5 < 1{,}000p \times £10$

$1{,}250 + 5{,}000p < 10{,}000p$

$1{,}250 < 5{,}000p$

$\dfrac{1{,}250}{5{,}000} < p$

$0.25 < p$

The proportion of defective tridgets in a batch must be over 0.25 for it to be cheaper to test all of them.

(ii)   The standard error of a proportion is $\sqrt{\dfrac{pq}{n}}$ where p is the proportion of defectives,

q the proportion of good units and n the sample size.

$$se = \sqrt{\frac{0.2 \times 0.8}{100}} = 0.04$$

95% confidence limits for a proportion are $p \pm 1.96se$.

$0.20 \pm 1.96 \times 0.04$ gives limits of 0.1216 and 0.2784.

95% confidence limits for the proportion of defectives in the batch from which the sample was taken are approximately 0.12 and 0.28.

(iii)   To calculate the sample size it is necessary first of all to calculate the number of the standard deviations which allow 95% of the area under the normal curve to be to the left of 0.25.

The value of 0.25 must be 1.64 standard deviations to the right of the sample estimated proportion (0.20). This value is derived from normal distribution tables.

$$n = \frac{1.64^2 \times pq}{r^2}$$

$$n = \frac{1.64^2 \times 0.2 \times 0.8}{0.05^2}$$

$$= 172.13 \text{ units}$$

A sample size of 173 (remember that we must round up) is required to indicate with 95% confidence that the proportion of defective units is less than 25% assuming that the sample continues to indicate 20% defectives.

(b)

Mid-point of class interval x	Frequency f	fx	fx^2
50	20	1,000	50,000
150	18	2,700	405,000
250	22	5,500	1,375,000
350	15	5,250	1,837,500
450	9	4,050	1,822,500
550	8	4,400	2,420,000
650	4	2,600	1,690,000
750	2	1,500	1,125,000
850	2	1,700	1,445,000
	100	28,700	12,170,000

(i) **Mean of sample** = £28,700/100 = £287.

Variance of sample = $(12,170,000/100) - 287^2 = 39,331$.

Standard deviation of sample = $\sqrt{39,331}$ = £198.32.

(ii) The **standard error of the sample mean is** $\sigma/\sqrt{n} = 198.32/\sqrt{100}$ = £19.832.

(1) At the **95% confidence level**, the confidence interval for the average value of all invoices is

$\bar{x} \pm 1.96$ se
= £$(287 \pm 1.96 \times 19.832)$ = £(287 ± 38.87)
= £248.13 to £325.87.

(2) At the **99% confidence level** the confidence interval for the average value of all invoices is

$\bar{x} \pm 2.58$ se
= £$(287 \pm 2.58 \times 19.832)$ = £(287 ± 51.17)
= £235.83 to £338.17.

27 DRY GULCH LTD

The standard deviation of the sample, s, is 2 minutes, so the estimated standard deviation of the population is 2 minutes.

The standard error of the sample mean is $2/\sqrt{49}$ = 0.2857 minutes.

(a) The **null hypothesis** is that the population mean is 48 minutes. The alternative hypothesis is that it is more than 48 minutes. This is a one-tail test at 1% significance, so the cut-off level is 2.33 standard errors.

$50 - 48 = 2$ minutes $= 2/0.2857 = 7$ standard errors

We therefore reject the null hypothesis and conclude that the average time per unit in January 20X3 was longer than 48 minutes. The claim of the factory manager is rejected.

(b) 95% confidence limits would be 1.96 standard errors either side of the sample mean of 50 minutes.

Confidence limits = $50 \pm (1.96 \times 0.2857)$ minutes
= 50 ± 0.56 minutes
= 49.44 and 50.56 minutes

28 SOLVE

(a) Since $2x + y - 4z = -20$
$y = 4z - 2x - 20$

Substitute this value for y in the other two equations.

(i) $x - 2(4z - 2x - 20) + 3z = -5$
$x - 8z + 4x + 40 + 3z = -5$
$5x - 5z = -45$
$x - z = -9$ (1)

(ii) $3x - 3(4z - 2x - 20) - z = -37$
$3x - 12z + 6x + 60 - z = -37$
$9x - 13z = -97$ (2)

Multiply equation (1) by 9.

$9x - 9z = -81$ (3)

Subtract equation (3) from equation (2)

$$-4z = -16$$
$$z = 4$$

$$x - z = -9 \quad (1)$$
$$x - 4 = -9$$
$$x = -5$$

$$y = 4z - 2x - 20$$
$$y = 16 + 10 - 20$$
$$y = 6$$

The solution is $x = -5$, $y = 6$, $z = 4$.

(b) Let the two positive numbers be x and y.

$$x^2 + y^2 = 890 \quad (1)$$
$$x - y = 4 \quad (2)$$
$$y = x - 4 \quad (3) \text{ (from (2))}.$$

Substituting in (1) we get
$$x^2 + (x - 4)^2 = 890$$
$$x^2 + (x^2 - 8x + 16) = 890$$
$$2x^2 - 8x - 874 = 0$$
$$x^2 - 4x - 437 = 0$$

Solve the quadratic equation.

$$x = \frac{-(-4) \pm \sqrt{[16 - (4 \times 1 \times (-437))]}}{2 \times 1}$$

$$= \frac{4 \pm \sqrt{1{,}764}}{2}$$

$$= \frac{4 + 42}{2} \text{ or } \frac{4 - 42}{2}$$

$$= 23 \text{ or } -19$$

Since x must be positive, $x = 23$

Since $y = x - 4$, $y = 19$

(c) Let the length and breadth of the rectangle be a and b.

$$2a + 2b = 44$$
$$a + b = 22 \quad (1)$$
$$ab = 112 \quad (2)$$

From (1) we get $a = 22 - b$

Substituting in (2) we get
$$b(22 - b) = 112$$
$$-b^2 + 22b - 112 = 0$$

Solve the quadratic equation.

$$b = \frac{-22 \pm \sqrt{[484 - (4 \times (-1) \times (-112))]}}{2 \times (-1)}$$

$$= \frac{-22 \pm \sqrt{36}}{-2}$$

$$= \frac{-22 + 6}{-2} \text{ or } \frac{-22 - 6}{-2}$$

$$b = 8 \text{ or } 14$$

Since $a + b = 22$, the sides of the rectangle are 8 metres and 14 metres.

29   QUADRATIC EQUATIONS

(a)   (i) $x = [+1.28 \pm \sqrt{((-1.28)^2 + 4 \times 1 \times 5.16)}]/(2 \times 1)$

  $= [+1.28 \pm \sqrt{22.2784}]/2$

  $= [+1.28 \pm 4.72]/2$

  $= 3 \text{ or } -1.72.$

(ii) $x = [-33 \pm \sqrt{(33^2 - 4 \times 4 \times 68)}]/(2 \times 4)$

  $= [-33 \pm \sqrt{1}]/8$

  $= [-33 \pm 1]/8$

  $= -4 \text{ or } -4.25.$

(iii) $-3x^2 + 6x + 24 = 0$

  $x = [-6 \pm \sqrt{(6^2 + 4 \times 3 \times 24)}]/(2 \times -3)$

  $= [-6 \pm \sqrt{324}]/(-6)$

  $= [-6 \pm 18]/(-6)$

  $= -2 \text{ or } +4.$

(iv) $x = [+4.8 \pm \sqrt{((-4.8)^2 - 4 \times 1 \times 5.76)}]/(2 \times 1)$

  $= (+4.8 \pm \sqrt{0})/2$

  $= 2.4.$

(b)   **Total revenue** $= pq = 600q - 0.15q^2 = 450,000$

  $-0.15q^2 + 600q - 450,000 = 0$

  $q = [-600 \pm \sqrt{(600^2 - 4 \times 0.15 \times 450,000)}]/(2 \times -0.15)$

  $= [-600 \pm \sqrt{90,000}]/(-0.3)$

  $= [-600 \pm 300]/(-0.3)$

  $= 1,000 \text{ or } 3,000 \text{ units.}$

(c)   (i) $y = ax + b$

When x = £16.40:

  $16,100 = 16.4a + b$ (1)

When x = £12.80:

  $24,200 = 12.8a + b$ (2)

Subtract (2) from (1).

  $-8,100 = 3.6a$

  $a = -2,250$

Substitute in equation (1).

  $16,100 = -36,900 + b$

  $b = 53,000$

The equation we require is

  $y = -2,250x + 53,000$

(ii)   **Revenue** $=$ volume of demand $\times$ price per unit

  $= \quad y \quad \times \quad x$

  $y = -2,250x + 53,000$

  Revenue $= x(-2,250x + 53,000)$

  $= -2,250x^2 + 53,000x$

  Costs $= 40,000 + 8y$

  $y = -2,250x + 53,000$

  Costs $= 40,000 + 8(-2,250x + 53,000)$

  $= 40,000 - 18,000x + 424,000$

  $= 464,000 - 18,000x$

Profit = revenue − costs $= -2,250x^2 + 71,000x - 464,000$

(iii)   A total profit of £89,000 will occur where

  $-2,250x^2 + 71,000x - 464,000 = 89,000$

  $-2,250x^2 + 71,000x - 553,000 = 0$

The solutions to this quadratic equation are as follows.

$$\frac{-71,000 \pm \sqrt{[(71,000)^2 - (4 \times (-2,250) \times (-553,000))]}}{2 \times (-2,250)}$$

$$= \frac{-71,000 + 8,000}{-4,500} \text{ or } \frac{-71,000 - 8,000}{-4,500}$$

x = +14   or +17.555

Since a price of £17.56 is outside the range for which the linear relationship given applies, it is not an acceptable solution. A profit of £89,000 will be obtained, however, at a price of £14 a unit.

Demand = y = −2,250x + 53,000 = 21,500 units.

30   REVENUES AND COSTS

(a)   Let q = the quantity of items produced.

    Total costs (£) = fixed costs + variable costs
            = 1,200 + 60q

(b)   We are told that the demand function is **linear**. To identify any straight line uniquely, it is sufficient to identify two points that lie on that line. We shall therefore demonstrate that the two points given satisfy the equation p = 160 − 2q.

    When p = 120, q = 20
       p = 160 − 2q = 160 − (2 × 20)
         = 160 − 40 = 120.

    When p = 100, q = 30
       p = 160 − 2q = 160 − (2 × 30)
         = 160 − 60 = 100.

    Both points satisfy the equation, so demand and price are indeed linked by the relation p = 160 − 2q.

(c)   **Revenue = Price × demand**
         = p × q
         = (160 − 2q)q
         = 160q − 2q²

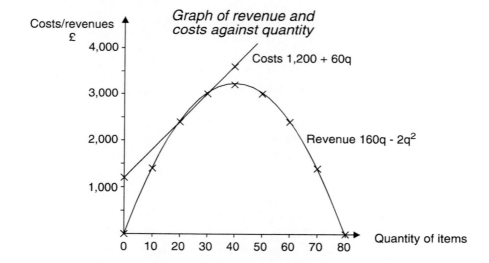

Graph of revenue and costs against quantity

Tabulation for graph

q	Costs $(1,200 + 60q)$	Revenues $(160q - 2q^2)$
0	1,200	0
10		1,400
20		2,400
30		3,000
40	3,600	3,200
50		3,000
60		2,400
70		1,400
80		0

(d) The graph shows breakeven points at outputs of 20 units and 30 units. We can verify this result algebraically.

Breakeven occurs when Revenue = Costs

$$\therefore\ 160q - 2q^2 = 1,200 + 60q$$

So we must solve the quadratic equation

$$2q^2 - 100q + 1,200 = 0$$

which simplifies to

$$q^2 - 50q + 600 = 0$$

We can see that this equation factorises into

$$(q - 20)(q - 30) = 0$$

and conclude that revenue = costs when q = 20 units and when q = 30 units.

31 **BRASS LTD**

(a) Let the number of units of Masso produced be   x
Let the number of units of Russo be   y.

The **optimal production plan** is assumed to be one which **maximises contribution and profit**.

The objective is to maximise 40x + 50y subject to the following constraints.

x + 2y	$\leq$	700	(Machining hours)
2.5x + 2y	$\leq$	1,000	(Assembly hours)
x	$\leq$	400	(Maximum output)
y	$\leq$	400	(Maximum output)
x,y	≥ 0		

The problem may be solved graphically. The **breakeven position** occurs where the total contribution equals fixed costs, that is, where 40x + 50y = 17,000.

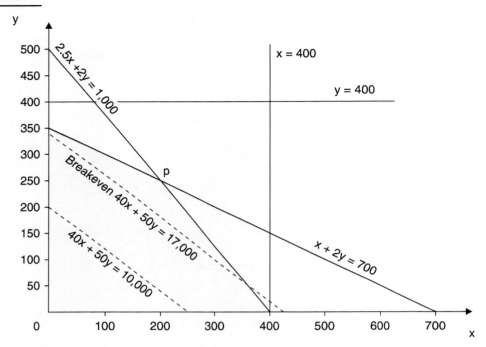

Contribution would be maximised at point P, where

2.5x + 2y = 1,000
x + 2y   = 700

Subtracting, 1.5x = 300
                      x = 200

Since x = 200 and x + 2y = 700
                               2y = 500
                                 y = 250

The **optimal production plan** is as follows.

	Units of production	Unit contribution £	Total £
Masso	200	40	8,000
Russo	250	50	12,500
Contribution			20,500
Less fixed costs			17,000
Profit			3,500

(b) The principal assumptions used in (a) are as follows.

(i) **The relationship between variables is linear**. In other words, the selling price per unit, resources consumed per unit and variable costs per unit are the same at all levels of output. This is a simplification which may not be realistic especially in the case of selling prices.

(ii) **The cost function relies on an accurate division of costs into fixed and variable elements**. Using historical costs to predict costs is a hazardous exercise, very prone to error.

(iii) **All constraints and coefficients are known with certainty**. Our solution does not allow for uncertainties and probabilities.

(iv) **There is no interdependence** between demand for Masso and Russo, so that the production mix selected can ignore problems of sales mix.

These assumptions might seem seriously to restrict the usefulness of linear programming, because none of them (especially items (i) and (iii)) is likely to apply. Nevertheless, provided that the assumptions are stated and understood, linear programming might help to provide better budgeting decisions when resources are scarce.

32   WALLOP LTD

(a)
	Hake	*Pane*
Hours per unit		
Labour	8 hrs	6 hrs
Machining	5 hrs	8 hrs

The linear programming problem may be formulated as follows.

Let x be the number of hakes produced per month
Let y be the number of panes produced per month.

The objective is to maximise 16x + 20y subject to the following constraints.

$$8x + 6y \leq 9,600 \quad \text{(labour hours)}$$
$$5x + 8y \leq 8,125 \quad \text{(machine hours)}$$
$$x \leq 1,000 \quad \text{(demand)}$$
$$x, y \geq 0$$

(b)

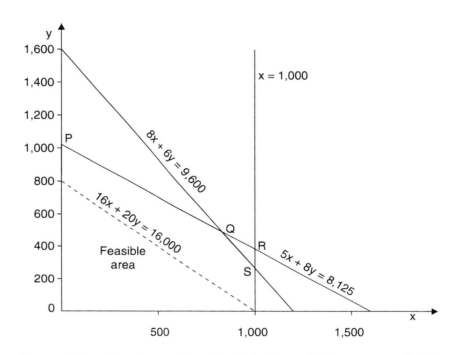

Using an **iso-profit line** 16x + 20y = 16,000 to obtain the gradient, we can see that the **optimal solution** is at point Q.

5x + 8y	=	8,125	(1)
8x + 6y	=	9,600	(2)
40x + 64y	=	65,000	(3) ((1) × 8)
40x + 30y	=	48,000	(4) ((2) × 5)
34y	=	17,000	(5) ((3) − (4))
y	=	500	(6)
8x + 3,000	=	9,600	(substituting (6) in (2))
8x	=	6,600	
x	=	825	

The **optimal solution** is as follows.

	Contribution
	£
825 units of hake (× £16)	13,200
500 units of pane (× £20)	10,000
Total monthly contribution	23,200

33   HITECH

(a)   The **regression equation** indicates that Hitech's overheads consist of:

£4,000   per week fixed overhead
£0.50   per hour spent on production of HT01
£0.70   per hour spent on production of HT02
£0.80   per hour spent on production of HT03

The total variable product costs are therefore as follows.

	HT01 £	HT02 £	HT03 £
Direct labour	100.0	120	132.0
Direct material	20.0	40	40.0
Variable overhead:			
HT01 (£100/£4 × £0.50)	12.5		
HT02 (£120/£4 × £0.70)		21	
HT03 (£132/£4 × £0.80)			26.4
	132.5	181	198.4

(b)   **Contribution earned by each product**

	HT01 £	HT02 £	HT03 £
Price	150.0	200	220.0
Variable production costs	132.5	181	198.4
(see part (a))	17.5	19	21.6

Let a,b,c be the number of HT01, HT02 and HT03 produced respectively. The objective function is to maximise contribution C, given by:

$C = 17.5a + 19b + 21.6c$

The **constraints** are as follows:

$25a + 30b + 33c \leq 257{,}600$ (labour hours)

$a + 2b + 2c \leq 20{,}000$ (materials)

$a \leq 16{,}000$ (demand for HT01)

$b \leq 10{,}000$ (demand for HT02)

$c \leq 6{,}000$ (demand for HT03)

$a,b,c \geq 0$

Let S_1 be the number of unused labour hours.
Let S_2 be the number of unused kilograms of material.
Let S_3, S_4, S_5 respectively be the number of units produced of HT01, HT02 and HT03 less than the maximum demand.

The **constraints** may be formulated:

$25a + 30b + 33c + S_1 = 257{,}600$

$a + 2b + 2c + S_2 = 20{,}000$

$a + S_3 = 16{,}000$

$b + S_4 = 10{,}000$

$c + S_5 = 6{,}000$

$a,b,c \geq 0$

The **objective function** is to maximise C, given by:

$C - 17.5a - 19b - 21.6c + 0S_1 + 0S_2 + 0S_3 + 0S_4 + 0S_5 = 0$

This leads to a **first tableau** where the **slack variables** have the following values:

$S_1 = 257{,}600$

$S_2 = 20{,}000$

$S_3 = 16{,}000$

$S_4 = 10{,}000$

$S_5 = 6{,}000$

First tableau

Variables	a	b	c	S_1	S_2	S_3	S_4	S_5	Solution
S_1	25	30	33	1	0	0	0	0	257,600
S_2	1	2	2	0	1	0	0	0	20,000
S_3	1	0	0	0	0	1	0	0	16,000
S_4	0	1	0	0	0	0	1	0	10,000
S_5	0	0	1	0	0	0	0	1	6,000
Solution	−17.5	−19	−21.6	0	0	0	0	0	0

(c) **Overall contribution** = £180,320

The shadow prices of HT02 and HT03 are £2.00 and £1.50 respectively. This means that for every unit of HT02 or HT03 made, contribution would fall by £2 and £1.50 respectively. In other words, the contribution from HT02 and HT03 would need to rise by at least those respective amounts before it became profitable to manufacture them at the expense of HT01. The shadow price of one hour of labour (S_1) is £0.70. This means that for every extra hour of labour made available at its normal cost of £4 per hour, contribution would be increased by 70p. **This intepretation is only valid while labour hours are a constraint on production**.

34 HOUND CAMPING LTD

(a) The total value of each investment will be calculated. After deducting the original principal, the interest earned will be found.

                                  £

(i) Value at the end of three years = $£8,000 \times 1.11^3$ 10,941.05

(ii) Value at the end of five years = $£15,000 \times 1.14^5$ 28,881.22

(iii) Value at the end of four years = $£6,000 \times 1.1^2 \times 1.15^2$ 9,601.35

                                                      49,423.62

Less principal (8,000 + 15,000 + 6,000)   29,000.00

Interest earned, in total   20,423.62

(b) (i) The **effective annual rate of interest of investment A** is

$1.0525^2 − 1 = 0.1078 = 10.78\%$

This is a lower return than investment (a)(i), which is therefore preferable.

(ii) The **effective annual rate of interest of investment B** is

$1.01^{12} − 1 = 12.68\%$.

This is less than the return from investment (a)(ii) which is therefore preferable.

(iii) If investment C were £6,000, it would earn

$£6,000 \times 1.03^{16}$ by the end of year 4 =
$£6,000 \times 1.6047$
= £9,628

This would be a slightly better return than that from investment (a)(iii).

35 WILFRED AND MABEL

(a) **Using the formula** $P_n = P_0 (1 + i)^n$
                           $P_6 = £5,000 \times 1.08^6$
                              = £7,934.37

(b) **Investment** $= £7,934.37 + \dfrac{1,000 \times [1.08^6 − 1]}{1.08 − 1}$

                    = £7,934.37 + £7,335.93
                    = £15,270.30

Suggested answers

(c) **Investment** $= 2{,}000 \times 1.10^5 + \dfrac{1{,}500 \times [1.10^5 - 1]}{1.10 - 1}$

$= £3{,}221.02 + £9{,}157.65$

$= £12{,}378.67$

(d)

	£
Year 0 value	300,000
Add interest in first year (10%)	30,000
	330,000
Less withdrawal	40,000
	290,000
Add interest in second year (10%)	29,000
	319,000
Less withdrawal	40,000
	279,000
Add interest in third year (8%)	22,320
	301,320
Less withdrawal	40,000
	261,320
Add interest in fourth year (8%)	20,906
	282,226
Less withdrawal	40,000
Value of investment at end of year 4	242,226

(e) **The formula for a sinking fund** is $S_n = a\left[\dfrac{(1+i)^n - 1}{i}\right]$

where a is the annual payment into the fund and S_{n} is the value of the fund in year n.

$100{,}000 = a\left[\dfrac{(1.14^5 - 1)}{0.14}\right]$

$100{,}000 = \left[\dfrac{(1.92541 - 1)}{0.14}\right]a$

$100{,}000 = 6.61007a$

$a = £15{,}128.43$

(f) $S_6 = 10{,}000 \times \left(\dfrac{(1.08)^6 - 1}{0.08}\right) = 10{,}000 \times \left(\dfrac{0.58687}{0.08}\right)$

$= £73{,}358.75$

36 WITCHES CHEEPER LTD

(a) Using the first repayment scheme, the amount of the loan will be the present value of all future repayments, discounted at a cost of 3% interest per quarter.

In five years there will be 20 equal repayments, starting at the end of the first quarter.

$PV = \dfrac{a(1 - (1+i)^{-n})}{i}$

$= \dfrac{1{,}680.45 \times (1 - 1.03^{-20})}{0.03}$

$= \dfrac{1{,}680.45 \times (1 - 0.55368)}{0.03}$

$= £25{,}000.61$, say £25,000.

(b) Using the second repayment scheme, there are 40 equal quarterly repayments.

$$PV = \frac{1,081.60 \times (1 - 1.03^{-40})}{0.03}$$

$$= \frac{1,081.60 \times (1 - 0.30656)}{0.03}$$

$$= £25,000.82, \text{ say } £25,000.$$

37 DAISY HOOF LTD

(a) (i)

Year	Cash flow £	Discount factor 16%	Present value £
0	(50,000)	1.0	(50,000.00)
1	18,000	$\frac{1}{1.16}$	15,517.24
2	25,000	$\frac{1}{1.16^2}$	18,579.07
3	15,000	$\frac{1}{1.16^3}$	9,609.87
4	12,000	$\frac{1}{1.16^4}$	6,627.49
		NPV	333.67

(ii) The IRR is a little above 16%. Try 18%.

Year	Cash flow £	Discount factor 18%	Present value £
0	(50,000)	1.0	(50,000.00)
1	18,000	$\frac{1}{1.18}$	15,254.24
2	25,000	$\frac{1}{1.18^2}$	17,954.61
3	15,000	$\frac{1}{1.18^3}$	9,129.46
4	12,000	$\frac{1}{1.18^4}$	6,189.47
		NPV	(1,472.22)

Using **interpolation**, the IRR approximately equals

$$16\% + \left[\frac{333.67}{(333.67 + 1,472.22)} \times (18 - 16)] \right]\%$$

$$= 16.4\%.$$

(b) The cheapest method of financing will be the one which gives the **lowest present value of cost**, when cash flows are discounted at 12%.

(i) **The loan**

Cash flows are: Years 1-4 £6,000 (interest)
Year 4 £50,000 (loan repayment)

$$\textbf{Present value} = \frac{6,000(1 - (1.12)^{-4})}{0.12} + (50,000 \; \square \; (1.12)^{-4})$$

$$= \frac{6,000 \times (1 - 0.63552)}{0.12} + 50,000 \times 0.63552$$

$$= 18,224 + 31,776$$

$$= £50,000$$

Suggested answers

(ii)   **The lease**

Cash flows are: Years 1-4 £16,000

$$\text{Present value} \quad = \quad \frac{16,000 \times (1 - 0.63552)}{0.12}$$

$$= \quad £48,597$$

(iii) **Hire purchase**

Cash flows are: Years 0-4 £15,000

$$\text{Present value} \quad = 15,000 + \frac{15,000 \times (1 - 0.63552)}{0.12}$$

$$= \quad 15,000 + 45,560$$

$$= \quad £60,560$$

Conclusion

Leasing appears to be cheapest option, followed by the bank loan. Hire purchase is the most expensive option.

Glossary
and Index

Additive model A method of estimating seasonal variations using the absolute differences between trend and actual data.

Annual percentage rate (APR) A rate of interest, calculated annually, which is equivalent to a given rate of interest.

Annuity A series of constant cash flows received over a period of years.

Arithmetic mean An average.

Array A list of items in order of value.

Attribute A property which an object has either got or not got which cannot be measured, for example the sex of a person.

Average A representative figure that is used to give some impression of all the items in a population.

Band curve A graphical data presentation method which is a form of time series graph in which the total figure is broken down into its various components.

Bar chart A method of presenting data in which quantities are shown in the form of bars on a chart, the length of the bars being proportional to the quantities.

Base period The point in time given the value of 100 in an index.

Binomial distribution A probability distribution used to answer questions like: what is the probability that 6 new cars in a batch of 100 will be faulty, given that 3% of all new cars are faulty? The binomial distribution applies where there are two possible outcomes, each with a constant probability. It follows that the outcome of one event has no effect on the outcomes of other events: the events are independent. The binomial distribution is for discrete variables.

Breakeven analysis See cost-volume-profit (CVP) analysis.

Breakeven point The level of activity at which neither a profit nor a loss is made.

Cartogram A method of displaying geographical data.

Census Enumeration of an entire population.

Central limit theorem The statistical rule that a sampling distribution of sample means is normally distributed.

Chain base method A method of indexing in which changes are taken as percentages of values in the period immediately before

Chart A method of visual display of data.

Class interval A subdivision within a frequency distribution.

Cluster sampling A cheap sampling method which can be used when no satisfactory sampling frame exists. It is similar to multistage sampling in that it involves the random selection of a number of small areas from the population but every item in the small areas is then examined.

Coefficient of determination A measure of the proportion of the change in the value of one variable that can be explained by variations in the value of the other variable.

Coefficient of mean deviation A measure of dispersion calculated as the mean deviation expressed as a proportion of the arithmetic mean.

Coefficient of skewness A measure of the skewness of a frequency distribution curve.

Coefficient of variation A relative measure of dispersion which compares the dispersion of two distributions.

Combination A set of items, selected from a larger collection of items, regardless of the order in which they are selected.

Complementary event A term used in probability when determining the probability of an event *not* occurring.

Component bar chart A bar chart that gives the breakdown of each total into its components (by splitting each bar into sections).

Compound annual rate of interest (CAR) Another name for the APR .

Compound bar chart A bar chart in which two or more separate bars are used to present components of each total.

Compound interest Interest accrued on the principal plus the reinvested interest.

Compounding An application of financial mathematics. If £P is invested now for n years at i% interest per annum, we should obtain $£P(1+i)^n$ in n years time.

Conditional probability The probability of an event occurring, conditional on another event having occurred.

Confidence interval A range of values between which a predetermined percentage of sample statistics will fall.

Confidence levels Degrees of certainty in hypothesis testing, for example 95% probability or 99% probability.

Confidence limits In hypothesis testing, the ends of the ranges around the sample mean.

Constraint A limit on the values that variables can take in linear programming.

Continuous variable A variable which can (theoretically) take on any value between two given values (eg height).

Glossary

Correlation The degree to which change in one variable is related to change in another. The interdependence between variables.

Correlation coefficient A measure of the degree of correlation between two variables.

Cost-volume-profit (CVP)/breakeven analysis The study of the interrelationships between costs, volume and profit at various levels of activity.

Cumulative frequency curve An ogive drawn as a curve.

Cumulative frequency distribution Shows the total number of times a value above or below a certain amount occurs.

Cumulative frequency polygon An ogive drawn with straight lines.

Cyclical variations Medium-term changes in result caused by circumstances which repeat in cycles.

Data Scientific term for facts, figures and measurements which are available or have been collected, usually for some form of statistical analysis.

Decile The value of each dividing point when a population is divided into ten equal groups.

Dependent variable A variable whose value is influenced by the value of another variable.

Discount factor The factor to be applied to a future sum of money to change it into a present value amount.

Discounted cash flow A cash flow represented in present value terms.

Discounting An application of financial mathematics. If we wish to have £P_n in n years' time, we need to invest a certain sum now (year 0) at an interest rate of i% in order to obtain the required sum of money in the future. If P_0 is the sum invested now, $P_0 = P_n \times 1/(1+i)^n$.

Discrete variable A variable that can only take a finite or countable number of values within a given range.

Dispersion The extent to which the values taken by the variables in a distribution deviate from the average.

Dual price See shadow price.

Effective annual rate of interest The equivalent annual rate of interest when interest is calculated at intervals shorter than annually.

Expected value A weighted average value based on probabilities.

Extrapolation Process of predicting a value outside a range of known data.

Feasible area/region The area on a graphical model of a linear programming problem in which all of the constraints are satisfied.

First quartile See lower quartile.

Frequency distribution The distribution of the number of times the value of a particular variable occurs.

Frequency distribution curve A frequency polygon of a grouped frequency distribution, the class intervals being very small.

Frequency polygon A chart, derived from a histogram, which makes the assumption that the frequency of occurrence of data items is not evenly spread.

Gantt chart A form of bar chart/line chart which records progress over time.

Graph A form of visual display showing, by means of a straight line or curve, the relationship between two variables.

Grouped frequency distribution The distribution of the number of times values within ranges of particular variables occur.

Histogram A data presentation method for (usually) grouped data of a continuous variable. Visually similar to a bar chart but frequencies are represented by areas covered by the bar rather than by their height.

Historigram The graph of a time series.

Hypothesis testing Process of establishing the significance of the results of sample data for beliefs about a population.

Independent variable A variable whose value affects the value of another variable.

Index numbers Numbers which measure the magnitude of change (usually of prices or of quantities) over a period of time.

Internal rate of return The rate of return at which the net present value of an investment is zero.

Interpolation Process of finding a value within a range of known data.

Interquartile range The difference between the lower and upper quartiles.

Iso-profit lines In linear programming, lines which are parallel to the slope or gradient of the line graphing the objective function

Laspeyre index An index using prices/quantities from the base year as weights.

Layer graph See band curve.

Least squares method A technique used to predict values for one variable (y) given values for the other variable (x), by finding the line (y = a + bx) which is a good fit for the points on a scattergraph, and then using that line to find the value of y corresponding to each given value of x.

Line chart A method of data presentation, similar to a bar chart but using lines instead of bars, the length of line being proportional to the value represented.

Line of best fit Represents the best linear relationship between two variables.

Line of uniform distribution Straight line on a Lorenz curve joining the points (0%, 0%) to (100%, 100%).

Linear equation Equation in which the highest power of the unknown variable(s) is one.

Linear programming The method whereby a decision is reduced to an objective function which must be optimised subject to a number of linear constraints.

Log-linear graph See semi-logarithmic graph.

Lorenz curve Graphical means of data presentation which measure one cumulative amount against another.

Lower quartile The value of the item below which 25% of the population falls.

Margin of safety Difference between budgeted sales volume/revenue and breakeven sales volume/revenue.

Mean deviation Measure of the average amount by which values in a distribution differ from the arithmetic mean.

Median The value of the middle member of an array or distribution

Mode An average, being the most frequently occurring value.

Moving averages A technique involving the calculation of consecutive averages over time to establish the trend of a time series.

Multiple bar chart See compound bar chart.

Multiplicative model A method of estimating seasonal variations whereby each actual figure is expressed as a percentage of the trend.

Multistage sampling A sampling method involving (usually)the division of a geographical area into a number of small areas, the selection of a small sample of these, the division of the small areas into even smaller areas and again a random selection of these areas. The process is repeated until a random sample of the smallest units is taken.

Mutually exclusive outcomes Outcomes such that the occurrence of one excludes the possibility of the other occurring.

Negative correlation Relationship such that low values of one variable are associated with high values of the other, and high values of one variable are associated with low values of the other.

Net present value method A capital expenditure appraisal method which works out the present value of all items of income and expenditure related to an investment at a given rate of return and then works out a net total. If the total is

positive the investment is acceptable but if negative it is not.

Nominal rate of interest An annual rate of interest quoted when interest is compounded over periods of less than one year.

Non-linear equation Equation in which one variable varies with the nth power of another, where n > 1.

Normal distribution A probability distribution most often applied to continuous variables.

Null hypothesis A hypothesis that proposes that the difference between statistical samples does not imply a difference between populations.

Objective function The mathematical equation which states the maximisation or minimisation objective of a linear programming problem.

Ogive A graph which shows the cumulative number of items with a value less than or equal to, or alternatively greater than or equal to, a certain amount.

One-tail test Type of hypothesis test used to determine whether results from a sample differ from expected results in one 'direction' only.

Paasche index An index using prices/quantities from the current year as weights.

Percentage component bar chart A component bar chart in which the length of each bar is equal but the length of the sections of the bar vary according to the relative size of the components of the total.

Percentile The value of each dividing part when a population is divided into 100 equal groups.

Perfect correlation An exact linear relationship existing between two variables.

Permutation A set of items, selected from a larger groups of items, the order of selection or arrangement being significant.

Perpetuity An annuity which lasts for ever.

Pictogram Statistical diagram in which quantities are represented by pictures or symbols.

Pie chart Shows pictorially the relative sizes of the component elements of a total.

Poisson distribution A probability distribution used to answer questions like: what is the probability of receiving five letters tomorrow, given that on average two letters a day are received? The Poisson distribution applies where events occur randomly within an interval, for example defects in a 100m length of rope, or telephone sales order received in an hour. It can also be used as an approximation to the binomial distribution, when n is large (say ten or more) and p is small (say 0.1 or less). The Poisson distribution is for discrete variables.

Population Any finite or infinite collection of individuals, measurements etc, defined by some characteristic common to those individuals, measurements etc.

Positive correlation Relationship such that low values of one variable are associated with low values of the other, and high values of one variable are associated with high values of the other.

Present value The amount of money which must be invested now for n years at an interest rate of r% to earn a given future sum of money at the time it will be due.

Primary data Data collected specifically for a current purpose.

Principal Original investment before interest added.

Probability A measure of likelihood.

Probability distribution An analysis of the proportion of times each particular value occurs in a set of items.

Proportion In sampling, the sampling proportion is the percentage of times an event occurs in a sample (for example, the proportion of faulty items out of the total number of items produced in a manufacturing department).

Proportional model See multiplicative model.

Quadratic equation Type of non-linear equation in which one variable varies with the square of the other variable.

Quantiles Collective name for the dividing points used to analyse a population.

Quartile The value of each dividing point when a population is divided into four equal groups.

Quartile coefficient of dispersion A measure of dispersion using quartiles.

Quartile deviation Half the difference between the lower and upper quartiles.

Quasi-random sampling Provides a good approximation to random sampling.

Quota sampling Commonly used by market researchers, this sampling method involves stratifying the population and restricting the sample to a fixed number in each strata. The interviewer controls the choice of sample respondents.

Random sampling Sampling such that every item in the population has an equal chance of being included.

Range Difference between highest observation and lowest observation.

Reciprocal The reciprocal of a number is one divided by that number.

Regression A method of predicting values of one variable given values for another variable.

Regression analysis A technique used to predict values for one variable (y) given values for the other variable (x), by finding a line $y = a + bx$ which is a good fit for the points on a scattergraph, and then using that line to find the value of y corresponding to each given value of x.

Residual The difference between the result that would have been predicted by a trend line adjusted for the average seasonal variation and the actual result.

Root The nth root of a number is a value which, when multiplied by itself (n−1) times equals that original number.

Sample A collection of information (ideally representative of the population from which it is taken).

Sampling distribution of a proportion A frequency distribution of the required proportion in a large number of samples.

Sampling distribution of the mean A frequency distribution of the mean of a large number of samples.

Sampling frame Numbered list of all items in a population.

Seasonal variations Short-term fluctuations in recorded values, due to different circumstances which affect results at different times of the year, month or whatever.

Secondary data Data which are already in existence that are used, adapted or adopted for a current purpose.

Semi-interquartile range See quartile deviation.

Semi-logarithmic graph A graph in which the logarithm of the dependent variable is plotted against the value of the independent variable.

Shadow price The amount by which the value of total contribution will go up (or down) if one unit more (or less) of a scarce resource is made available.

Simple interest Interest earned in equal amounts very year (or month) and which is a given proportion of the original investment.

Simple random sample Sample selected in such a way that every item in the population has an equal chance of being included.

Simplex technique A technique which tests a number of feasible solutions to the problem until the optimal solution is found. The technique is a repetitive step-by-step process and therefore an ideal computer application. However, if the manual process is used this is done in the form of a tableau (or 'table' or 'matrix') of figures.

Simultaneous equations Two or more equations which are satisfied by the same variable values.

Sinking fund An investment into which equal annual instalments are paid in order to earn interest, so that by the end of a given number of years, the investment is large enough to pay off a known commitment at that time.

Skewness The asymmetry of a frequency distribution curve.

Slack variable A variable introduced into the equation for a constraint in the Simplex approach to a linear programming problem to turn the inequality into an equation.

Spearman's rank correlation coefficient A measure of the degree of correlation between two variables when the data are given in terms of order or rank rather than actual values.

Standard deviation Square root of the variance.

Standard error Standard deviation of a sampling distribution.

Statistical map See cartogram.

Stratified sampling A sampling method whereby the population is divided into strata or categories and random samples are taken from each strata.

Systematic sampling A sampling method which selects every nth item after a random start.

Table A matrix of data in rows and columns, the rows and columns having titles.

Tally marks A simple way of presenting data, each tally mark reflecting the occurrence of an event, value etc once.

Terminal value The value of an investment at the end of an investment period.

Third quartile See upper quartile.

Time series A series of figures or values recorded over time.

Time series analysis A technique used in forecasting to eliminate seasonal variations.

Time value of money The concept that £1 earned or spent sooner is worth more than £1 earned or spent later.

Trend The underlying long-term movement over time in the values of data recorded.

Two-tail test Type of hypothesis test used to determine whether results from a sample differ from expected results in two 'directions'.

Upper quartile The value of the item above which 25% of the population falls.

Variable Something that can be measured.

Variance Average of the squared mean deviation for each value in a distribution.

Venn diagram A pictorial representation of divisions and subdivisions of a universal set.

Z chart A data presentation method which shows the value of a variable plotted against time over a period, the cumulative sum of values for that variable over the period to date and the period moving total for that variable.

$\bar{x}$ **('x bar')** The mathematical notation for the arithmetic mean.

BPP
PUBLISHING